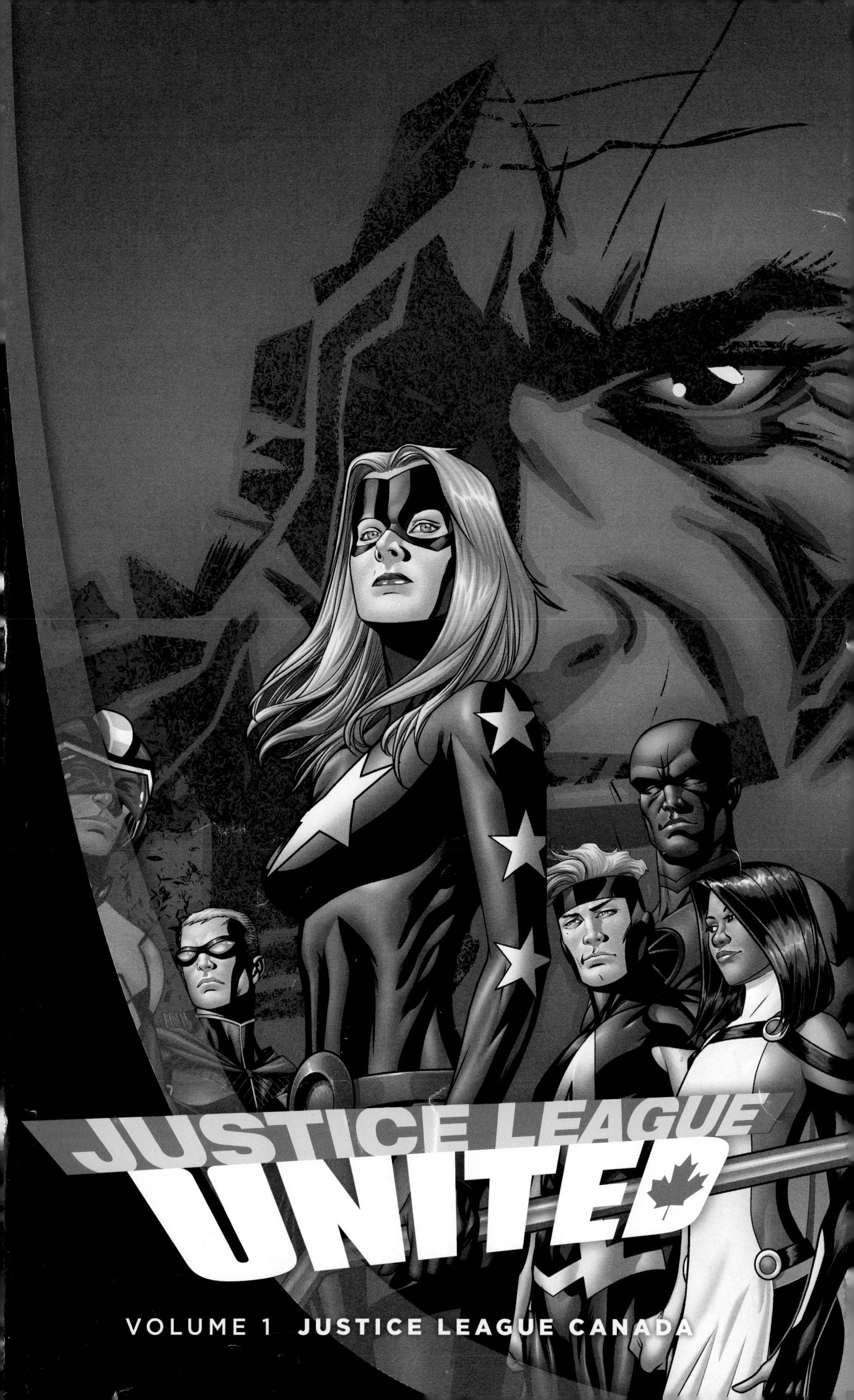
JUSTICE LEAGUE
UNITED
VOLUME 1 JUSTICE LEAGUE CANADA

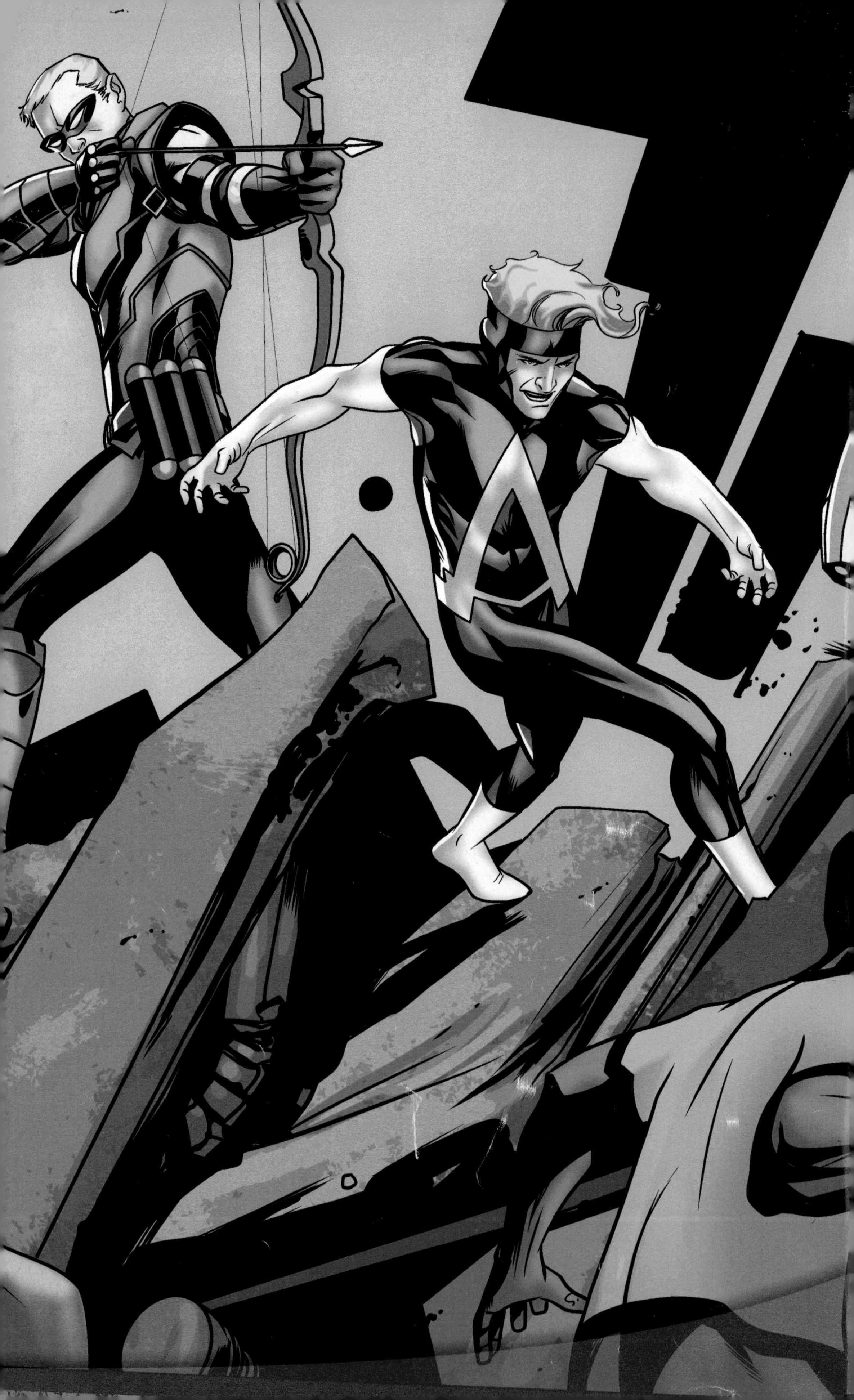

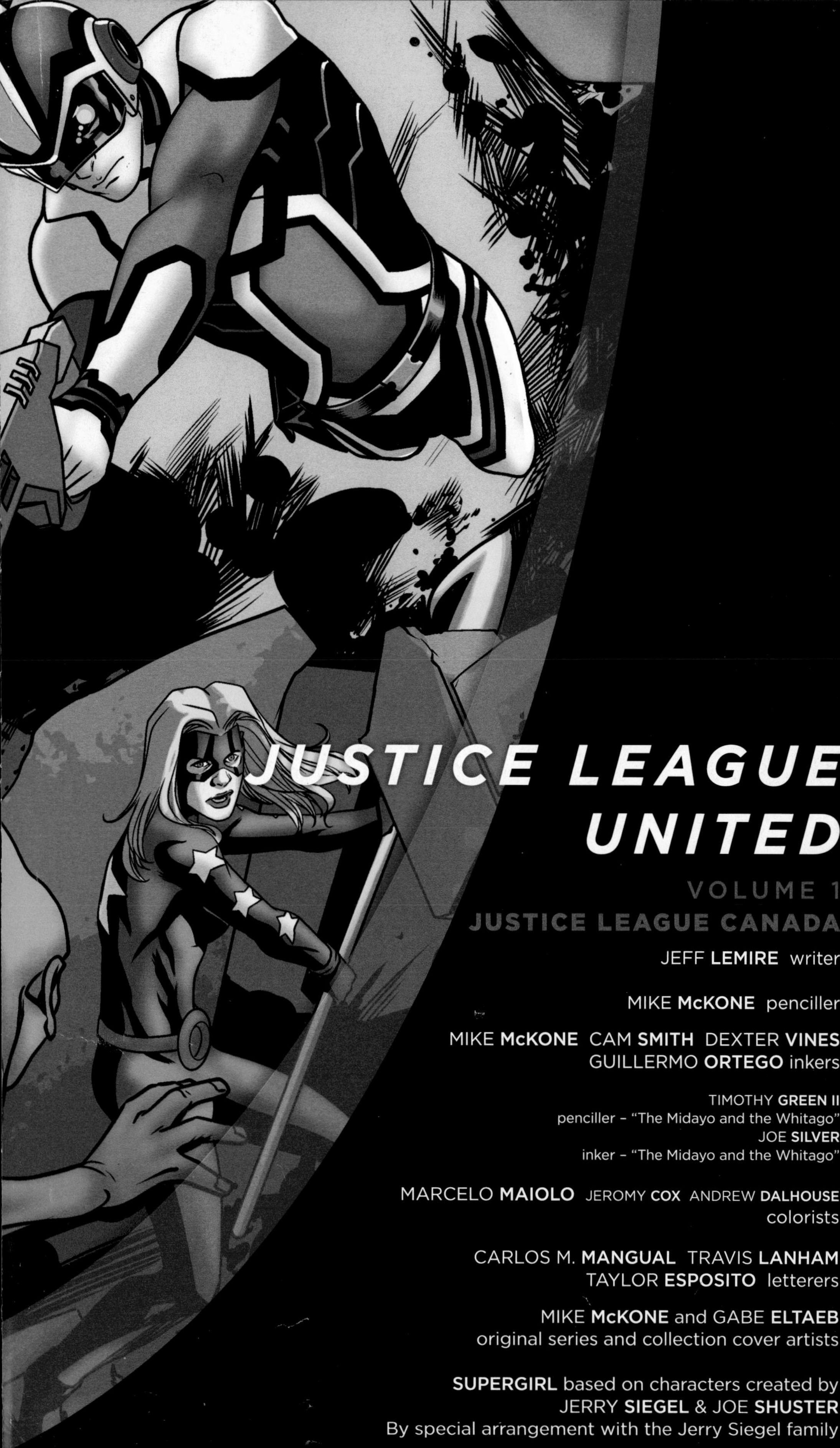

JUSTICE LEAGUE UNITED

VOLUME 1

JUSTICE LEAGUE CANADA

JEFF **LEMIRE** writer

MIKE **McKONE** penciller

MIKE **McKONE** CAM **SMITH** DEXTER **VINES**
GUILLERMO **ORTEGO** inkers

TIMOTHY **GREEN II**
penciller – "The Midayo and the Whitago"
JOE **SILVER**
inker – "The Midayo and the Whitago"

MARCELO **MAIOLO** JEROMY **COX** ANDREW **DALHOUSE**
colorists

CARLOS M. **MANGUAL** TRAVIS **LANHAM**
TAYLOR **ESPOSITO** letterers

MIKE **McKONE** and GABE **ELTAEB**
original series and collection cover artists

SUPERGIRL based on characters created by
JERRY **SIEGEL** & JOE **SHUSTER**
By special arrangement with the Jerry Siegel family

EDDIE BERGANZA RICKEY PURDIN Editors – Original Series ROBIN WILDMAN Editor
ROBBIN BROSTERMAN Design Director – Books ROBBIE BIEDERMAN Publication Design

BOB HARRAS Senior VP – Editor-in-Chief, DC Comics

DIANE NELSON President DAN DIDIO and JIM LEE Co-Publishers GEOFF JOHNS Chief Creative Officer
AMIT DESAI Senior VP – Marketing and Franchise Management
AMY GENKINS Senior VP – Business and Legal Affairs NAIRI GARDINER Senior VP – Finance
JEFF BOISON VP – Publishing Planning MARK CHIARELLO VP – Art Direction and Design
JOHN CUNNINGHAM VP – Marketing TERRI CUNNINGHAM VP – Editorial Administration
LARRY GANEM VP – Talent Relations and Services ALISON GILL Senior VP – Manufacturing and Operations
HANK KANALZ Senior VP – Vertigo and Integrated Publishing JAY KOGAN VP – Business and Legal Affairs, Publishing
JACK MAHAN VP – Business Affairs, Talent NICK NAPOLITANO VP – Manufacturing Administration SUE POHJA VP – Book Sales
FRED RUIZ VP – Manufacturing Operations COURTNEY SIMMONS Senior VP – Publicity BOB WAYNE Senior VP – Sales

JUSTICE LEAGUE UNITED VOLUME 1: JUSTICE LEAGUE CANADA

DC Comics, 1700 Broadway, New York, NY 10019
A Warner Bros. Entertainment Company.
Printed by RR Donnelley, Salem, VA, USA. 1/30/15. First Printing.

HC ISBN: 978-1-4012-5235-9

Library of Congress Cataloging-in-Publication Data is Available.

SUSTAINABLE
FORESTRY
INITIATIVE

Certified Chain of Custody
20% Certified Forest Content,
80% Certified Sourcing
www.sfiprogram.org
SFI-01042
APPLIES TO TEXT STOCK ONLY

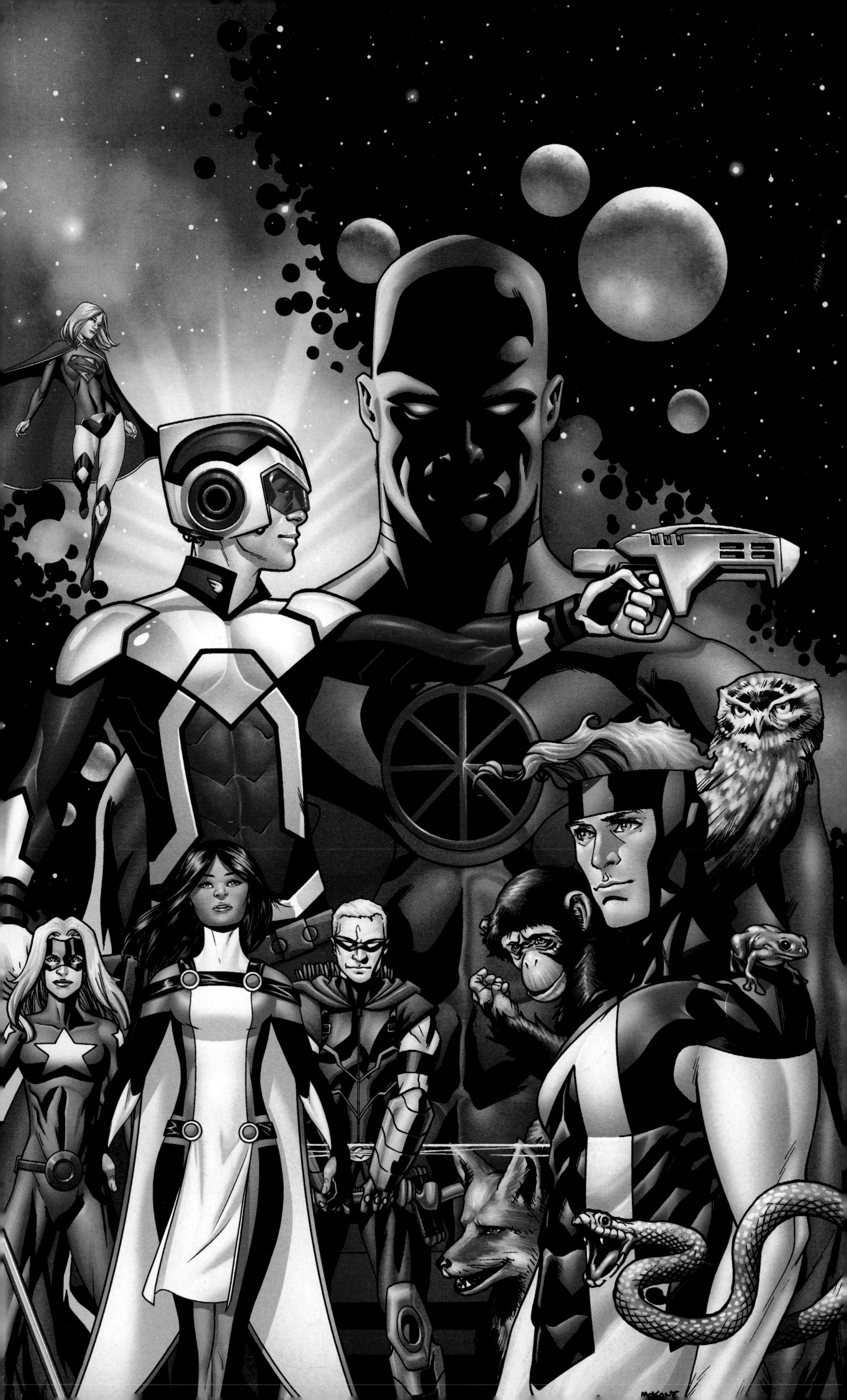

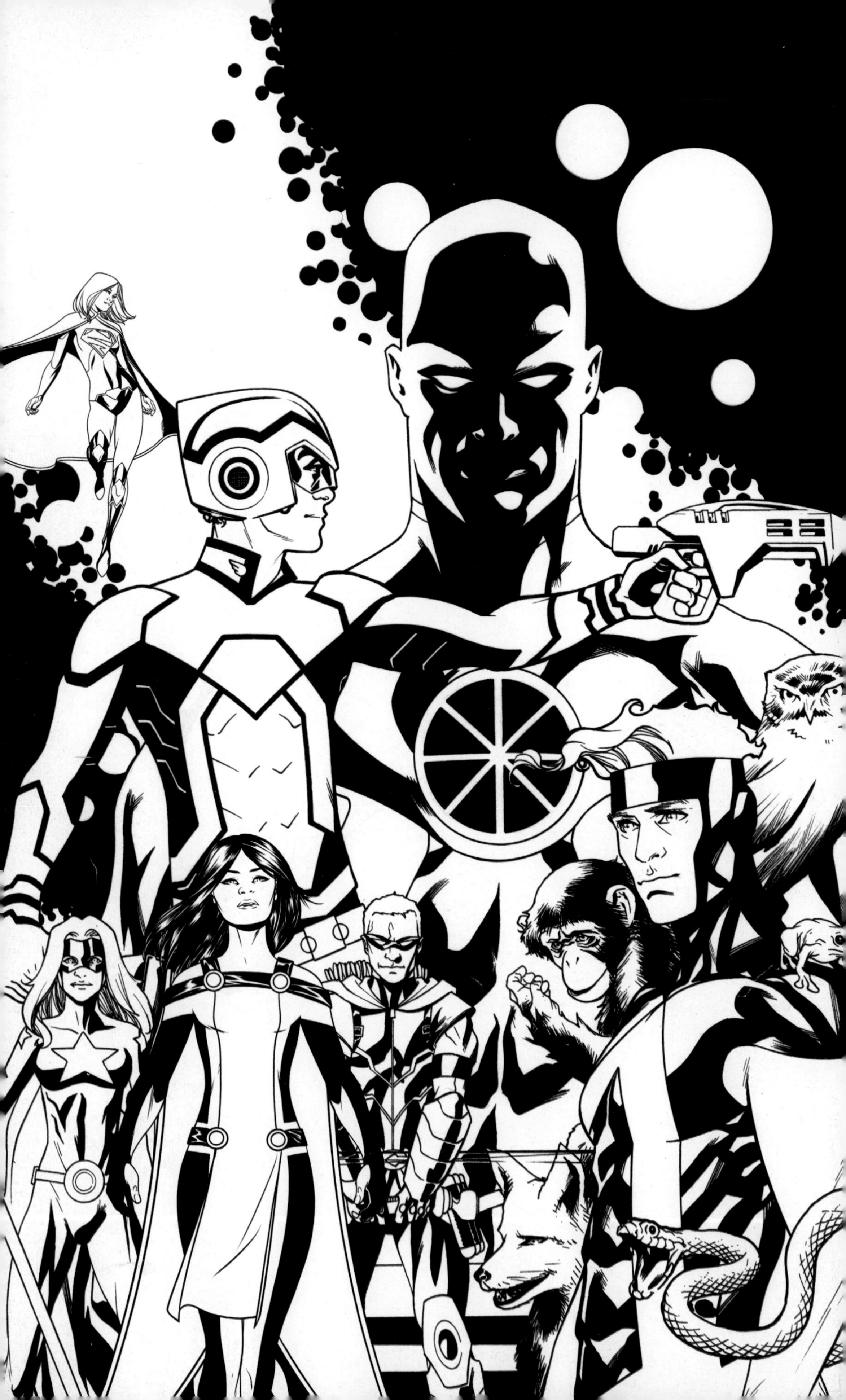

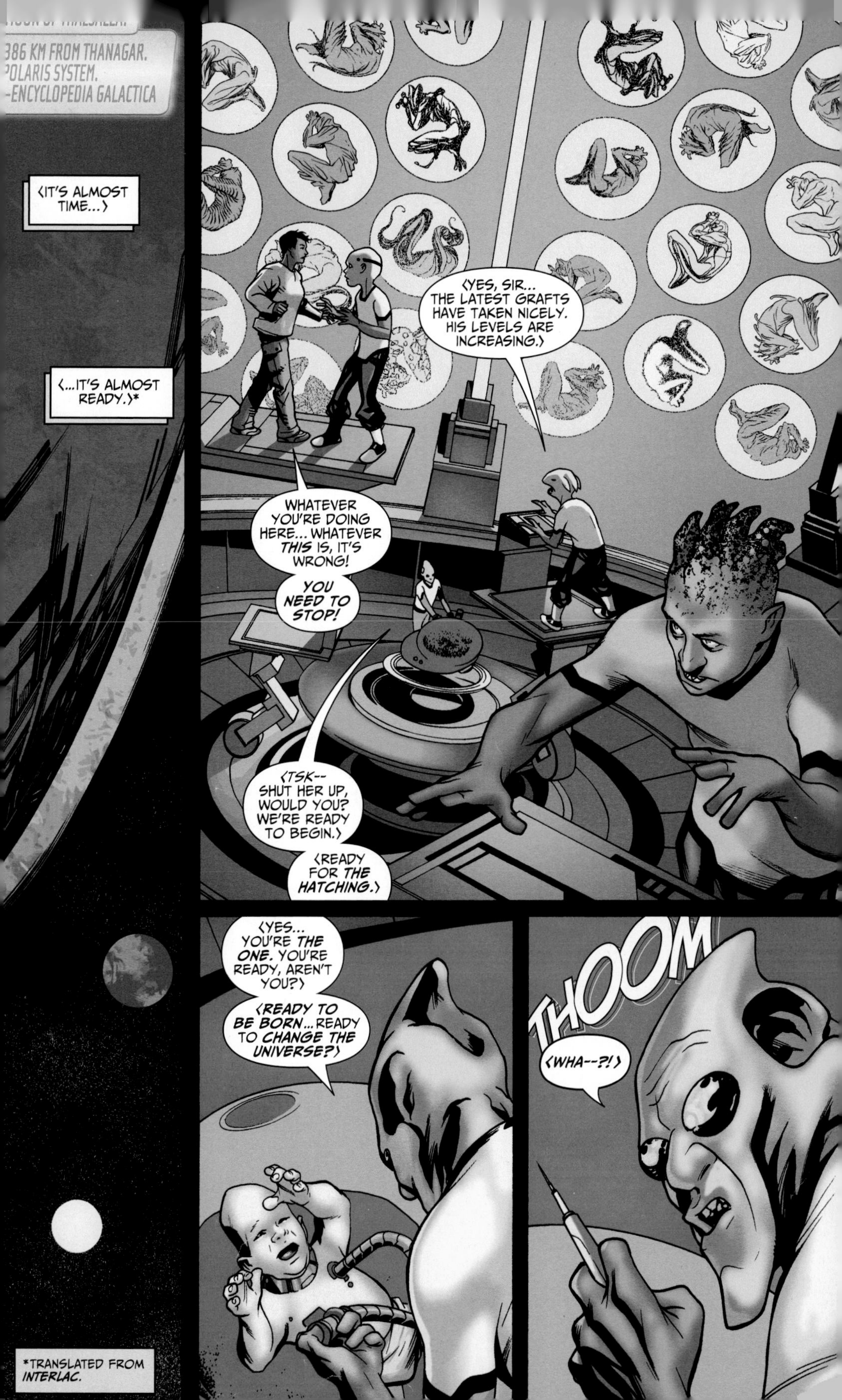
386 KM FROM THANAGAR.
POLARIS SYSTEM.
-ENCYCLOPEDIA GALACTICA
‹IT'S ALMOST TIME...›
‹...IT'S ALMOST READY.›*
‹YES, SIR... THE LATEST GRAFTS HAVE TAKEN NICELY. HIS LEVELS ARE INCREASING.›
WHATEVER YOU'RE DOING HERE... WHATEVER *THIS* IS, IT'S WRONG!
YOU NEED TO STOP!
‹TSK-- SHUT HER UP, WOULD YOU? WE'RE READY TO BEGIN.›
‹READY FOR *THE HATCHING.*›
‹YES... YOU'RE *THE ONE.* YOU'RE READY, AREN'T YOU?›
‹*READY TO BE BORN*... READY TO *CHANGE THE UNIVERSE?*›
THOOM
‹*WHA--?!*›
*TRANSLATED FROM *INTERLAC.*

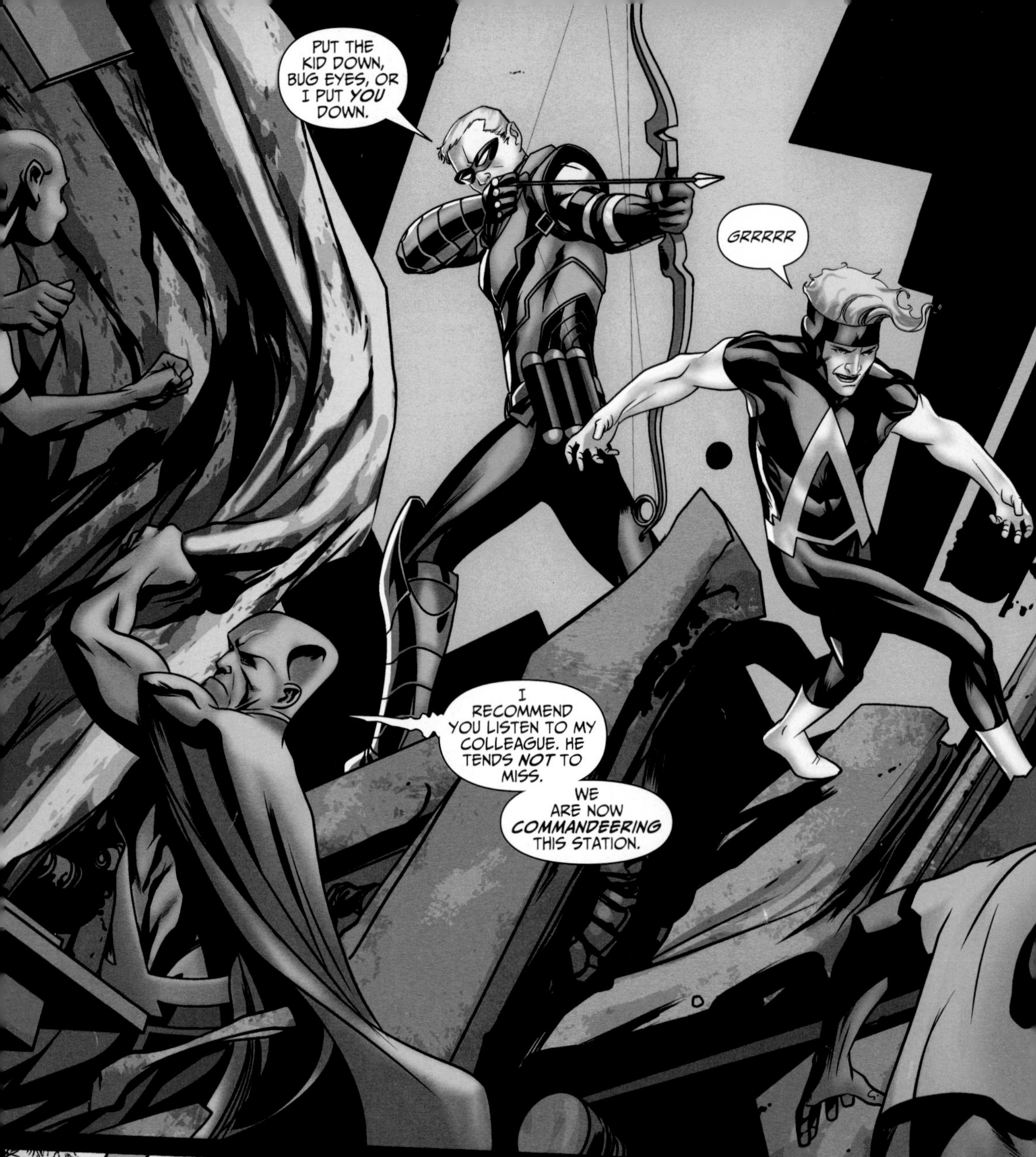
PUT THE KID DOWN, BUG EYES, OR I PUT *YOU* DOWN.
GRRRRR
I RECOMMEND YOU LISTEN TO MY COLLEAGUE. HE TENDS *NOT* TO MISS.
WE ARE NOW *COMMANDEERING* THIS STATION.

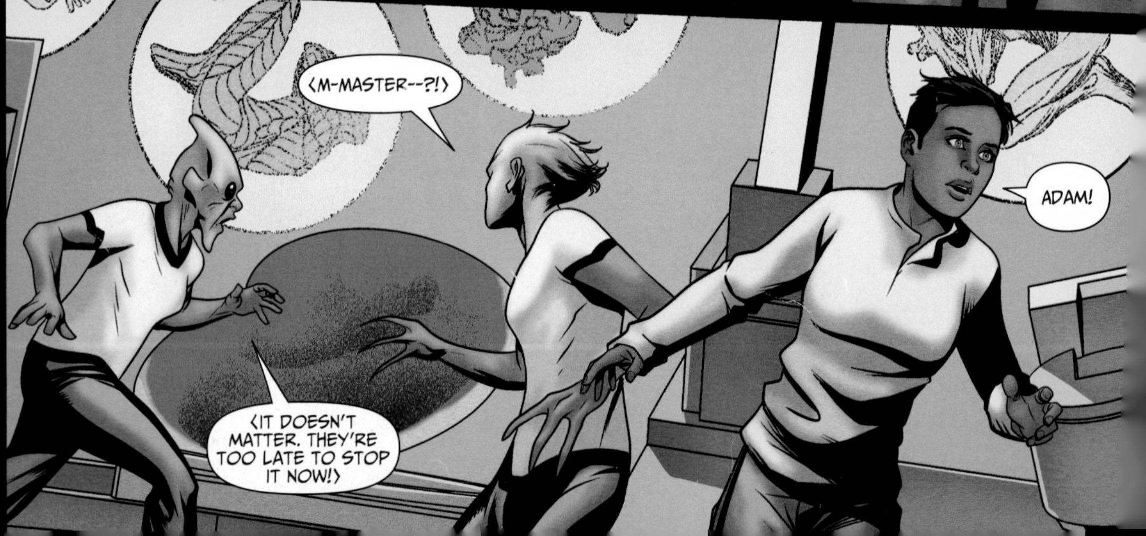
⟨M-MASTER--?!⟩
ADAM!
⟨IT DOESN'T MATTER. THEY'RE TOO LATE TO STOP IT NOW!⟩

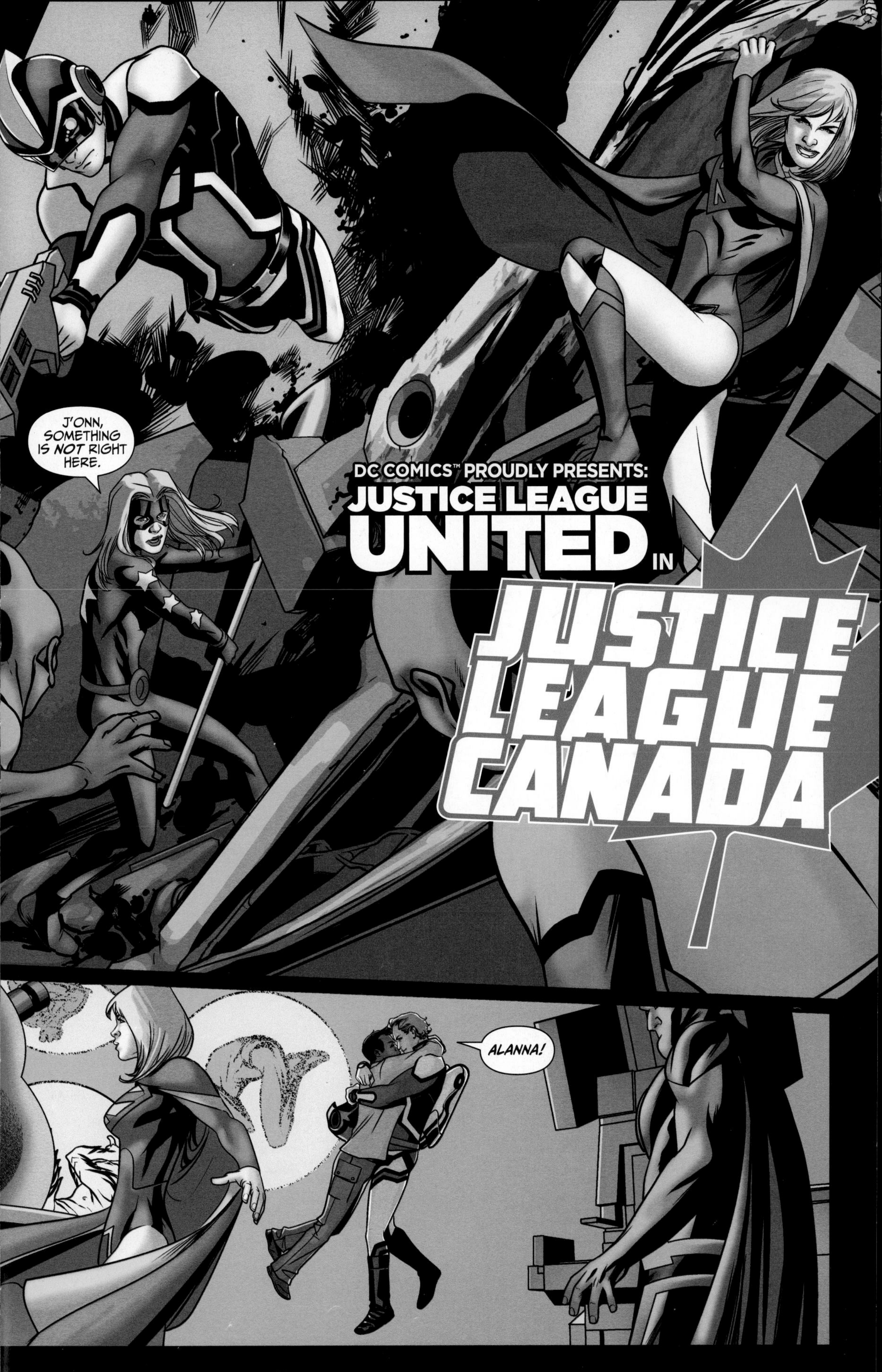
J'ONN, SOMETHING IS NOT RIGHT HERE.
DC COMICS™ PROUDLY PRESENTS:
JUSTICE LEAGUE UNITED IN
JUSTICE LEAGUE CANADA
ALANNA!

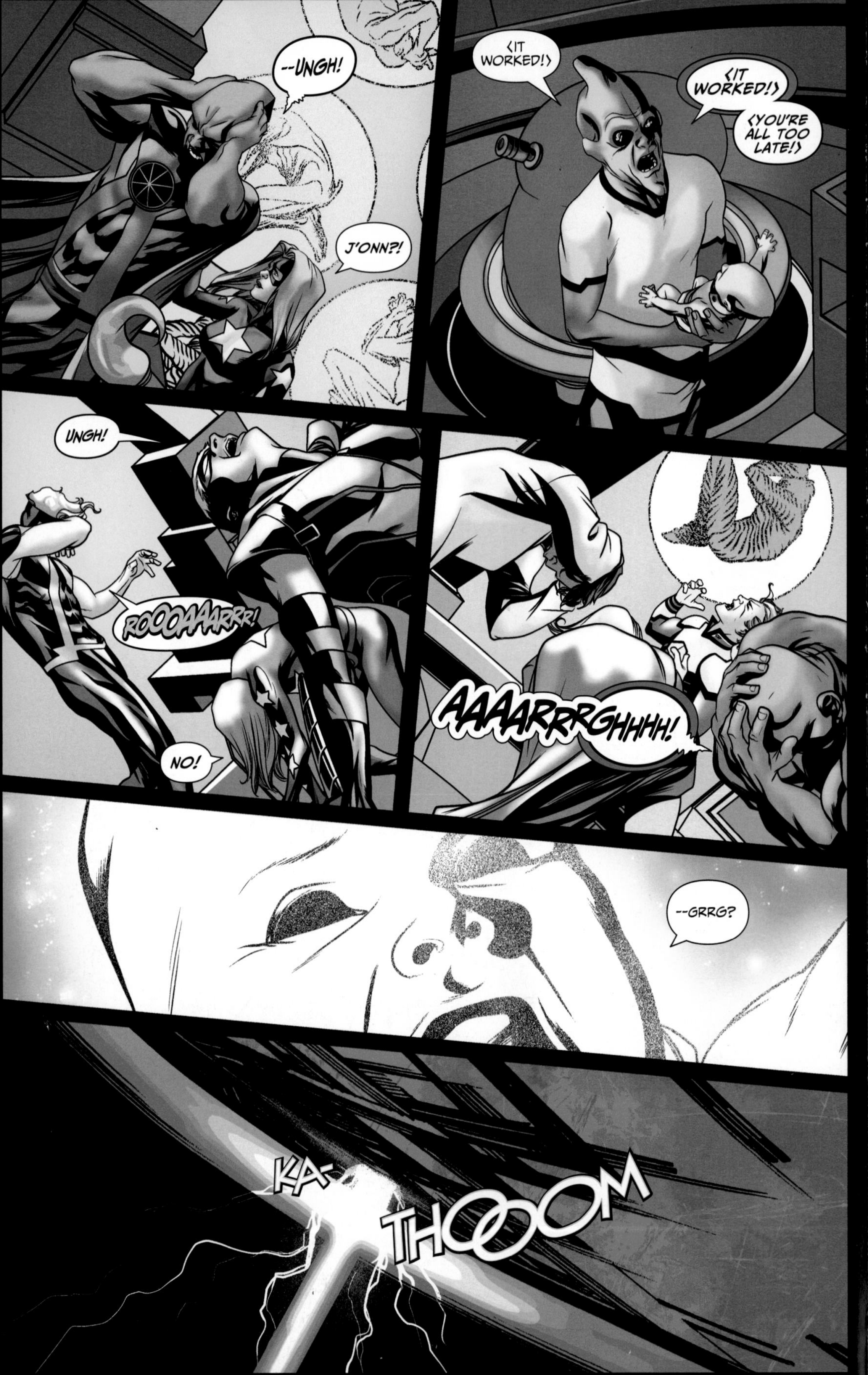

--UNGH!
J'ONN?!
<IT WORKED!>
<IT WORKED!>
<YOU'RE ALL TOO LATE!>
UNGH!
ROOOAAARRR!
NO!
AAAARRRRGHHHH!
--GRRG?
KA-THOOOM

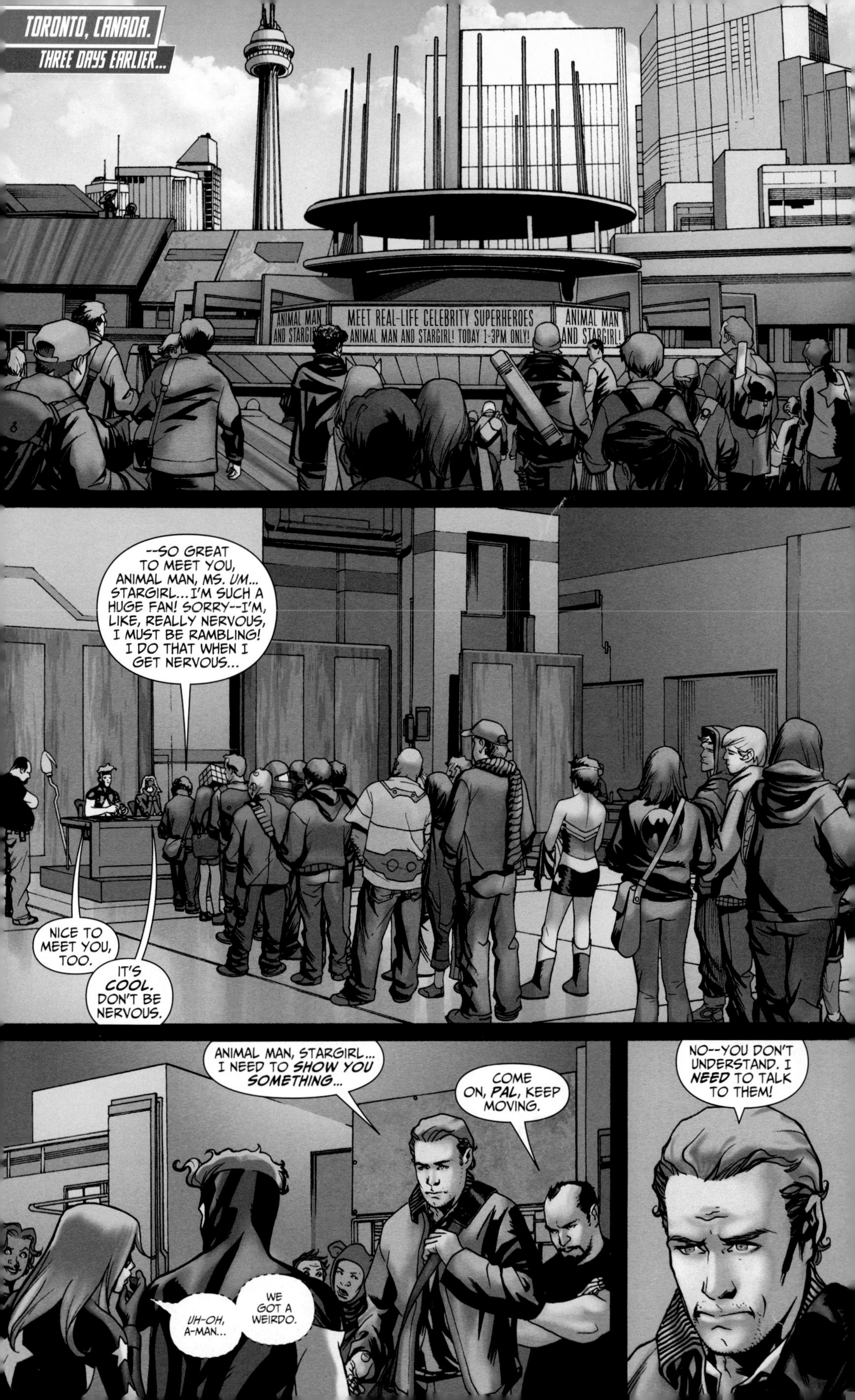
TORONTO, CANADA.
THREE DAYS EARLIER...
ANIMAL MAN AND STARGIRL!
MEET REAL-LIFE CELEBRITY SUPERHEROES ANIMAL MAN AND STARGIRL! TODAY 1-3PM ONLY!
ANIMAL MAN AND STARGIRL!
--SO GREAT TO MEET YOU, ANIMAL MAN, MS. UM... STARGIRL... I'M SUCH A HUGE FAN! SORRY--I'M, LIKE, REALLY NERVOUS, I MUST BE RAMBLING! I DO THAT WHEN I GET NERVOUS...
NICE TO MEET YOU, TOO.
IT'S COOL. DON'T BE NERVOUS.
ANIMAL MAN, STARGIRL... I NEED TO SHOW YOU SOMETHING...
COME ON, PAL, KEEP MOVING.
UH-OH, A-MAN...
WE GOT A WEIRDO.
NO--YOU DON'T UNDERSTAND. I NEED TO TALK TO THEM!

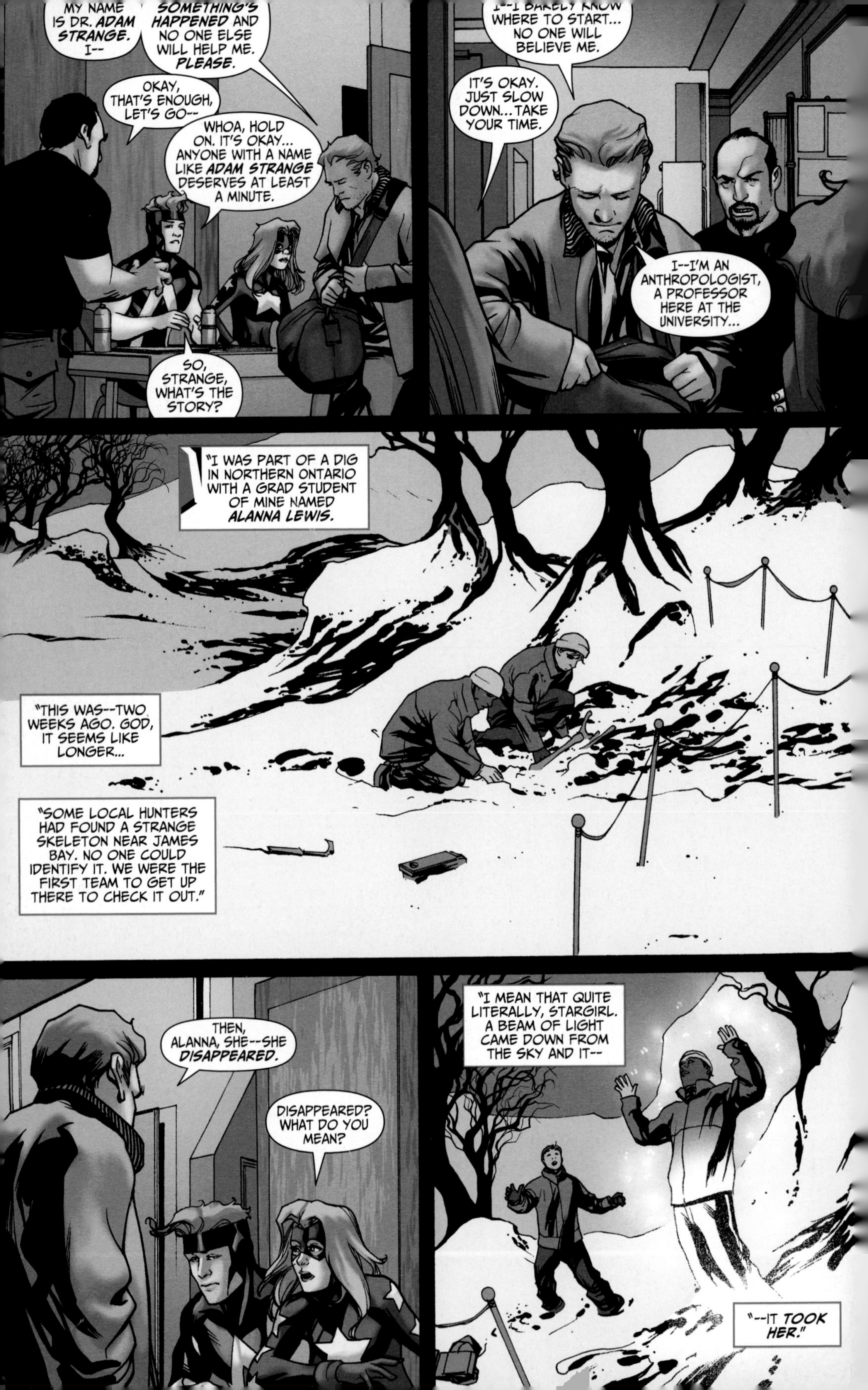
MY NAME IS DR. ADAM STRANGE. I--
SOMETHING'S HAPPENED AND NO ONE ELSE WILL HELP ME. PLEASE.
OKAY, THAT'S ENOUGH, LET'S GO--
WHOA, HOLD ON. IT'S OKAY... ANYONE WITH A NAME LIKE ADAM STRANGE DESERVES AT LEAST A MINUTE.
SO, STRANGE, WHAT'S THE STORY?
I--I BARELY KNOW WHERE TO START... NO ONE WILL BELIEVE ME.
IT'S OKAY. JUST SLOW DOWN... TAKE YOUR TIME.
I--I'M AN ANTHROPOLOGIST, A PROFESSOR HERE AT THE UNIVERSITY...
"I WAS PART OF A DIG IN NORTHERN ONTARIO WITH A GRAD STUDENT OF MINE NAMED ALANNA LEWIS.
"THIS WAS--TWO WEEKS AGO. GOD, IT SEEMS LIKE LONGER...
"SOME LOCAL HUNTERS HAD FOUND A STRANGE SKELETON NEAR JAMES BAY. NO ONE COULD IDENTIFY IT. WE WERE THE FIRST TEAM TO GET UP THERE TO CHECK IT OUT."
THEN, ALANNA, SHE--SHE DISAPPEARED.
DISAPPEARED? WHAT DO YOU MEAN?
"I MEAN THAT QUITE LITERALLY, STARGIRL. A BEAM OF LIGHT CAME DOWN FROM THE SKY AND IT--
"--IT TOOK HER."

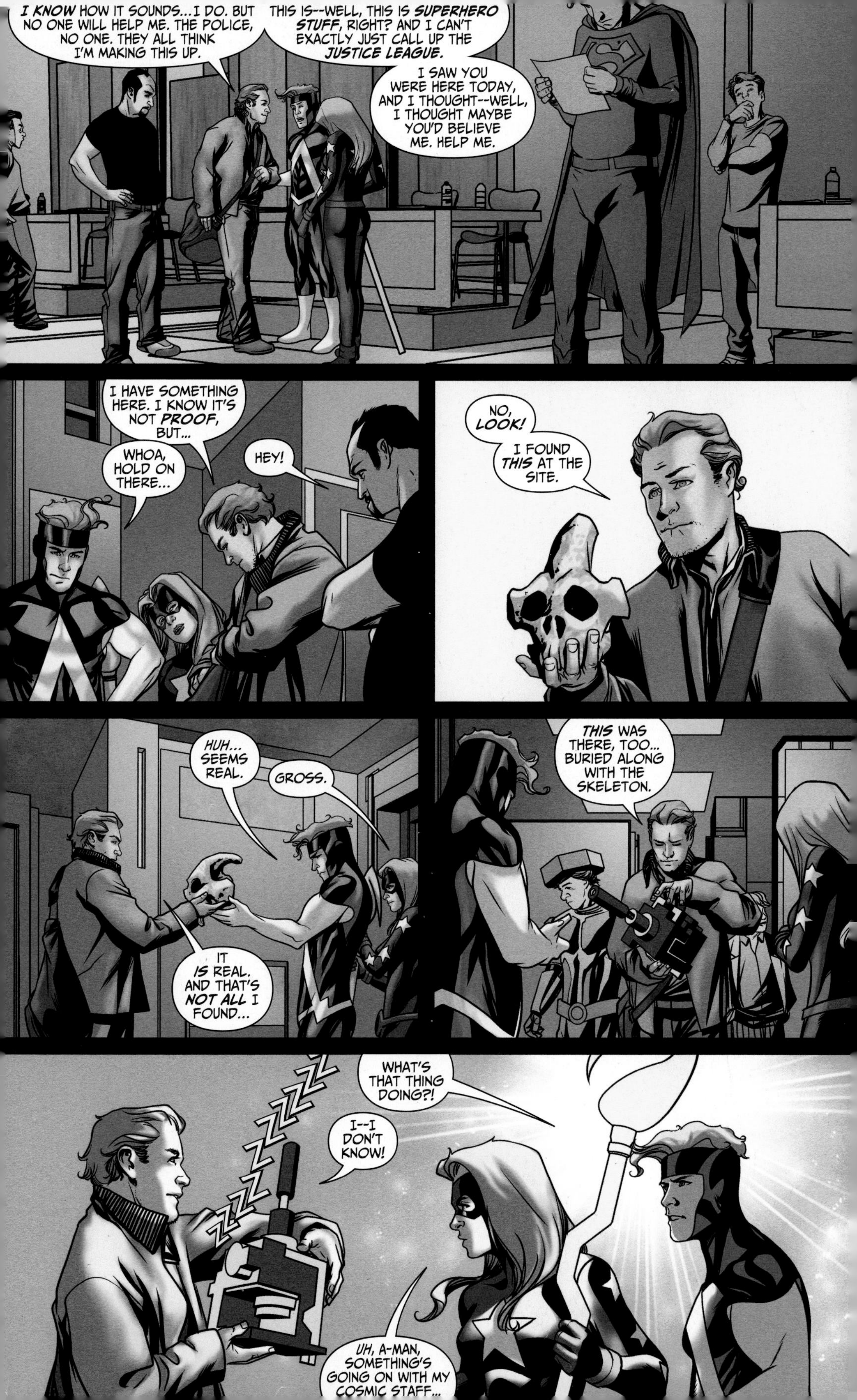
I KNOW HOW IT SOUNDS...I DO. BUT NO ONE WILL HELP ME. THE POLICE, NO ONE. THEY ALL THINK I'M MAKING THIS UP.
THIS IS--WELL, THIS IS SUPERHERO STUFF, RIGHT? AND I CAN'T EXACTLY JUST CALL UP THE JUSTICE LEAGUE.
I SAW YOU WERE HERE TODAY, AND I THOUGHT--WELL, I THOUGHT MAYBE YOU'D BELIEVE ME. HELP ME.
I HAVE SOMETHING HERE. I KNOW IT'S NOT PROOF, BUT...
WHOA, HOLD ON THERE...
HEY!
NO, LOOK!
I FOUND THIS AT THE SITE.
HUH... SEEMS REAL.
GROSS.
IT IS REAL. AND THAT'S NOT ALL I FOUND...
THIS WAS THERE, TOO... BURIED ALONG WITH THE SKELETON.
WHAT'S THAT THING DOING?!
I--I DON'T KNOW!
UH, A-MAN, SOMETHING'S GOING ON WITH MY COSMIC STAFF...

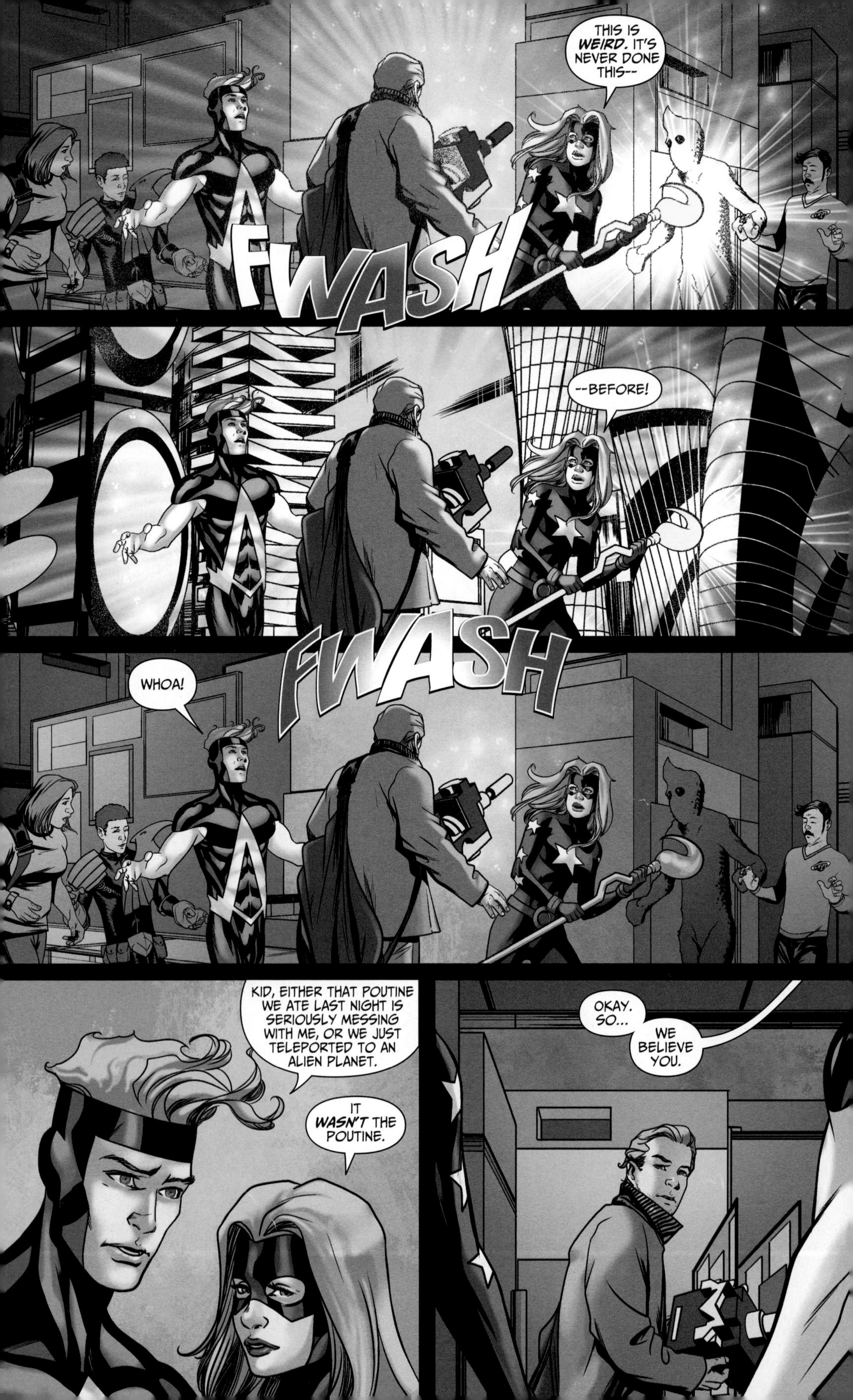
THIS IS WEIRD. IT'S NEVER DONE THIS--
FWASH
--BEFORE!
FWASH
WHOA!
KID, EITHER THAT POUTINE WE ATE LAST NIGHT IS SERIOUSLY MESSING WITH ME, OR WE JUST TELEPORTED TO AN ALIEN PLANET.
IT WASN'T THE POUTINE.
OKAY. SO...
WE BELIEVE YOU.

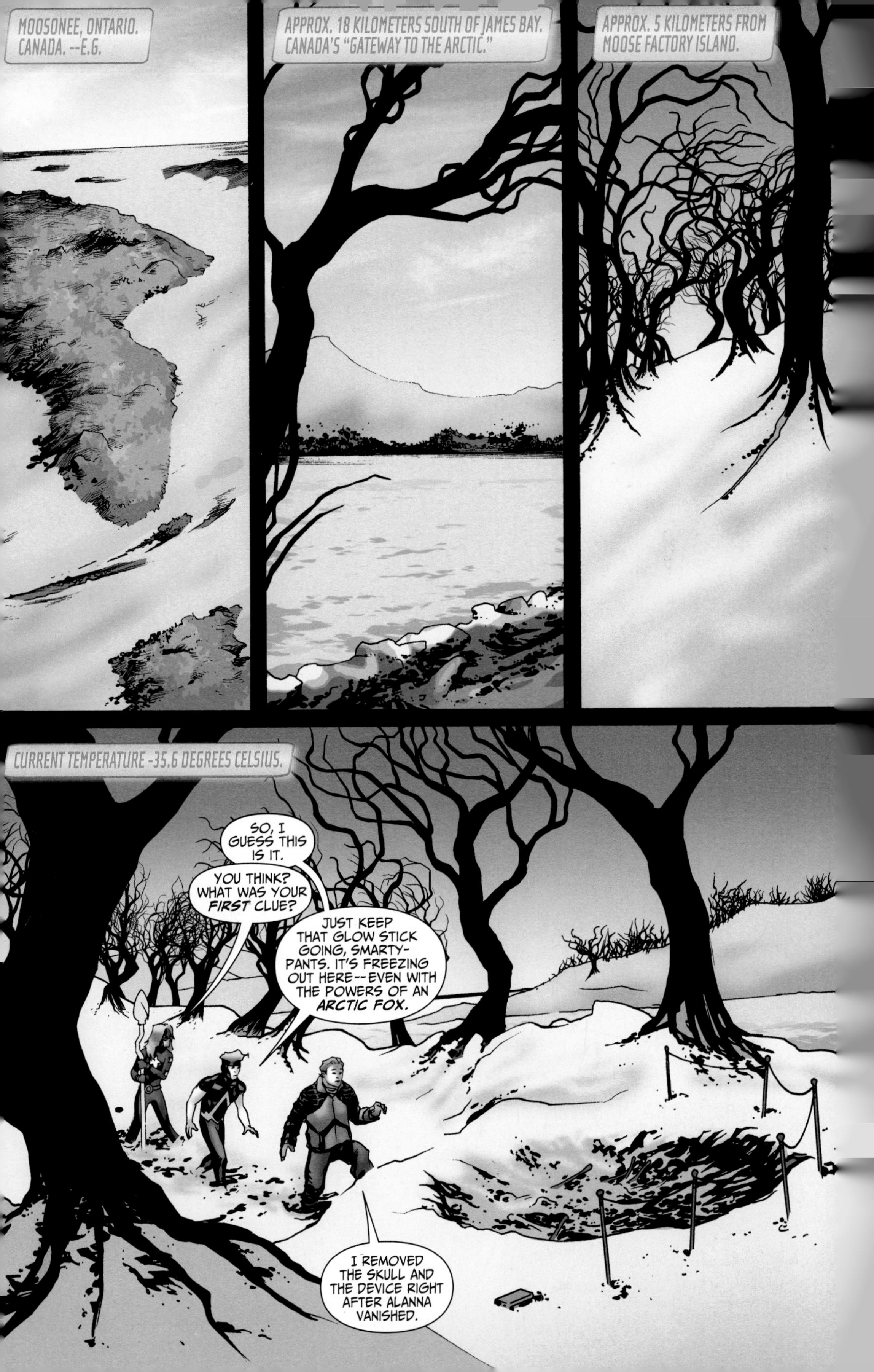

MOOSONEE, ONTARIO. CANADA. --E.G.
APPROX. 18 KILOMETERS SOUTH OF JAMES BAY. CANADA'S "GATEWAY TO THE ARCTIC."
APPROX. 5 KILOMETERS FROM MOOSE FACTORY ISLAND.
CURRENT TEMPERATURE -35.6 DEGREES CELSIUS.
SO, I GUESS THIS IS IT.
YOU THINK? WHAT WAS YOUR FIRST CLUE?
JUST KEEP THAT GLOW STICK GOING, SMARTY-PANTS. IT'S FREEZING OUT HERE--EVEN WITH THE POWERS OF AN ARCTIC FOX.
I REMOVED THE SKULL AND THE DEVICE RIGHT AFTER ALANNA VANISHED.

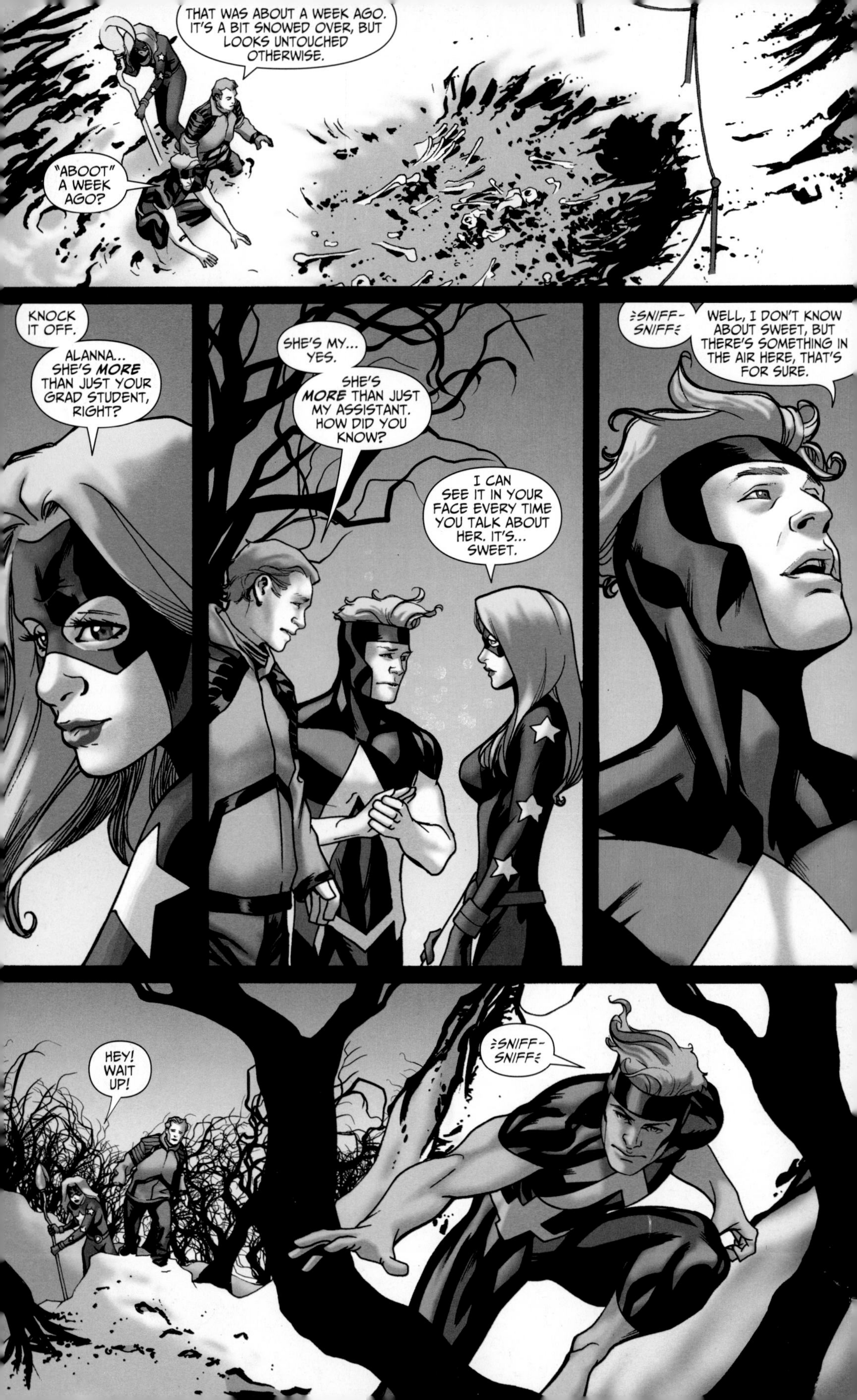
THAT WAS ABOUT A WEEK AGO. IT'S A BIT SNOWED OVER, BUT LOOKS UNTOUCHED OTHERWISE.
"ABOOT" A WEEK AGO?
KNOCK IT OFF.
ALANNA... SHE'S MORE THAN JUST YOUR GRAD STUDENT, RIGHT?
SHE'S MY... YES.
SHE'S MORE THAN JUST MY ASSISTANT. HOW DID YOU KNOW?
I CAN SEE IT IN YOUR FACE EVERY TIME YOU TALK ABOUT HER. IT'S... SWEET.
SNIFF-SNIFF
WELL, I DON'T KNOW ABOUT SWEET, BUT THERE'S SOMETHING IN THE AIR HERE, THAT'S FOR SURE.
HEY! WAIT UP!
SNIFF-SNIFF

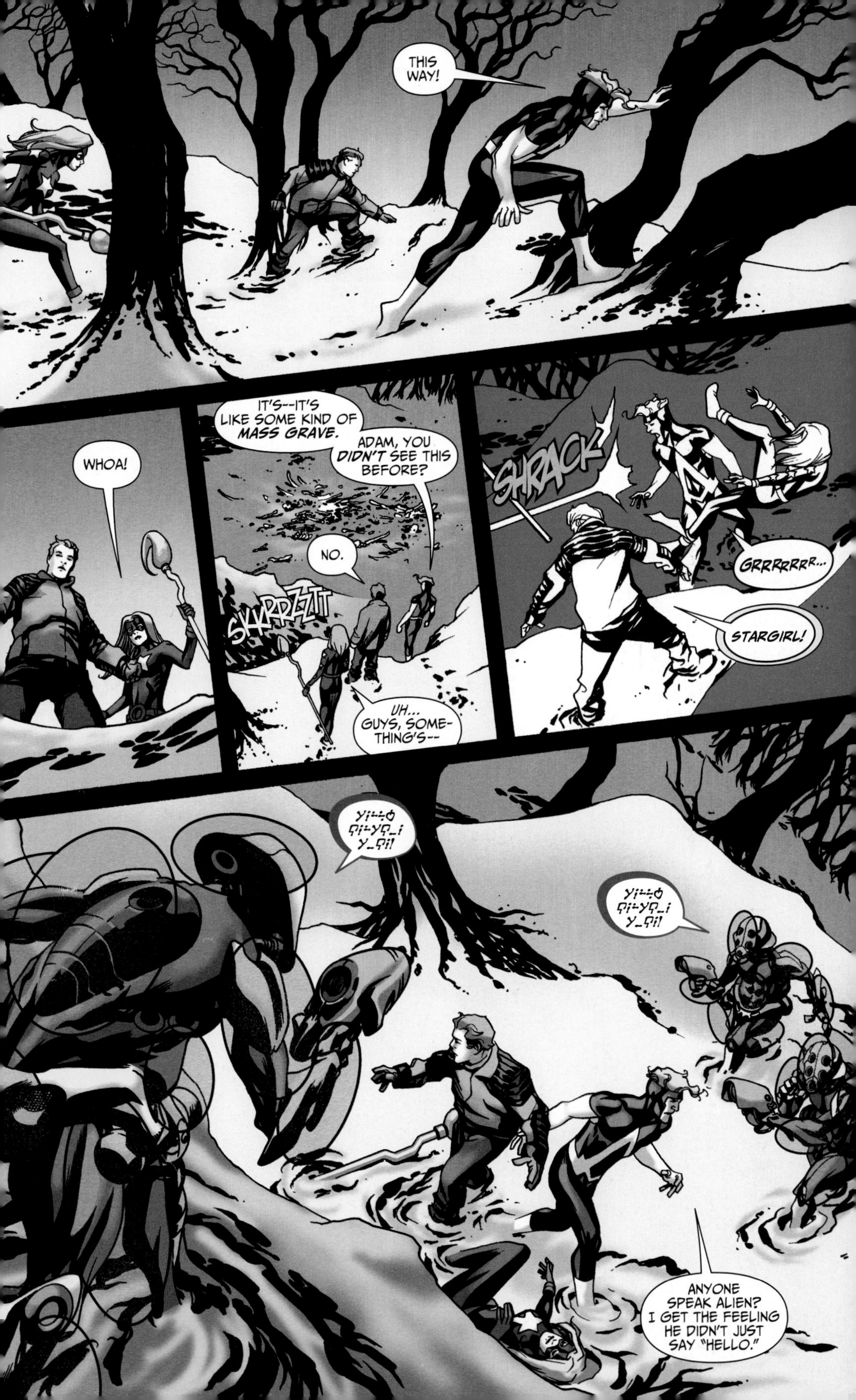
THIS WAY!
WHOA!
IT'S--IT'S LIKE SOME KIND OF MASS GRAVE.
ADAM, YOU DIDN'T SEE THIS BEFORE?
NO.
SKKRRZZZTT
UH... GUYS, SOME-THING'S--
SHRACK
GRRRRRRR...
STARGIRL!
ANYONE SPEAK ALIEN? I GET THE FEELING HE DIDN'T JUST SAY "HELLO."

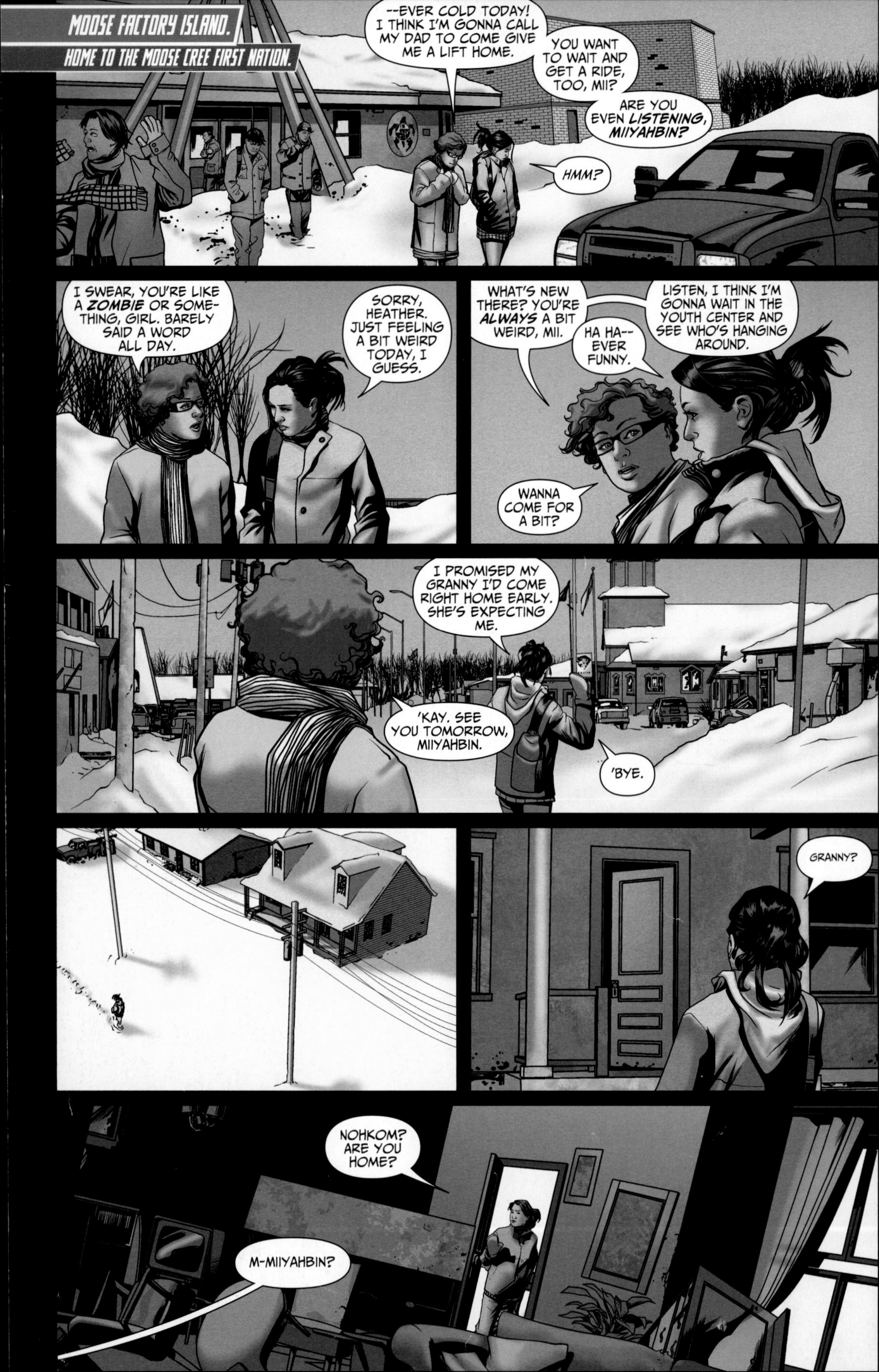
MOOSE FACTORY ISLAND.
HOME TO THE MOOSE CREE FIRST NATION.
--EVER COLD TODAY! I THINK I'M GONNA CALL MY DAD TO COME GIVE ME A LIFT HOME.
YOU WANT TO WAIT AND GET A RIDE, TOO, MII?
ARE YOU EVEN LISTENING, MIIYAHBIN?
HMM?
I SWEAR, YOU'RE LIKE A ZOMBIE OR SOME-THING, GIRL. BARELY SAID A WORD ALL DAY.
SORRY, HEATHER. JUST FEELING A BIT WEIRD TODAY, I GUESS.
WHAT'S NEW THERE? YOU'RE ALWAYS A BIT WEIRD, MII.
HA HA-- EVER FUNNY.
LISTEN, I THINK I'M GONNA WAIT IN THE YOUTH CENTER AND SEE WHO'S HANGING AROUND.
WANNA COME FOR A BIT?
I PROMISED MY GRANNY I'D COME RIGHT HOME EARLY. SHE'S EXPECTING ME.
'KAY. SEE YOU TOMORROW, MIIYAHBIN.
'BYE.
GRANNY?
NOHKOM? ARE YOU HOME?
M-MIIYAHBIN?

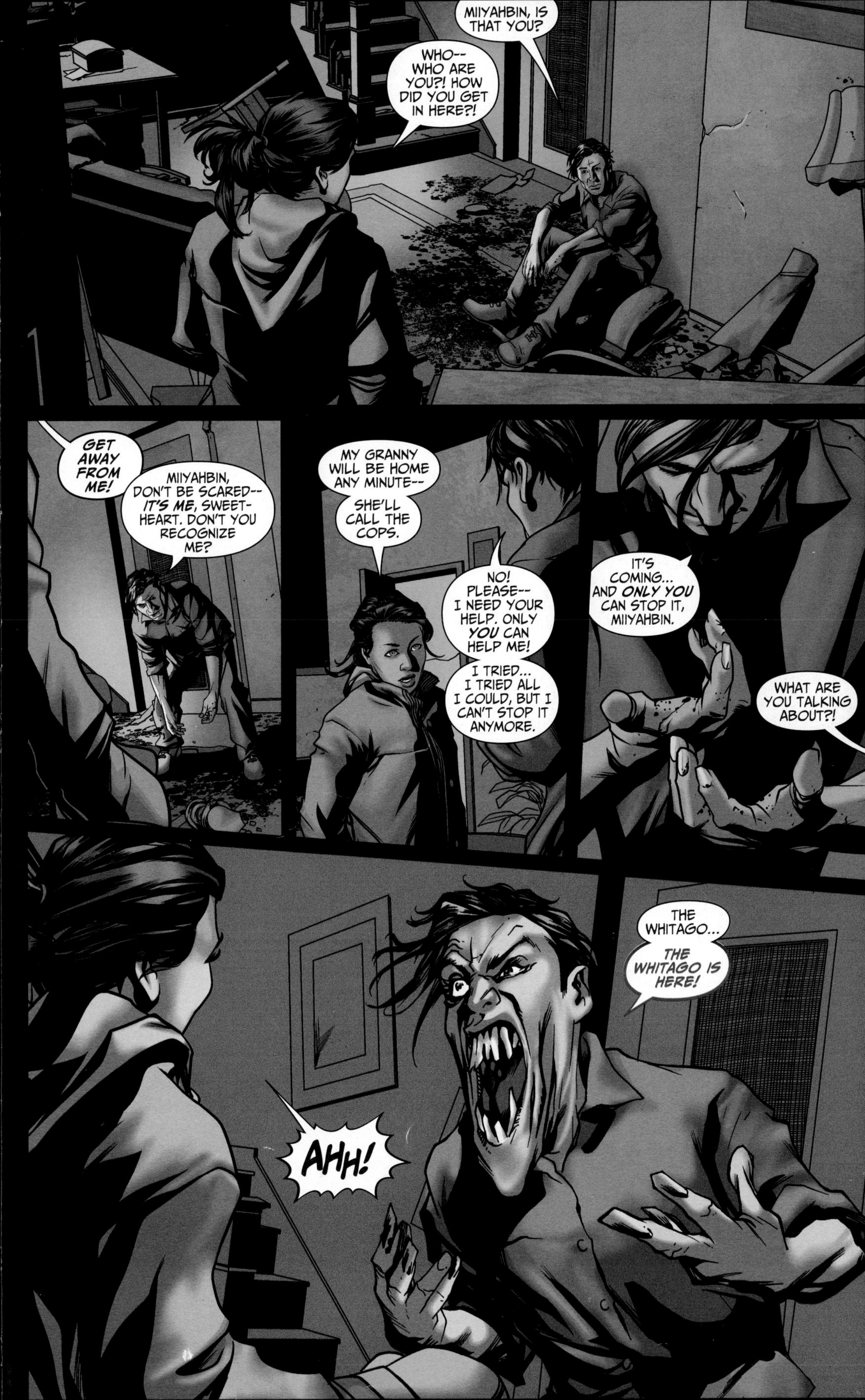
MIIYAHBIN, IS THAT YOU?
WHO-- WHO ARE YOU?! HOW DID YOU GET IN HERE?!
GET AWAY FROM ME!
MIIYAHBIN, DON'T BE SCARED-- IT'S ME, SWEET-HEART. DON'T YOU RECOGNIZE ME?
MY GRANNY WILL BE HOME ANY MINUTE--
SHE'LL CALL THE COPS.
NO! PLEASE-- I NEED YOUR HELP. ONLY YOU CAN HELP ME!
I TRIED... I TRIED ALL I COULD, BUT I CAN'T STOP IT ANYMORE.
IT'S COMING... AND ONLY YOU CAN STOP IT, MIIYAHBIN.
WHAT ARE YOU TALKING ABOUT?!
THE WHITAGO...
THE WHITAGO IS HERE!
AHH!

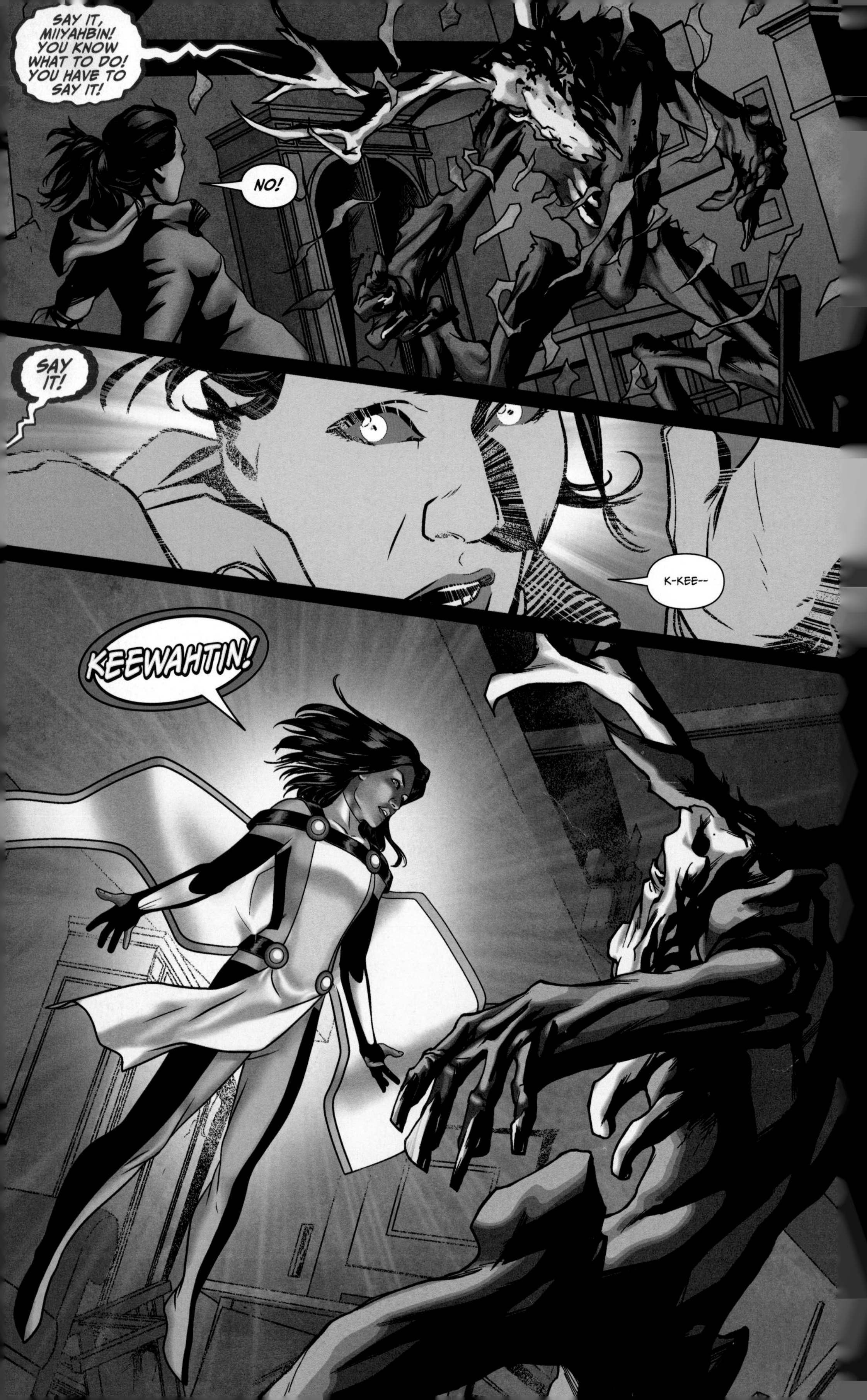
SAY IT, MIIYAHBIN! YOU KNOW WHAT TO DO! YOU HAVE TO SAY IT!
NO!
SAY IT!
K-KEE--
KEEWAHTIN!

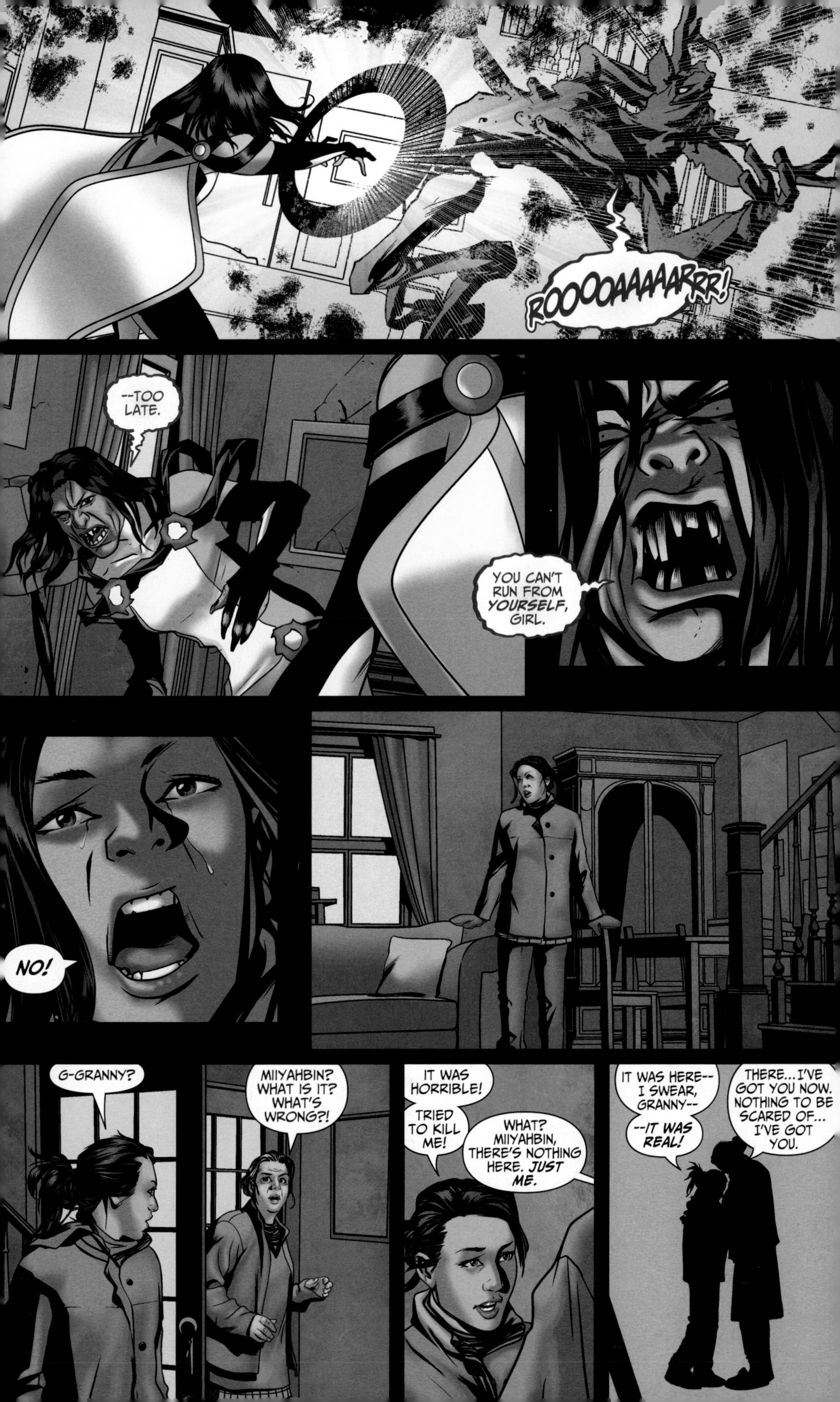
ROOOOAAAAARRR!
--TOO LATE.
YOU CAN'T RUN FROM *YOURSELF*, GIRL.
NO!
G-GRANNY?
MIIYAHBIN? WHAT IS IT? WHAT'S WRONG?!
IT WAS HORRIBLE!
TRIED TO KILL ME!
WHAT? MIIYAHBIN, THERE'S NOTHING HERE. *JUST ME.*
IT WAS HERE-- I SWEAR, GRANNY--
--*IT WAS REAL!*
THERE... I'VE GOT YOU NOW. NOTHING TO BE SCARED OF... I'VE GOT YOU.

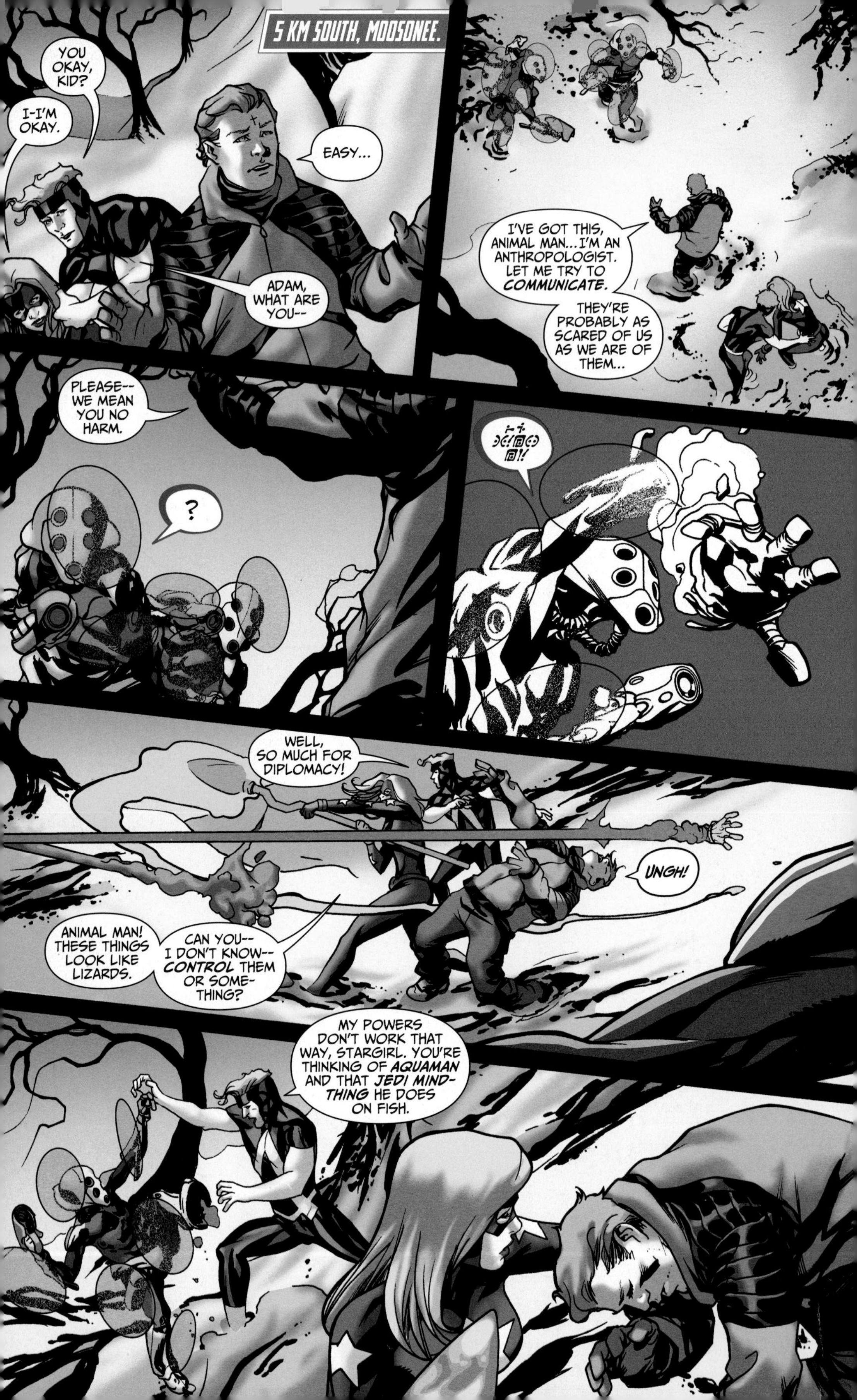
5 KM SOUTH, MOOSONEE.
YOU OKAY, KID?
I-I'M OKAY.
EASY...
ADAM, WHAT ARE YOU--
I'VE GOT THIS, ANIMAL MAN...I'M AN ANTHROPOLOGIST. LET ME TRY TO COMMUNICATE.
THEY'RE PROBABLY AS SCARED OF US AS WE ARE OF THEM...
PLEASE-- WE MEAN YOU NO HARM.
?
WELL, SO MUCH FOR DIPLOMACY!
UNGH!
ANIMAL MAN! THESE THINGS LOOK LIKE LIZARDS.
CAN YOU-- I DON'T KNOW-- CONTROL THEM OR SOME-THING?
MY POWERS DON'T WORK THAT WAY, STARGIRL. YOU'RE THINKING OF AQUAMAN AND THAT JEDI MIND-THING HE DOES ON FISH.

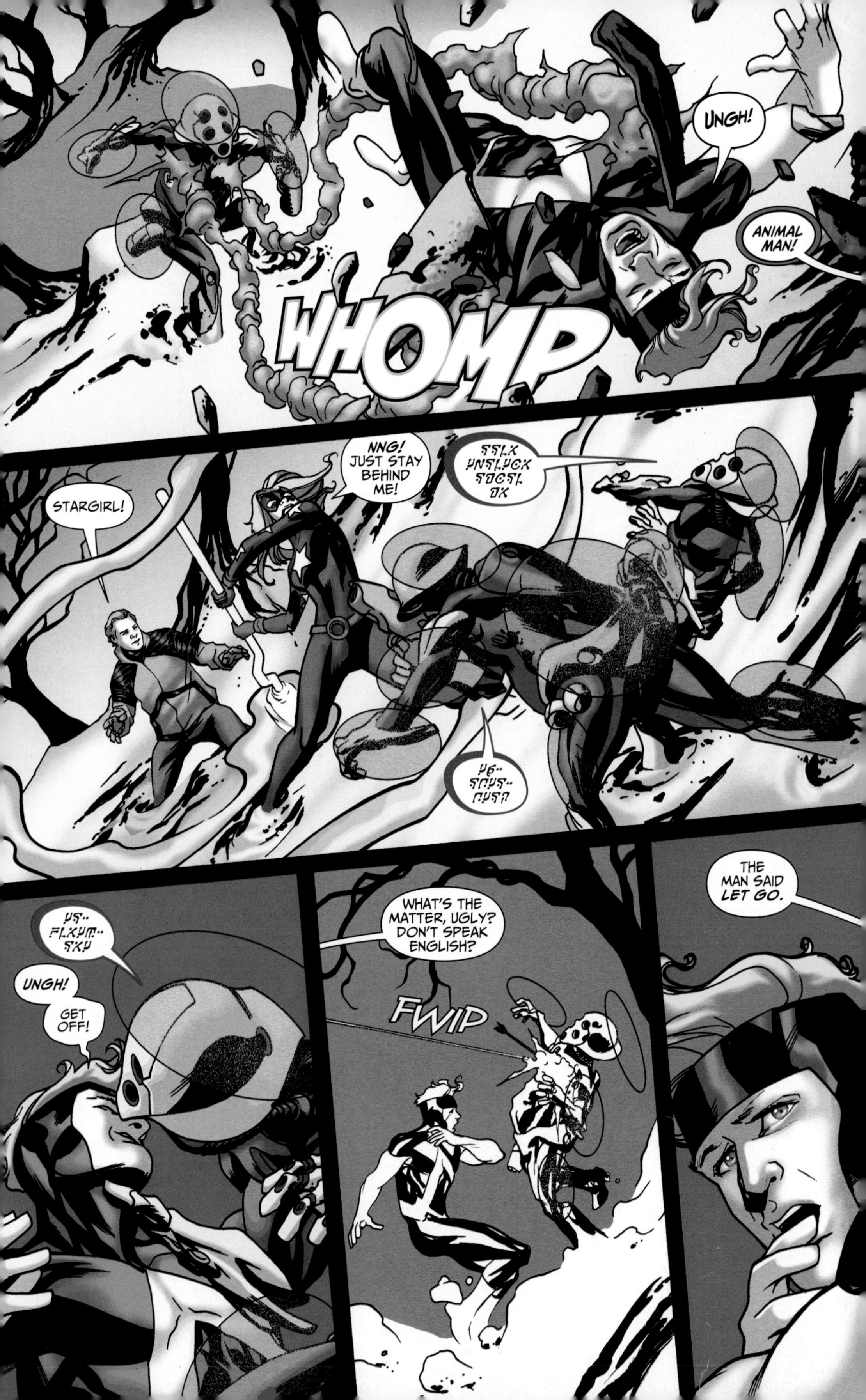
UNGH!
ANIMAL MAN!
WHOMP
STARGIRL!
NNG! JUST STAY BEHIND ME!
UNGH!
GET OFF!
WHAT'S THE MATTER, UGLY? DON'T SPEAK ENGLISH?
FWIP
THE MAN SAID LET GO.

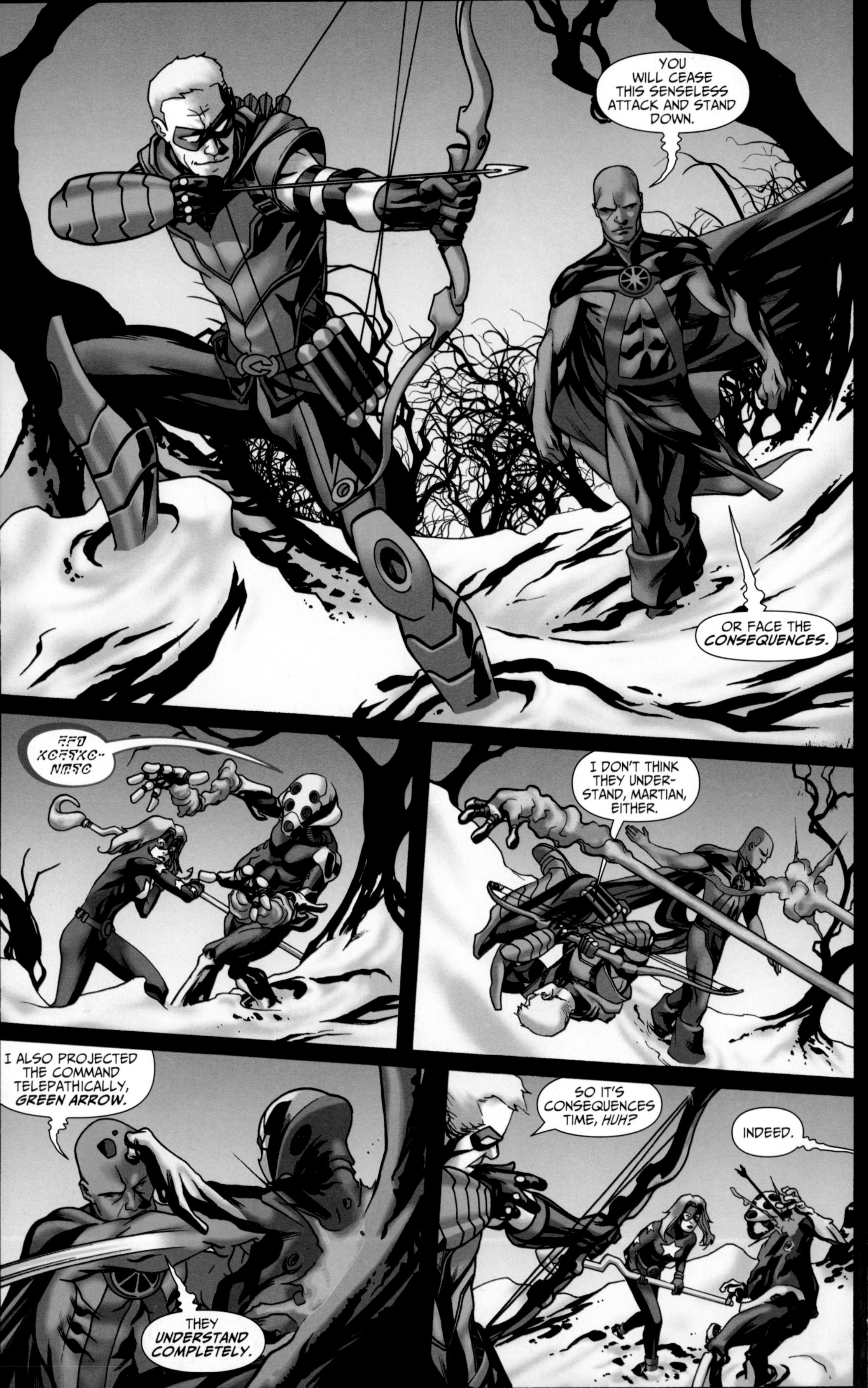
YOU WILL CEASE THIS SENSELESS ATTACK AND STAND DOWN.
OR FACE THE CONSEQUENCES.
I DON'T THINK THEY UNDER-STAND, MARTIAN, EITHER.
I ALSO PROJECTED THE COMMAND TELEPATHICALLY, GREEN ARROW.
THEY UNDERSTAND COMPLETELY.
SO IT'S CONSEQUENCES TIME, HUH?
INDEED.

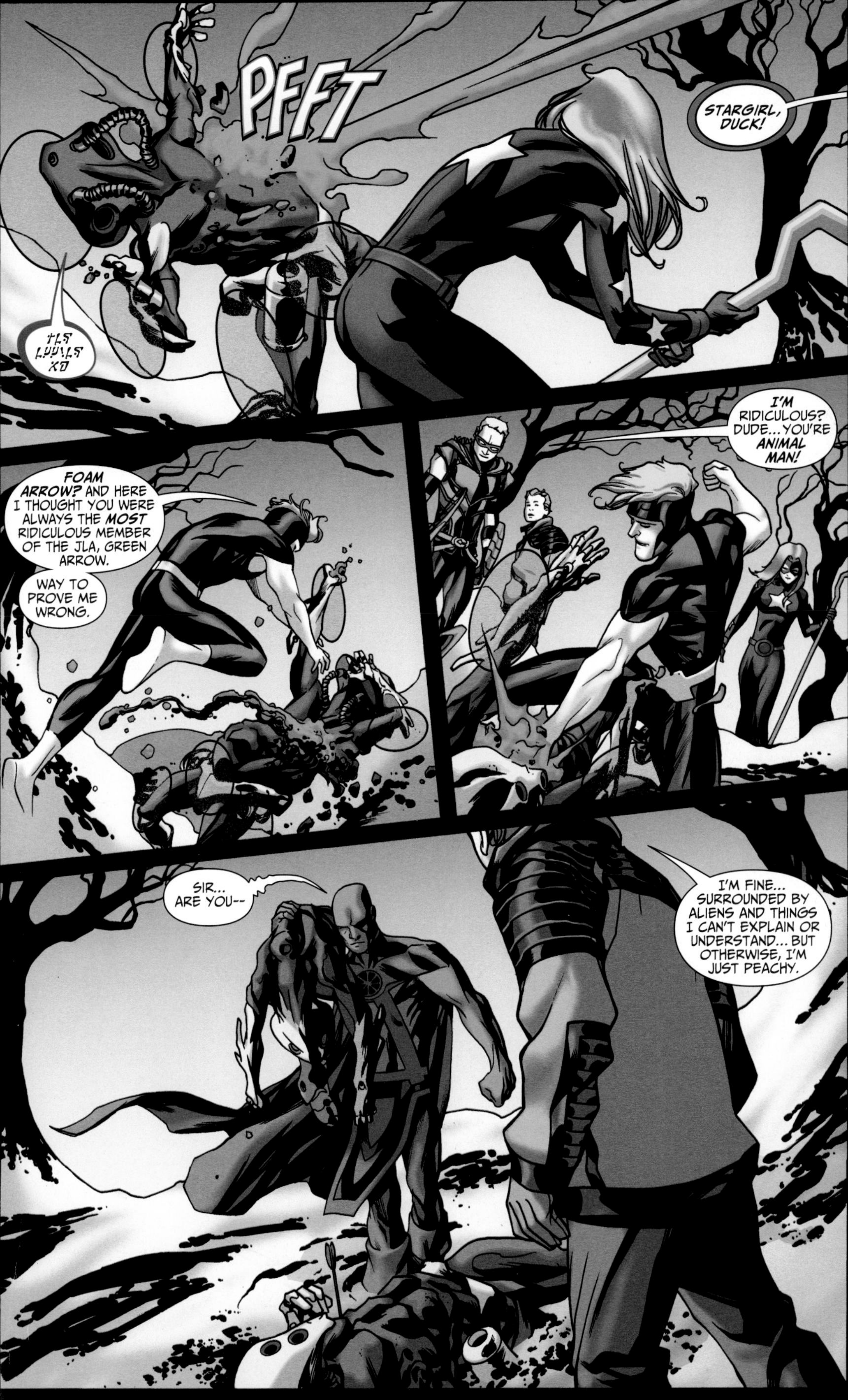
PFFT
STARGIRL, DUCK!
FOAM ARROW? AND HERE I THOUGHT YOU WERE ALWAYS THE MOST RIDICULOUS MEMBER OF THE JLA, GREEN ARROW.
WAY TO PROVE ME WRONG.
I'M RIDICULOUS? DUDE... YOU'RE ANIMAL MAN!
SIR... ARE YOU--
I'M FINE... SURROUNDED BY ALIENS AND THINGS I CAN'T EXPLAIN OR UNDERSTAND... BUT OTHERWISE, I'M JUST PEACHY.

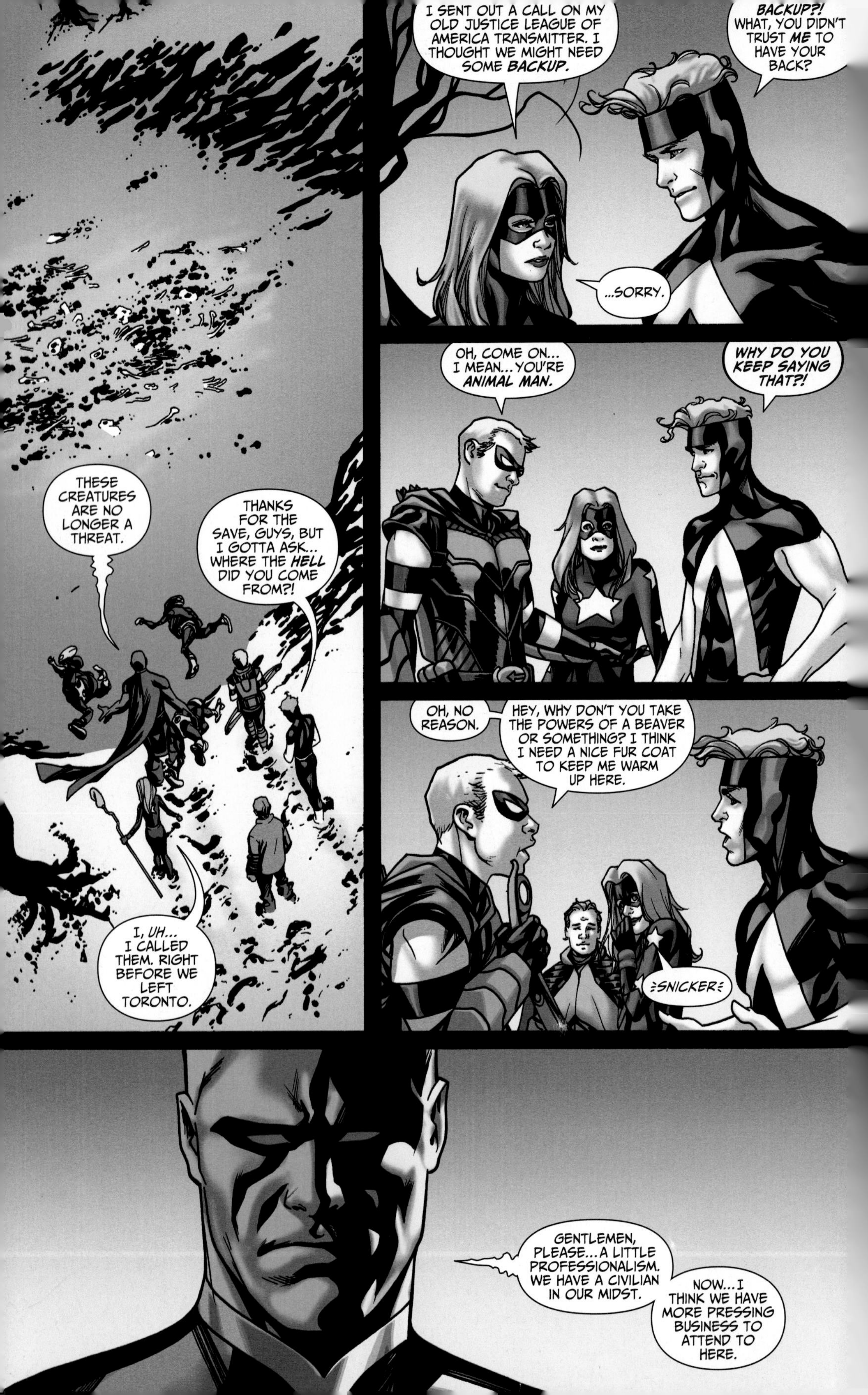
THESE CREATURES ARE NO LONGER A THREAT.
THANKS FOR THE SAVE, GUYS, BUT I GOTTA ASK... WHERE THE HELL DID YOU COME FROM?!
I, UH... I CALLED THEM. RIGHT BEFORE WE LEFT TORONTO.
I SENT OUT A CALL ON MY OLD JUSTICE LEAGUE OF AMERICA TRANSMITTER. I THOUGHT WE MIGHT NEED SOME BACKUP.
BACKUP?! WHAT, YOU DIDN'T TRUST ME TO HAVE YOUR BACK?
...SORRY.
OH, COME ON... I MEAN... YOU'RE ANIMAL MAN.
WHY DO YOU KEEP SAYING THAT?!
OH, NO REASON.
HEY, WHY DON'T YOU TAKE THE POWERS OF A BEAVER OR SOMETHING? I THINK I NEED A NICE FUR COAT TO KEEP ME WARM UP HERE.
SNICKER
GENTLEMEN, PLEASE... A LITTLE PROFESSIONALISM. WE HAVE A CIVILIAN IN OUR MIDST.
NOW... I THINK WE HAVE MORE PRESSING BUSINESS TO ATTEND TO HERE.

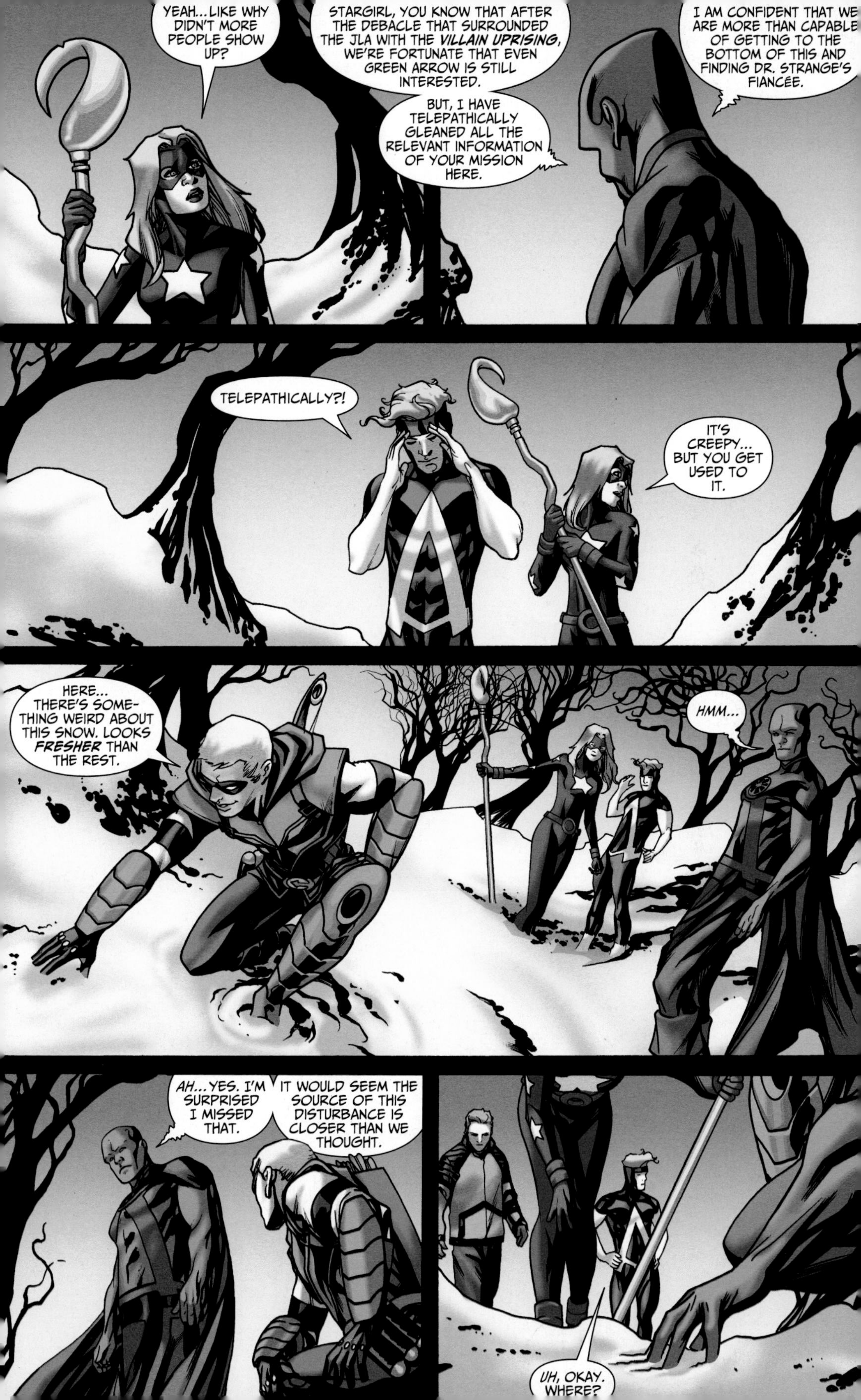
YEAH...LIKE WHY DIDN'T MORE PEOPLE SHOW UP?
STARGIRL, YOU KNOW THAT AFTER THE DEBACLE THAT SURROUNDED THE JLA WITH THE *VILLAIN UPRISING*, WE'RE FORTUNATE THAT EVEN GREEN ARROW IS STILL INTERESTED.
BUT, I HAVE TELEPATHICALLY GLEANED ALL THE RELEVANT INFORMATION OF YOUR MISSION HERE.
I AM CONFIDENT THAT WE ARE MORE THAN CAPABLE OF GETTING TO THE BOTTOM OF THIS AND FINDING DR. STRANGE'S FIANCÉE.
TELEPATHICALLY?!
IT'S CREEPY... BUT YOU GET USED TO IT.
HERE... THERE'S SOME-THING WEIRD ABOUT THIS SNOW. LOOKS *FRESHER* THAN THE REST.
HMM...
AH...YES. I'M SURPRISED I MISSED THAT.
IT WOULD SEEM THE SOURCE OF THIS DISTURBANCE IS CLOSER THAN WE THOUGHT.
UH, OKAY. WHERE?

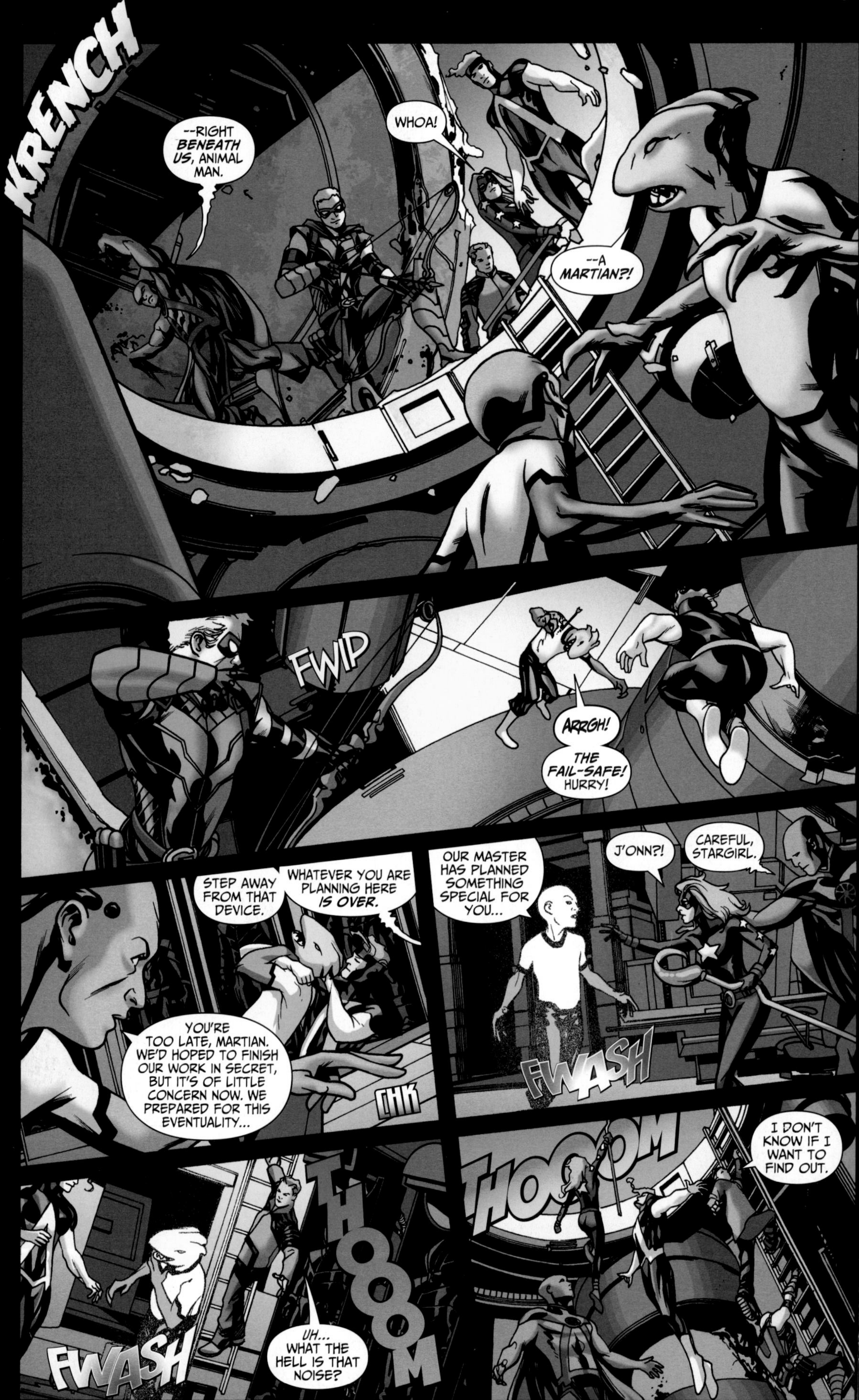
KRENCH
--RIGHT BENEATH US, ANIMAL MAN.
WHOA!
--A MARTIAN?!
FWIP
ARRGH!
THE FAIL-SAFE! HURRY!
STEP AWAY FROM THAT DEVICE.
WHATEVER YOU ARE PLANNING HERE IS OVER.
YOU'RE TOO LATE, MARTIAN. WE'D HOPED TO FINISH OUR WORK IN SECRET, BUT IT'S OF LITTLE CONCERN NOW. WE PREPARED FOR THIS EVENTUALITY...
CHK
OUR MASTER HAS PLANNED SOMETHING SPECIAL FOR YOU...
J'ONN?!
CAREFUL, STARGIRL.
FWASH
FWASH
TH88M
UH... WHAT THE HELL IS THAT NOISE?
THOOOM
I DON'T KNOW IF I WANT TO FIND OUT.

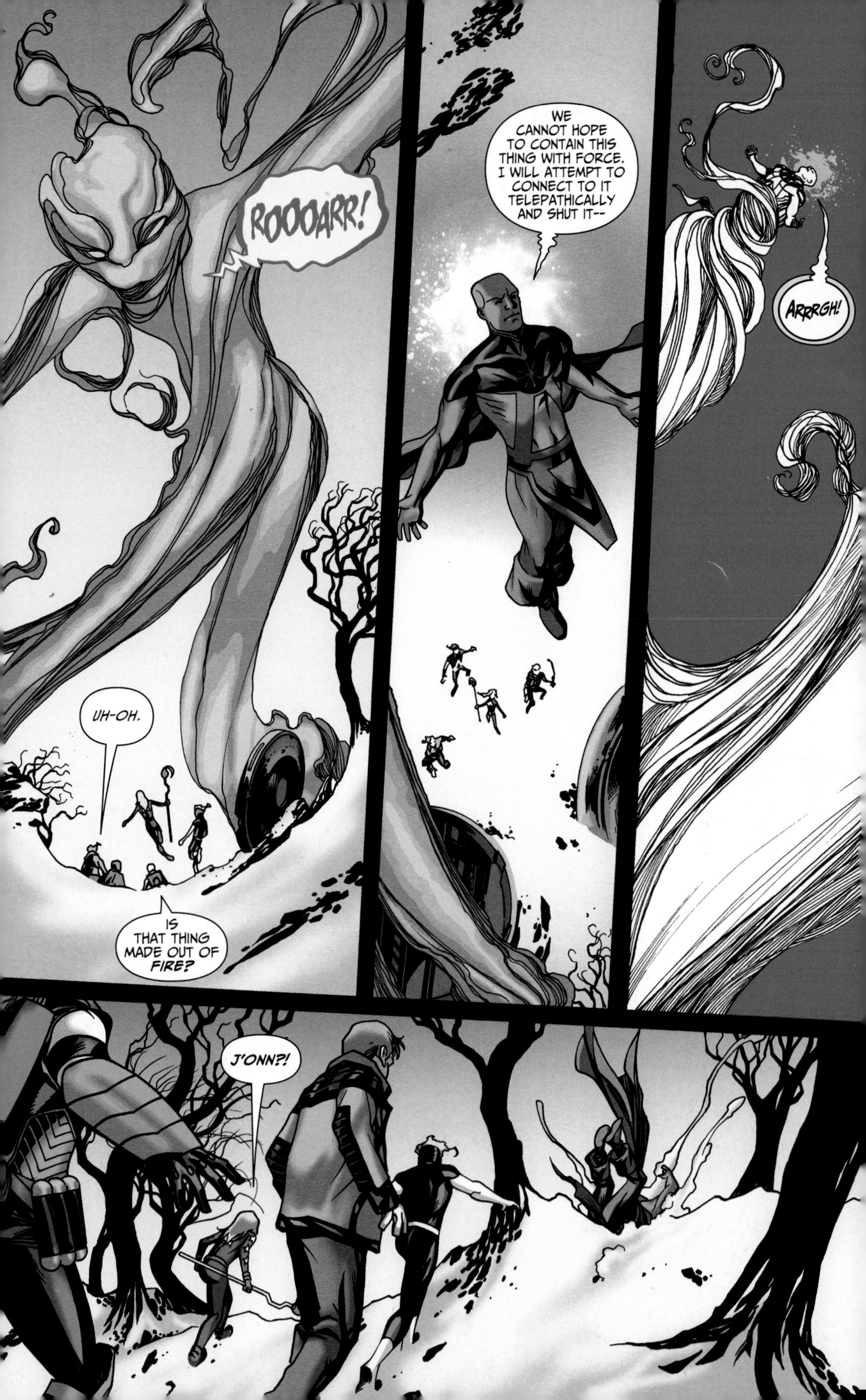
ROOOARR!
UH-OH.
IS THAT THING MADE OUT OF FIRE?
WE CANNOT HOPE TO CONTAIN THIS THING WITH FORCE. I WILL ATTEMPT TO CONNECT TO IT TELEPATHICALLY AND SHUT IT--
ARRRGH!
J'ONN?!

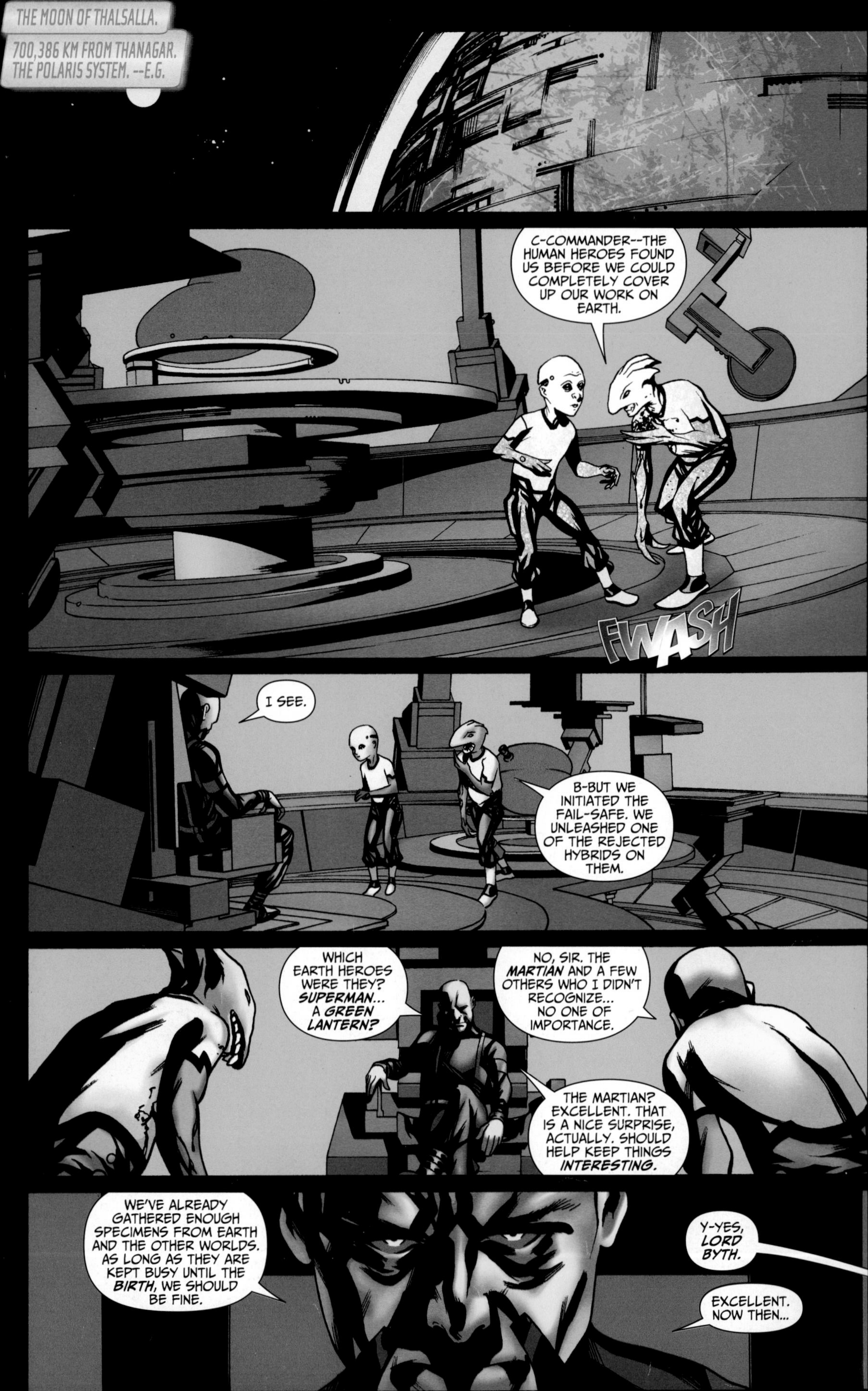
THE MOON OF THALSALLA.
700,386 KM FROM THANAGAR. THE POLARIS SYSTEM. --E.G.
C-COMMANDER--THE HUMAN HEROES FOUND US BEFORE WE COULD COMPLETELY COVER UP OUR WORK ON EARTH.
FWASH
I SEE.
B-BUT WE INITIATED THE FAIL-SAFE. WE UNLEASHED ONE OF THE REJECTED HYBRIDS ON THEM.
WHICH EARTH HEROES WERE THEY? SUPERMAN... A GREEN LANTERN?
NO, SIR. THE MARTIAN AND A FEW OTHERS WHO I DIDN'T RECOGNIZE... NO ONE OF IMPORTANCE.
THE MARTIAN? EXCELLENT. THAT IS A NICE SURPRISE, ACTUALLY. SHOULD HELP KEEP THINGS INTERESTING.
WE'VE ALREADY GATHERED ENOUGH SPECIMENS FROM EARTH AND THE OTHER WORLDS. AS LONG AS THEY ARE KEPT BUSY UNTIL THE BIRTH, WE SHOULD BE FINE.
Y-YES, LORD BYTH.
EXCELLENT. NOW THEN...

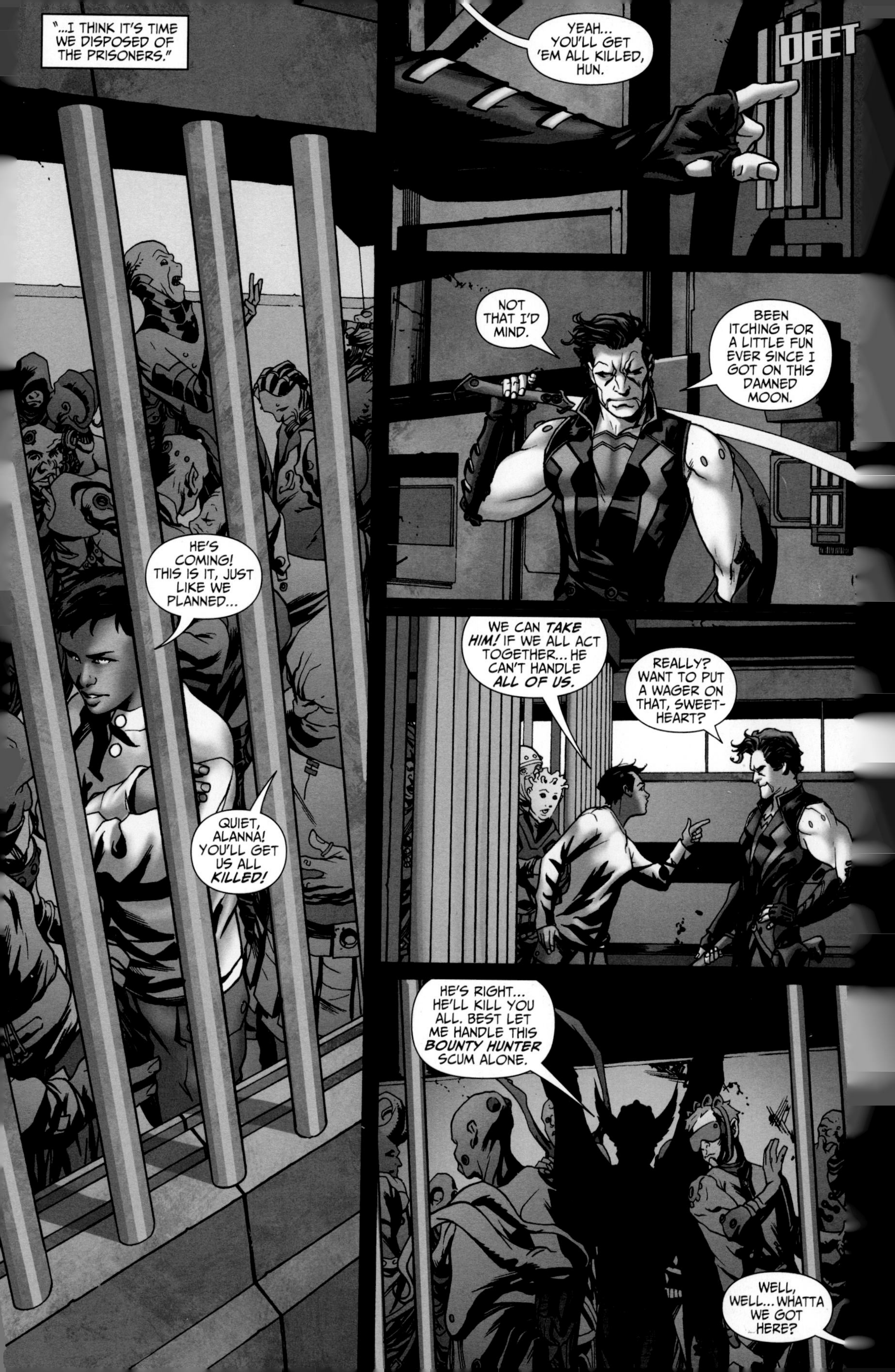
"...I THINK IT'S TIME WE DISPOSED OF THE PRISONERS."
YEAH... YOU'LL GET 'EM ALL KILLED, HUN.
DEET
HE'S COMING! THIS IS IT, JUST LIKE WE PLANNED...
QUIET, ALANNA! YOU'LL GET US ALL KILLED!
NOT THAT I'D MIND.
BEEN ITCHING FOR A LITTLE FUN EVER SINCE I GOT ON THIS DAMNED MOON.
WE CAN TAKE HIM! IF WE ALL ACT TOGETHER... HE CAN'T HANDLE ALL OF US.
REALLY? WANT TO PUT A WAGER ON THAT, SWEET-HEART?
HE'S RIGHT... HE'LL KILL YOU ALL. BEST LET ME HANDLE THIS BOUNTY HUNTER SCUM ALONE.
WELL, WELL... WHATTA WE GOT HERE?

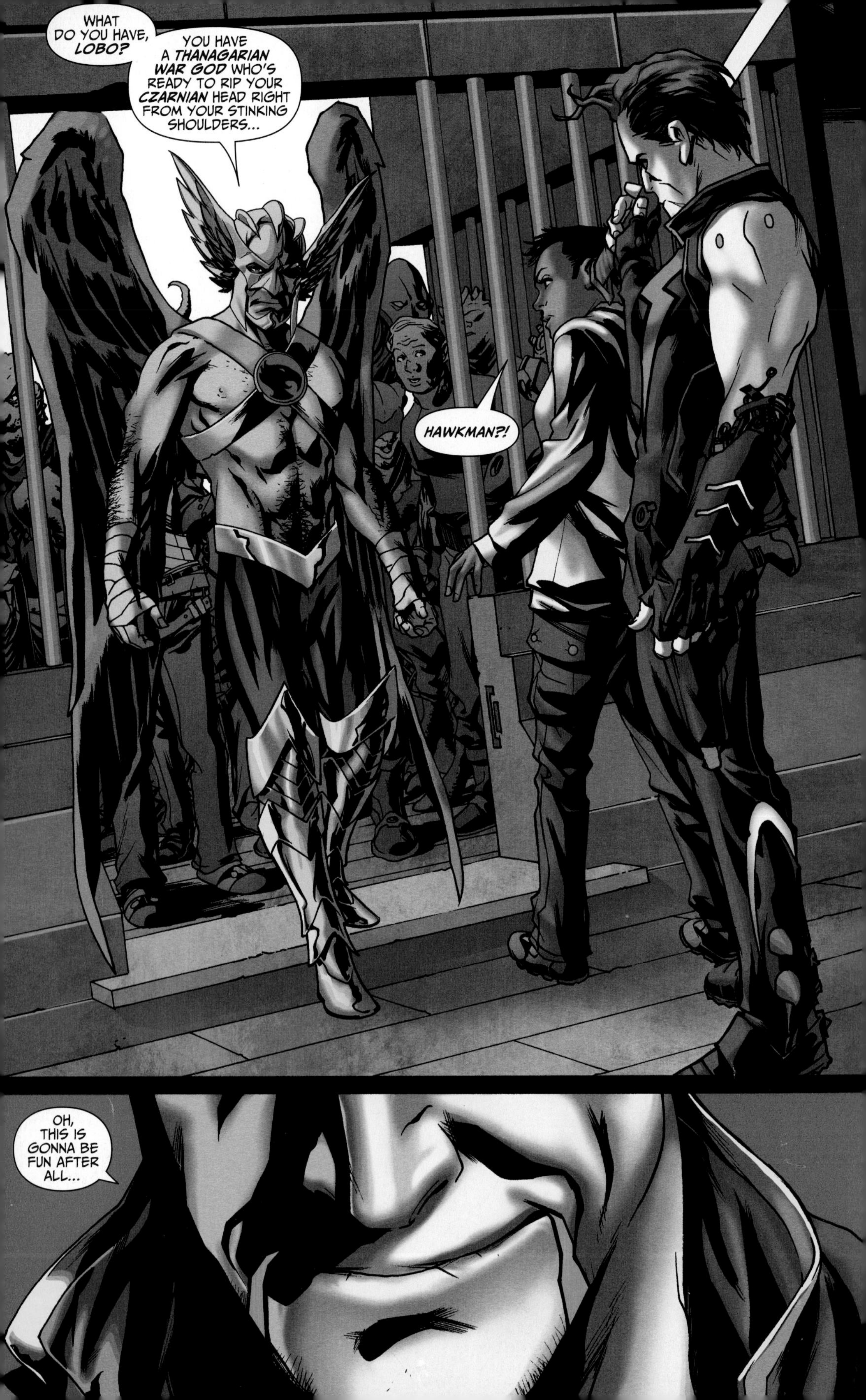
WHAT DO YOU HAVE, LOBO?
YOU HAVE A THANAGARIAN WAR GOD WHO'S READY TO RIP YOUR CZARNIAN HEAD RIGHT FROM YOUR STINKING SHOULDERS...
HAWKMAN?!
OH, THIS IS GONNA BE FUN AFTER ALL...

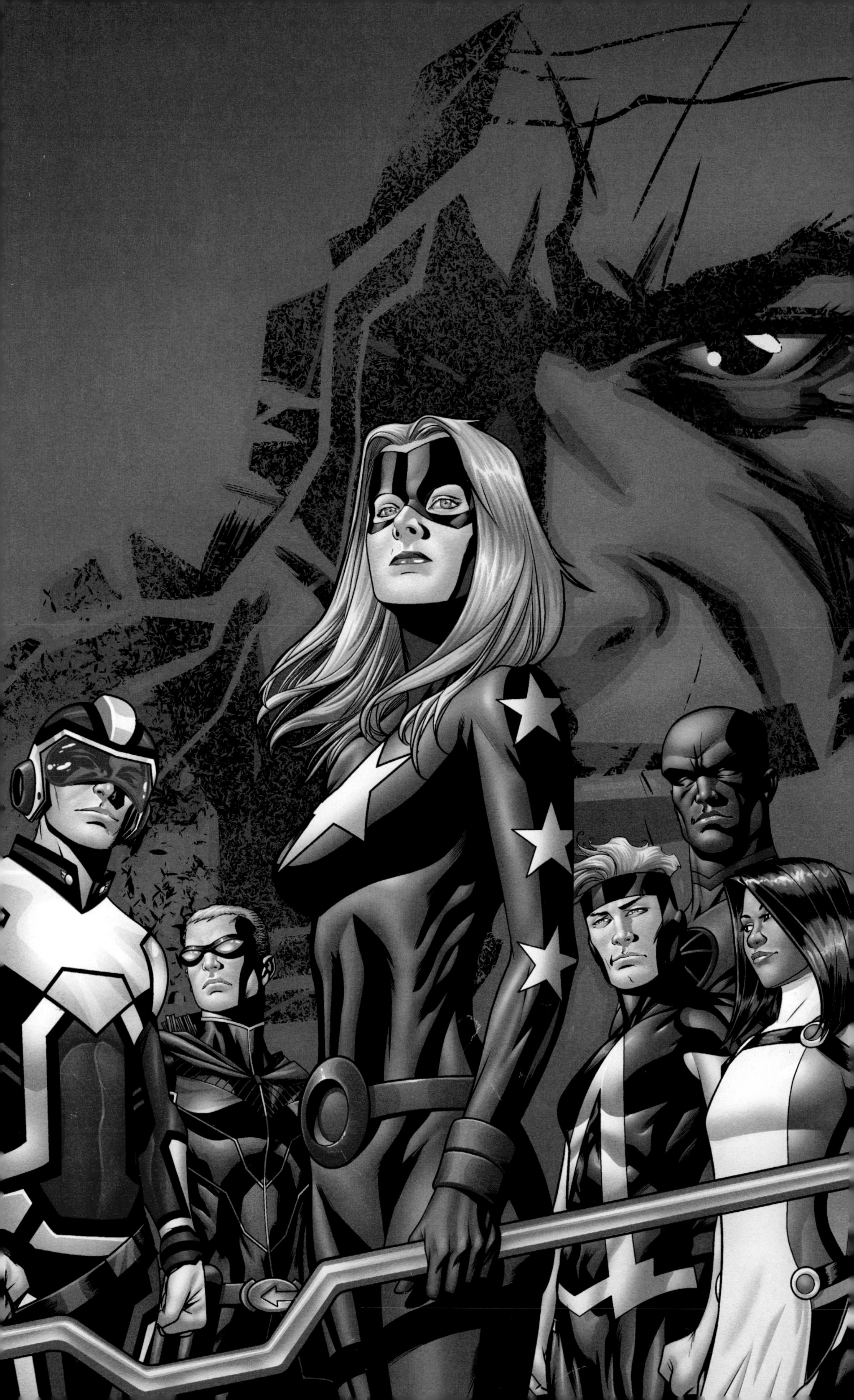

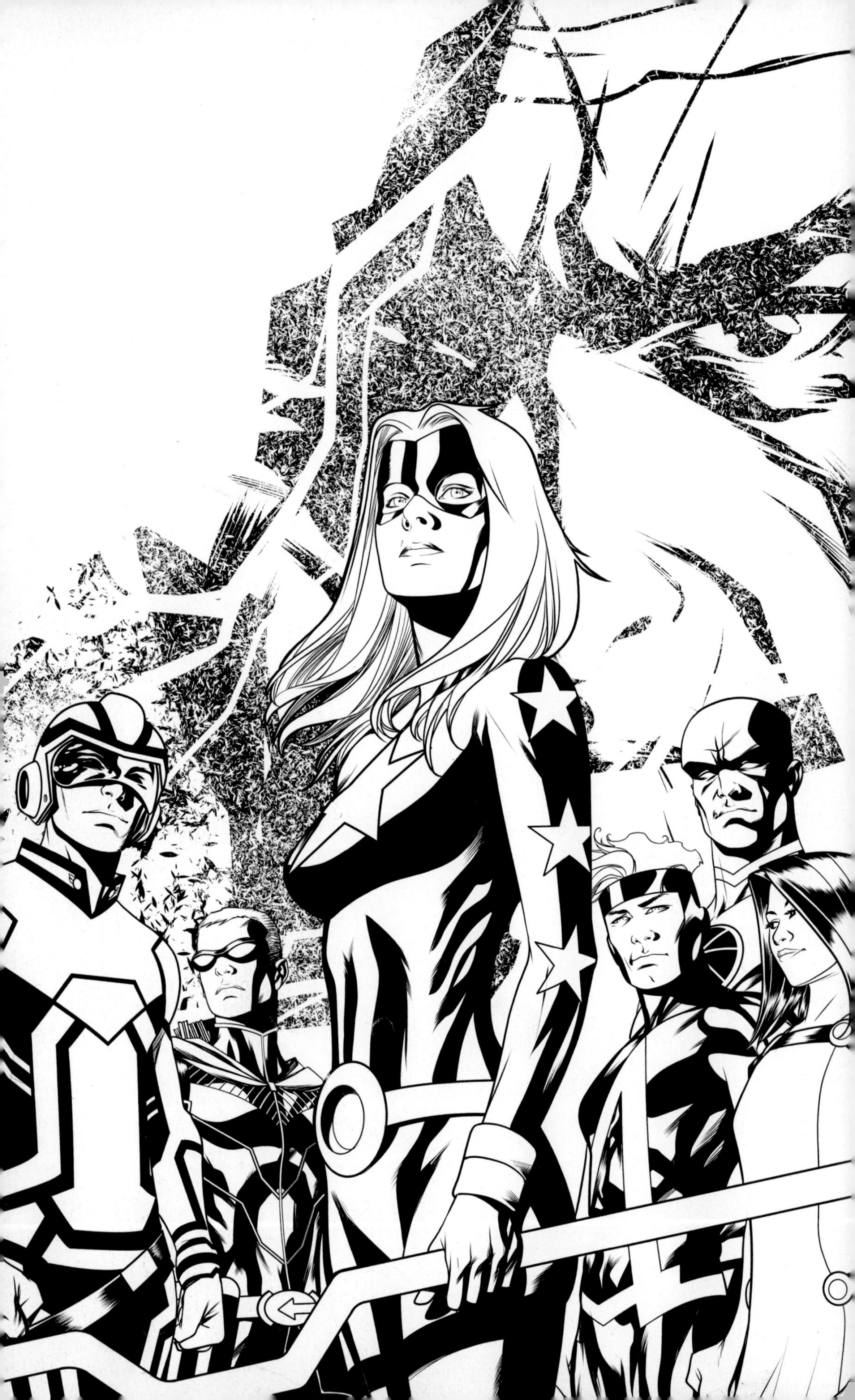

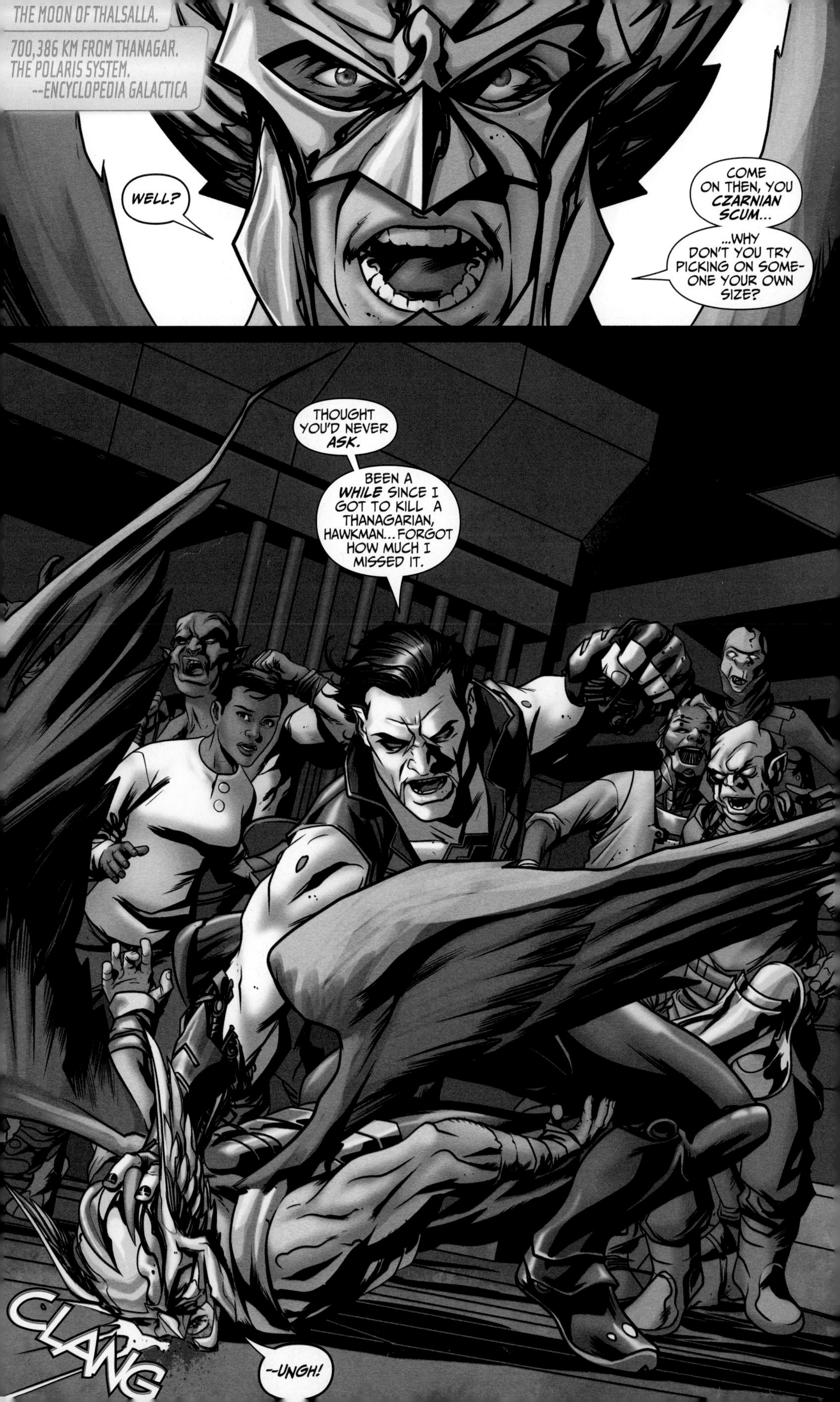
THE MOON OF THALSALLA.
700,386 KM FROM THANAGAR. THE POLARIS SYSTEM. --ENCYCLOPEDIA GALACTICA
WELL?
COME ON THEN, YOU CZARNIAN SCUM...
...WHY DON'T YOU TRY PICKING ON SOME-ONE YOUR OWN SIZE?
THOUGHT YOU'D NEVER ASK.
BEEN A WHILE SINCE I GOT TO KILL A THANAGARIAN, HAWKMAN...FORGOT HOW MUCH I MISSED IT.
CLANG
--UNGH!

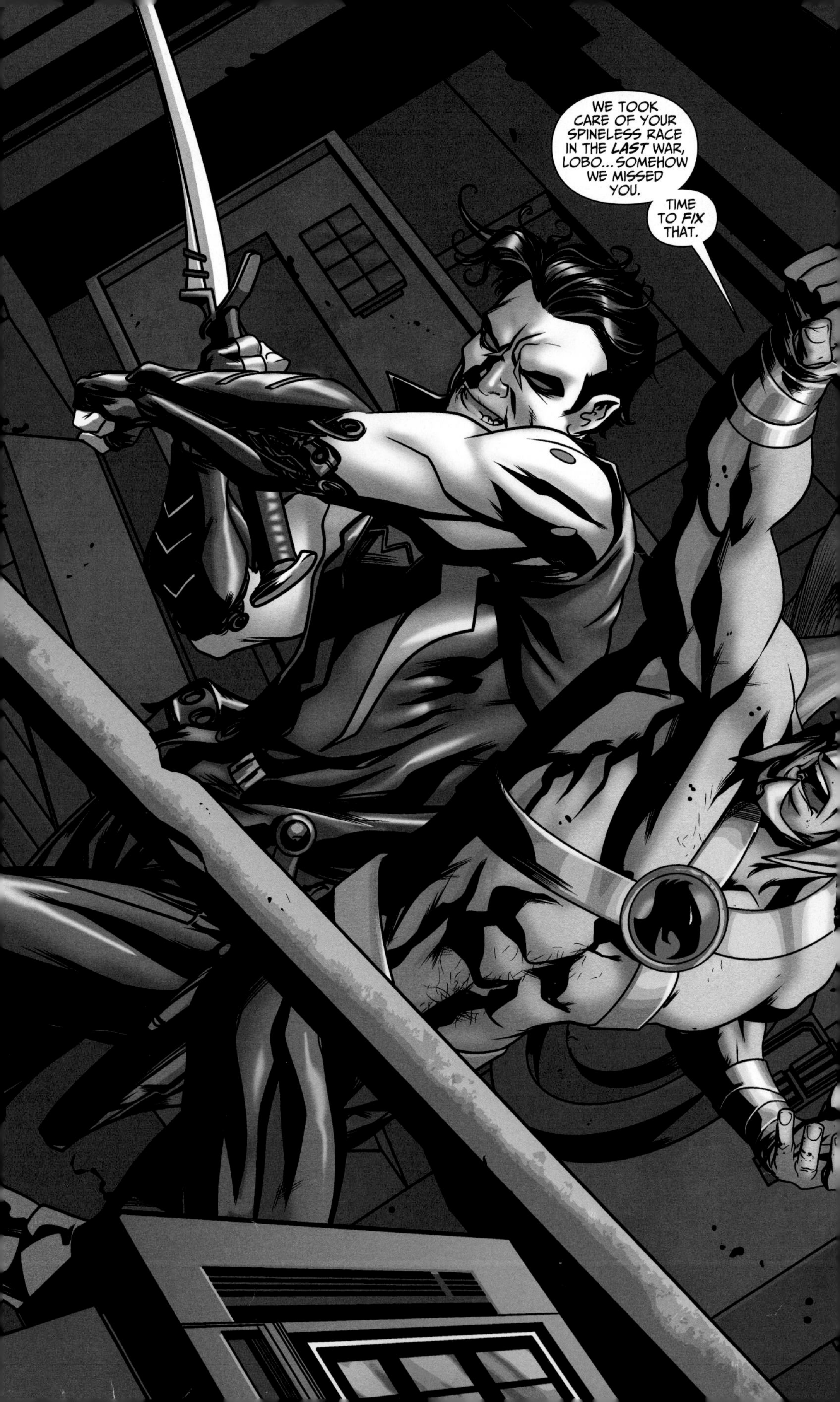
WE TOOK CARE OF YOUR SPINELESS RACE IN THE LAST WAR, LOBO...SOMEHOW WE MISSED YOU.
TIME TO FIX THAT.

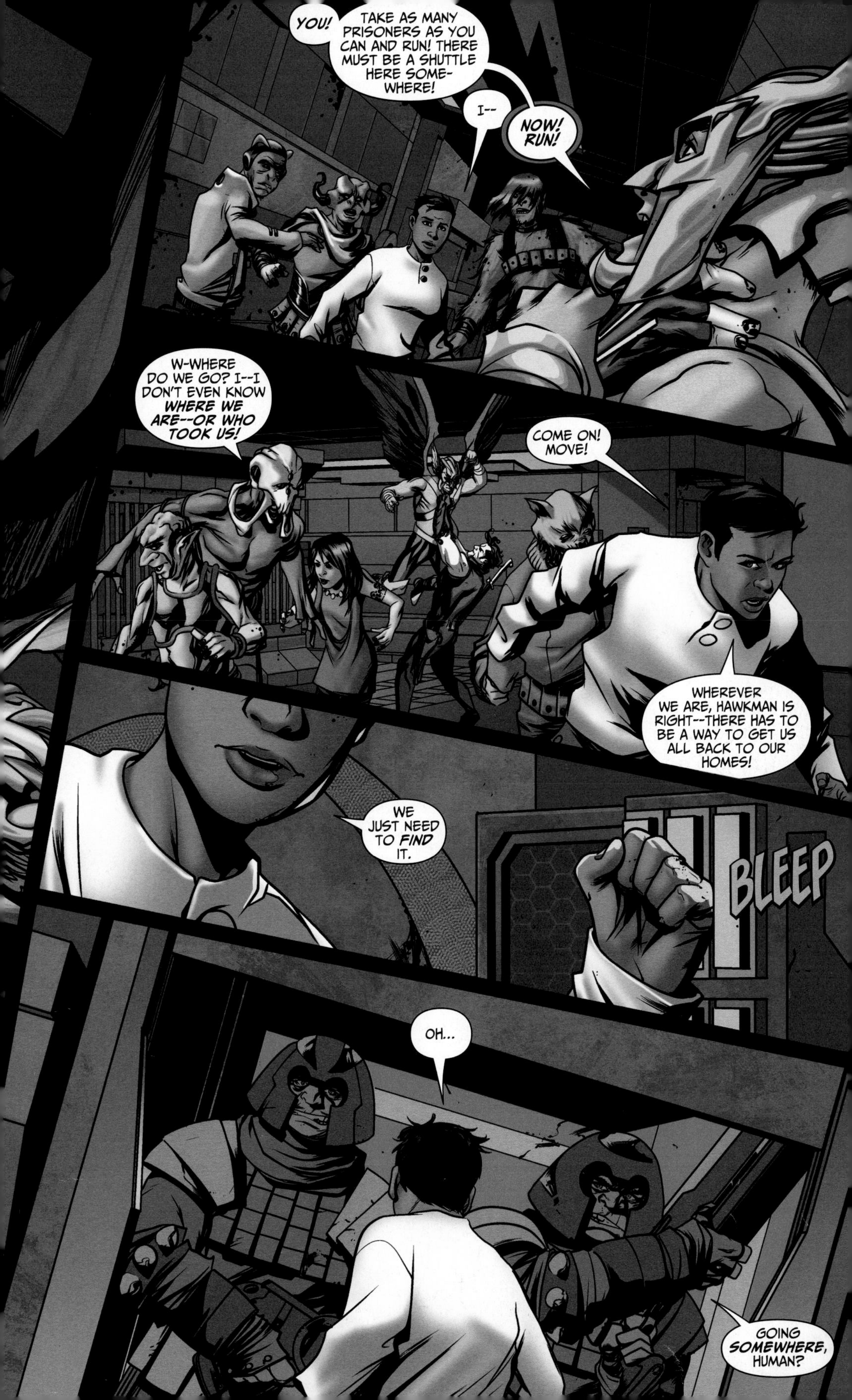
YOU!
TAKE AS MANY PRISONERS AS YOU CAN AND RUN! THERE MUST BE A SHUTTLE HERE SOME-WHERE!
I--
NOW! RUN!
W-WHERE DO WE GO? I--I DON'T EVEN KNOW WHERE WE ARE--OR WHO TOOK US!
COME ON! MOVE!
WHEREVER WE ARE, HAWKMAN IS RIGHT--THERE HAS TO BE A WAY TO GET US ALL BACK TO OUR HOMES!
WE JUST NEED TO FIND IT.
BLEEP
OH...
GOING SOMEWHERE, HUMAN?

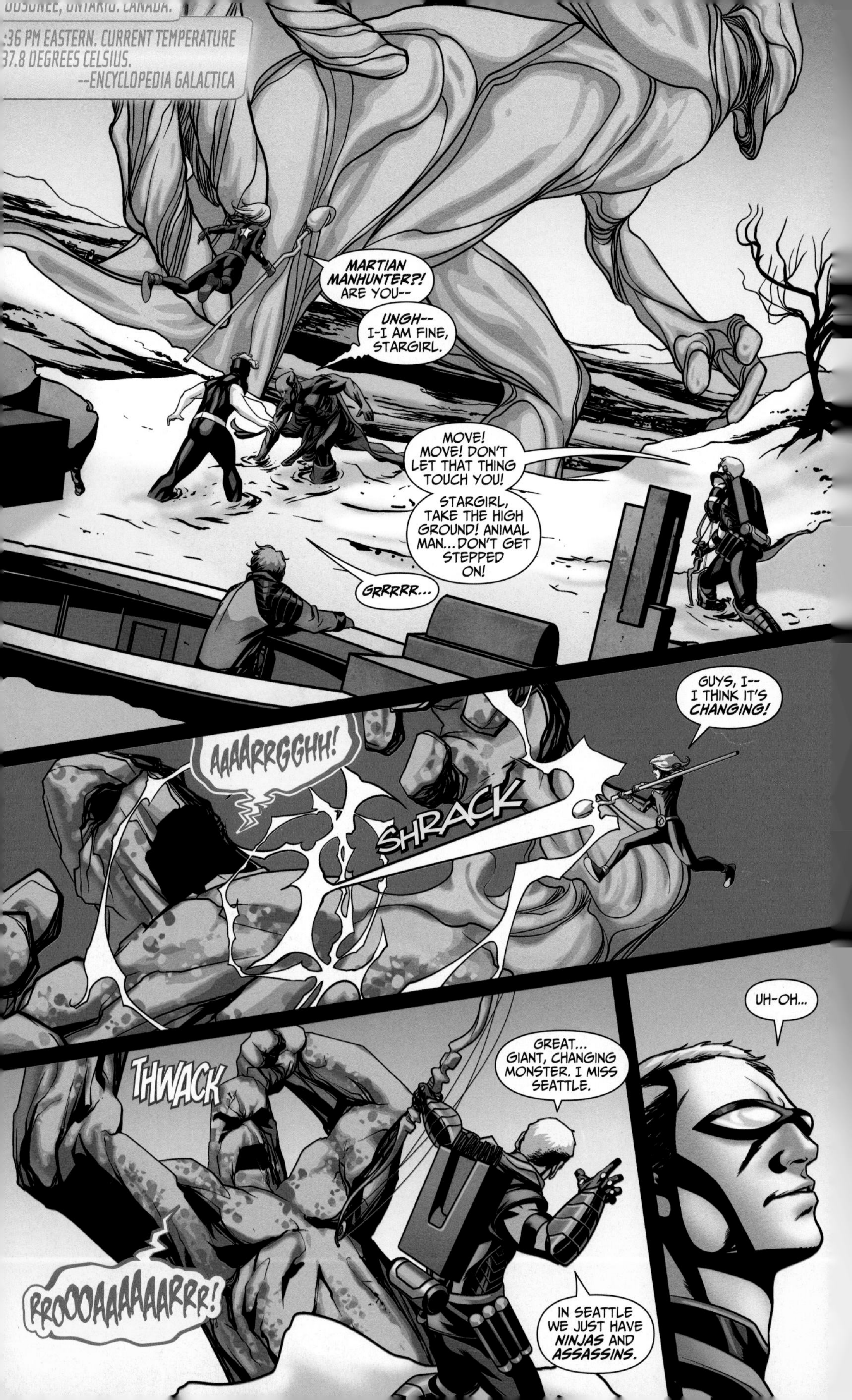
OOSONEE, ONTARIO. CANADA.
:36 PM EASTERN. CURRENT TEMPERATURE 37.8 DEGREES CELSIUS.
--ENCYCLOPEDIA GALACTICA
MARTIAN MANHUNTER?! ARE YOU--
UNGH-- I-I AM FINE, STARGIRL.
MOVE! MOVE! DON'T LET THAT THING TOUCH YOU!
STARGIRL, TAKE THE HIGH GROUND! ANIMAL MAN... DON'T GET STEPPED ON!
GRRRRR...
GUYS, I-- I THINK IT'S CHANGING!
AAAARRGGHH!
SHRACK
THWACK
GREAT... GIANT, CHANGING MONSTER. I MISS SEATTLE.
UH-OH...
RROOOAAAAAARRR!
IN SEATTLE WE JUST HAVE NINJAS AND ASSASSINS.

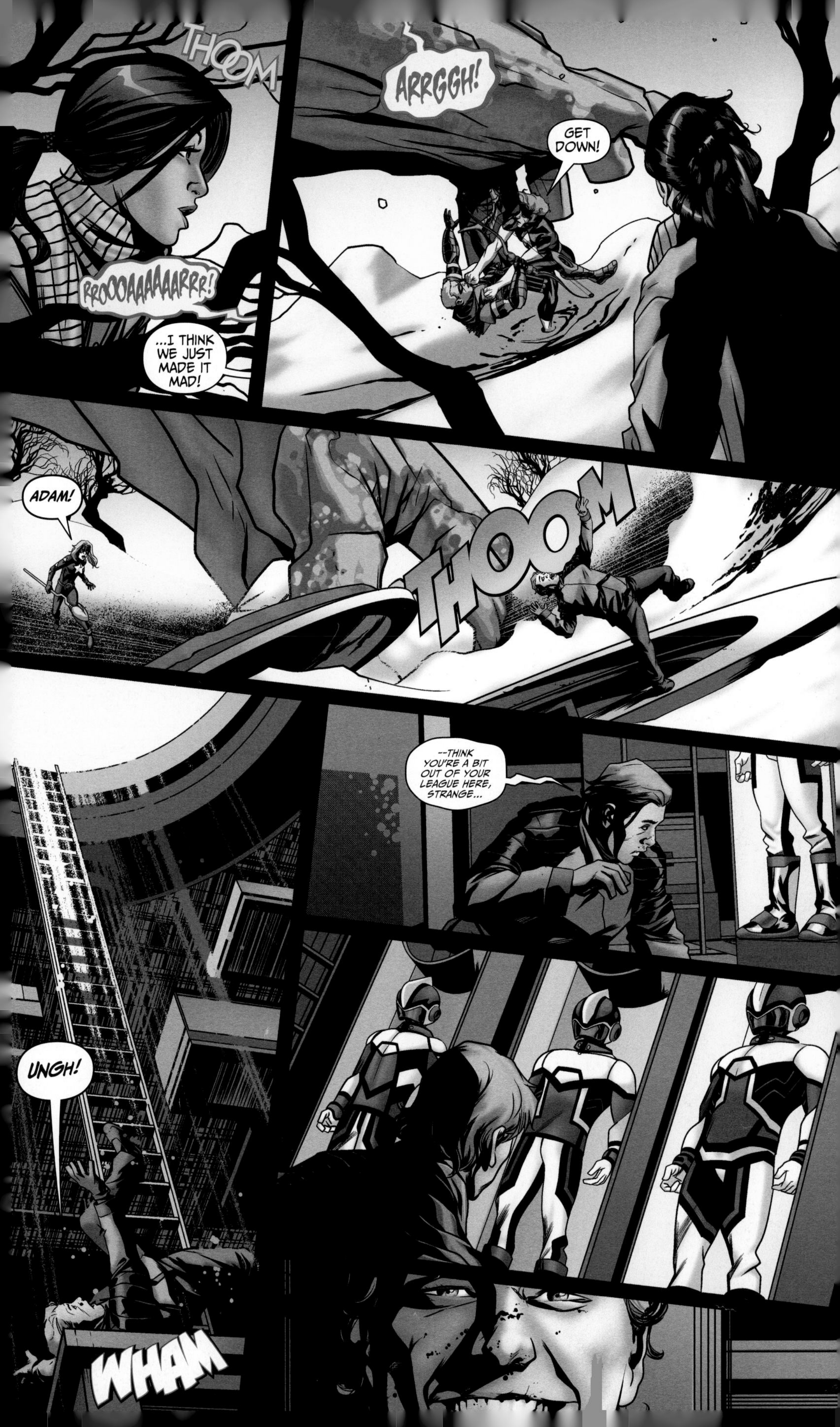
THOOM
RROOOAAAAAAARRR!
...I THINK WE JUST MADE IT MAD!
ARRGGH!
GET DOWN!
ADAM!
THOOM
--THINK YOU'RE A BIT OUT OF YOUR LEAGUE HERE, STRANGE...
UNGH!
WHAM

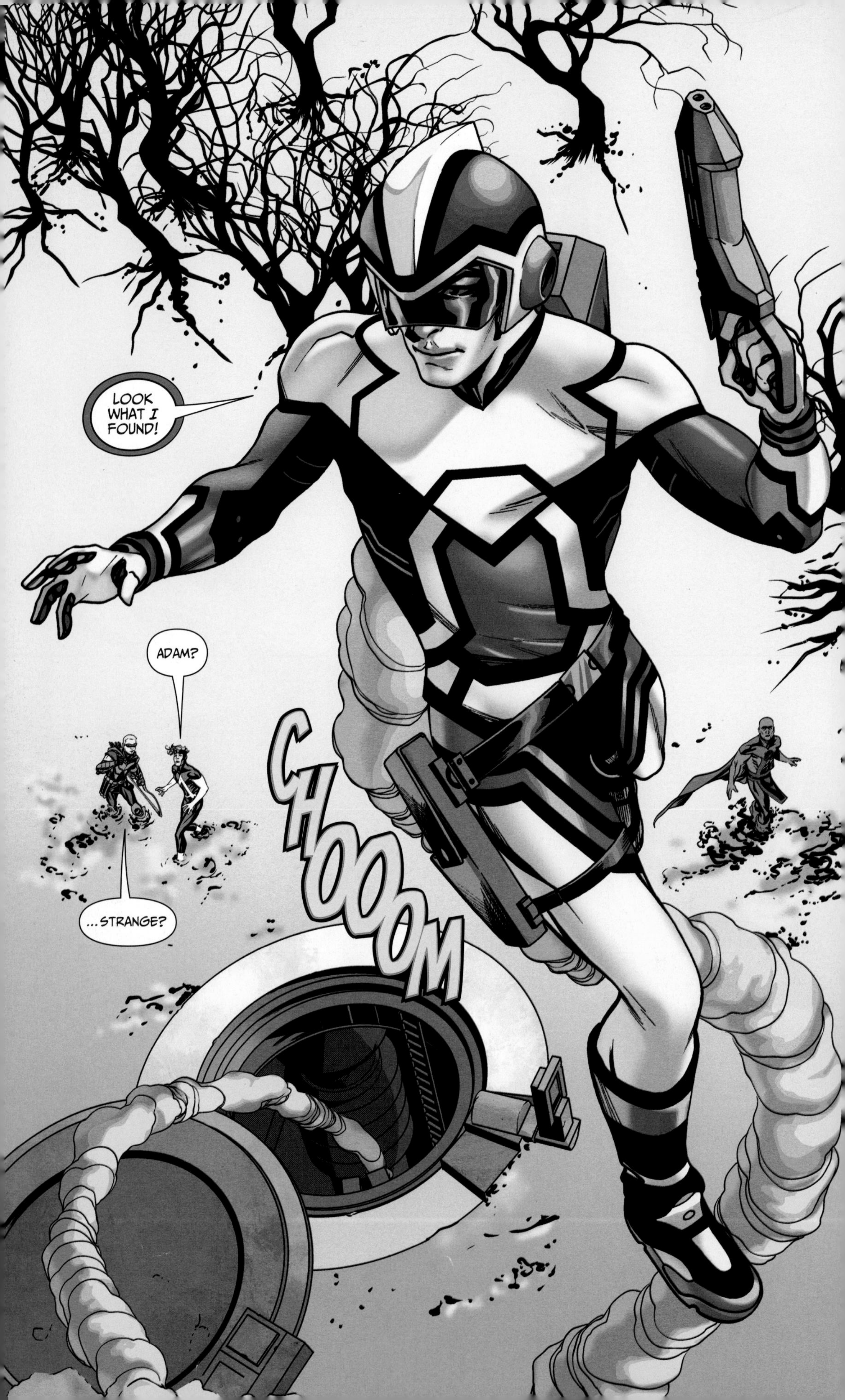
LOOK WHAT I FOUND!
ADAM?
...STRANGE?
CHOOOM

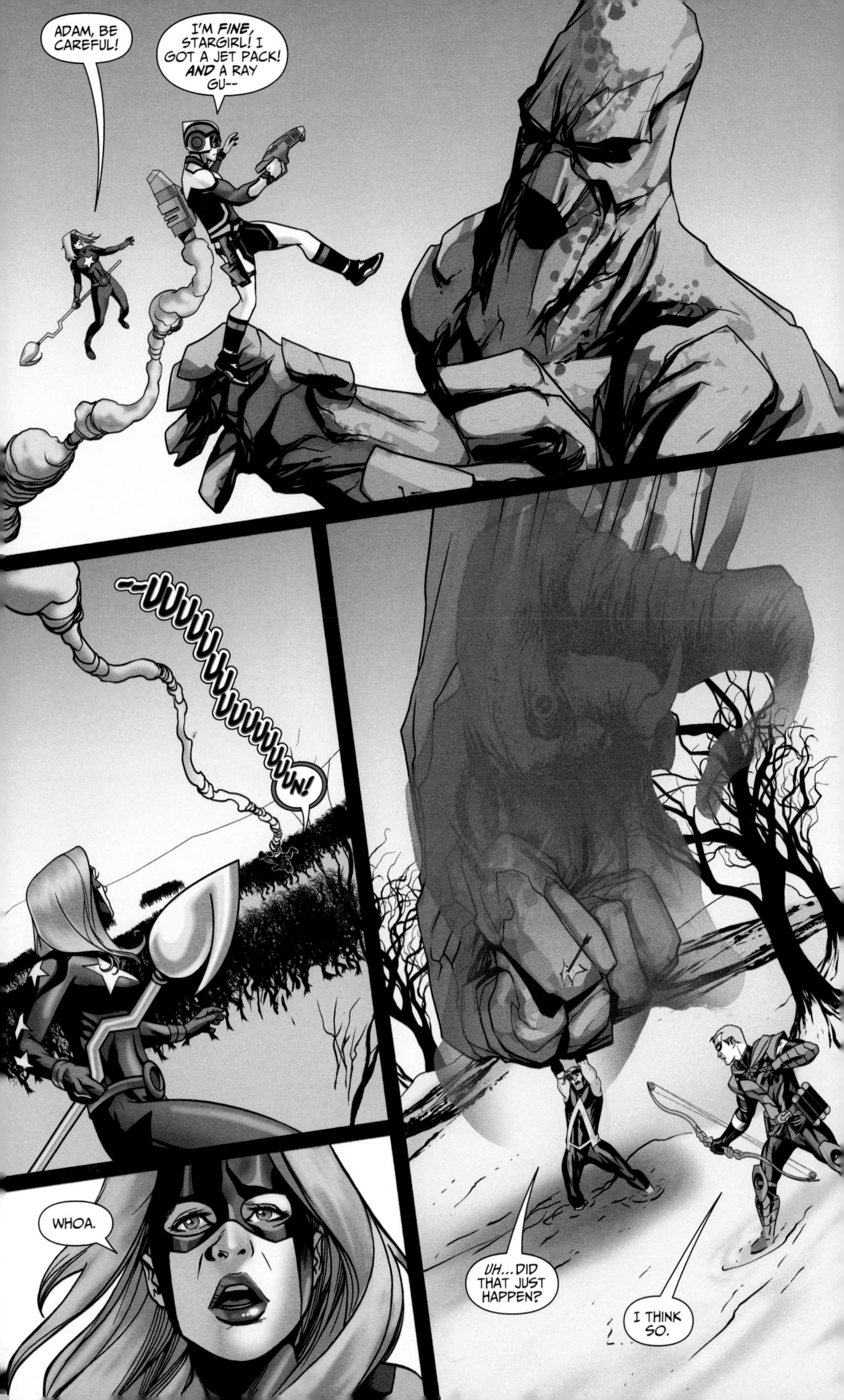
ADAM, BE CAREFUL!
I'M FINE, STARGIRL! I GOT A JET PACK! AND A RAY GU--
--VVVVVVVVVVVVVVVUUUN!
WHOA.
UH...DID THAT JUST HAPPEN?
I THINK SO.

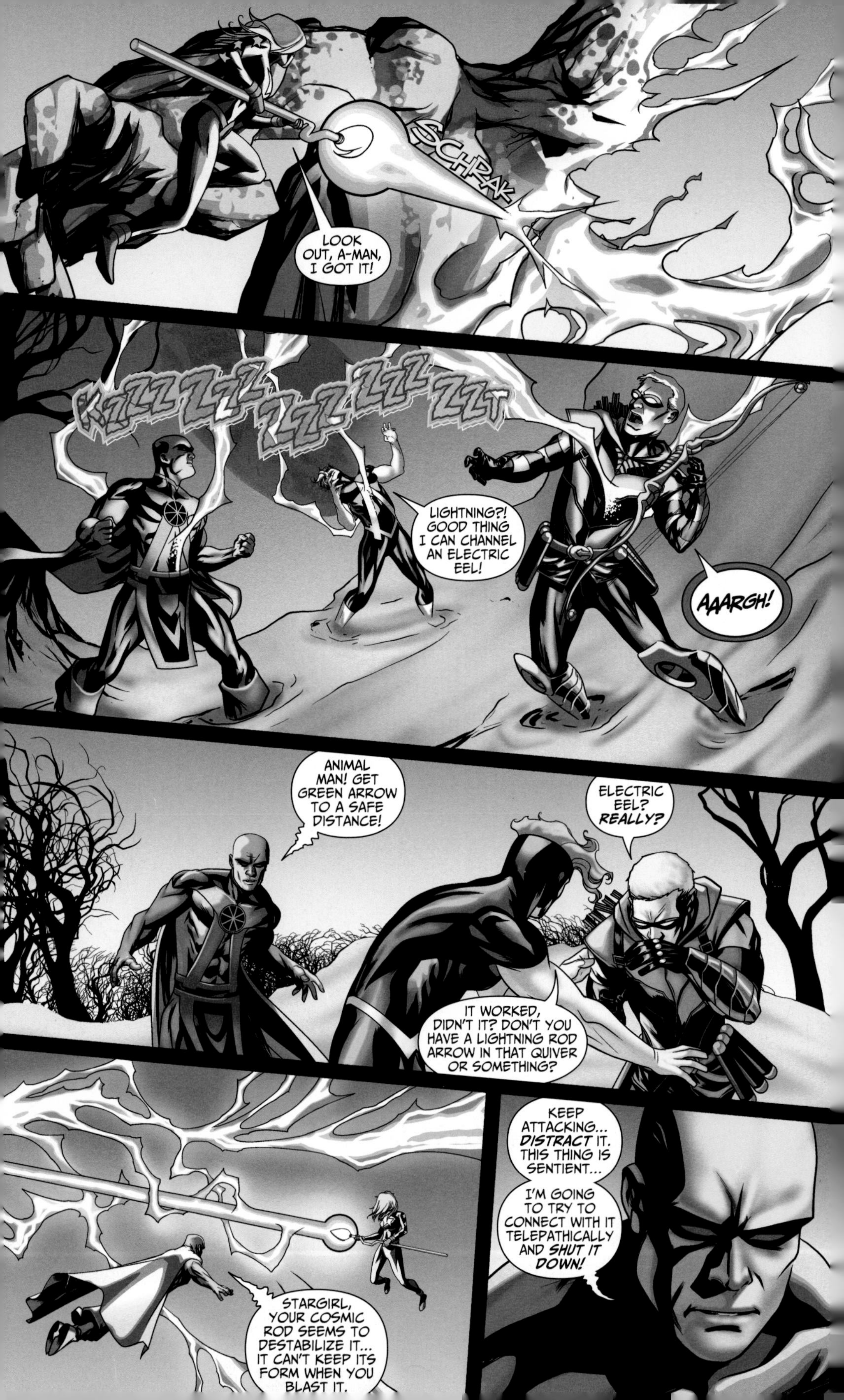
SCHRAK
LOOK OUT, A-MAN, I GOT IT!
KZZZZZZZZZZZZZZZT
LIGHTNING?! GOOD THING I CAN CHANNEL AN ELECTRIC EEL!
AAARGH!
ANIMAL MAN! GET GREEN ARROW TO A SAFE DISTANCE!
ELECTRIC EEL? REALLY?
IT WORKED, DIDN'T IT? DON'T YOU HAVE A LIGHTNING ROD ARROW IN THAT QUIVER OR SOMETHING?
STARGIRL, YOUR COSMIC ROD SEEMS TO DESTABILIZE IT... IT CAN'T KEEP ITS FORM WHEN YOU BLAST IT.
KEEP ATTACKING... DISTRACT IT. THIS THING IS SENTIENT...
I'M GOING TO TRY TO CONNECT WITH IT TELEPATHICALLY AND SHUT IT DOWN!

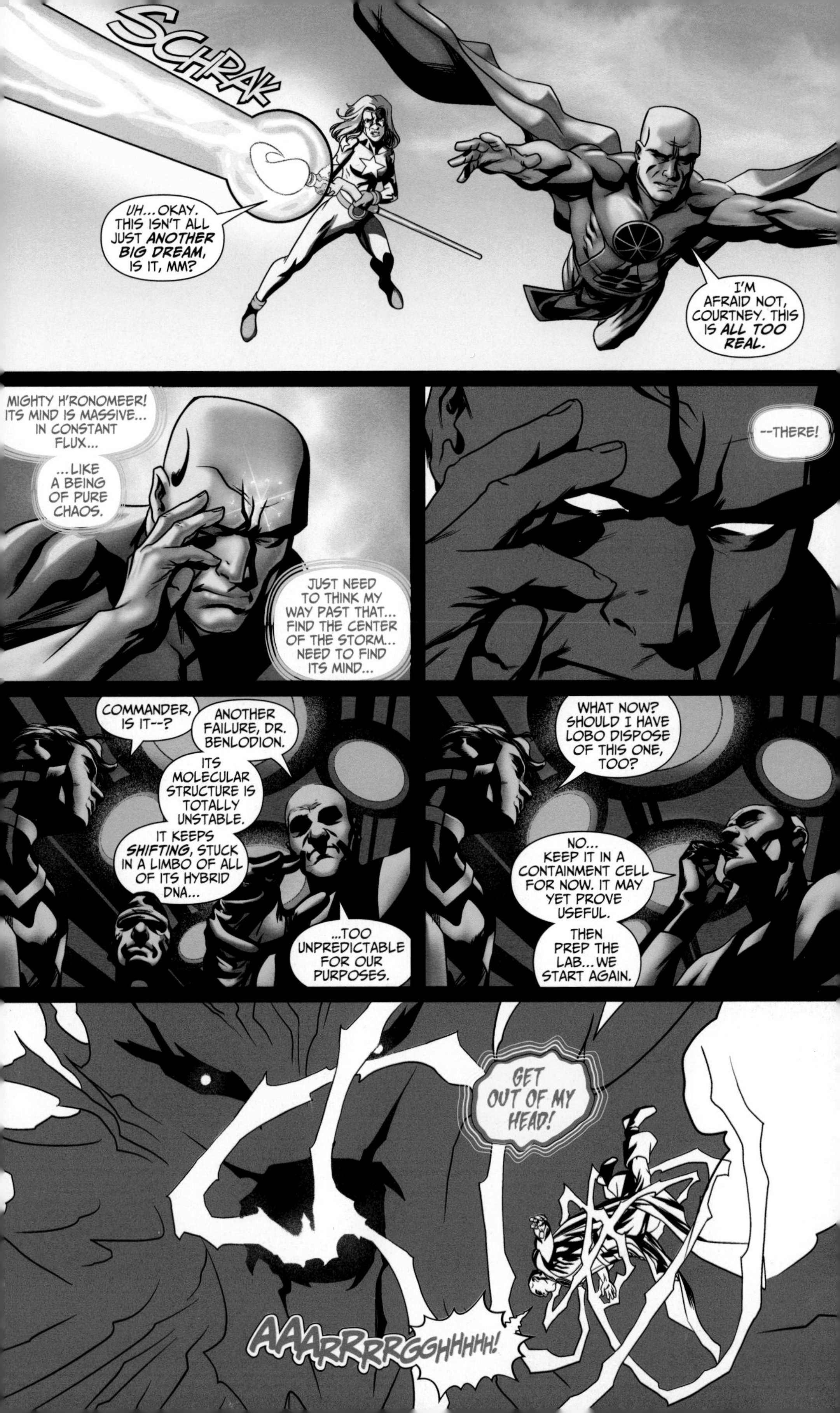
SCHRAK
UH...OKAY. THIS ISN'T ALL JUST ANOTHER BIG DREAM, IS IT, MM?
I'M AFRAID NOT, COURTNEY. THIS IS ALL TOO REAL.
MIGHTY H'RONOMEER! ITS MIND IS MASSIVE... IN CONSTANT FLUX...
...LIKE A BEING OF PURE CHAOS.
JUST NEED TO THINK MY WAY PAST THAT... FIND THE CENTER OF THE STORM... NEED TO FIND ITS MIND...
--THERE!
COMMANDER, IS IT--?
ANOTHER FAILURE, DR. BENLODION.
ITS MOLECULAR STRUCTURE IS TOTALLY UNSTABLE.
IT KEEPS SHIFTING, STUCK IN A LIMBO OF ALL OF ITS HYBRID DNA...
...TOO UNPREDICTABLE FOR OUR PURPOSES.
WHAT NOW? SHOULD I HAVE LOBO DISPOSE OF THIS ONE, TOO?
NO... KEEP IT IN A CONTAINMENT CELL FOR NOW. IT MAY YET PROVE USEFUL.
THEN PREP THE LAB...WE START AGAIN.
GET OUT OF MY HEAD!
AAARRRRGGHHHHH!

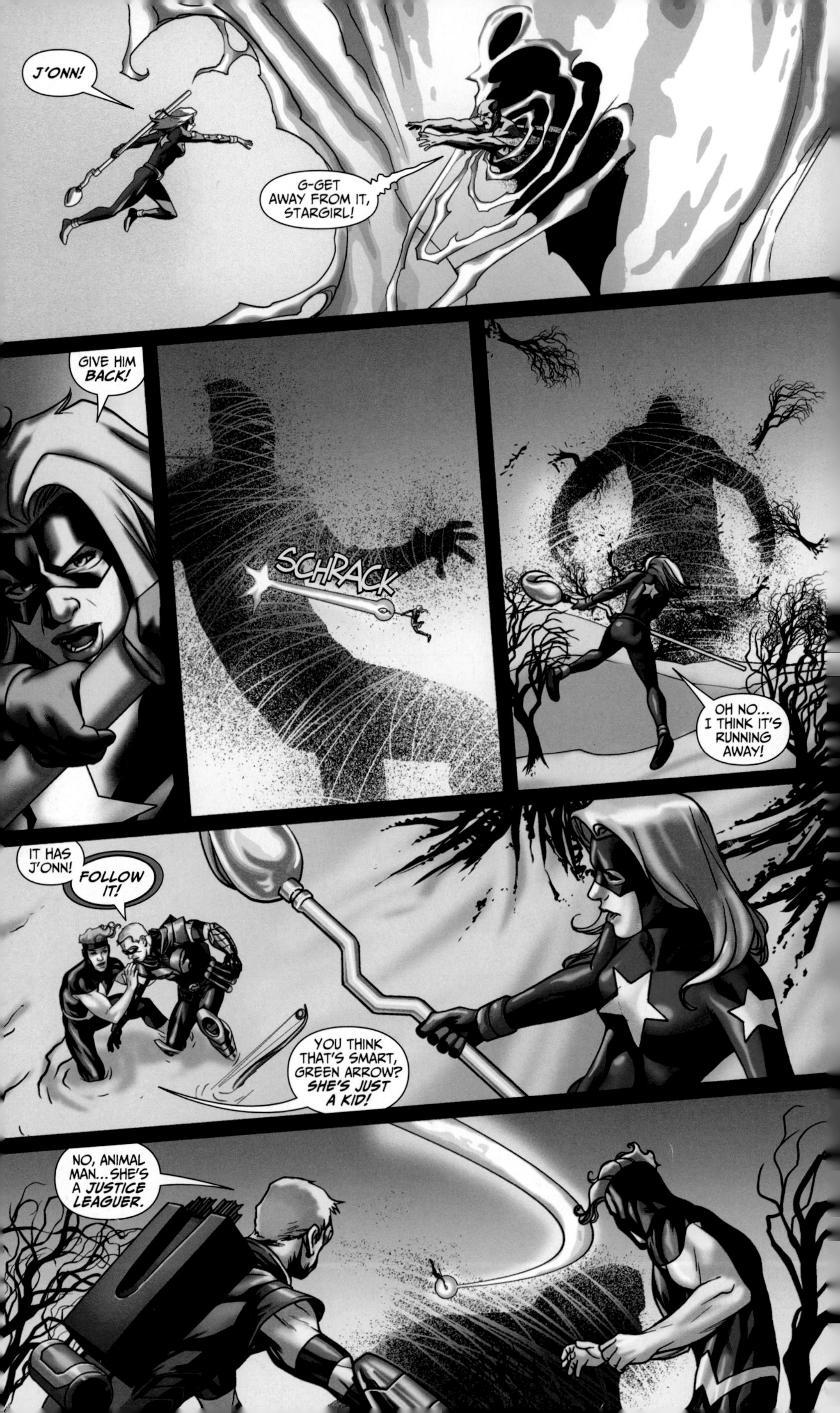
J'ONN!
G-GET AWAY FROM IT, STARGIRL!
GIVE HIM BACK!
SCHRACK
OH NO... I THINK IT'S RUNNING AWAY!
IT HAS J'ONN!
FOLLOW IT!
YOU THINK THAT'S SMART, GREEN ARROW? SHE'S JUST A KID!
NO, ANIMAL MAN...SHE'S A JUSTICE LEAGUER.

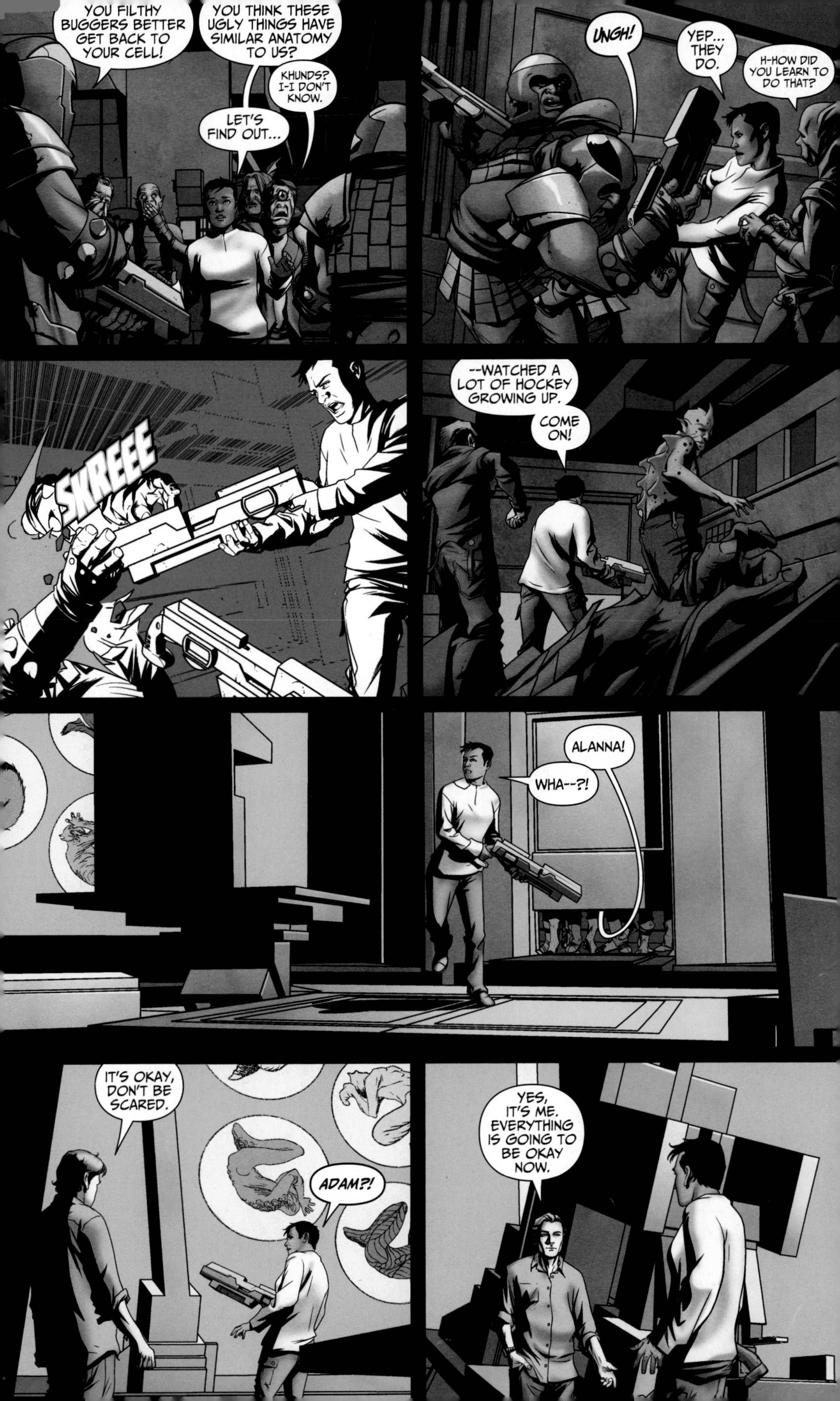
YOU FILTHY BUGGERS BETTER GET BACK TO YOUR CELL!
YOU THINK THESE UGLY THINGS HAVE SIMILAR ANATOMY TO US?
KHUNDS? I-I DON'T KNOW.
LET'S FIND OUT...
UNGH!
YEP... THEY DO.
H-HOW DID YOU LEARN TO DO THAT?
SKREEE
--WATCHED A LOT OF HOCKEY GROWING UP.
COME ON!
ALANNA!
WHA--?!
IT'S OKAY, DON'T BE SCARED.
ADAM?!
YES, IT'S ME. EVERYTHING IS GOING TO BE OKAY NOW.

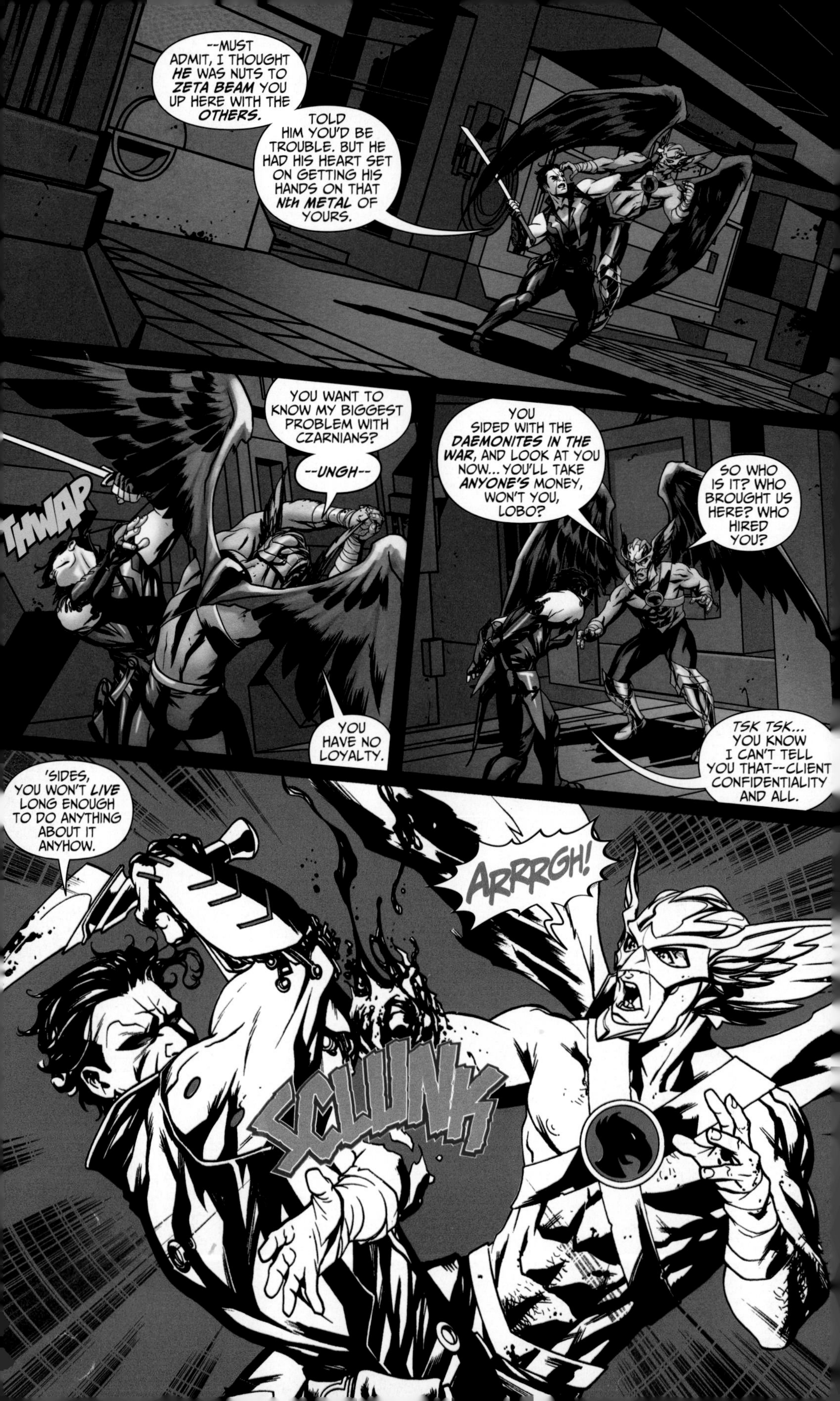
--MUST ADMIT, I THOUGHT HE WAS NUTS TO ZETA BEAM YOU UP HERE WITH THE OTHERS.
TOLD HIM YOU'D BE TROUBLE. BUT HE HAD HIS HEART SET ON GETTING HIS HANDS ON THAT Nth METAL OF YOURS.
THWAP
YOU WANT TO KNOW MY BIGGEST PROBLEM WITH CZARNIANS?
--UNGH--
YOU HAVE NO LOYALTY.
YOU SIDED WITH THE DAEMONITES IN THE WAR, AND LOOK AT YOU NOW... YOU'LL TAKE ANYONE'S MONEY, WON'T YOU, LOBO?
SO WHO IS IT? WHO BROUGHT US HERE? WHO HIRED YOU?
TSK TSK... YOU KNOW I CAN'T TELL YOU THAT--CLIENT CONFIDENTIALITY AND ALL.
'SIDES, YOU WON'T LIVE LONG ENOUGH TO DO ANYTHING ABOUT IT ANYHOW.
ARRRGH!
SCLUNK

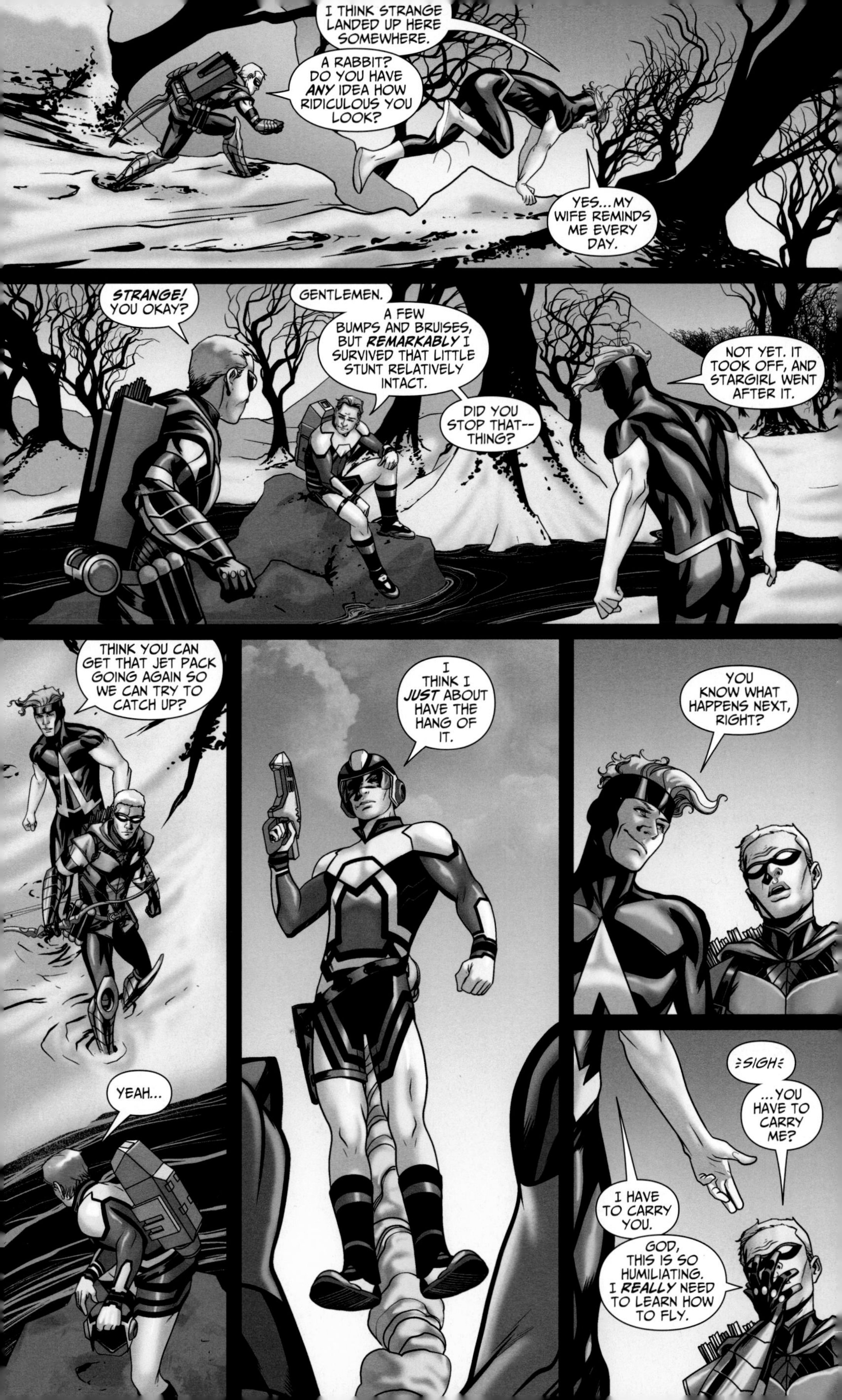
I THINK STRANGE LANDED UP HERE SOMEWHERE.
A RABBIT? DO YOU HAVE *ANY* IDEA HOW RIDICULOUS YOU LOOK?
YES...MY WIFE REMINDS ME EVERY DAY.
STRANGE! YOU OKAY?
GENTLEMEN.
A FEW BUMPS AND BRUISES, BUT *REMARKABLY* I SURVIVED THAT LITTLE STUNT RELATIVELY INTACT.
DID YOU STOP THAT--THING?
NOT YET. IT TOOK OFF, AND STARGIRL WENT AFTER IT.
THINK YOU CAN GET THAT JET PACK GOING AGAIN SO WE CAN TRY TO CATCH UP?
YEAH...
I THINK I *JUST* ABOUT HAVE THE HANG OF IT.
YOU KNOW WHAT HAPPENS NEXT, RIGHT?
SIGH
...YOU HAVE TO CARRY ME?
I HAVE TO CARRY YOU.
GOD, THIS IS SO HUMILIATING. I *REALLY* NEED TO LEARN HOW TO FLY.

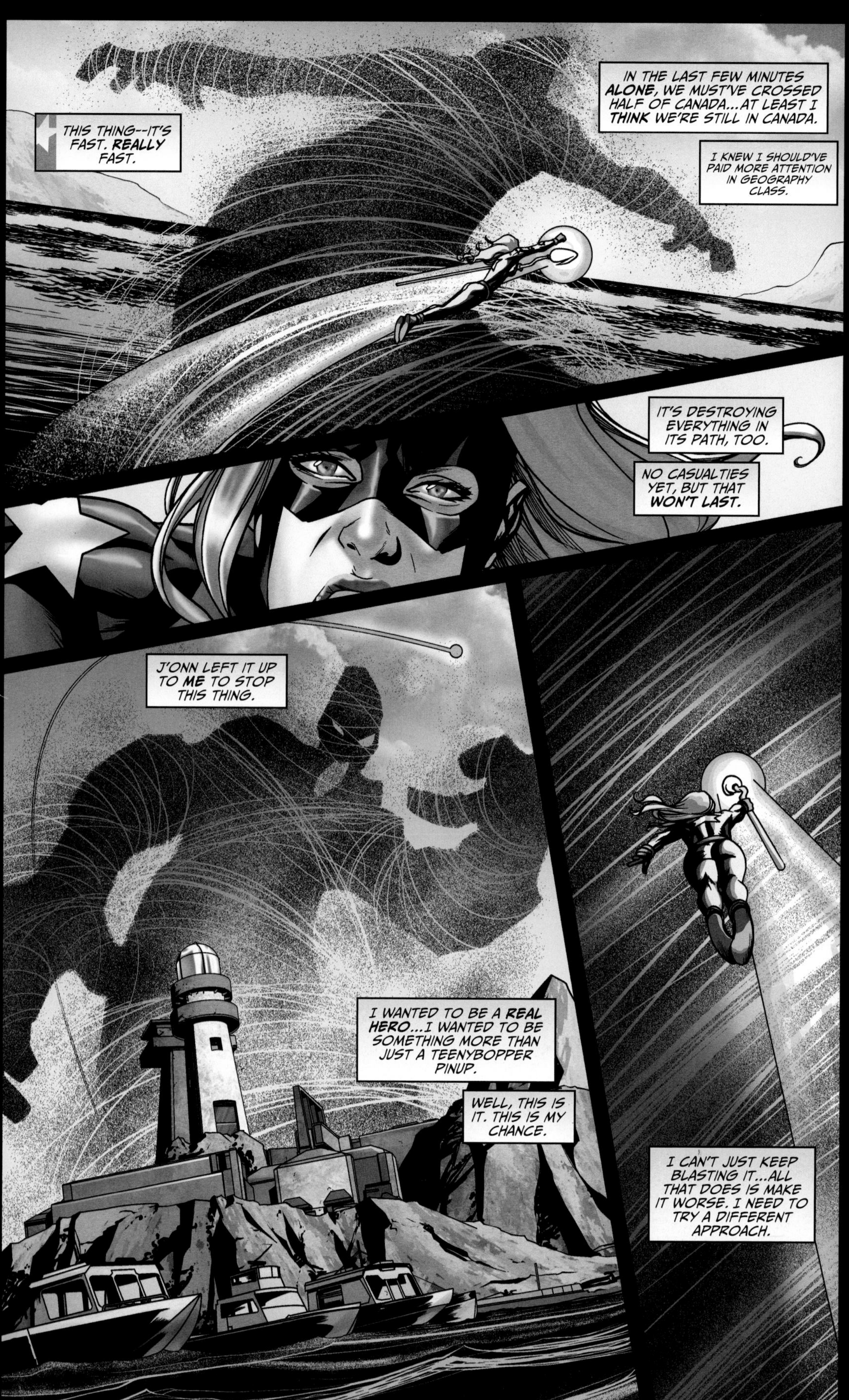

THIS THING--IT'S FAST. **REALLY** FAST.
IN THE LAST FEW MINUTES **ALONE**, WE MUST'VE CROSSED HALF OF CANADA...AT LEAST I **THINK** WE'RE STILL IN CANADA.
I KNEW I SHOULD'VE PAID MORE ATTENTION IN GEOGRAPHY CLASS.
IT'S DESTROYING EVERYTHING IN ITS PATH, TOO.
NO CASUALTIES YET, BUT THAT **WON'T LAST.**
J'ONN LEFT IT UP TO **ME** TO STOP THIS THING.
I WANTED TO BE A **REAL HERO**...I WANTED TO BE SOMETHING MORE THAN JUST A TEENYBOPPER PINUP.
WELL, THIS IS IT. THIS IS MY CHANCE.
I CAN'T JUST KEEP BLASTING IT...ALL THAT DOES IS MAKE IT WORSE. I NEED TO TRY A DIFFERENT APPROACH.

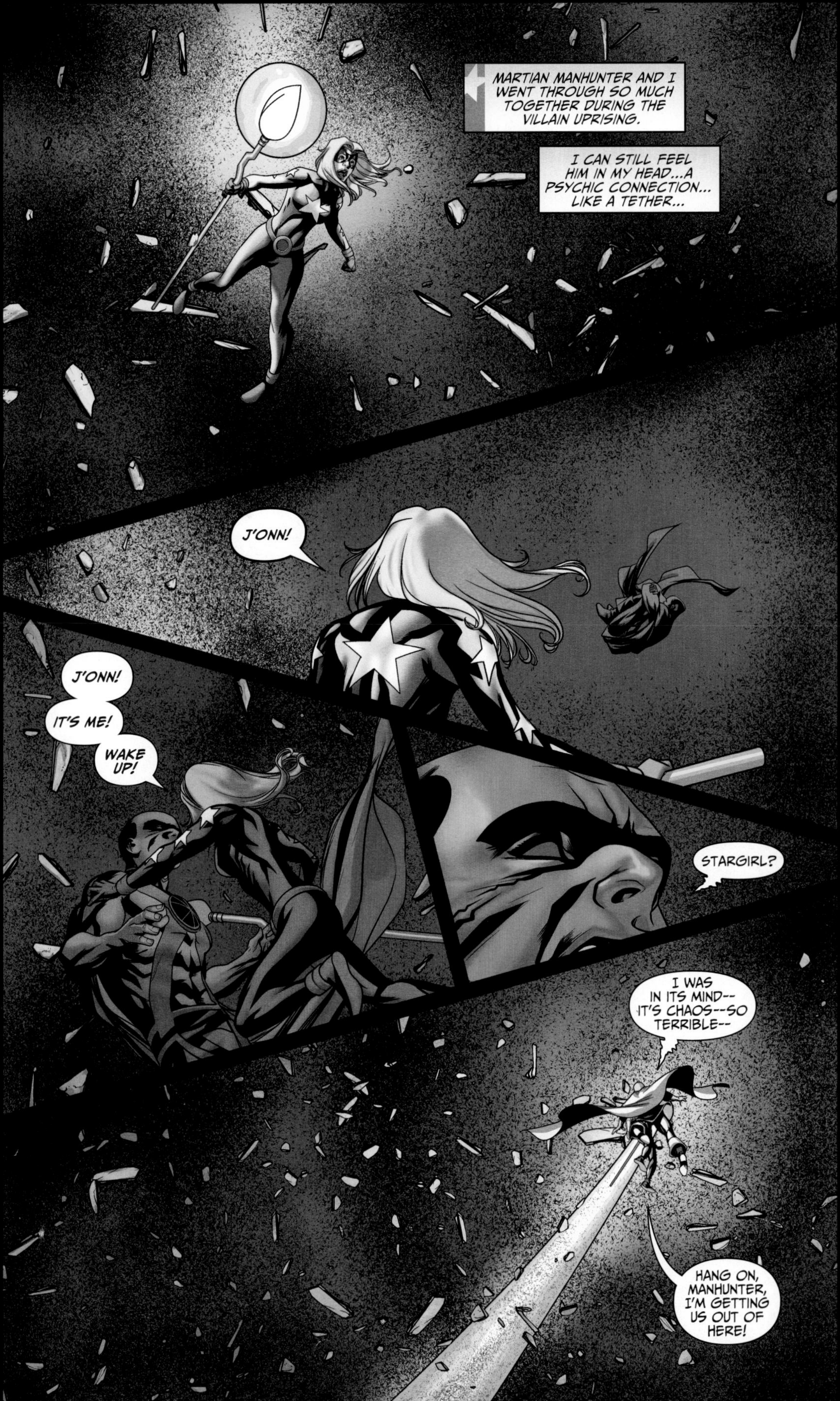
MARTIAN MANHUNTER AND I WENT THROUGH SO MUCH TOGETHER DURING THE VILLAIN UPRISING.
I CAN STILL FEEL HIM IN MY HEAD...A PSYCHIC CONNECTION... LIKE A TETHER...
J'ONN!
J'ONN!
IT'S ME!
WAKE UP!
STARGIRL?
I WAS IN ITS MIND-- IT'S CHAOS--SO TERRIBLE--
HANG ON, MANHUNTER, I'M GETTING US OUT OF HERE!

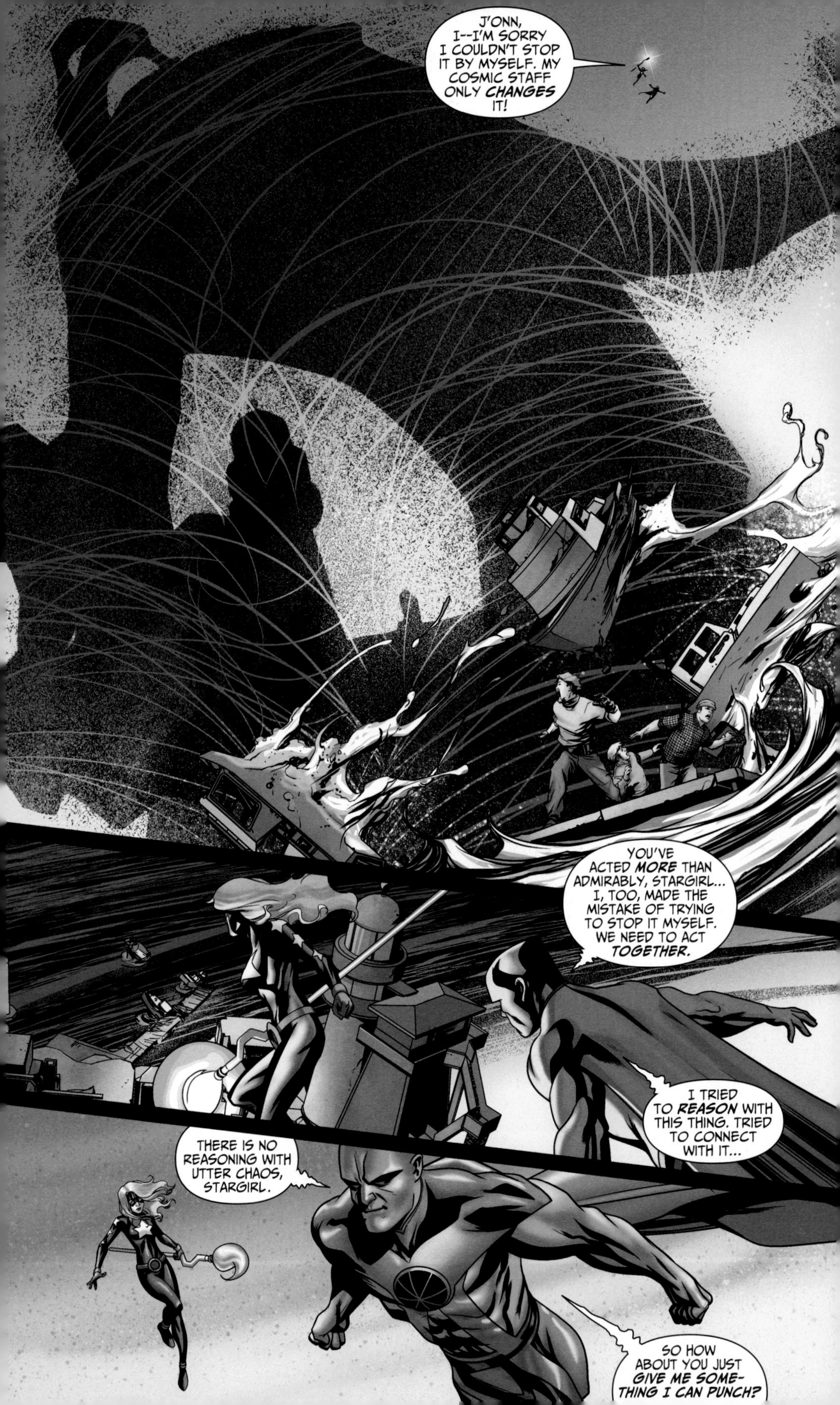
J'ONN, I--I'M SORRY I COULDN'T STOP IT BY MYSELF. MY COSMIC STAFF ONLY *CHANGES* IT!
YOU'VE ACTED *MORE* THAN ADMIRABLY, STARGIRL... I, TOO, MADE THE MISTAKE OF TRYING TO STOP IT MYSELF. WE NEED TO ACT *TOGETHER.*
I TRIED TO *REASON* WITH THIS THING. TRIED TO CONNECT WITH IT...
THERE IS NO REASONING WITH UTTER CHAOS, STARGIRL.
SO HOW ABOUT YOU JUST *GIVE ME SOME-THING I CAN PUNCH?*

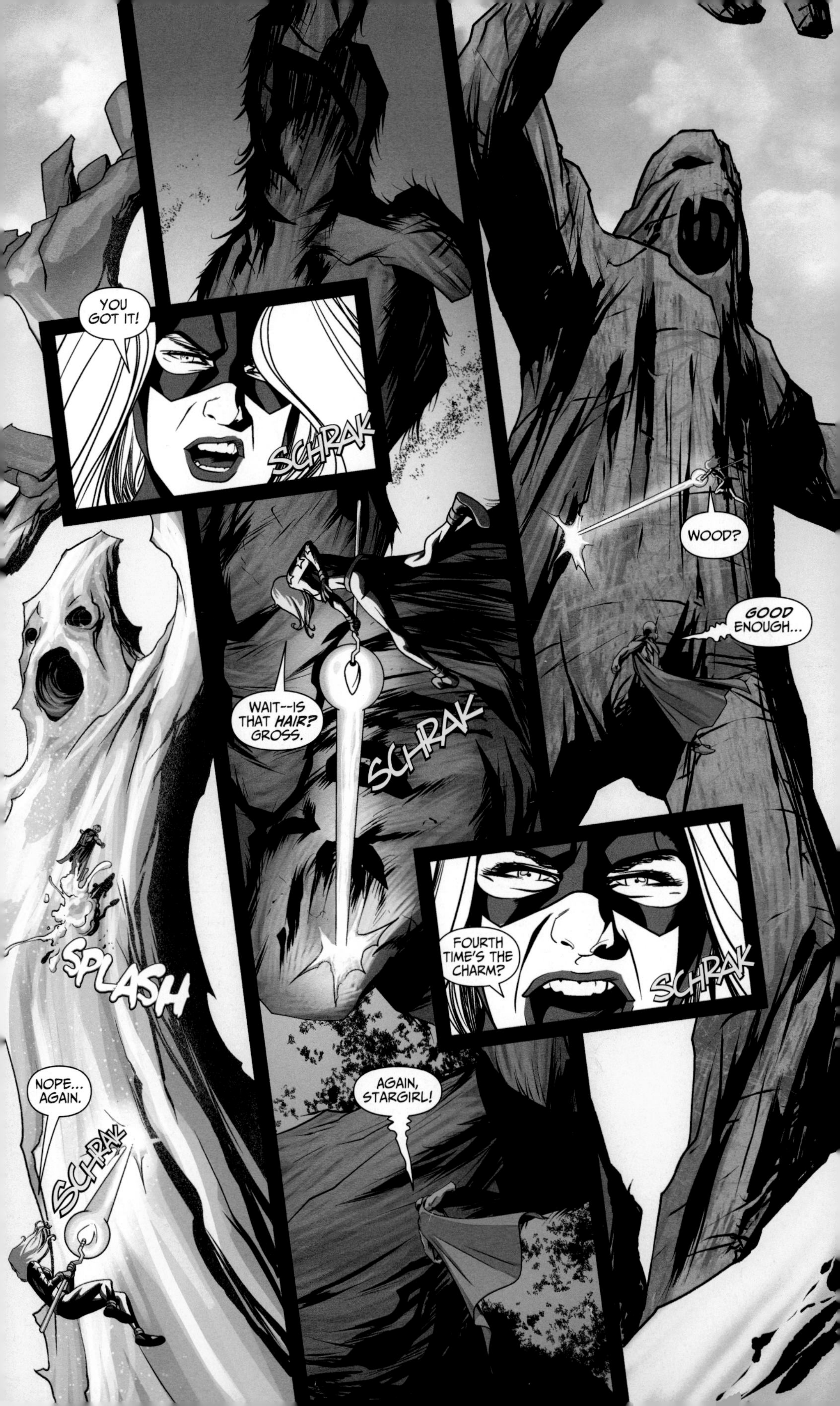
YOU GOT IT!
SCHRAK
WOOD?
GOOD ENOUGH...
WAIT--IS THAT HAIR? GROSS.
SCHRAK
FOURTH TIME'S THE CHARM?
SCHRAK
SPLASH
NOPE... AGAIN.
SCHRAK
AGAIN, STARGIRL!

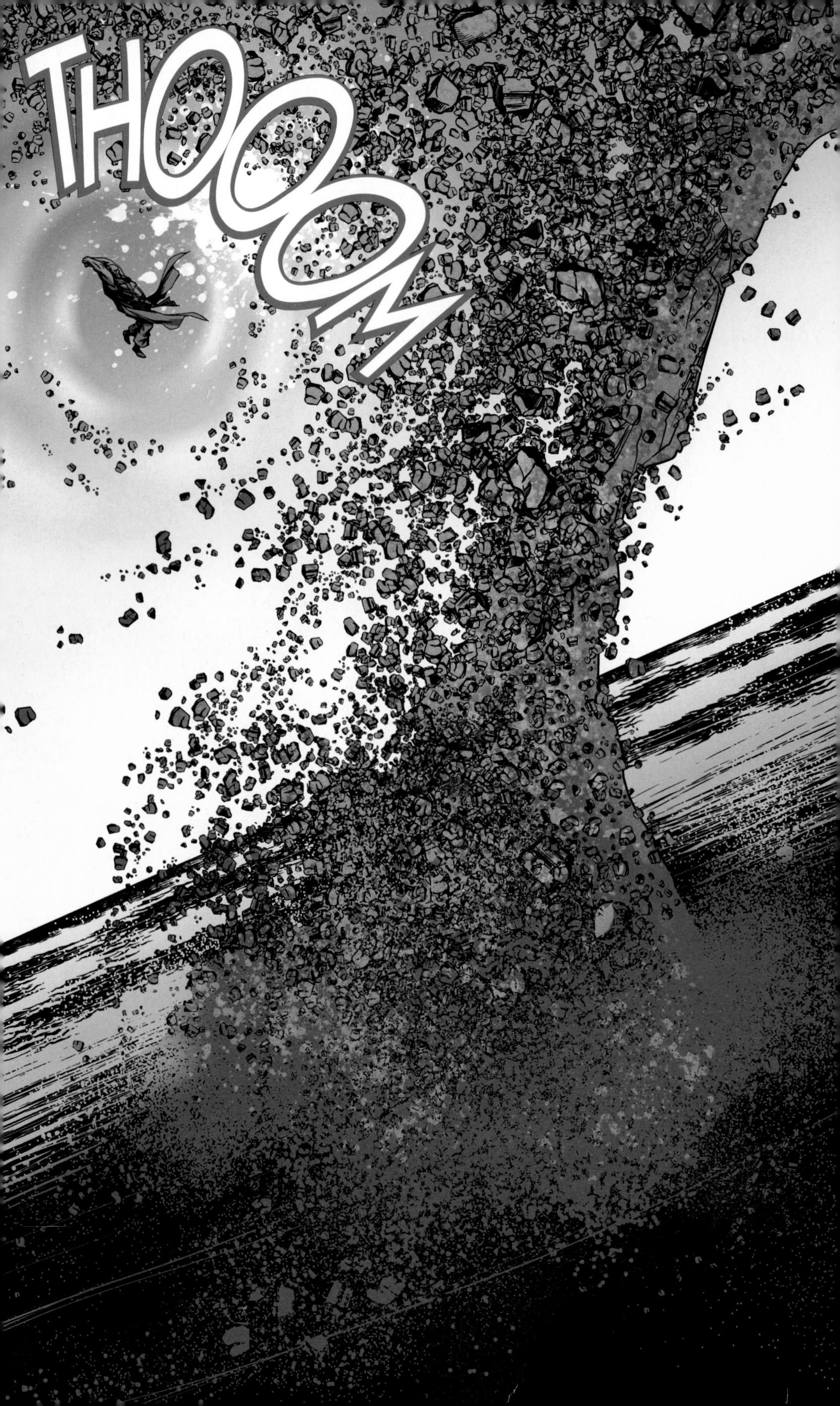
THOOOOM

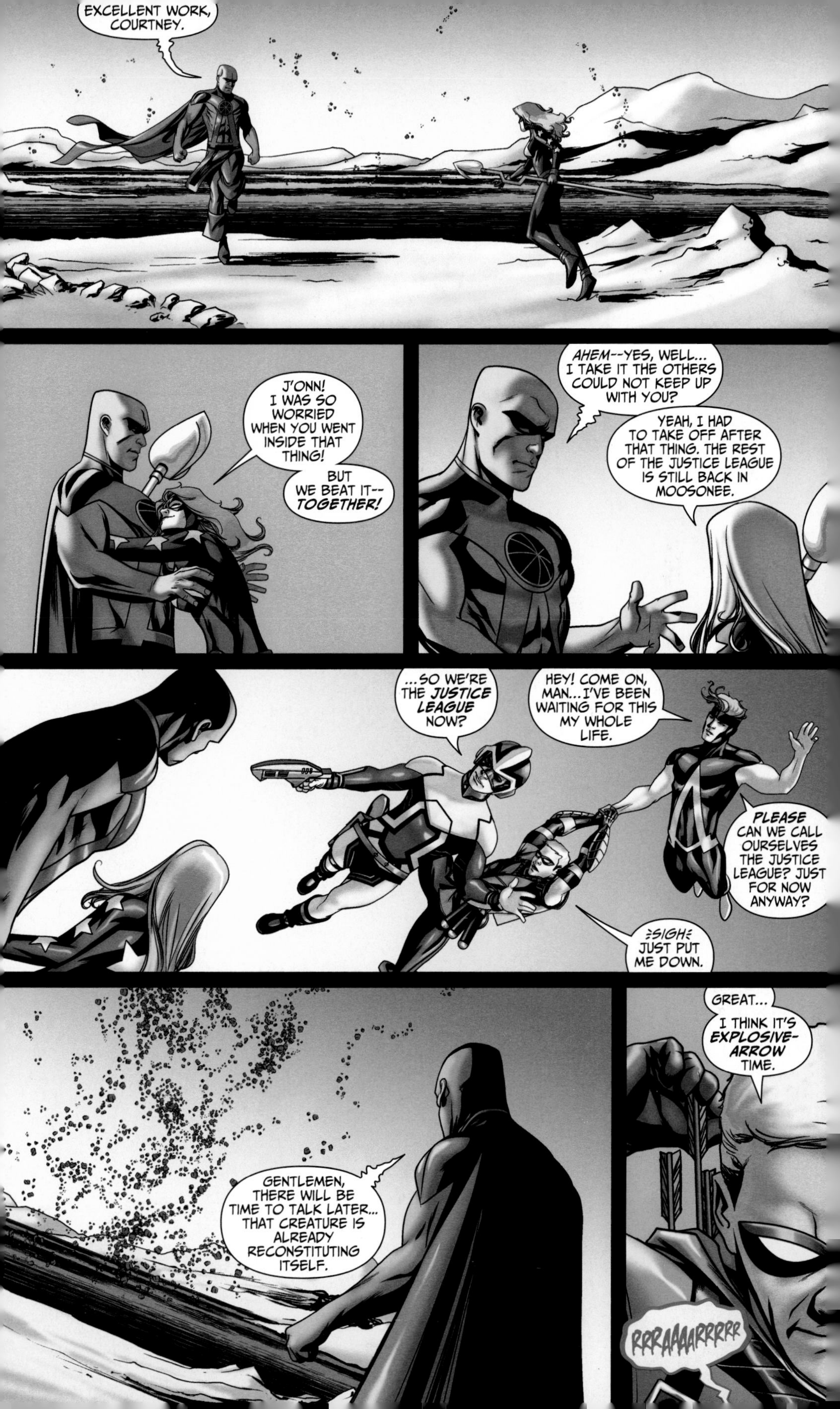

EXCELLENT WORK, COURTNEY.
J'ONN! I WAS SO WORRIED WHEN YOU WENT INSIDE THAT THING!
BUT WE BEAT IT-- TOGETHER!
AHEM--YES, WELL... I TAKE IT THE OTHERS COULD NOT KEEP UP WITH YOU?
YEAH, I HAD TO TAKE OFF AFTER THAT THING. THE REST OF THE JUSTICE LEAGUE IS STILL BACK IN MOOSONEE.
...SO WE'RE THE JUSTICE LEAGUE NOW?
HEY! COME ON, MAN...I'VE BEEN WAITING FOR THIS MY WHOLE LIFE.
PLEASE CAN WE CALL OURSELVES THE JUSTICE LEAGUE? JUST FOR NOW ANYWAY?
SIGH JUST PUT ME DOWN.
GENTLEMEN, THERE WILL BE TIME TO TALK LATER... THAT CREATURE IS ALREADY RECONSTITUTING ITSELF.
GREAT...
I THINK IT'S EXPLOSIVE-ARROW TIME.
RRRAAAARRRRR

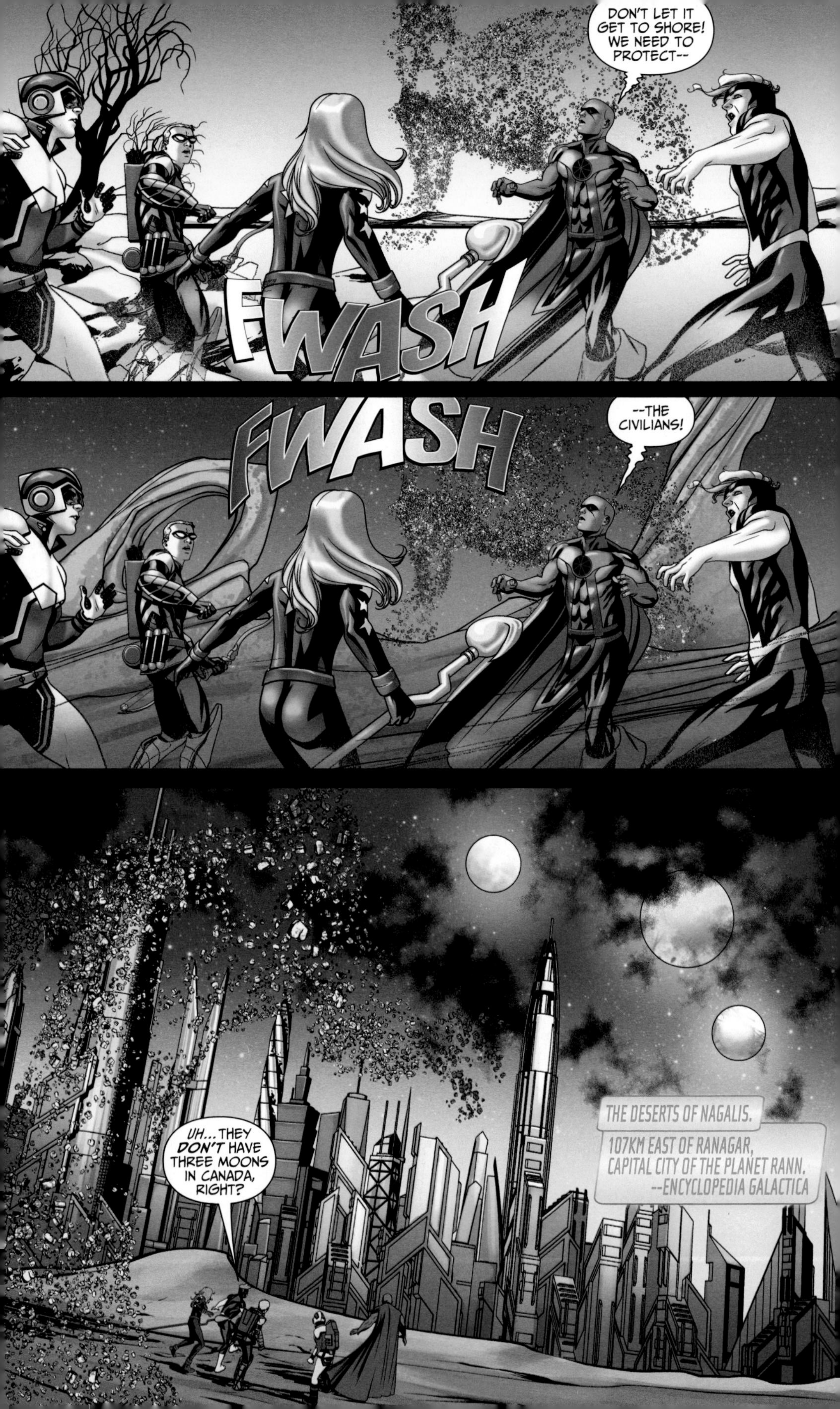
DON'T LET IT GET TO SHORE! WE NEED TO PROTECT--
FWASH
FWASH
--THE CIVILIANS!
THE DESERTS OF NAGALIS.
107KM EAST OF RANAGAR, CAPITAL CITY OF THE PLANET RANN. --ENCYCLOPEDIA GALACTICA
UH... THEY DON'T HAVE THREE MOONS IN CANADA, RIGHT?

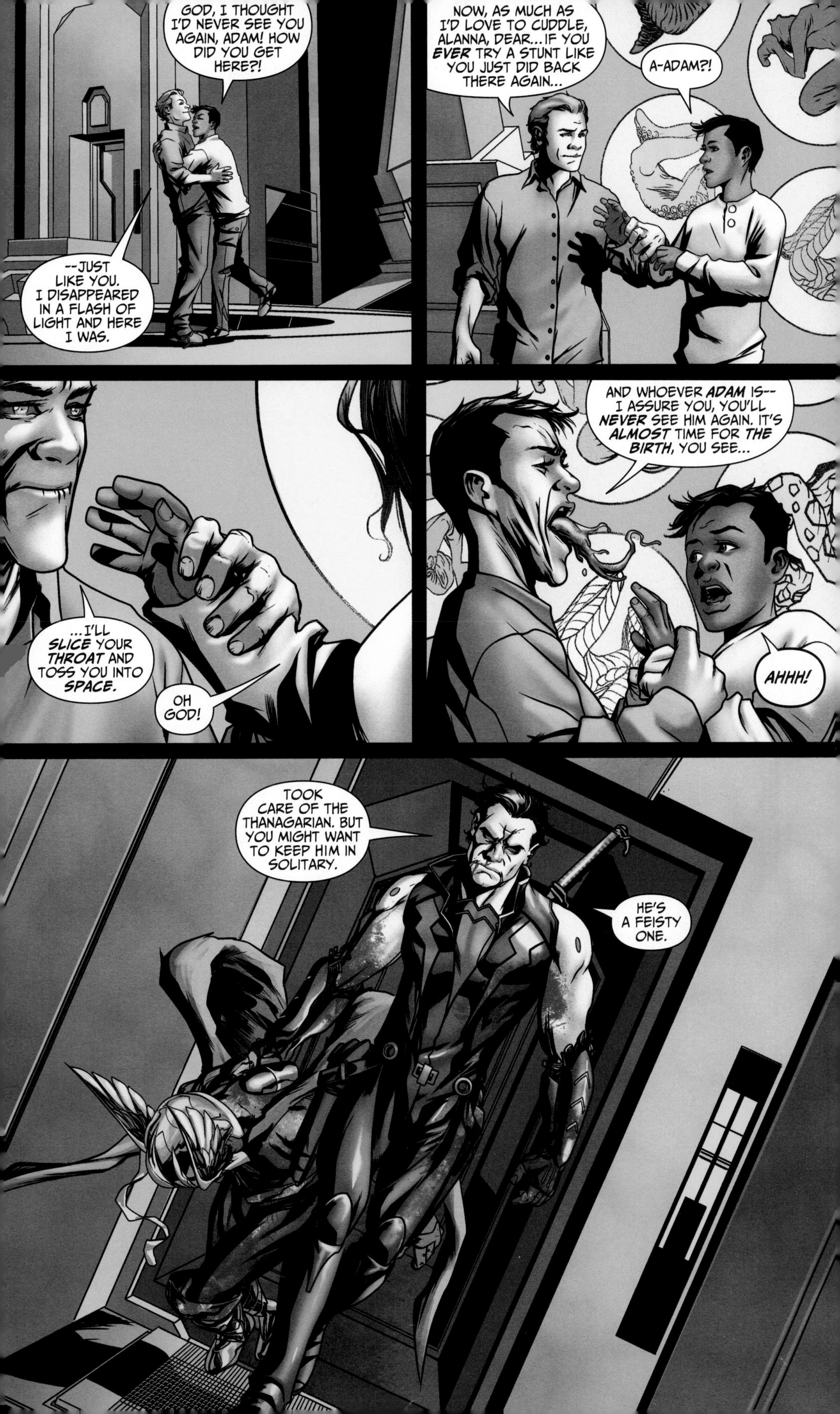
GOD, I THOUGHT I'D NEVER SEE YOU AGAIN, ADAM! HOW DID YOU GET HERE?!
--JUST LIKE YOU. I DISAPPEARED IN A FLASH OF LIGHT AND HERE I WAS.
NOW, AS MUCH AS I'D LOVE TO CUDDLE, ALANNA, DEAR... IF YOU EVER TRY A STUNT LIKE YOU JUST DID BACK THERE AGAIN...
A-ADAM?!
...I'LL SLICE YOUR THROAT AND TOSS YOU INTO SPACE.
OH GOD!
AND WHOEVER ADAM IS-- I ASSURE YOU, YOU'LL NEVER SEE HIM AGAIN. IT'S ALMOST TIME FOR THE BIRTH, YOU SEE...
AHHH!
TOOK CARE OF THE THANAGARIAN. BUT YOU MIGHT WANT TO KEEP HIM IN SOLITARY.
HE'S A FEISTY ONE.

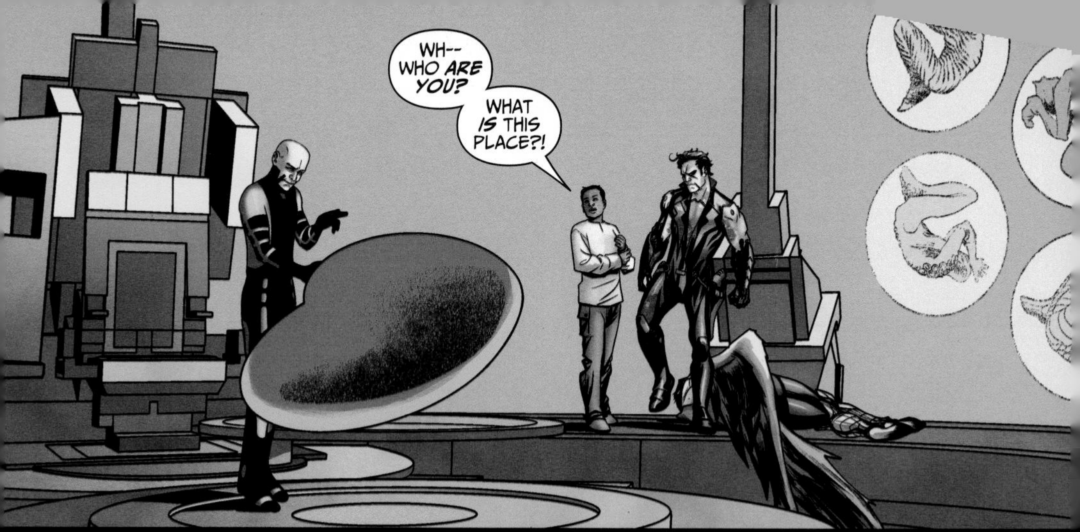
WH-- WHO ARE YOU?
WHAT IS THIS PLACE?!

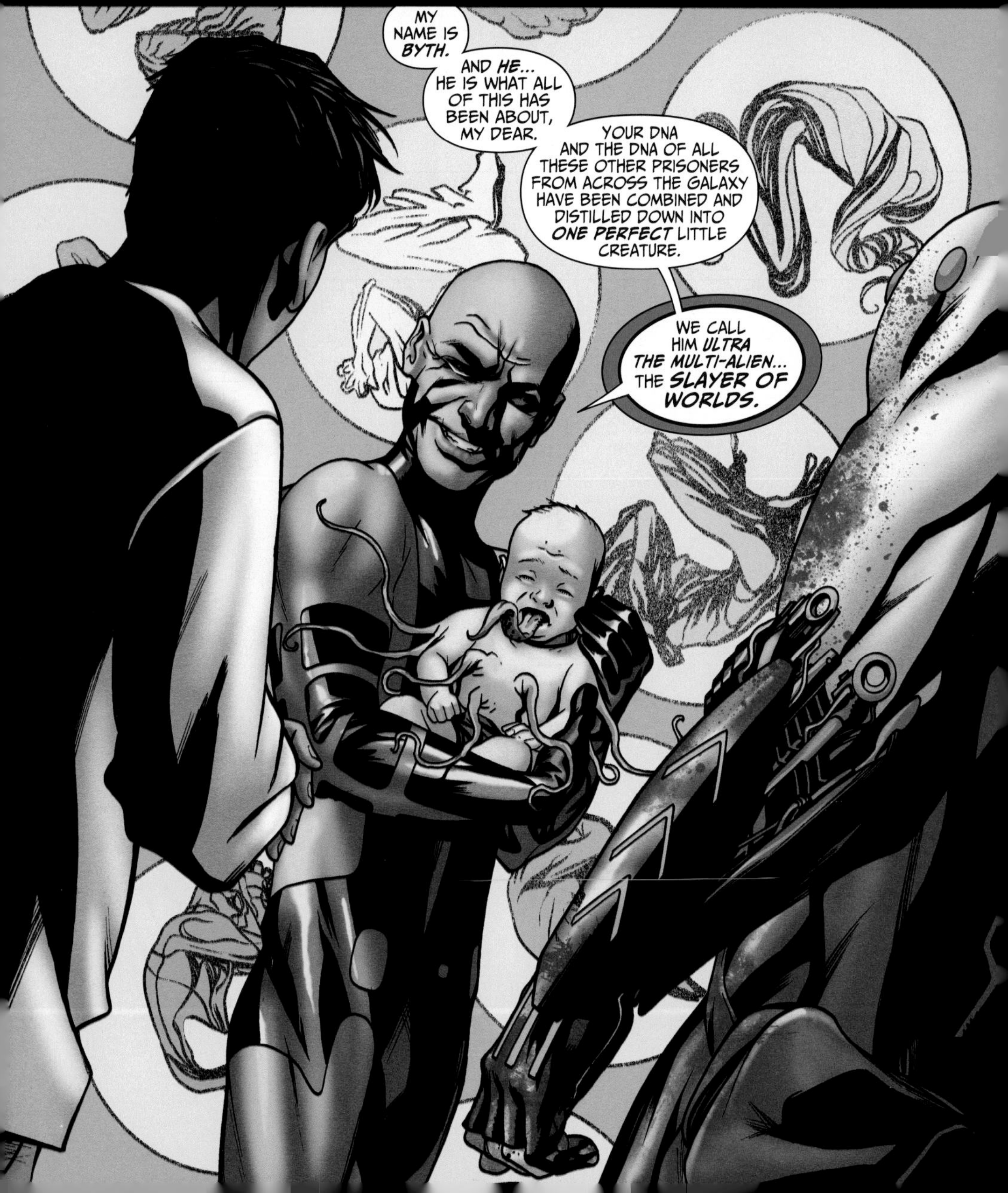
MY NAME IS BYTH.
AND HE... HE IS WHAT ALL OF THIS HAS BEEN ABOUT, MY DEAR.
YOUR DNA AND THE DNA OF ALL THESE OTHER PRISONERS FROM ACROSS THE GALAXY HAVE BEEN COMBINED AND DISTILLED DOWN INTO ONE PERFECT LITTLE CREATURE.
WE CALL HIM ULTRA THE MULTI-ALIEN... THE SLAYER OF WORLDS.

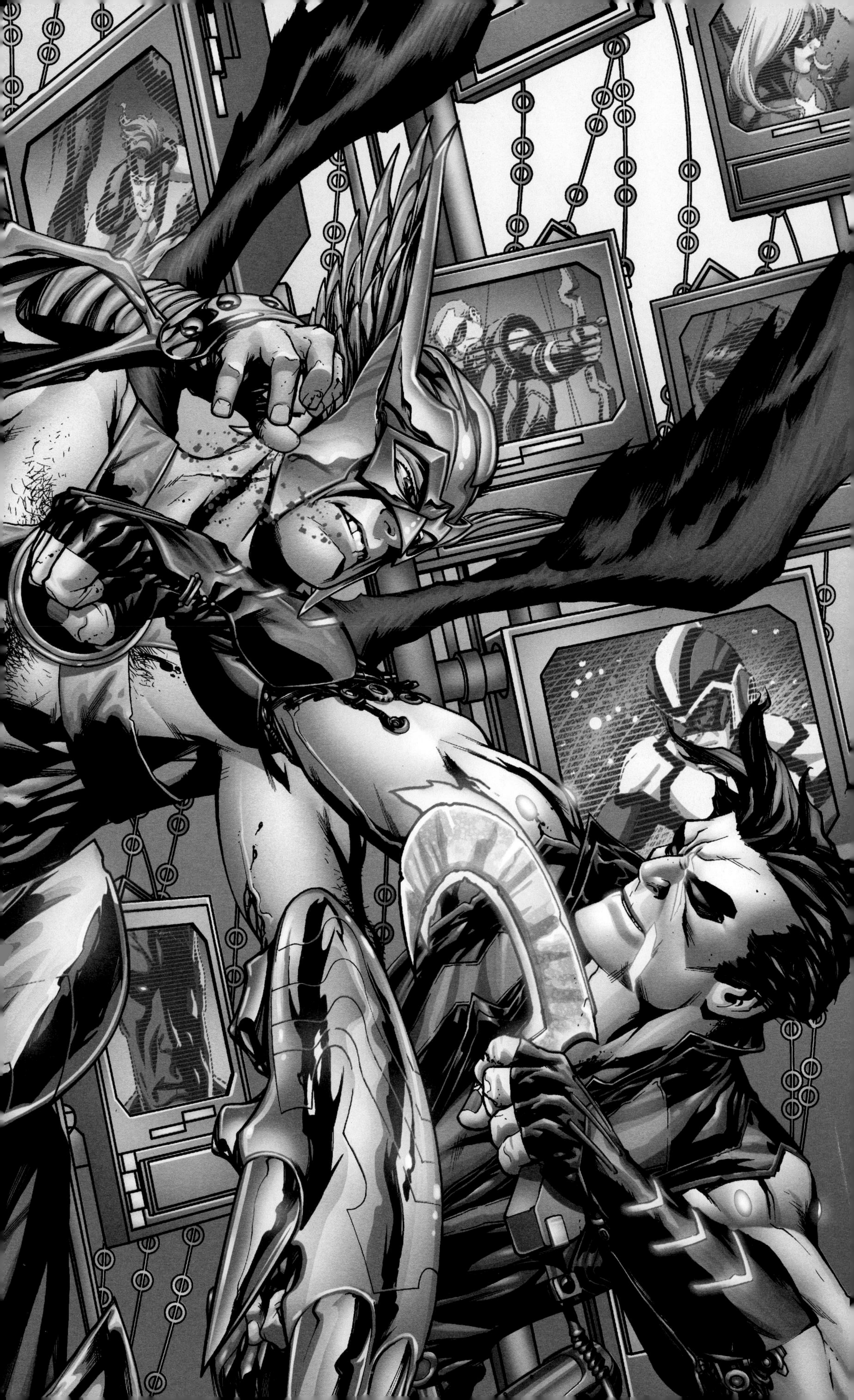

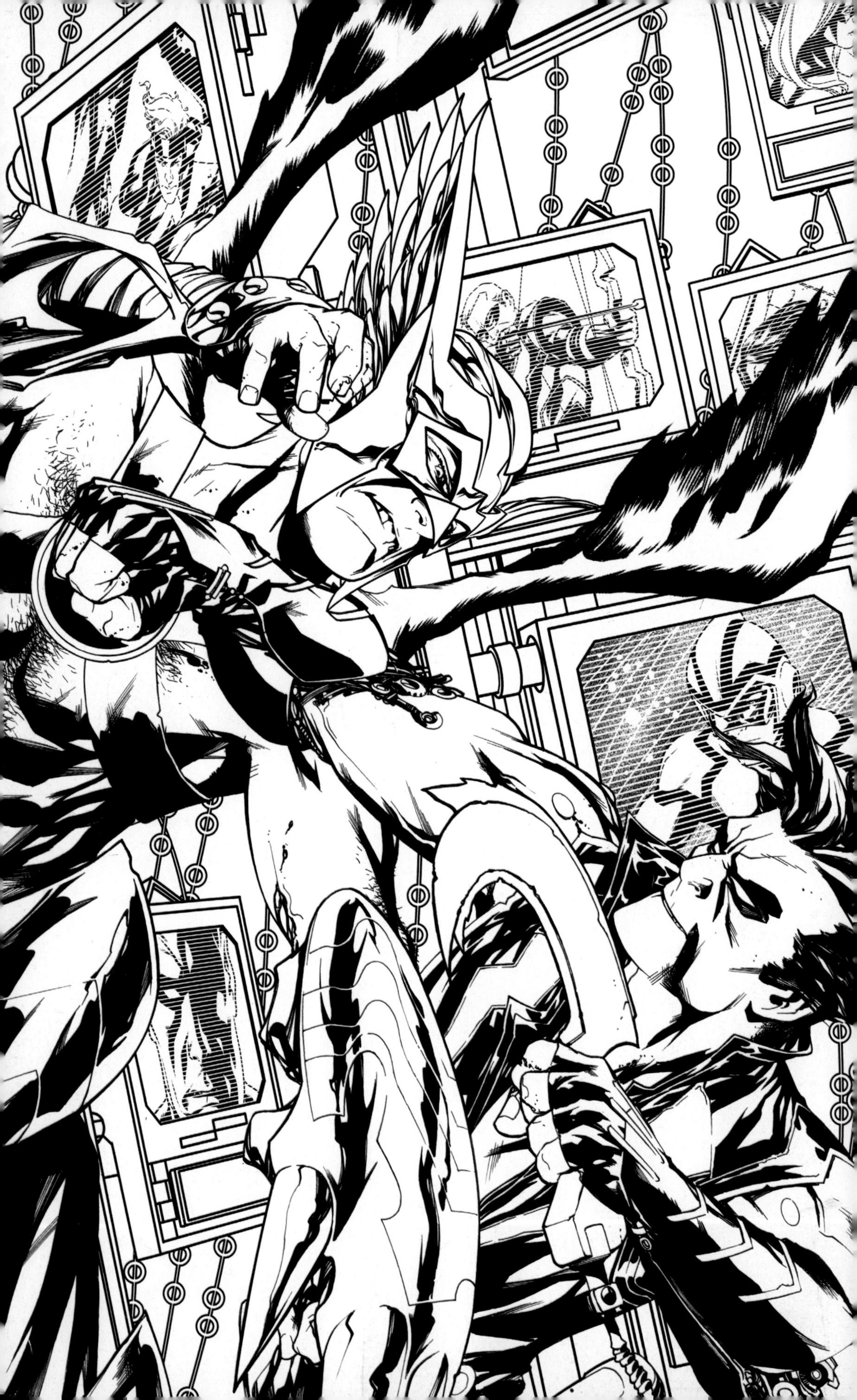

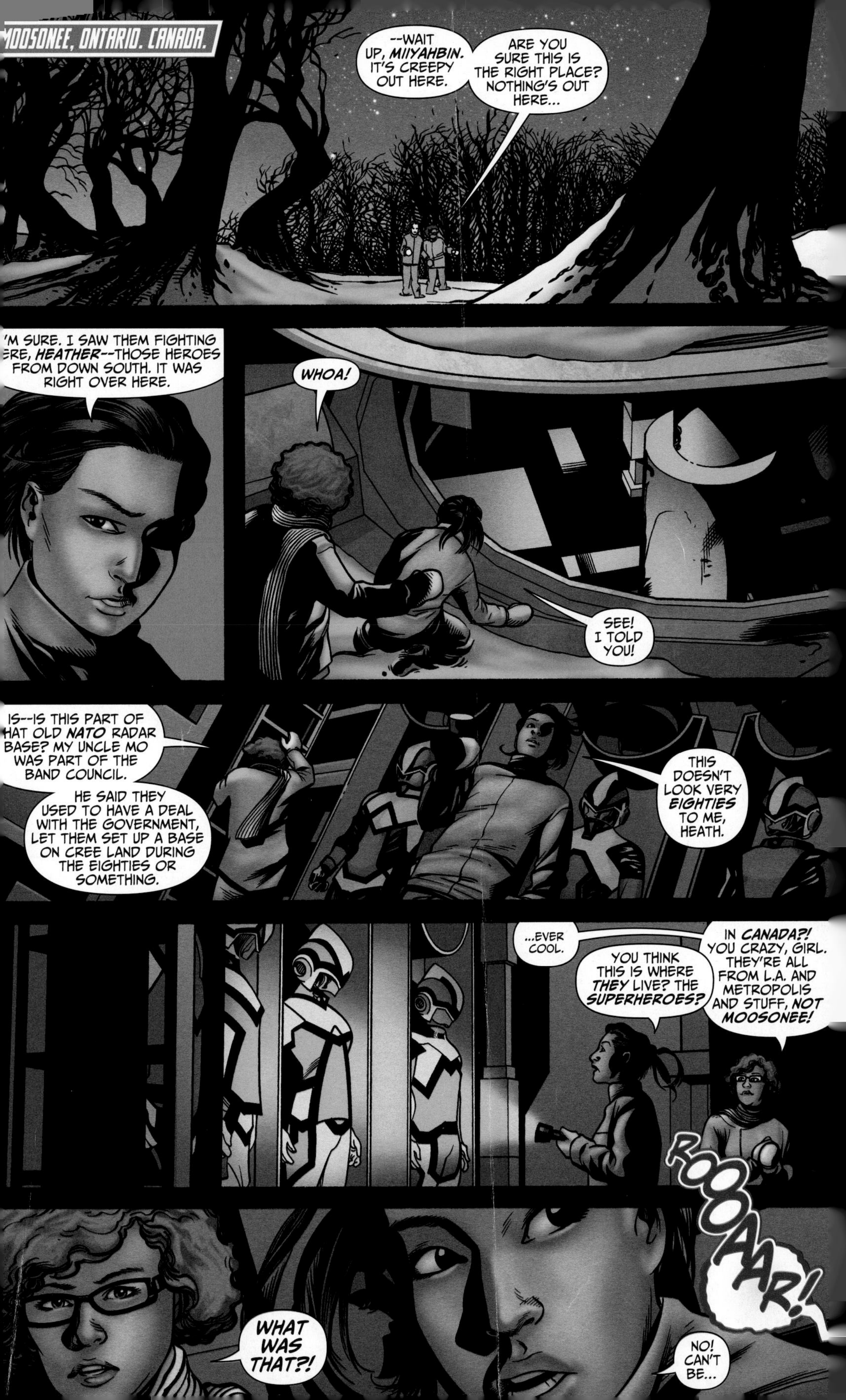
MOOSONEE, ONTARIO. CANADA.
--WAIT UP, MIIYAHBIN. IT'S CREEPY OUT HERE.
ARE YOU SURE THIS IS THE RIGHT PLACE? NOTHING'S OUT HERE...
'M SURE. I SAW THEM FIGHTING ERE, HEATHER--THOSE HEROES FROM DOWN SOUTH. IT WAS RIGHT OVER HERE.
WHOA!
SEE! I TOLD YOU!
IS--IS THIS PART OF HAT OLD NATO RADAR BASE? MY UNCLE MO WAS PART OF THE BAND COUNCIL.
HE SAID THEY USED TO HAVE A DEAL WITH THE GOVERNMENT, LET THEM SET UP A BASE ON CREE LAND DURING THE EIGHTIES OR SOMETHING.
THIS DOESN'T LOOK VERY EIGHTIES TO ME, HEATH.
...EVER COOL.
YOU THINK THIS IS WHERE THEY LIVE? THE SUPERHEROES?
IN CANADA?! YOU CRAZY, GIRL. THEY'RE ALL FROM L.A. AND METROPOLIS AND STUFF, NOT MOOSONEE!
ROOOAAR!
WHAT WAS THAT?!
NO! CAN'T BE...

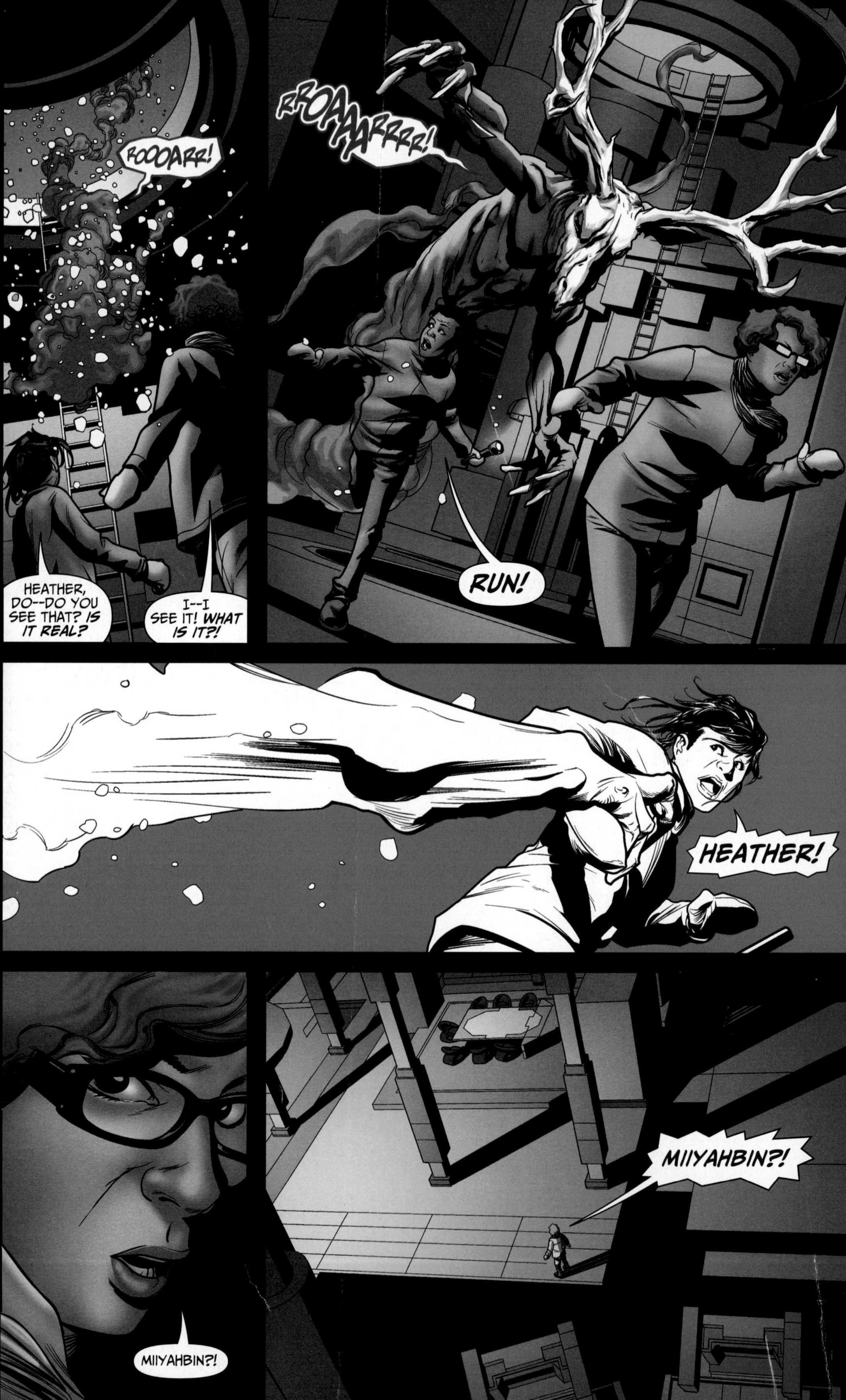
ROOOARR!
HEATHER, DO--DO YOU SEE THAT? IS IT REAL?
I--I SEE IT! WHAT IS IT?!
RROOAAAARRRR!
RUN!
HEATHER!
MIIYAHBIN?!
MIIYAHBIN?!

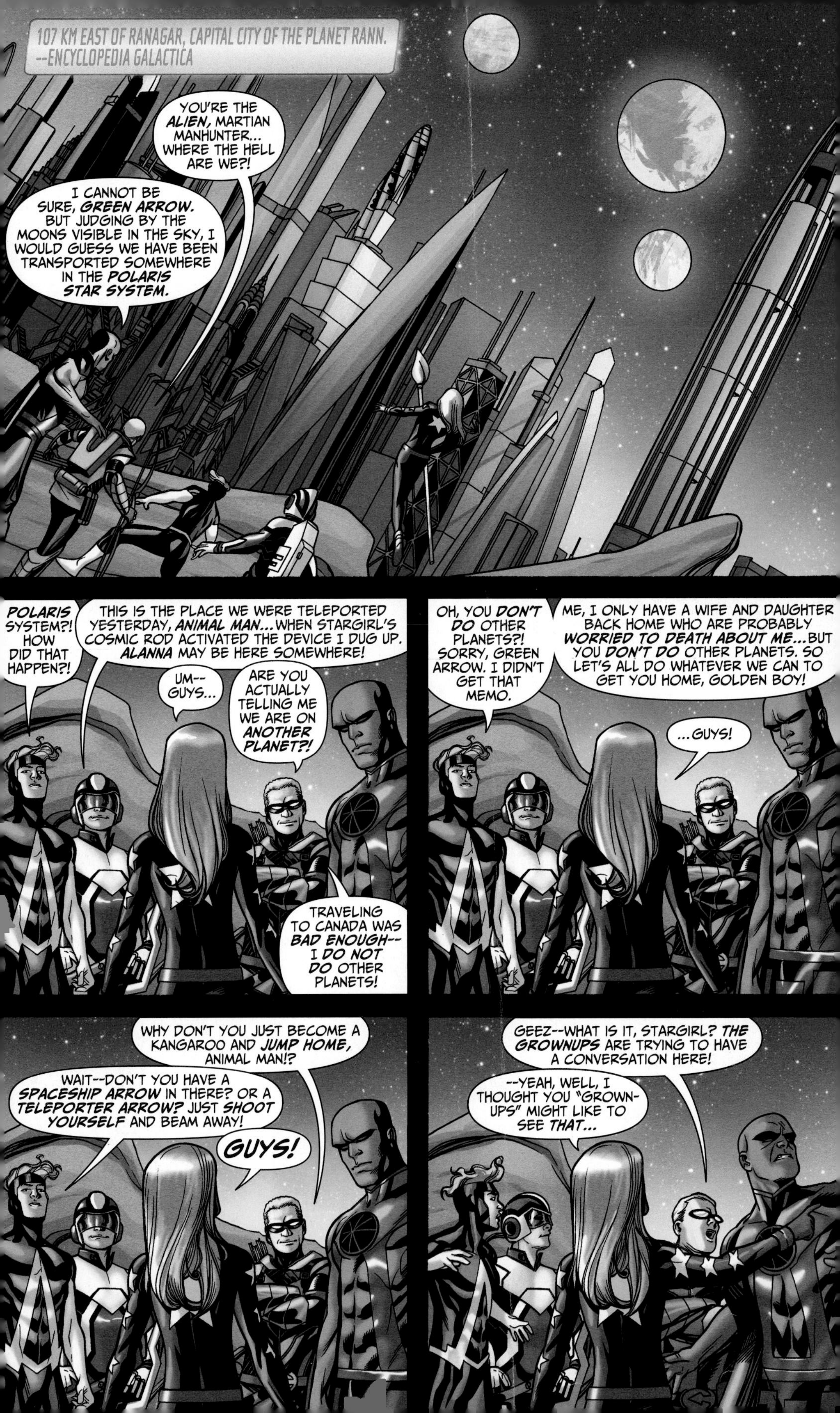

107 KM EAST OF RANAGAR, CAPITAL CITY OF THE PLANET RANN.
--ENCYCLOPEDIA GALACTICA
YOU'RE THE ALIEN, MARTIAN MANHUNTER... WHERE THE HELL ARE WE?!
I CANNOT BE SURE, GREEN ARROW. BUT JUDGING BY THE MOONS VISIBLE IN THE SKY, I WOULD GUESS WE HAVE BEEN TRANSPORTED SOMEWHERE IN THE POLARIS STAR SYSTEM.
POLARIS SYSTEM?! HOW DID THAT HAPPEN?!
THIS IS THE PLACE WE WERE TELEPORTED YESTERDAY, ANIMAL MAN...WHEN STARGIRL'S COSMIC ROD ACTIVATED THE DEVICE I DUG UP. ALANNA MAY BE HERE SOMEWHERE!
UM--GUYS...
ARE YOU ACTUALLY TELLING ME WE ARE ON ANOTHER PLANET?!
TRAVELING TO CANADA WAS BAD ENOUGH--I DO NOT DO OTHER PLANETS!
OH, YOU DON'T DO OTHER PLANETS?! SORRY, GREEN ARROW. I DIDN'T GET THAT MEMO.
ME, I ONLY HAVE A WIFE AND DAUGHTER BACK HOME WHO ARE PROBABLY WORRIED TO DEATH ABOUT ME...BUT YOU DON'T DO OTHER PLANETS. SO LET'S ALL DO WHATEVER WE CAN TO GET YOU HOME, GOLDEN BOY!
...GUYS!
WHY DON'T YOU JUST BECOME A KANGAROO AND JUMP HOME, ANIMAL MAN!?
WAIT--DON'T YOU HAVE A SPACESHIP ARROW IN THERE? OR A TELEPORTER ARROW? JUST SHOOT YOURSELF AND BEAM AWAY!
GUYS!
GEEZ--WHAT IS IT, STARGIRL? THE GROWNUPS ARE TRYING TO HAVE A CONVERSATION HERE!
--YEAH, WELL, I THOUGHT YOU "GROWN-UPS" MIGHT LIKE TO SEE THAT...

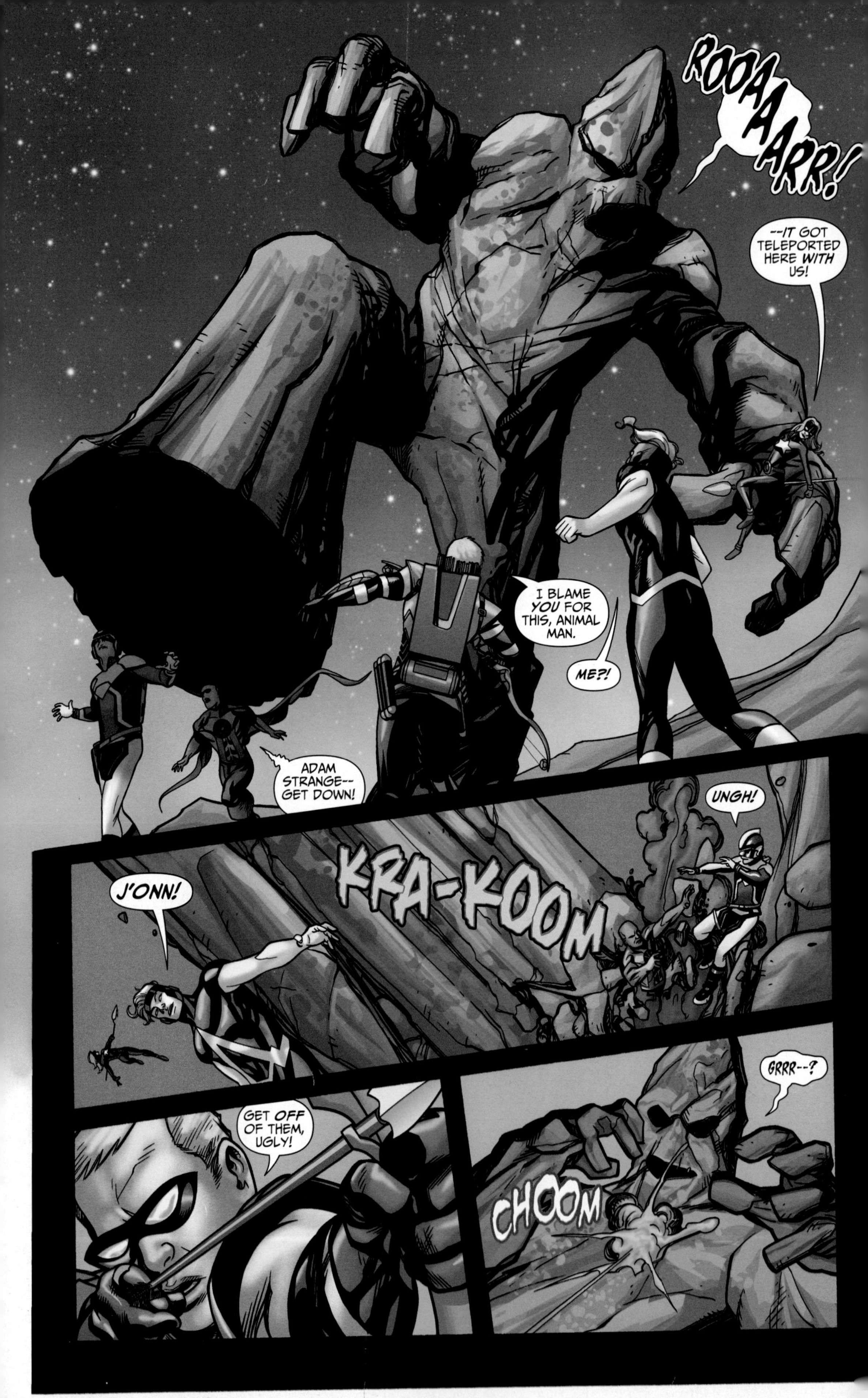
ROOAAAARR!
--IT GOT TELEPORTED HERE WITH US!
I BLAME YOU FOR THIS, ANIMAL MAN.
ME?!
ADAM STRANGE-- GET DOWN!
UNGH!
KRA-KOOM
J'ONN!
GRRR--?
GET OFF OF THEM, UGLY!
CHOOM

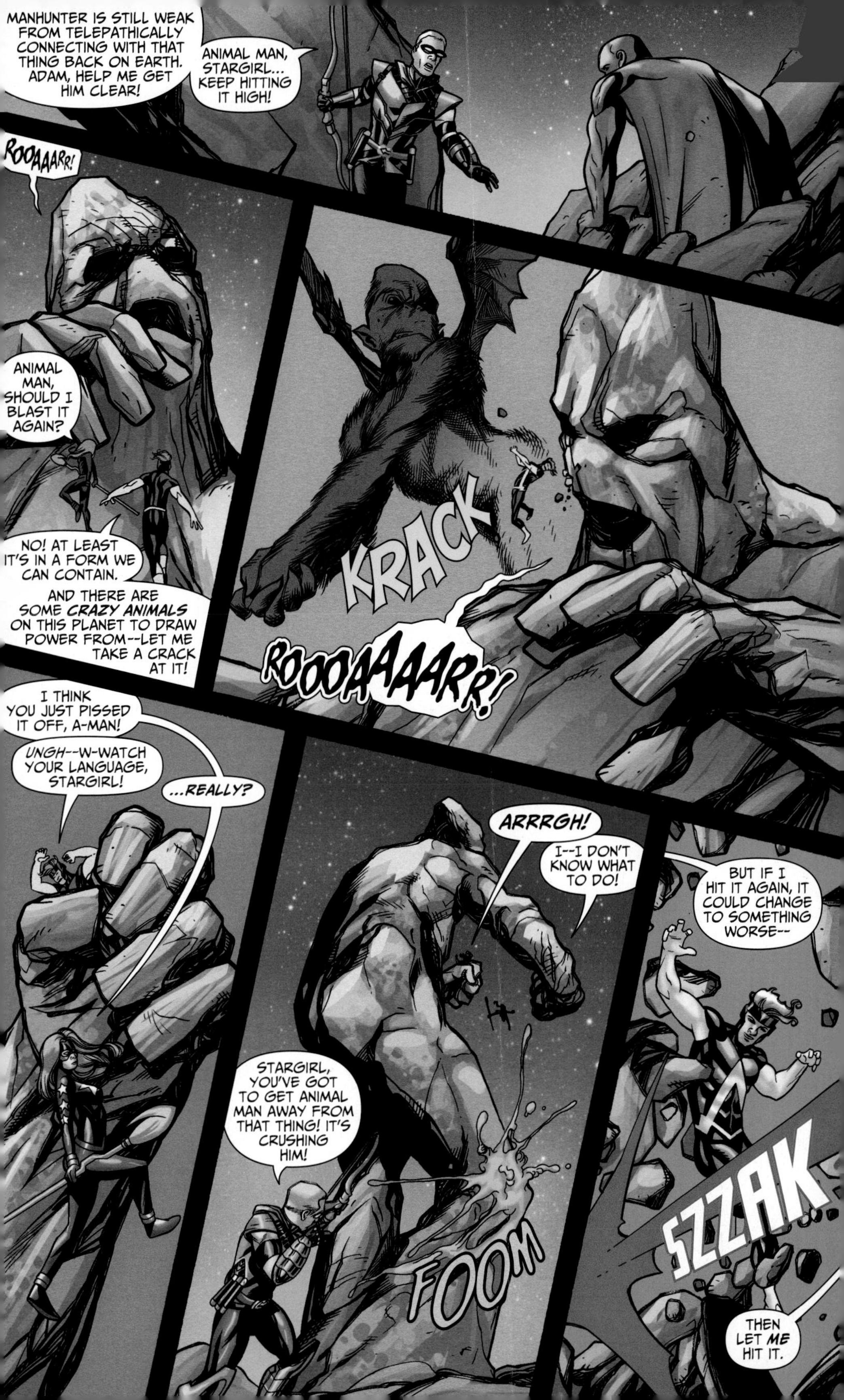

MANHUNTER IS STILL WEAK FROM TELEPATHICALLY CONNECTING WITH THAT THING BACK ON EARTH. ADAM, HELP ME GET HIM CLEAR!
ANIMAL MAN, STARGIRL... KEEP HITTING IT HIGH!
ROOAAARR!
ANIMAL MAN, SHOULD I BLAST IT AGAIN?
NO! AT LEAST IT'S IN A FORM WE CAN CONTAIN.
AND THERE ARE SOME *CRAZY ANIMALS* ON THIS PLANET TO DRAW POWER FROM--LET ME TAKE A CRACK AT IT!
KRACK
ROOOAAAARR!
I THINK YOU JUST PISSED IT OFF, A-MAN!
UNGH--W-WATCH YOUR LANGUAGE, STARGIRL!
...REALLY?
ARRRGH!
I--I DON'T KNOW WHAT TO DO!
BUT IF I HIT IT AGAIN, IT COULD CHANGE TO SOMETHING WORSE--
STARGIRL, YOU'VE GOT TO GET ANIMAL MAN AWAY FROM THAT THING! IT'S CRUSHING HIM!
FOOM
SZZAK
THEN LET *ME* HIT IT.

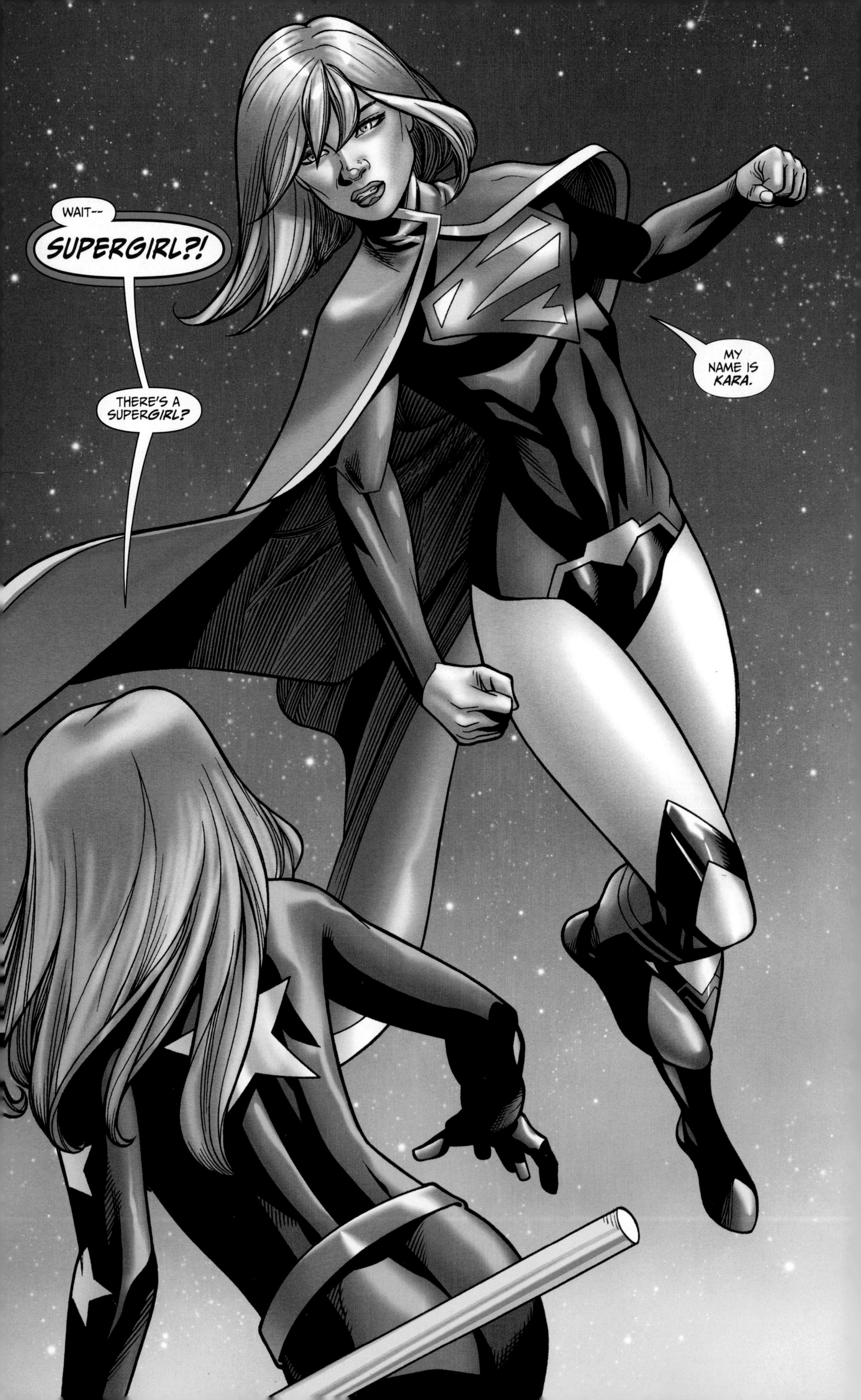
WAIT--
SUPERGIRL?!
THERE'S A SUPERGIRL?
MY NAME IS KARA.

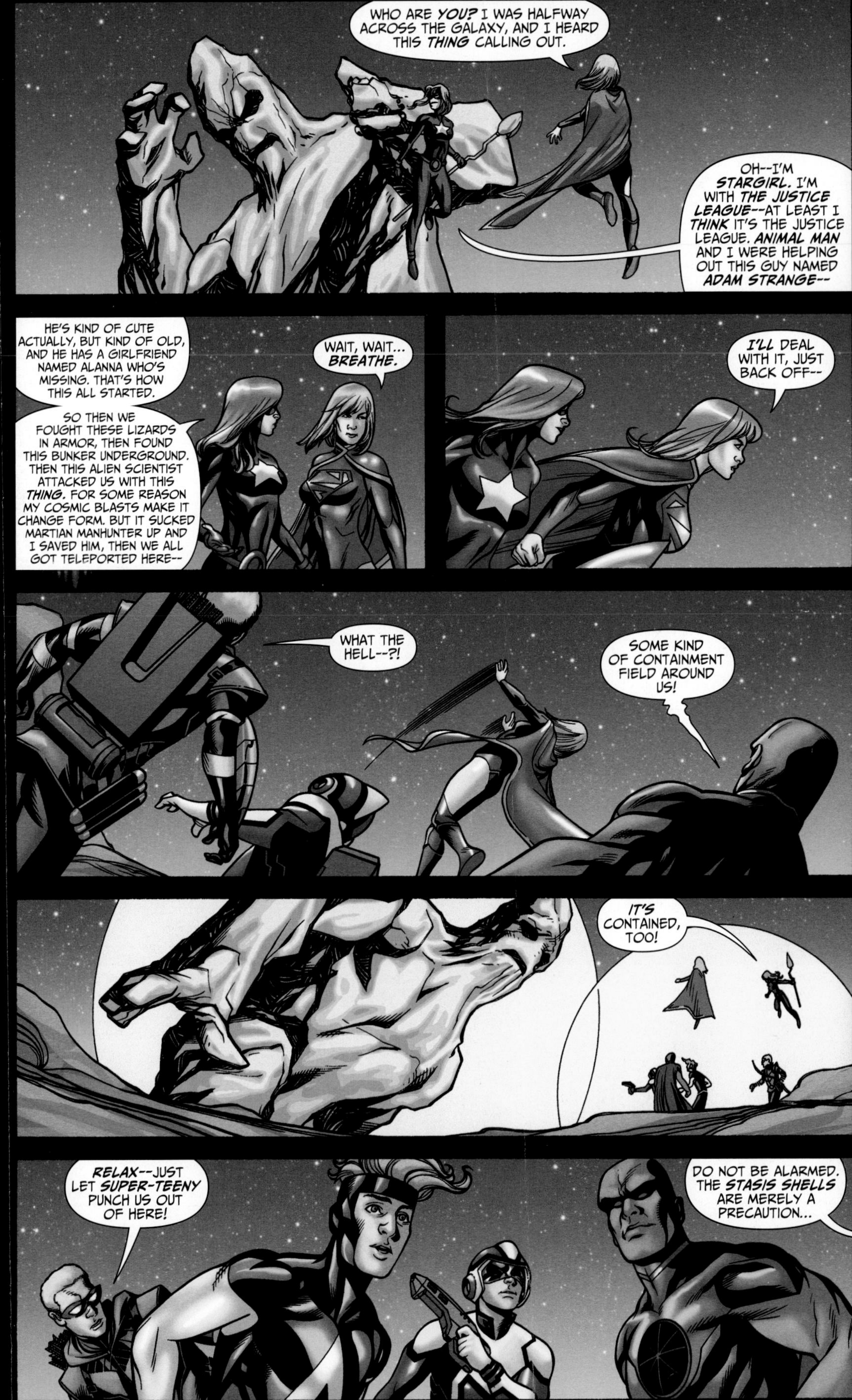
WHO ARE YOU? I WAS HALFWAY ACROSS THE GALAXY, AND I HEARD THIS THING CALLING OUT.
OH--I'M STARGIRL. I'M WITH THE JUSTICE LEAGUE--AT LEAST I THINK IT'S THE JUSTICE LEAGUE. ANIMAL MAN AND I WERE HELPING OUT THIS GUY NAMED ADAM STRANGE--
HE'S KIND OF CUTE ACTUALLY, BUT KIND OF OLD, AND HE HAS A GIRLFRIEND NAMED ALANNA WHO'S MISSING. THAT'S HOW THIS ALL STARTED.
SO THEN WE FOUGHT THESE LIZARDS IN ARMOR, THEN FOUND THIS BUNKER UNDERGROUND. THEN THIS ALIEN SCIENTIST ATTACKED US WITH THIS THING. FOR SOME REASON MY COSMIC BLASTS MAKE IT CHANGE FORM. BUT IT SUCKED MARTIAN MANHUNTER UP AND I SAVED HIM, THEN WE ALL GOT TELEPORTED HERE--
WAIT, WAIT... BREATHE.
I'LL DEAL WITH IT, JUST BACK OFF--
WHAT THE HELL--?!
SOME KIND OF CONTAINMENT FIELD AROUND US!
IT'S CONTAINED, TOO!
RELAX--JUST LET SUPER-TEENY PUNCH US OUT OF HERE!
DO NOT BE ALARMED. THE STASIS SHELLS ARE MERELY A PRECAUTION...

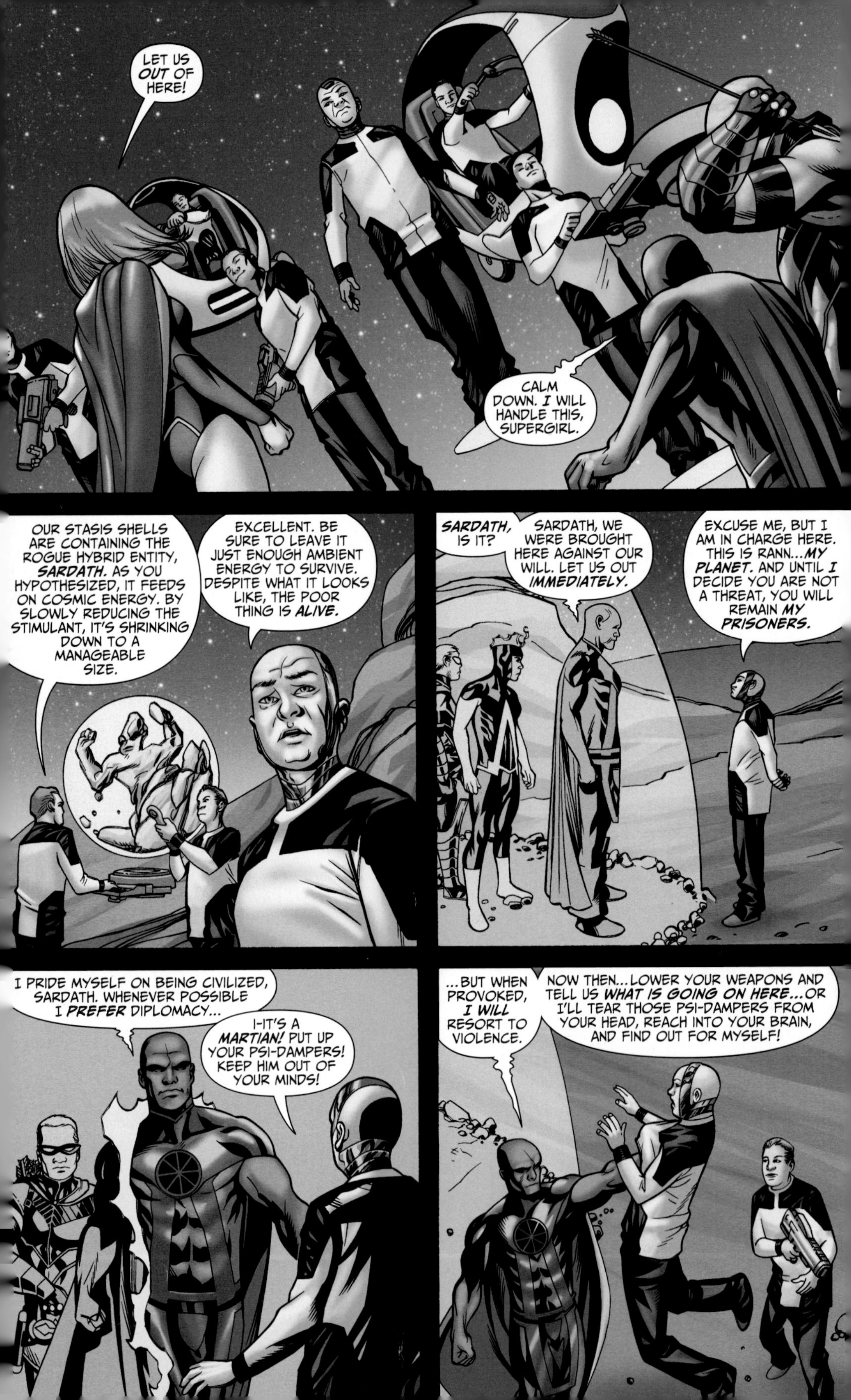
LET US OUT OF HERE!
CALM DOWN. I WILL HANDLE THIS, SUPERGIRL.
OUR STASIS SHELLS ARE CONTAINING THE ROGUE HYBRID ENTITY, SARDATH. AS YOU HYPOTHESIZED, IT FEEDS ON COSMIC ENERGY. BY SLOWLY REDUCING THE STIMULANT, IT'S SHRINKING DOWN TO A MANAGEABLE SIZE.
EXCELLENT. BE SURE TO LEAVE IT JUST ENOUGH AMBIENT ENERGY TO SURVIVE. DESPITE WHAT IT LOOKS LIKE, THE POOR THING IS ALIVE.
SARDATH, IS IT?
SARDATH, WE WERE BROUGHT HERE AGAINST OUR WILL. LET US OUT IMMEDIATELY.
EXCUSE ME, BUT I AM IN CHARGE HERE. THIS IS RANN...MY PLANET. AND UNTIL I DECIDE YOU ARE NOT A THREAT, YOU WILL REMAIN MY PRISONERS.
I PRIDE MYSELF ON BEING CIVILIZED, SARDATH. WHENEVER POSSIBLE I PREFER DIPLOMACY...
I-IT'S A MARTIAN! PUT UP YOUR PSI-DAMPERS! KEEP HIM OUT OF YOUR MINDS!
...BUT WHEN PROVOKED, I WILL RESORT TO VIOLENCE.
NOW THEN...LOWER YOUR WEAPONS AND TELL US WHAT IS GOING ON HERE...OR I'LL TEAR THOSE PSI-DAMPERS FROM YOUR HEAD, REACH INTO YOUR BRAIN, AND FIND OUT FOR MYSELF!

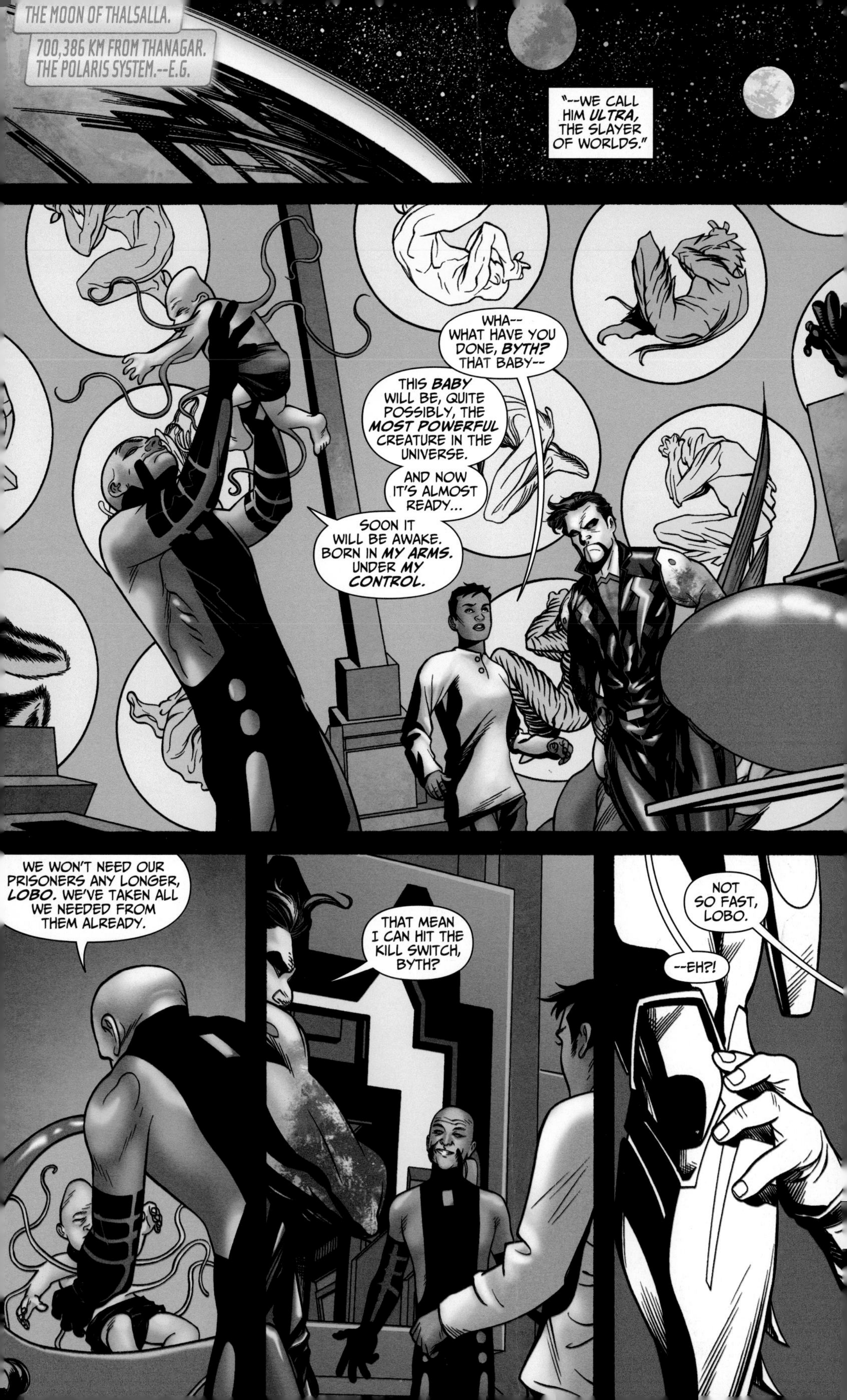

THE MOON OF THALSALLA.
700,386 KM FROM THANAGAR. THE POLARIS SYSTEM.--E.G.
"--WE CALL HIM ULTRA, THE SLAYER OF WORLDS."
WHA-- WHAT HAVE YOU DONE, BYTH? THAT BABY--
THIS BABY WILL BE, QUITE POSSIBLY, THE MOST POWERFUL CREATURE IN THE UNIVERSE.
AND NOW IT'S ALMOST READY...
SOON IT WILL BE AWAKE. BORN IN MY ARMS. UNDER MY CONTROL.
WE WON'T NEED OUR PRISONERS ANY LONGER, LOBO. WE'VE TAKEN ALL WE NEEDED FROM THEM ALREADY.
THAT MEAN I CAN HIT THE KILL SWITCH, BYTH?
NOT SO FAST, LOBO.
--EH?!

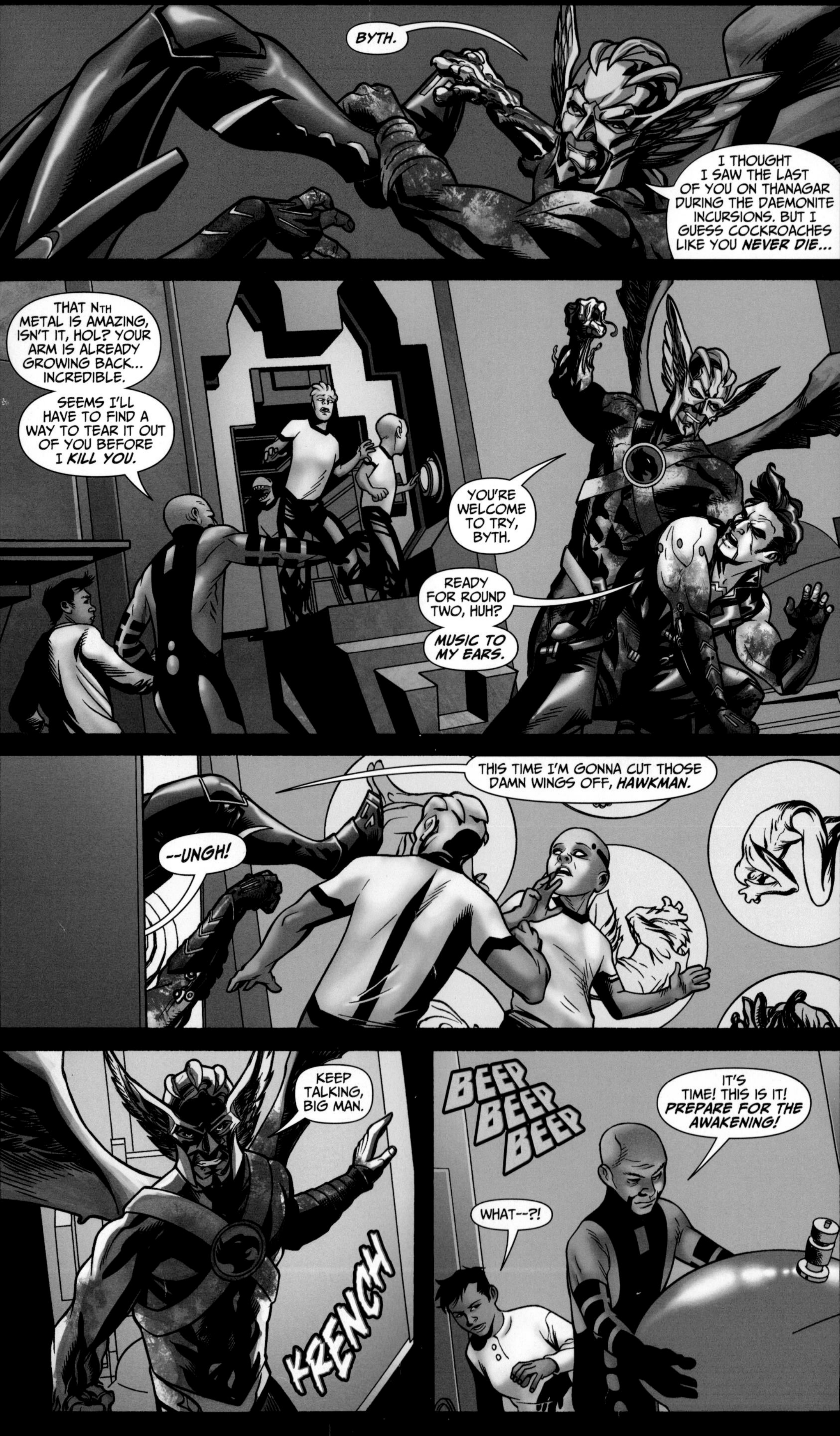
BYTH.
I THOUGHT I SAW THE LAST OF YOU ON THANAGAR DURING THE DAEMONITE INCURSIONS. BUT I GUESS COCKROACHES LIKE YOU NEVER DIE...
THAT NTH METAL IS AMAZING, ISN'T IT, HOL? YOUR ARM IS ALREADY GROWING BACK... INCREDIBLE.
SEEMS I'LL HAVE TO FIND A WAY TO TEAR IT OUT OF YOU BEFORE I KILL YOU.
YOU'RE WELCOME TO TRY, BYTH.
READY FOR ROUND TWO, HUH?
MUSIC TO MY EARS.
THIS TIME I'M GONNA CUT THOSE DAMN WINGS OFF, HAWKMAN.
--UNGH!
KEEP TALKING, BIG MAN.
KRENCH
BEEP BEEP BEEP
IT'S TIME! THIS IS IT! PREPARE FOR THE AWAKENING!
WHAT--?!

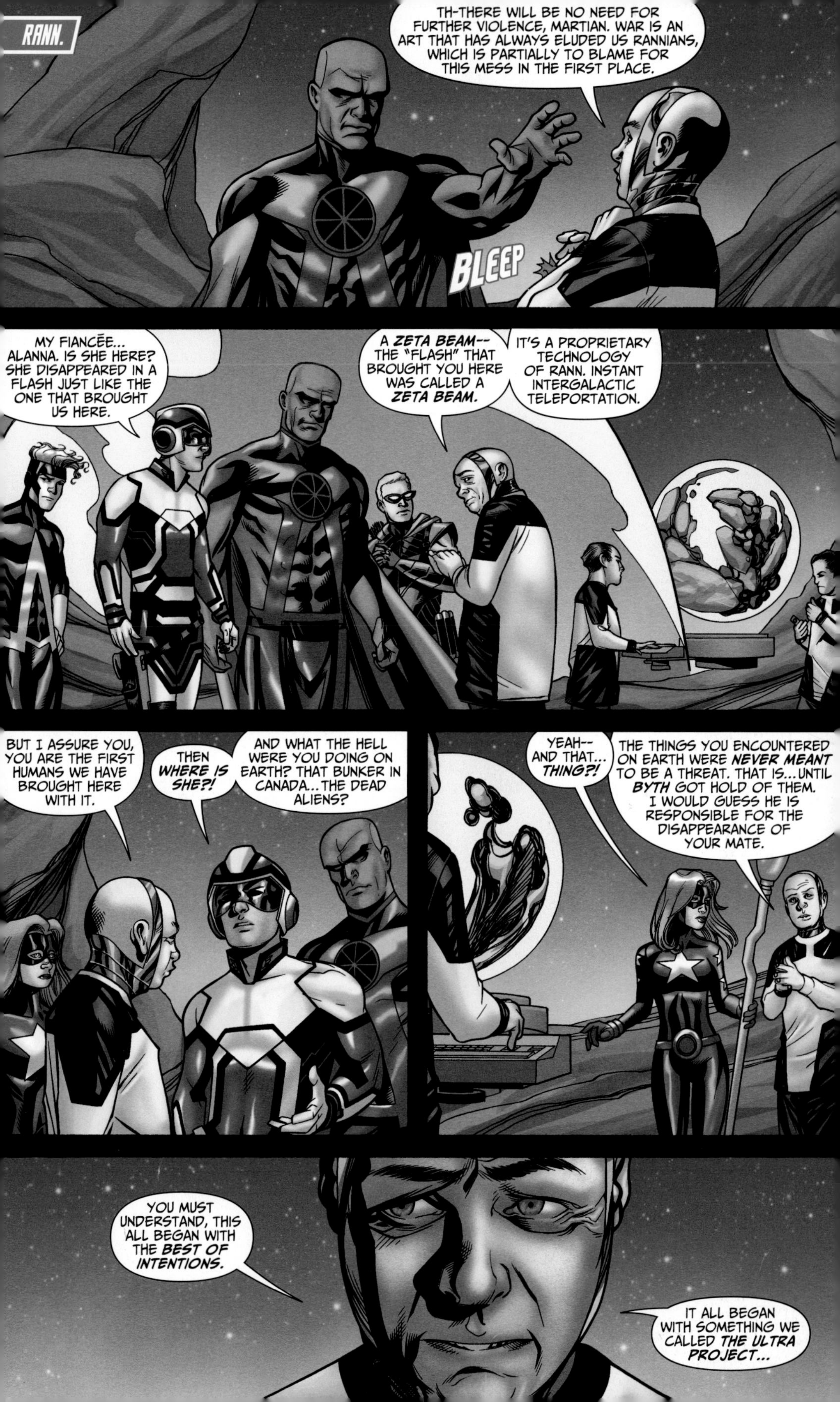
RANN.
TH-THERE WILL BE NO NEED FOR FURTHER VIOLENCE, MARTIAN. WAR IS AN ART THAT HAS ALWAYS ELUDED US RANNIANS, WHICH IS PARTIALLY TO BLAME FOR THIS MESS IN THE FIRST PLACE.
BLEEP
MY FIANCÉE... ALANNA. IS SHE HERE? SHE DISAPPEARED IN A FLASH JUST LIKE THE ONE THAT BROUGHT US HERE.
A ZETA BEAM-- THE "FLASH" THAT BROUGHT YOU HERE WAS CALLED A ZETA BEAM.
IT'S A PROPRIETARY TECHNOLOGY OF RANN. INSTANT INTERGALACTIC TELEPORTATION.
BUT I ASSURE YOU, YOU ARE THE FIRST HUMANS WE HAVE BROUGHT HERE WITH IT.
THEN WHERE IS SHE?!
AND WHAT THE HELL WERE YOU DOING ON EARTH? THAT BUNKER IN CANADA... THE DEAD ALIENS?
YEAH-- AND THAT... THING?!
THE THINGS YOU ENCOUNTERED ON EARTH WERE NEVER MEANT TO BE A THREAT. THAT IS... UNTIL BYTH GOT HOLD OF THEM. I WOULD GUESS HE IS RESPONSIBLE FOR THE DISAPPEARANCE OF YOUR MATE.
YOU MUST UNDERSTAND, THIS ALL BEGAN WITH THE BEST OF INTENTIONS.
IT ALL BEGAN WITH SOMETHING WE CALLED THE ULTRA PROJECT...

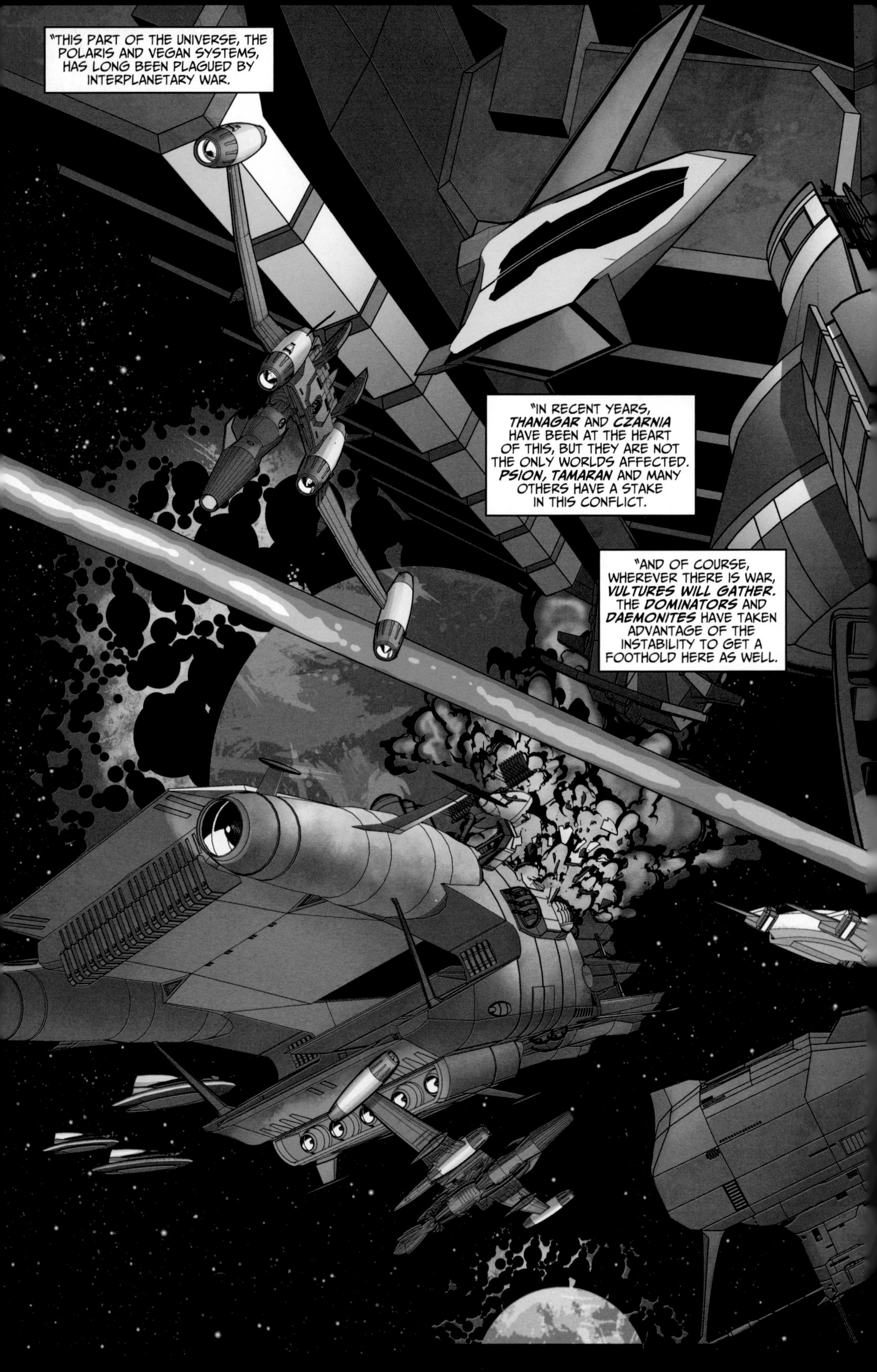
"THIS PART OF THE UNIVERSE, THE POLARIS AND VEGAN SYSTEMS, HAS LONG BEEN PLAGUED BY INTERPLANETARY WAR.
"IN RECENT YEARS, THANAGAR AND CZARNIA HAVE BEEN AT THE HEART OF THIS, BUT THEY ARE NOT THE ONLY WORLDS AFFECTED. PSION, TAMARAN AND MANY OTHERS HAVE A STAKE IN THIS CONFLICT.
"AND OF COURSE, WHEREVER THERE IS WAR, VULTURES WILL GATHER. THE DOMINATORS AND DAEMONITES HAVE TAKEN ADVANTAGE OF THE INSTABILITY TO GET A FOOTHOLD HERE AS WELL.

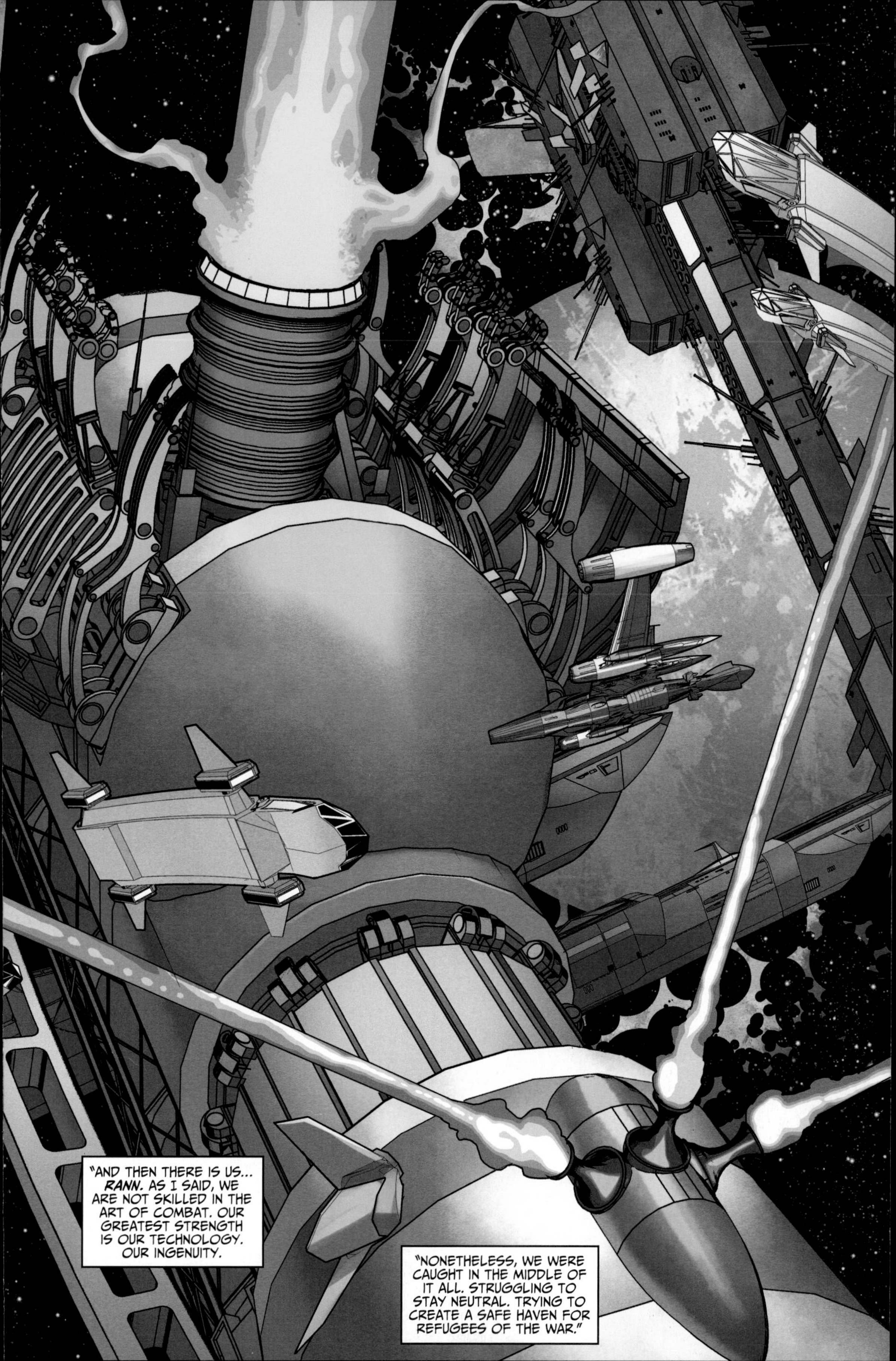
"AND THEN THERE IS US... *RANN.* AS I SAID, WE ARE NOT SKILLED IN THE ART OF COMBAT. OUR GREATEST STRENGTH IS OUR TECHNOLOGY. OUR INGENUITY.
"NONETHELESS, WE WERE CAUGHT IN THE MIDDLE OF IT ALL. STRUGGLING TO STAY NEUTRAL. TRYING TO CREATE A SAFE HAVEN FOR REFUGEES OF THE WAR."

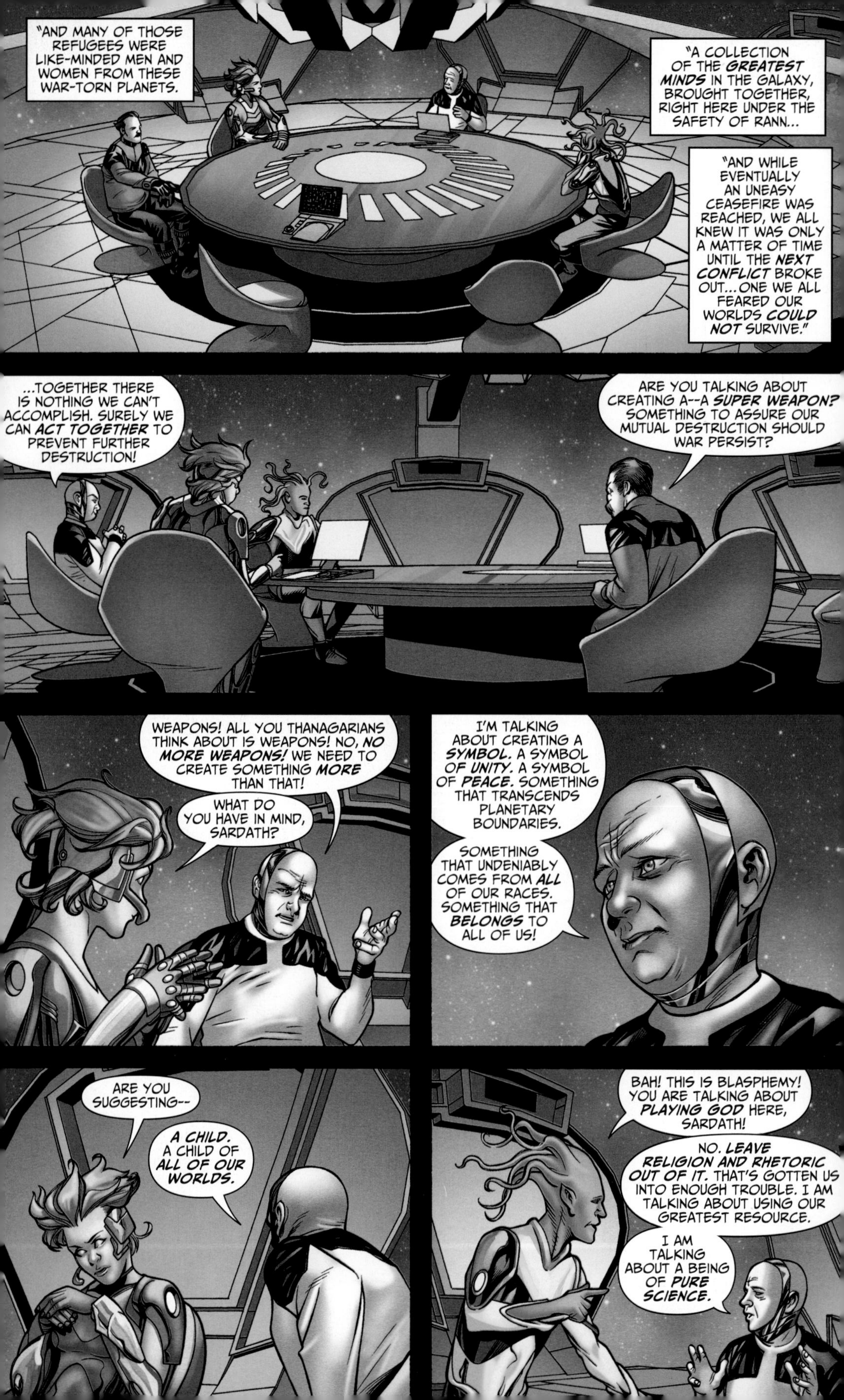
"AND MANY OF THOSE REFUGEES WERE LIKE-MINDED MEN AND WOMEN FROM THESE WAR-TORN PLANETS.
"A COLLECTION OF THE GREATEST MINDS IN THE GALAXY, BROUGHT TOGETHER, RIGHT HERE UNDER THE SAFETY OF RANN...
"AND WHILE EVENTUALLY AN UNEASY CEASEFIRE WAS REACHED, WE ALL KNEW IT WAS ONLY A MATTER OF TIME UNTIL THE NEXT CONFLICT BROKE OUT...ONE WE ALL FEARED OUR WORLDS COULD NOT SURVIVE."
...TOGETHER THERE IS NOTHING WE CAN'T ACCOMPLISH. SURELY WE CAN ACT TOGETHER TO PREVENT FURTHER DESTRUCTION!
ARE YOU TALKING ABOUT CREATING A--A SUPER WEAPON? SOMETHING TO ASSURE OUR MUTUAL DESTRUCTION SHOULD WAR PERSIST?
WEAPONS! ALL YOU THANAGARIANS THINK ABOUT IS WEAPONS! NO, NO MORE WEAPONS! WE NEED TO CREATE SOMETHING MORE THAN THAT!
WHAT DO YOU HAVE IN MIND, SARDATH?
I'M TALKING ABOUT CREATING A SYMBOL. A SYMBOL OF UNITY. A SYMBOL OF PEACE. SOMETHING THAT TRANSCENDS PLANETARY BOUNDARIES.
SOMETHING THAT UNDENIABLY COMES FROM ALL OF OUR RACES. SOMETHING THAT BELONGS TO ALL OF US!
ARE YOU SUGGESTING--
A CHILD. A CHILD OF ALL OF OUR WORLDS.
BAH! THIS IS BLASPHEMY! YOU ARE TALKING ABOUT PLAYING GOD HERE, SARDATH!
NO. LEAVE RELIGION AND RHETORIC OUT OF IT. THAT'S GOTTEN US INTO ENOUGH TROUBLE. I AM TALKING ABOUT USING OUR GREATEST RESOURCE.
I AM TALKING ABOUT A BEING OF PURE SCIENCE.

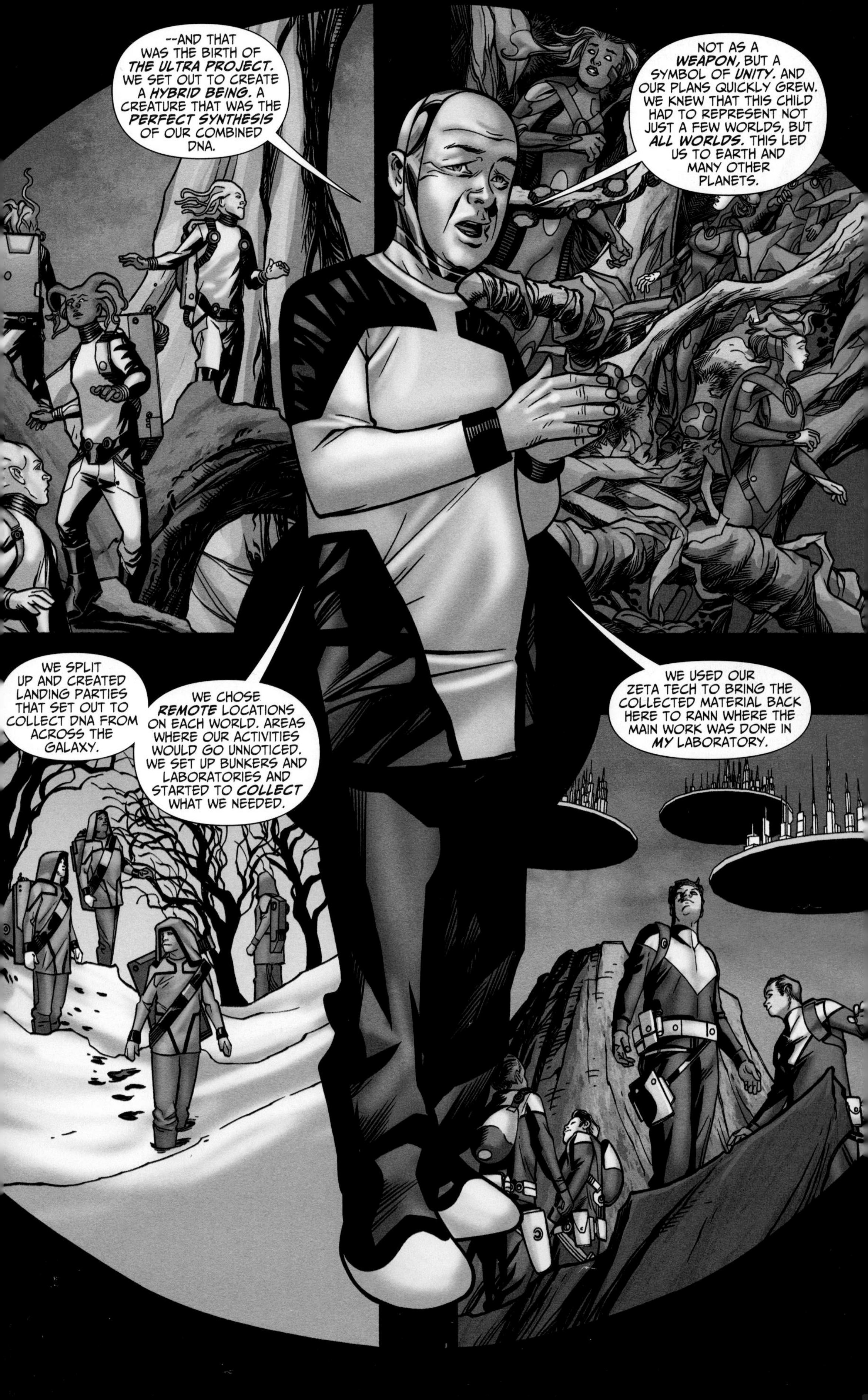
--AND THAT WAS THE BIRTH OF THE ULTRA PROJECT. WE SET OUT TO CREATE A HYBRID BEING. A CREATURE THAT WAS THE PERFECT SYNTHESIS OF OUR COMBINED DNA.
NOT AS A WEAPON, BUT A SYMBOL OF UNITY. AND OUR PLANS QUICKLY GREW. WE KNEW THAT THIS CHILD HAD TO REPRESENT NOT JUST A FEW WORLDS, BUT ALL WORLDS. THIS LED US TO EARTH AND MANY OTHER PLANETS.
WE SPLIT UP AND CREATED LANDING PARTIES THAT SET OUT TO COLLECT DNA FROM ACROSS THE GALAXY.
WE CHOSE REMOTE LOCATIONS ON EACH WORLD. AREAS WHERE OUR ACTIVITIES WOULD GO UNNOTICED. WE SET UP BUNKERS AND LABORATORIES AND STARTED TO COLLECT WHAT WE NEEDED.
WE USED OUR ZETA TECH TO BRING THE COLLECTED MATERIAL BACK HERE TO RANN WHERE THE MAIN WORK WAS DONE IN MY LABORATORY.

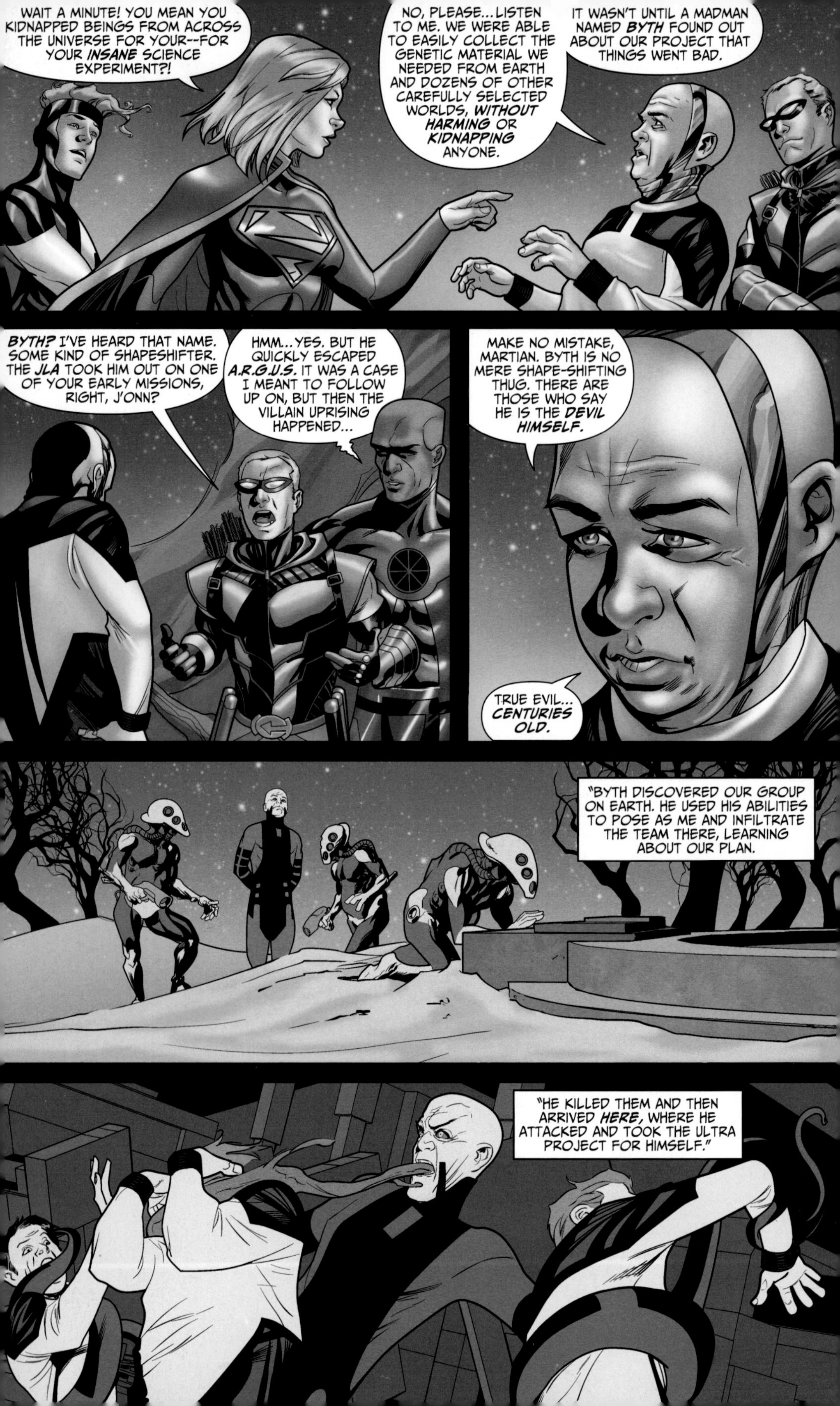
WAIT A MINUTE! YOU MEAN YOU KIDNAPPED BEINGS FROM ACROSS THE UNIVERSE FOR YOUR--FOR YOUR INSANE SCIENCE EXPERIMENT?!
NO, PLEASE... LISTEN TO ME. WE WERE ABLE TO EASILY COLLECT THE GENETIC MATERIAL WE NEEDED FROM EARTH AND DOZENS OF OTHER CAREFULLY SELECTED WORLDS, WITHOUT HARMING OR KIDNAPPING ANYONE.
IT WASN'T UNTIL A MADMAN NAMED BYTH FOUND OUT ABOUT OUR PROJECT THAT THINGS WENT BAD.
BYTH? I'VE HEARD THAT NAME. SOME KIND OF SHAPESHIFTER. THE JLA TOOK HIM OUT ON ONE OF YOUR EARLY MISSIONS, RIGHT, J'ONN?
HMM... YES. BUT HE QUICKLY ESCAPED A.R.G.U.S. IT WAS A CASE I MEANT TO FOLLOW UP ON, BUT THEN THE VILLAIN UPRISING HAPPENED...
MAKE NO MISTAKE, MARTIAN. BYTH IS NO MERE SHAPE-SHIFTING THUG. THERE ARE THOSE WHO SAY HE IS THE DEVIL HIMSELF.
TRUE EVIL... CENTURIES OLD.
"BYTH DISCOVERED OUR GROUP ON EARTH. HE USED HIS ABILITIES TO POSE AS ME AND INFILTRATE THE TEAM THERE, LEARNING ABOUT OUR PLAN.
"HE KILLED THEM AND THEN ARRIVED HERE, WHERE HE ATTACKED AND TOOK THE ULTRA PROJECT FOR HIMSELF."

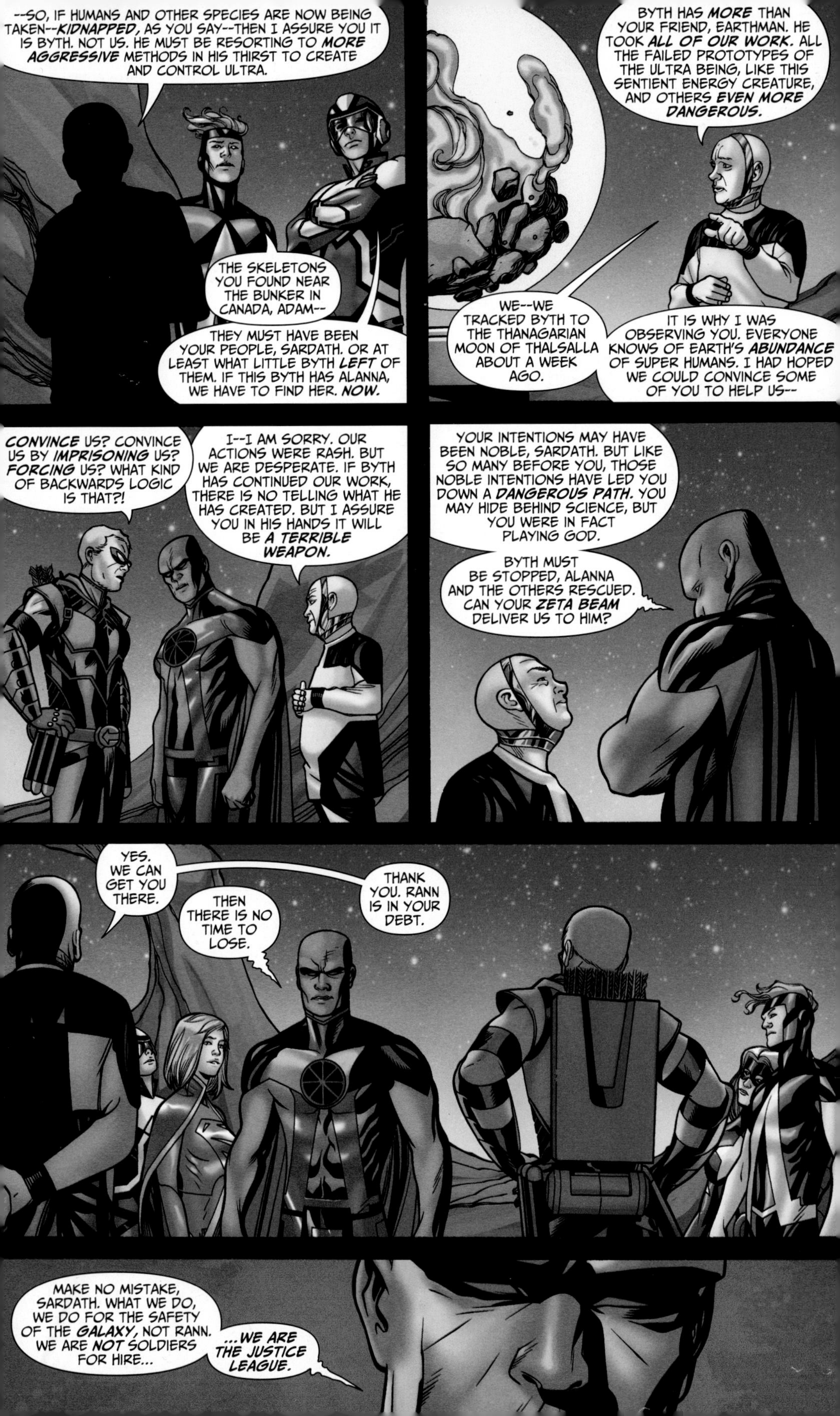
--SO, IF HUMANS AND OTHER SPECIES ARE NOW BEING TAKEN--KIDNAPPED, AS YOU SAY--THEN I ASSURE YOU IT IS BYTH. NOT US. HE MUST BE RESORTING TO MORE AGGRESSIVE METHODS IN HIS THIRST TO CREATE AND CONTROL ULTRA.
THE SKELETONS YOU FOUND NEAR THE BUNKER IN CANADA, ADAM--
THEY MUST HAVE BEEN YOUR PEOPLE, SARDATH. OR AT LEAST WHAT LITTLE BYTH LEFT OF THEM. IF THIS BYTH HAS ALANNA, WE HAVE TO FIND HER. NOW.
BYTH HAS MORE THAN YOUR FRIEND, EARTHMAN. HE TOOK ALL OF OUR WORK. ALL THE FAILED PROTOTYPES OF THE ULTRA BEING, LIKE THIS SENTIENT ENERGY CREATURE, AND OTHERS EVEN MORE DANGEROUS.
WE--WE TRACKED BYTH TO THE THANAGARIAN MOON OF THALSALLA ABOUT A WEEK AGO.
IT IS WHY I WAS OBSERVING YOU. EVERYONE KNOWS OF EARTH'S ABUNDANCE OF SUPER HUMANS. I HAD HOPED WE COULD CONVINCE SOME OF YOU TO HELP US--
CONVINCE US? CONVINCE US BY IMPRISONING US? FORCING US? WHAT KIND OF BACKWARDS LOGIC IS THAT?!
I--I AM SORRY. OUR ACTIONS WERE RASH. BUT WE ARE DESPERATE. IF BYTH HAS CONTINUED OUR WORK, THERE IS NO TELLING WHAT HE HAS CREATED. BUT I ASSURE YOU IN HIS HANDS IT WILL BE A TERRIBLE WEAPON.
YOUR INTENTIONS MAY HAVE BEEN NOBLE, SARDATH. BUT LIKE SO MANY BEFORE YOU, THOSE NOBLE INTENTIONS HAVE LED YOU DOWN A DANGEROUS PATH. YOU MAY HIDE BEHIND SCIENCE, BUT YOU WERE IN FACT PLAYING GOD.
BYTH MUST BE STOPPED, ALANNA AND THE OTHERS RESCUED. CAN YOUR ZETA BEAM DELIVER US TO HIM?
YES. WE CAN GET YOU THERE.
THEN THERE IS NO TIME TO LOSE.
THANK YOU. RANN IS IN YOUR DEBT.
MAKE NO MISTAKE, SARDATH. WHAT WE DO, WE DO FOR THE SAFETY OF THE GALAXY, NOT RANN. WE ARE NOT SOLDIERS FOR HIRE...
...WE ARE THE JUSTICE LEAGUE.

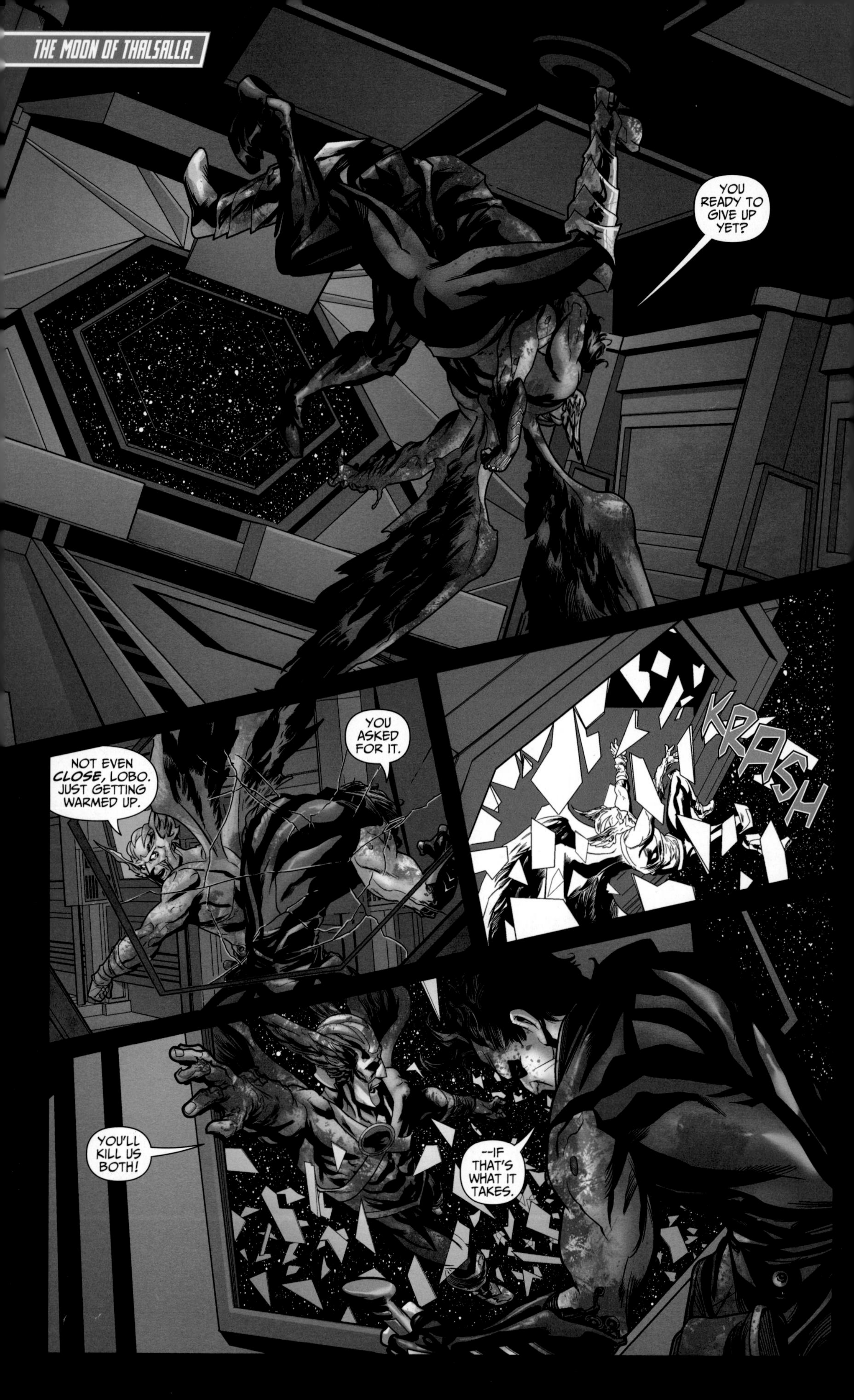
THE MOON OF THALSALLA.
YOU READY TO GIVE UP YET?
NOT EVEN CLOSE, LOBO. JUST GETTING WARMED UP.
YOU ASKED FOR IT.
KRASH
YOU'LL KILL US BOTH!
--IF THAT'S WHAT IT TAKES.

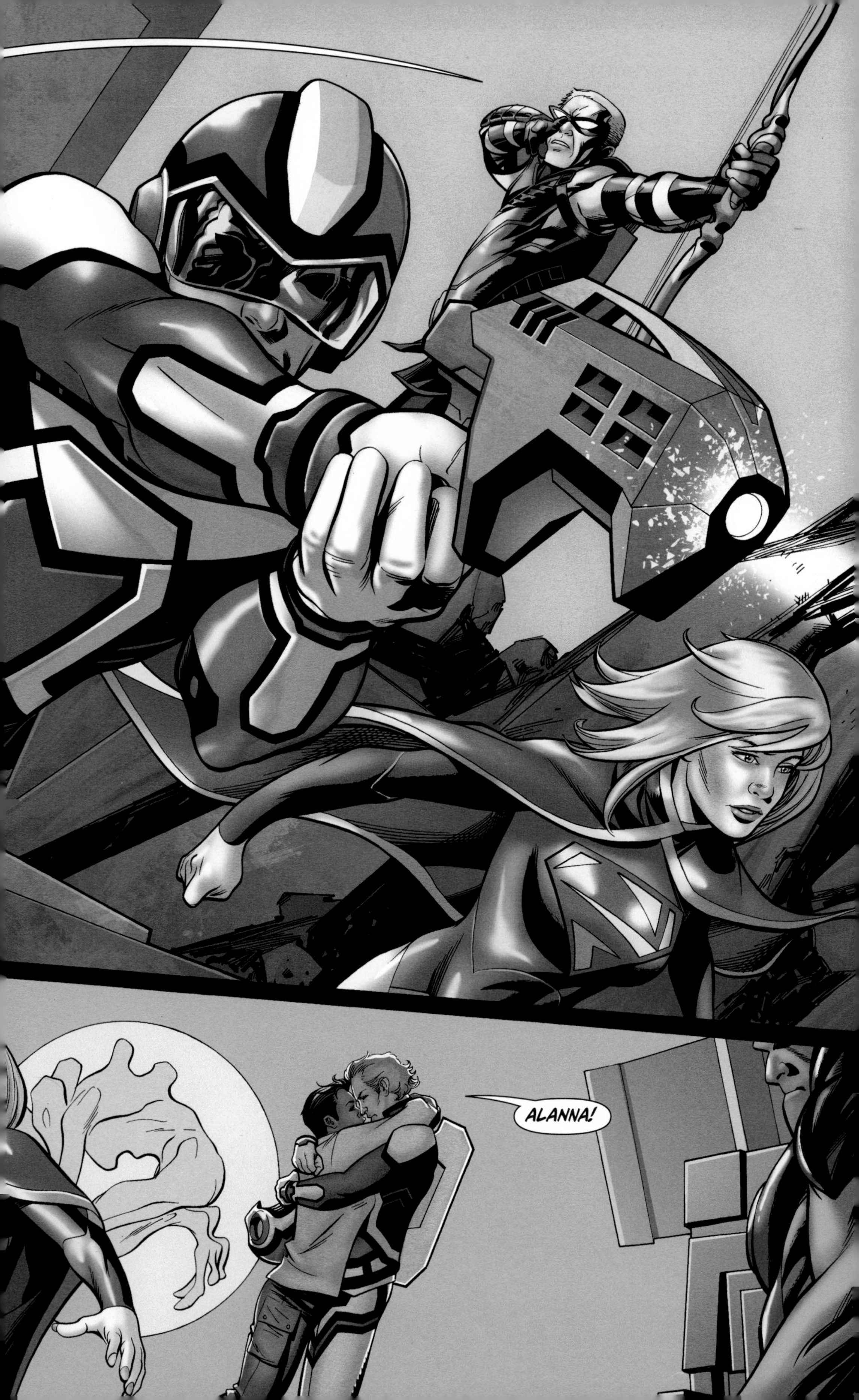
ALANNA!

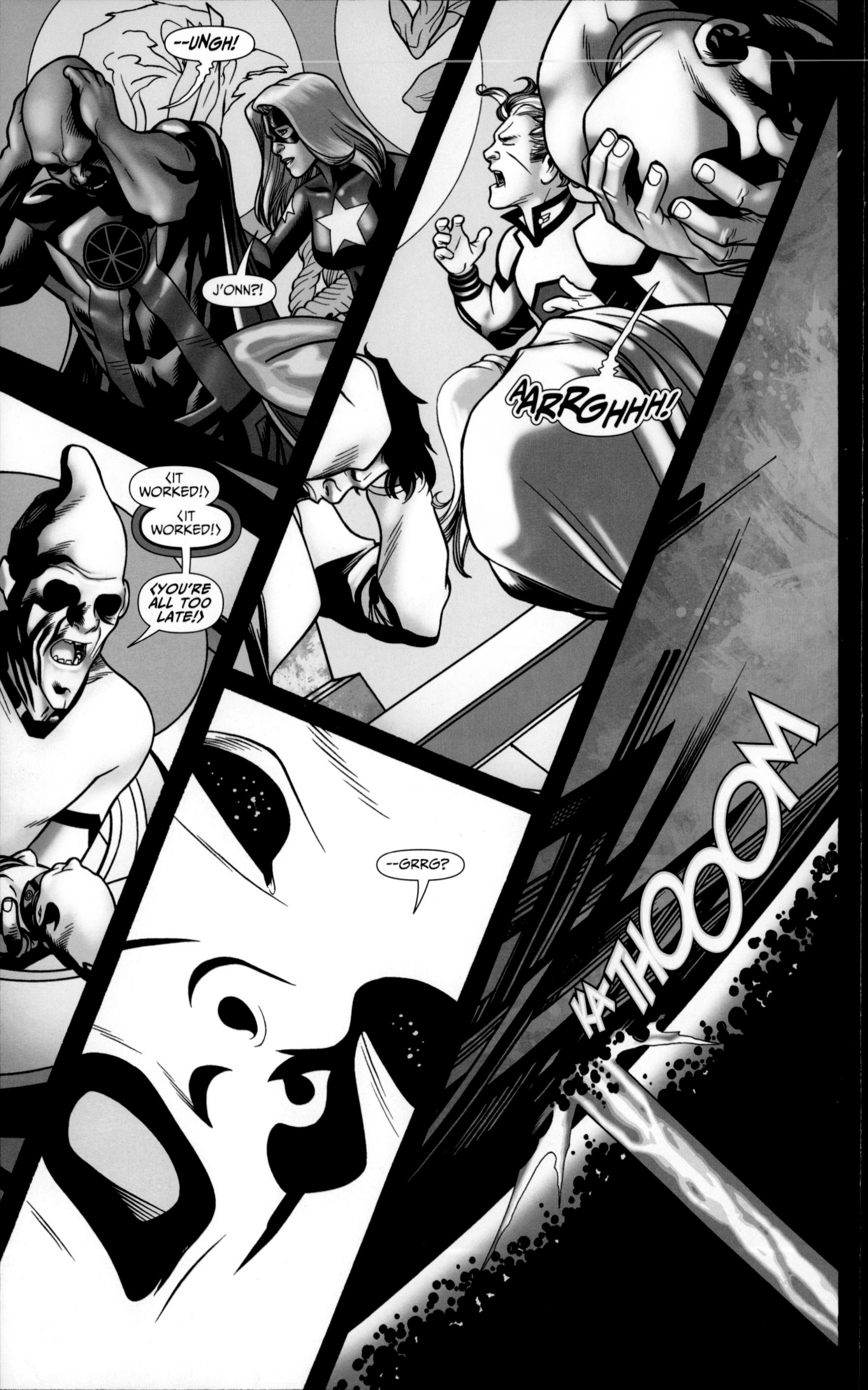
--UNGH!
J'ONN?!
AARRGHHH!
<IT WORKED!>
<IT WORKED!>
<YOU'RE ALL TOO LATE!>
--GRRG?
KA-THOOOM

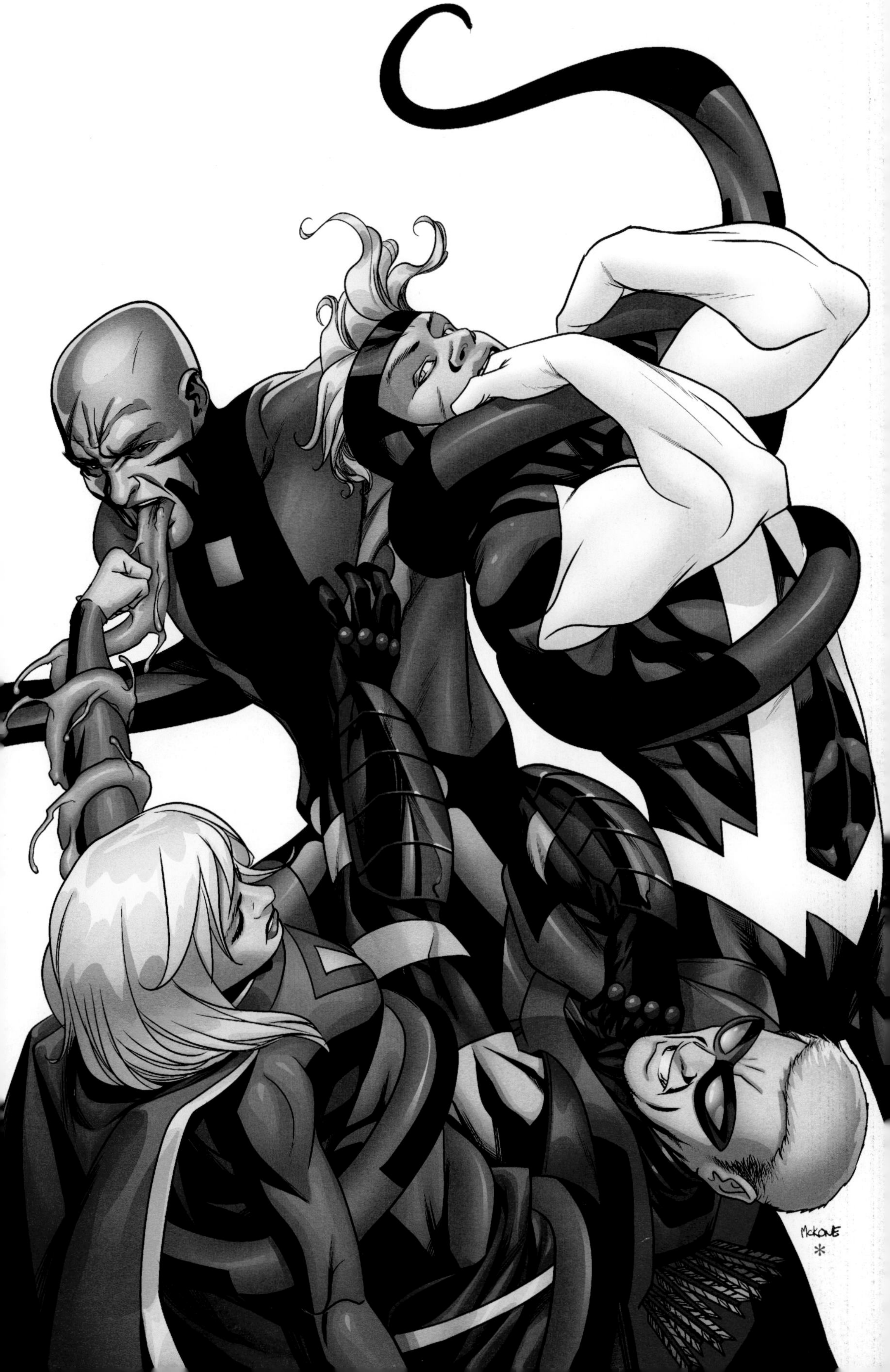
McKONE

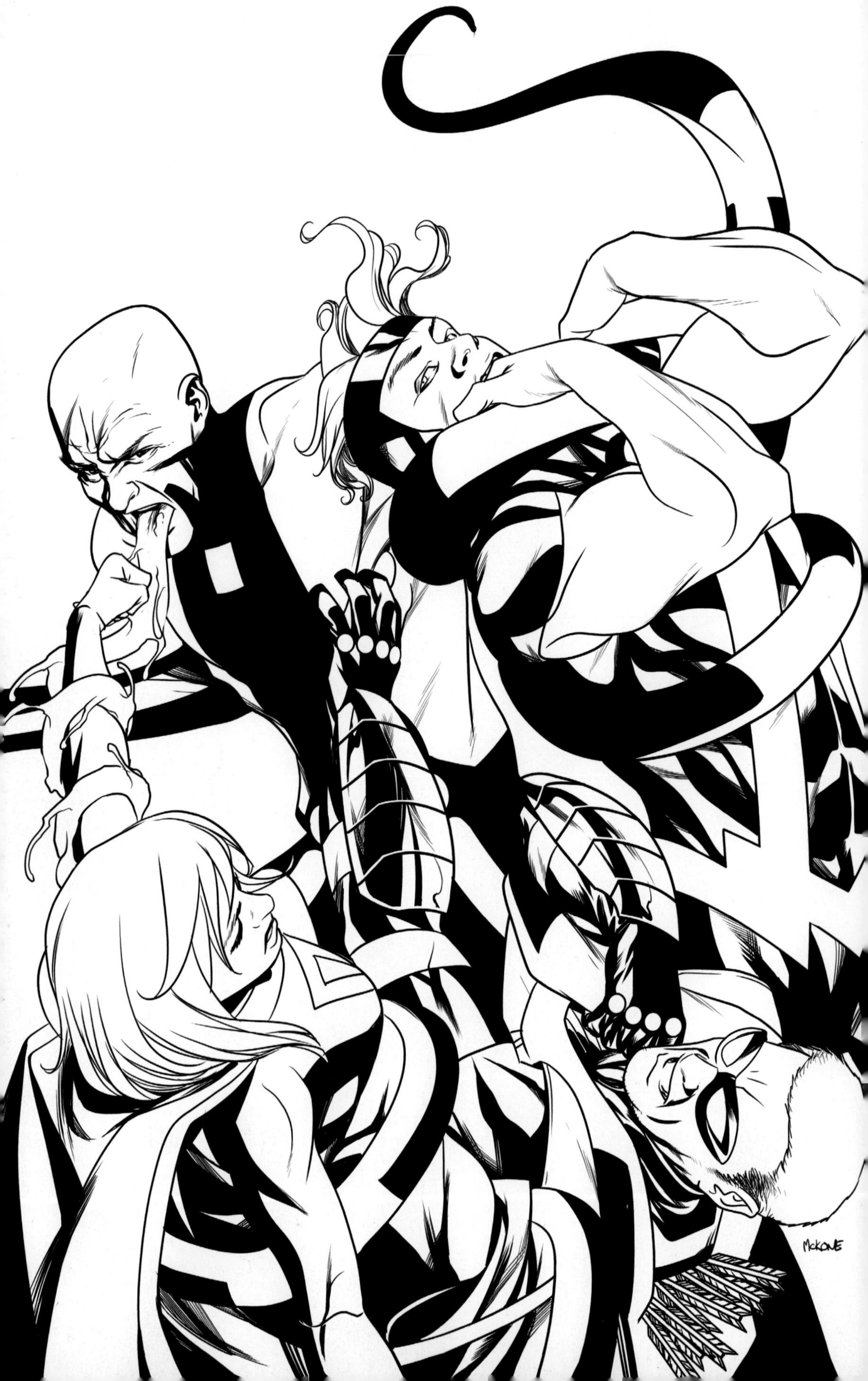
McKONE

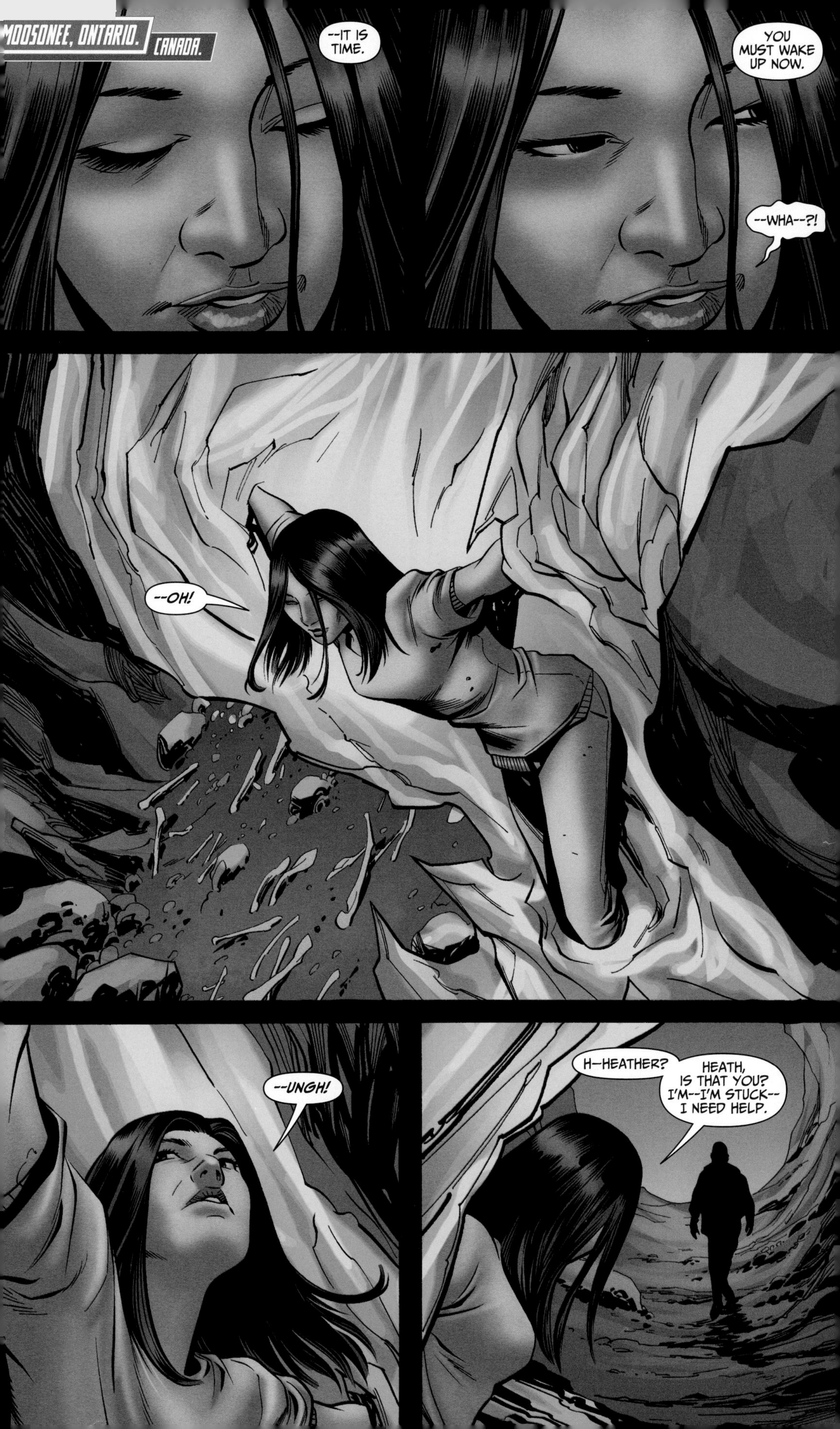
MOOSONEE, ONTARIO.
CANADA.
--IT IS TIME.
YOU MUST WAKE UP NOW.
--WHA--?!
--OH!
--UNGH!
H--HEATHER?
HEATH, IS THAT YOU? I'M--I'M STUCK-- I NEED HELP.

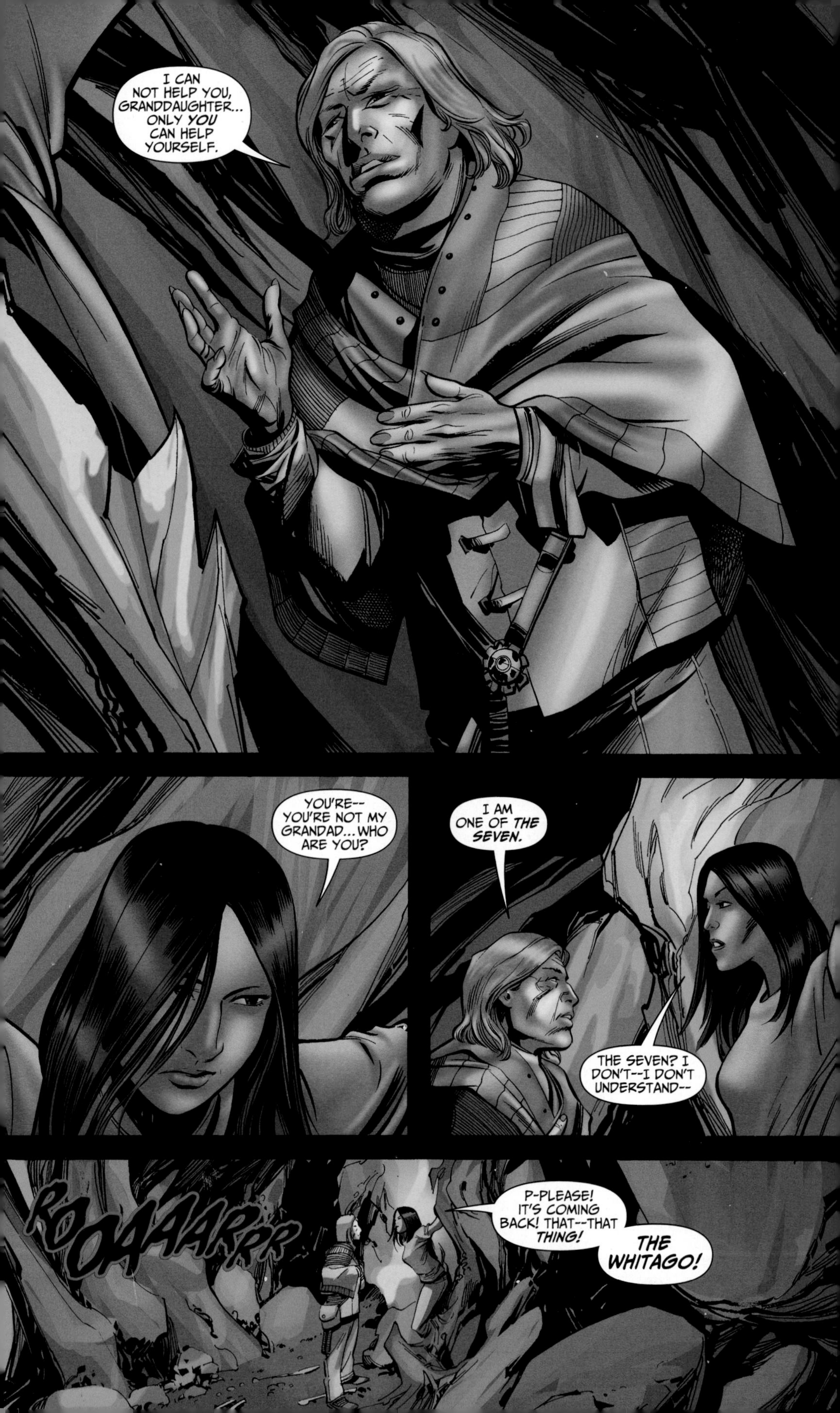
I CAN NOT HELP YOU, GRANDDAUGHTER... ONLY *YOU* CAN HELP YOURSELF.
YOU'RE-- YOU'RE NOT MY GRANDAD... WHO ARE YOU?
I AM ONE OF *THE SEVEN.*
THE SEVEN? I DON'T--I DON'T UNDERSTAND--
ROOAAAARRR
P-PLEASE! IT'S COMING BACK! THAT--THAT *THING!*
THE WHITAGO!

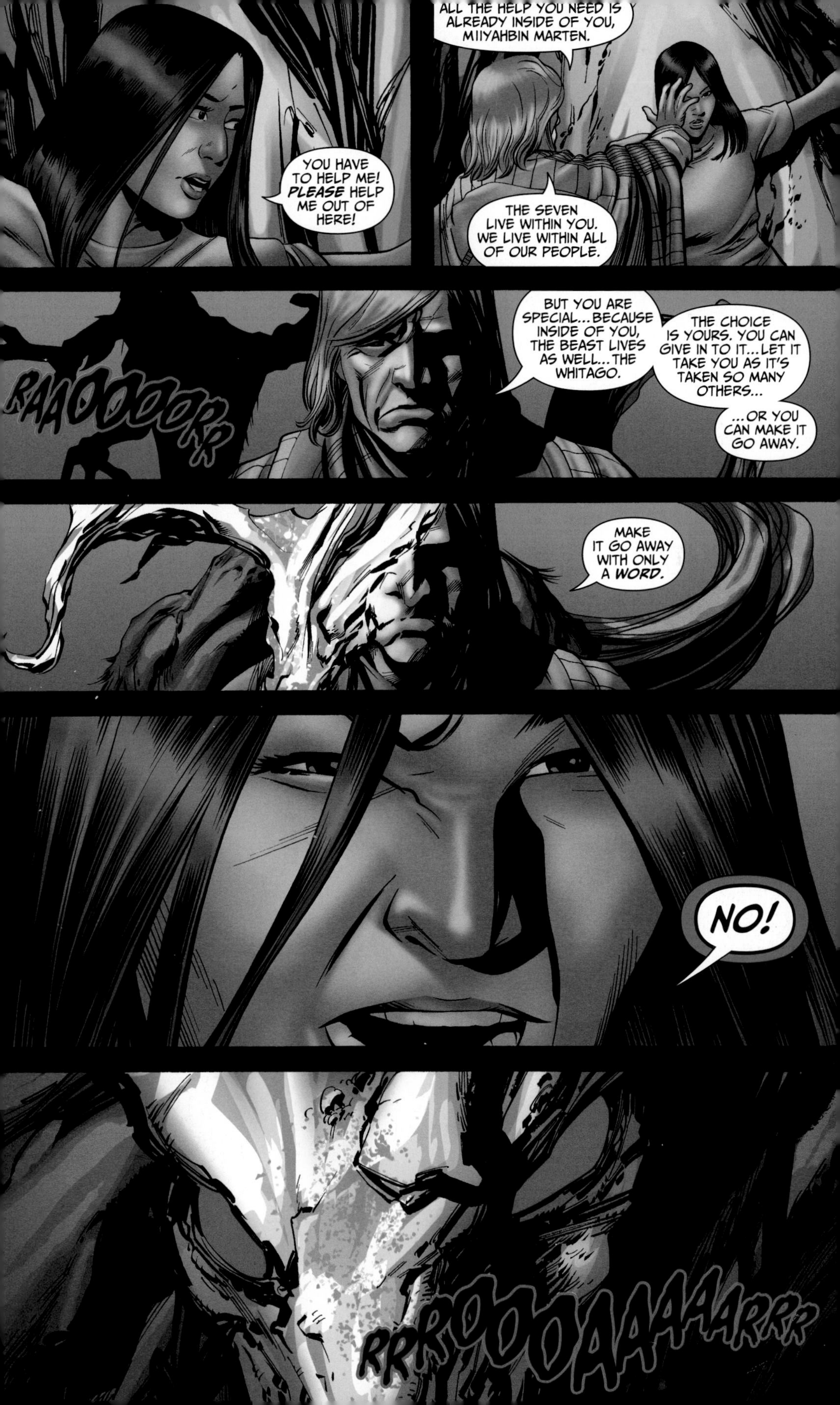

YOU HAVE TO HELP ME! *PLEASE* HELP ME OUT OF HERE!
ALL THE HELP YOU NEED IS ALREADY INSIDE OF YOU, MIIYAHBIN MARTEN.
THE SEVEN LIVE WITHIN YOU. WE LIVE WITHIN ALL OF OUR PEOPLE.
RAAOOOORR
BUT YOU ARE SPECIAL...BECAUSE INSIDE OF YOU, THE BEAST LIVES AS WELL...THE WHITAGO.
THE CHOICE IS YOURS. YOU CAN GIVE IN TO IT...LET IT TAKE YOU AS IT'S TAKEN SO MANY OTHERS...
...OR YOU CAN MAKE IT GO AWAY.
MAKE IT GO AWAY WITH ONLY A *WORD*.
NO!
RRRROOOAAAAARRR

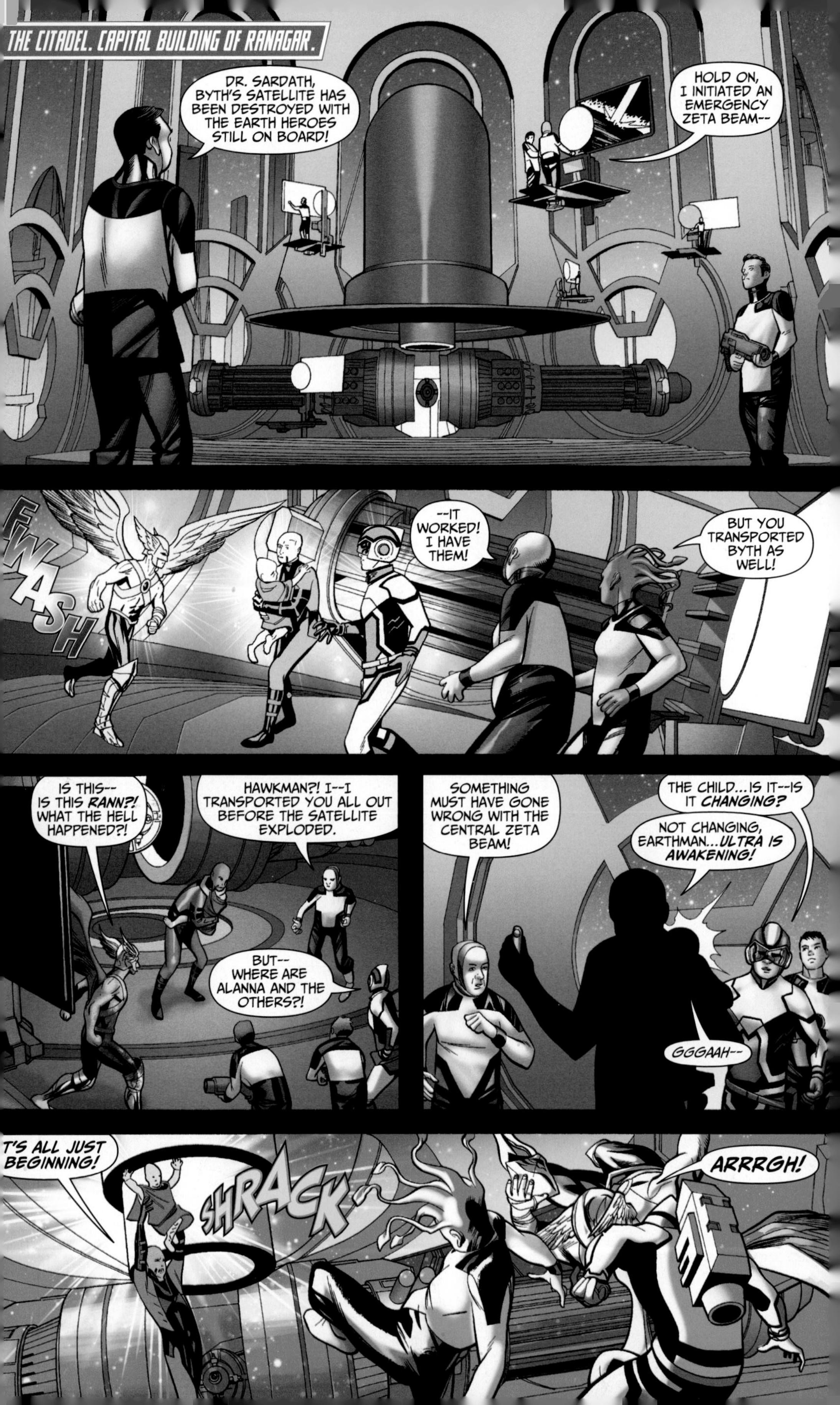
THE CITADEL. CAPITAL BUILDING OF RANAGAR.
DR. SARDATH, BYTH'S SATELLITE HAS BEEN DESTROYED WITH THE EARTH HEROES STILL ON BOARD!
HOLD ON, I INITIATED AN EMERGENCY ZETA BEAM--
FWASH
--IT WORKED! I HAVE THEM!
BUT YOU TRANSPORTED BYTH AS WELL!
IS THIS-- IS THIS *RANN?!* WHAT THE HELL HAPPENED?!
HAWKMAN?! I--I TRANSPORTED YOU ALL OUT BEFORE THE SATELLITE EXPLODED.
BUT-- WHERE ARE ALANNA AND THE OTHERS?!
SOMETHING MUST HAVE GONE WRONG WITH THE CENTRAL ZETA BEAM!
THE CHILD...IS IT--IS IT *CHANGING?*
NOT CHANGING, EARTHMAN...*ULTRA IS AWAKENING!*
GGGAAH--
T'S ALL JUST BEGINNING!
SHRACK
ARRRGH!

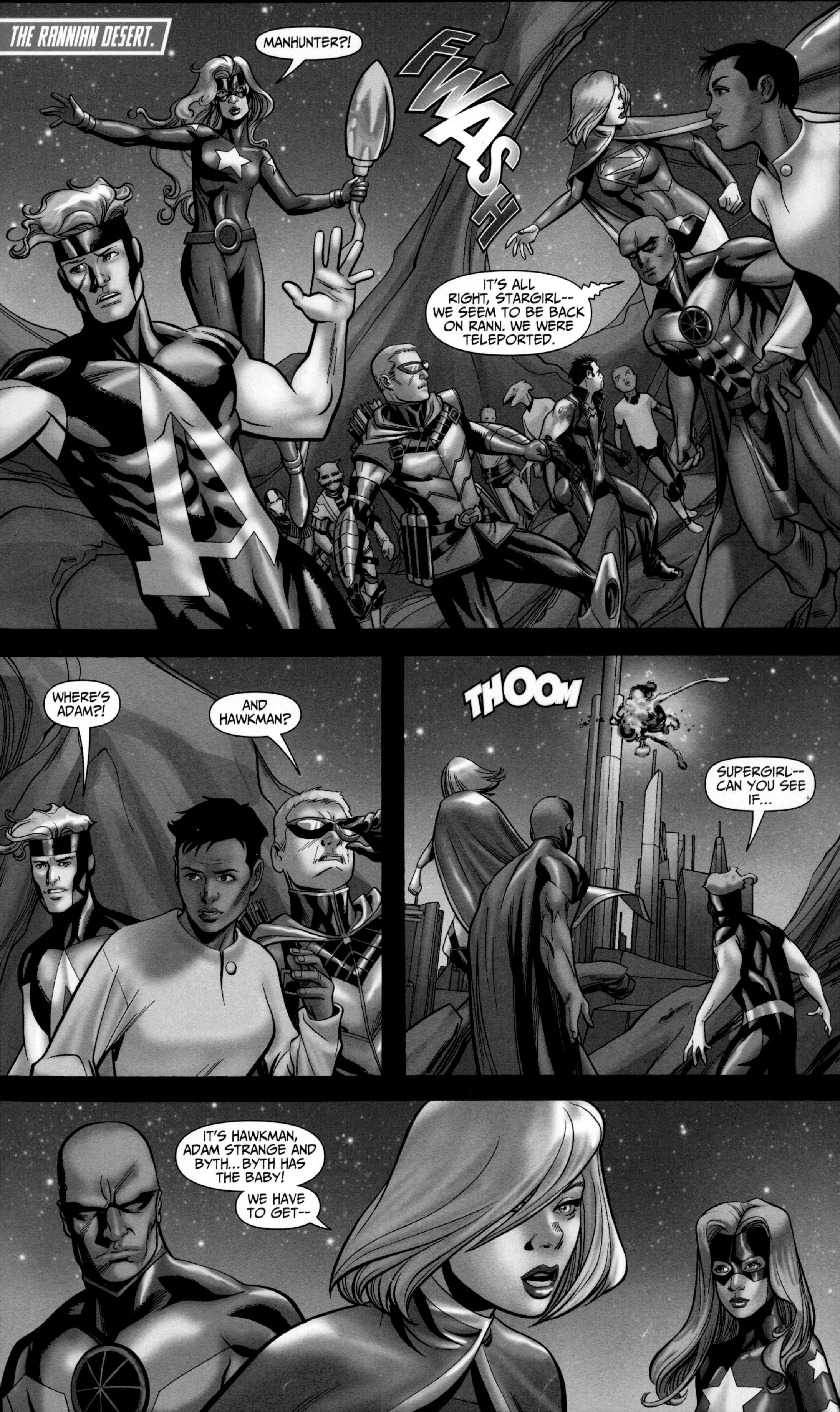
THE RANNIAN DESERT.
MANHUNTER?!
FWASH
IT'S ALL RIGHT, STARGIRL-- WE SEEM TO BE BACK ON RANN. WE WERE TELEPORTED.
WHERE'S ADAM?!
AND HAWKMAN?
THOOM
SUPERGIRL-- CAN YOU SEE IF...
IT'S HAWKMAN, ADAM STRANGE AND BYTH... BYTH HAS THE BABY!
WE HAVE TO GET--

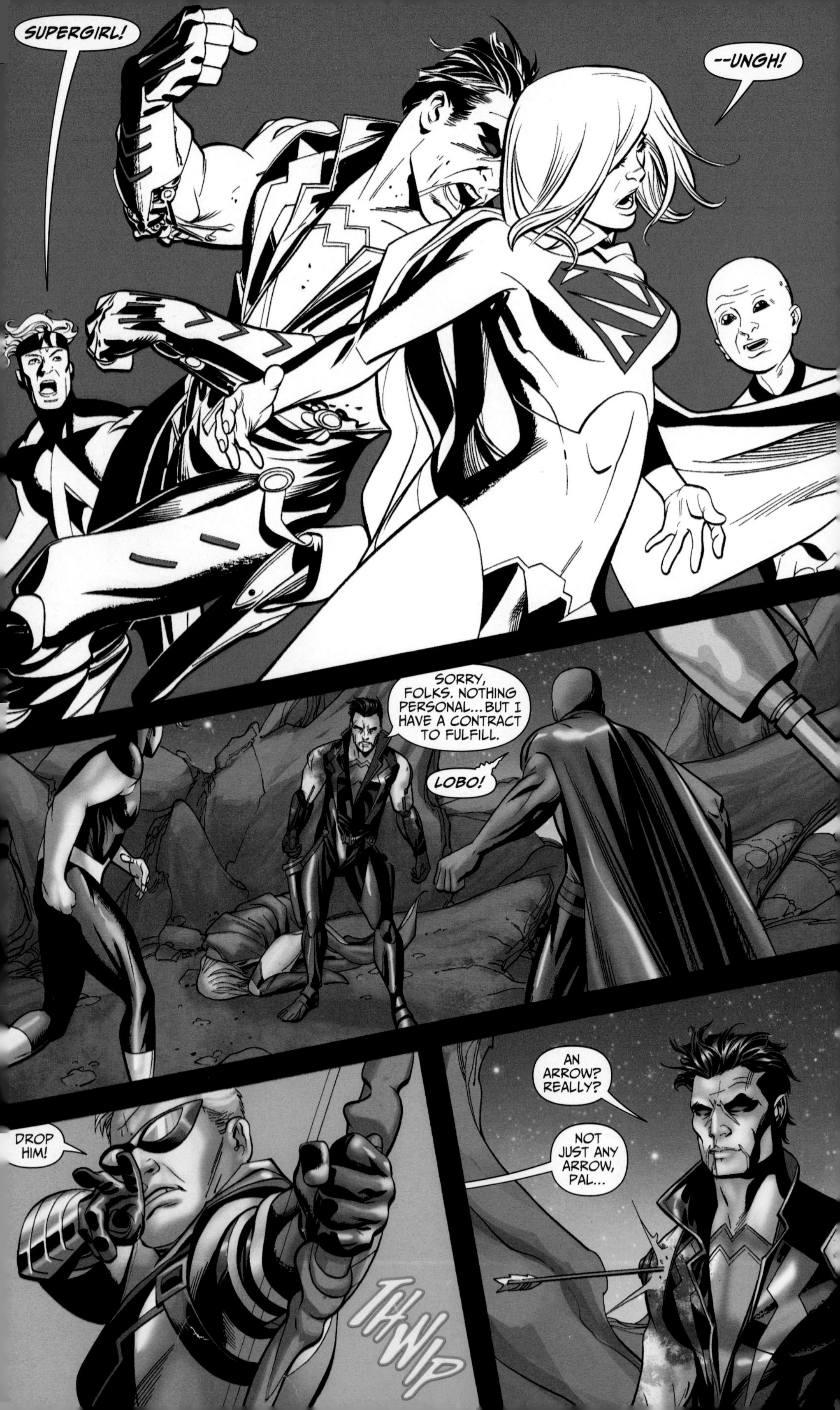
SUPERGIRL!
--UNGH!
SORRY, FOLKS. NOTHING PERSONAL...BUT I HAVE A CONTRACT TO FULFILL.
LOBO!
DROP HIM!
AN ARROW? REALLY?
NOT JUST ANY ARROW, PAL...
THWIP

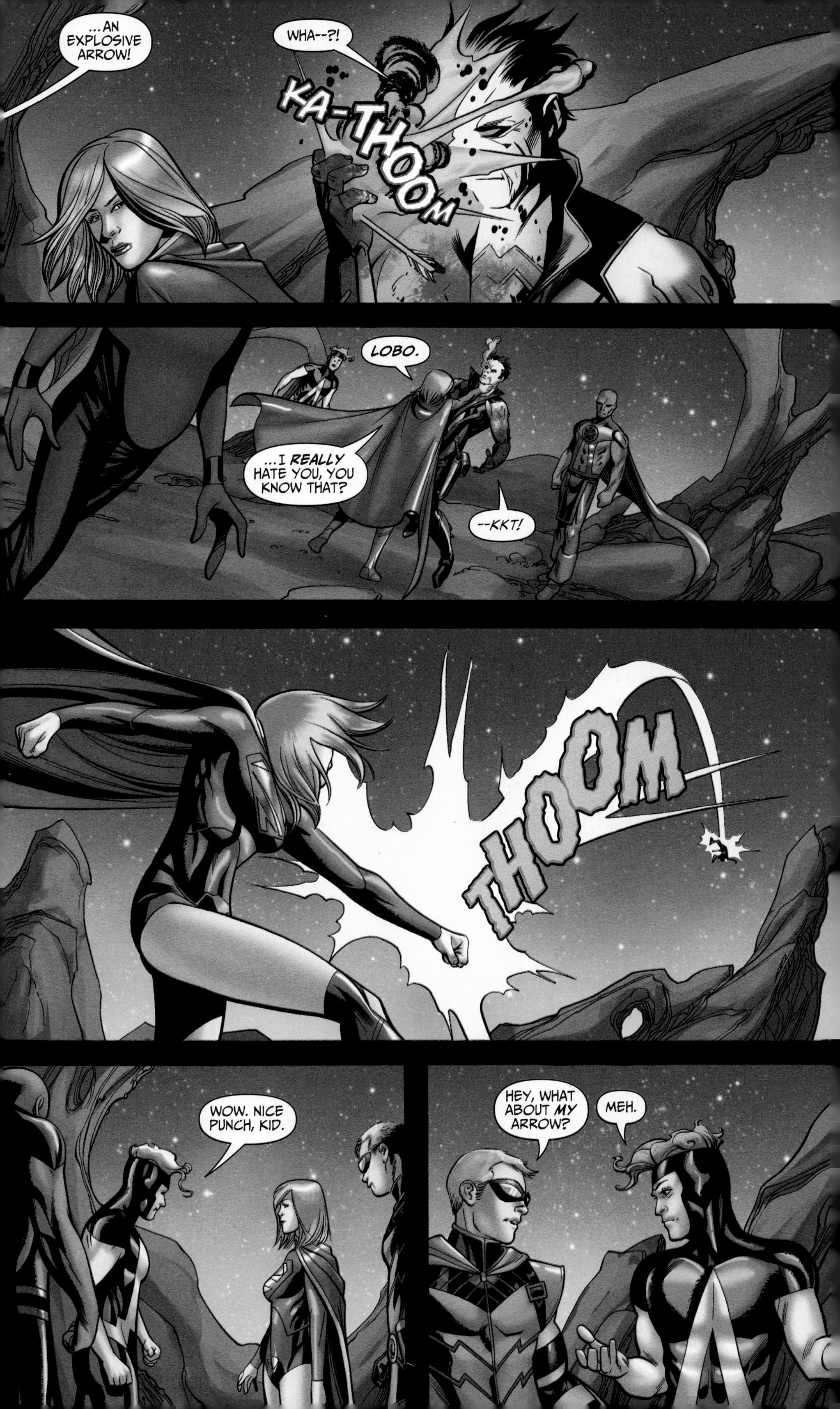
...AN EXPLOSIVE ARROW!
WHA--?!
KA-THOOM
LOBO.
...I *REALLY* HATE YOU, YOU KNOW THAT?
--KKT!
THOOM
WOW. NICE PUNCH, KID.
HEY, WHAT ABOUT *MY* ARROW?
MEH.

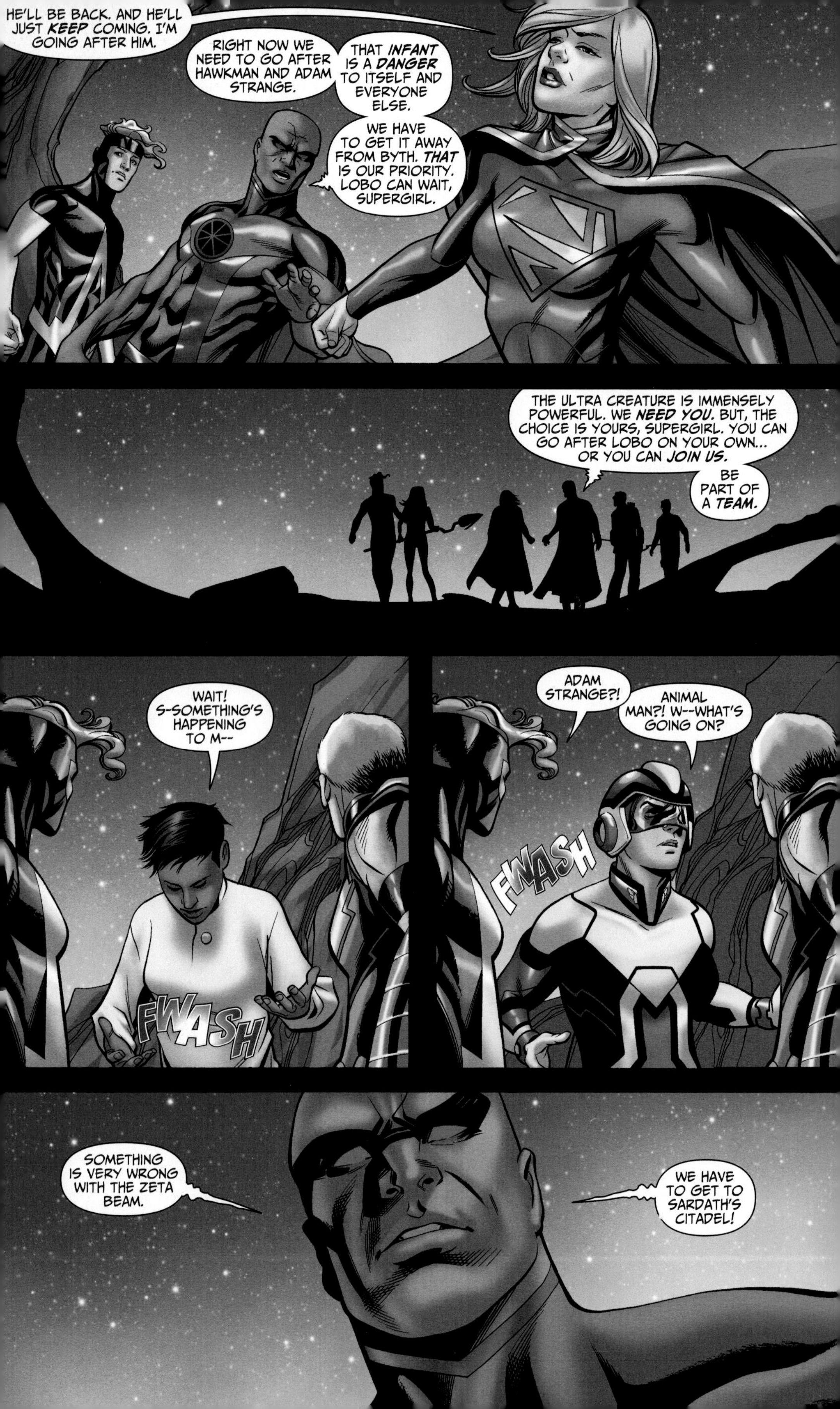
HE'LL BE BACK. AND HE'LL JUST KEEP COMING. I'M GOING AFTER HIM.
RIGHT NOW WE NEED TO GO AFTER HAWKMAN AND ADAM STRANGE.
THAT INFANT IS A DANGER TO ITSELF AND EVERYONE ELSE.
WE HAVE TO GET IT AWAY FROM BYTH. THAT IS OUR PRIORITY. LOBO CAN WAIT, SUPERGIRL.
THE ULTRA CREATURE IS IMMENSELY POWERFUL. WE NEED YOU. BUT, THE CHOICE IS YOURS, SUPERGIRL. YOU CAN GO AFTER LOBO ON YOUR OWN... OR YOU CAN JOIN US.
BE PART OF A TEAM.
WAIT! S-SOMETHING'S HAPPENING TO M--
FWASH
ADAM STRANGE?!
ANIMAL MAN?! W--WHAT'S GOING ON?
FWASH
SOMETHING IS VERY WRONG WITH THE ZETA BEAM.
WE HAVE TO GET TO SARDATH'S CITADEL!

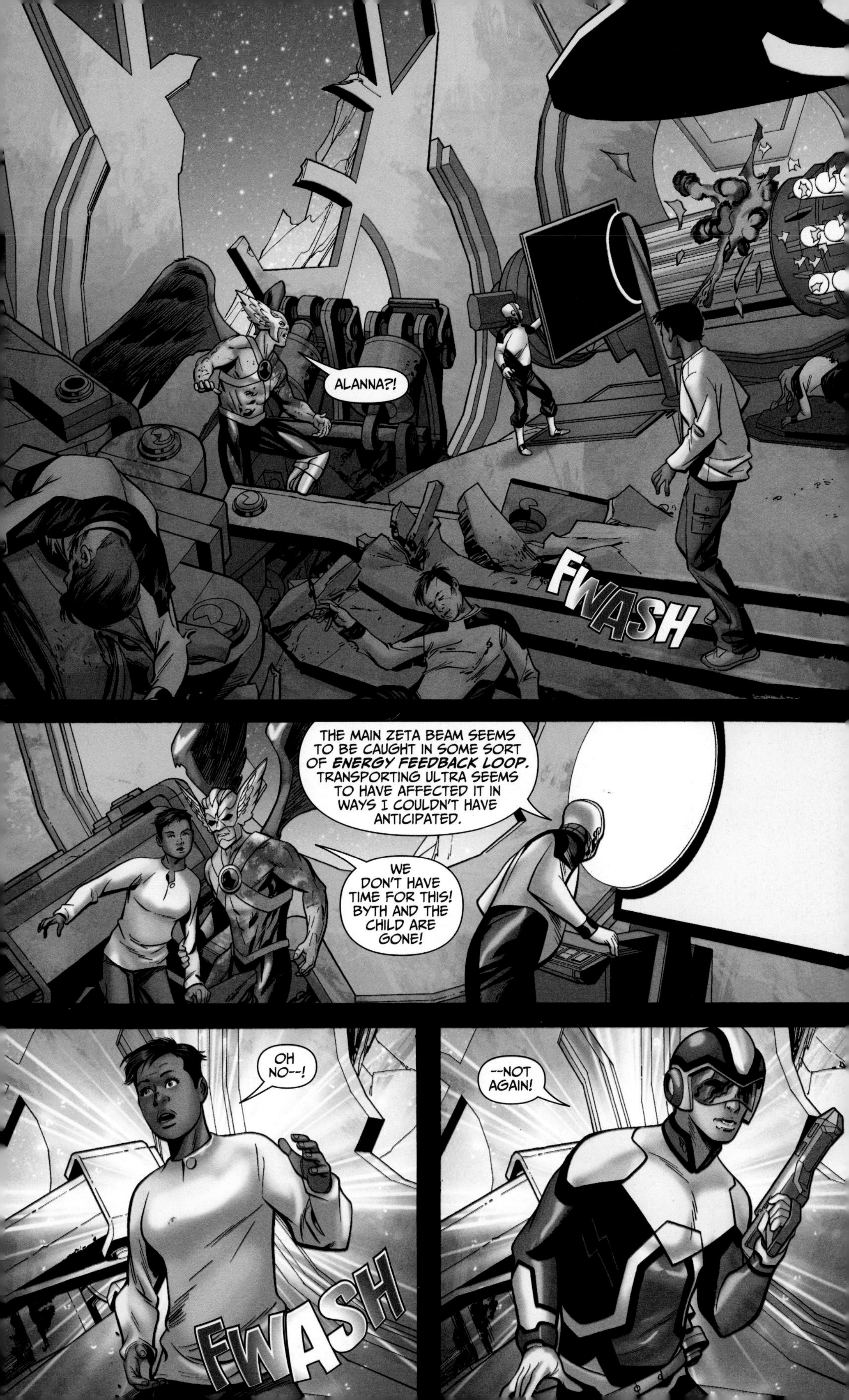
ALANNA?!
FWASH
THE MAIN ZETA BEAM SEEMS TO BE CAUGHT IN SOME SORT OF ENERGY FEEDBACK LOOP. TRANSPORTING ULTRA SEEMS TO HAVE AFFECTED IT IN WAYS I COULDN'T HAVE ANTICIPATED.
WE DON'T HAVE TIME FOR THIS! BYTH AND THE CHILD ARE GONE!
OH NO--!
FWASH
--NOT AGAIN!

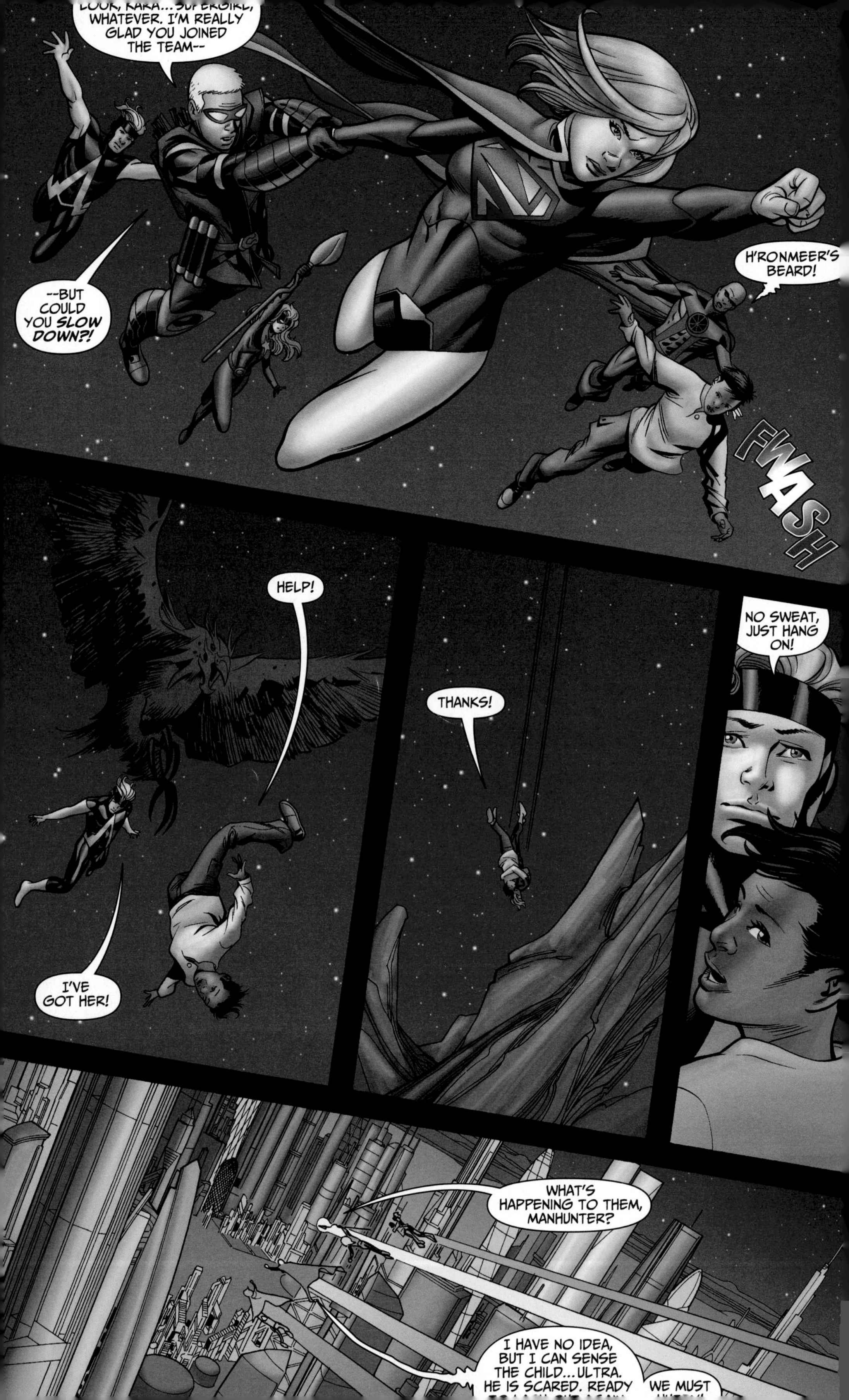
LOOK, KARA... SUPERGIRL, WHATEVER. I'M REALLY GLAD YOU JOINED THE TEAM--
--BUT COULD YOU SLOW DOWN?!
H'RONMEER'S BEARD!
FWASH
HELP!
I'VE GOT HER!
THANKS!
NO SWEAT, JUST HANG ON!
WHAT'S HAPPENING TO THEM, MANHUNTER?
I HAVE NO IDEA, BUT I CAN SENSE THE CHILD... ULTRA. HE IS SCARED. READY
WE MUST

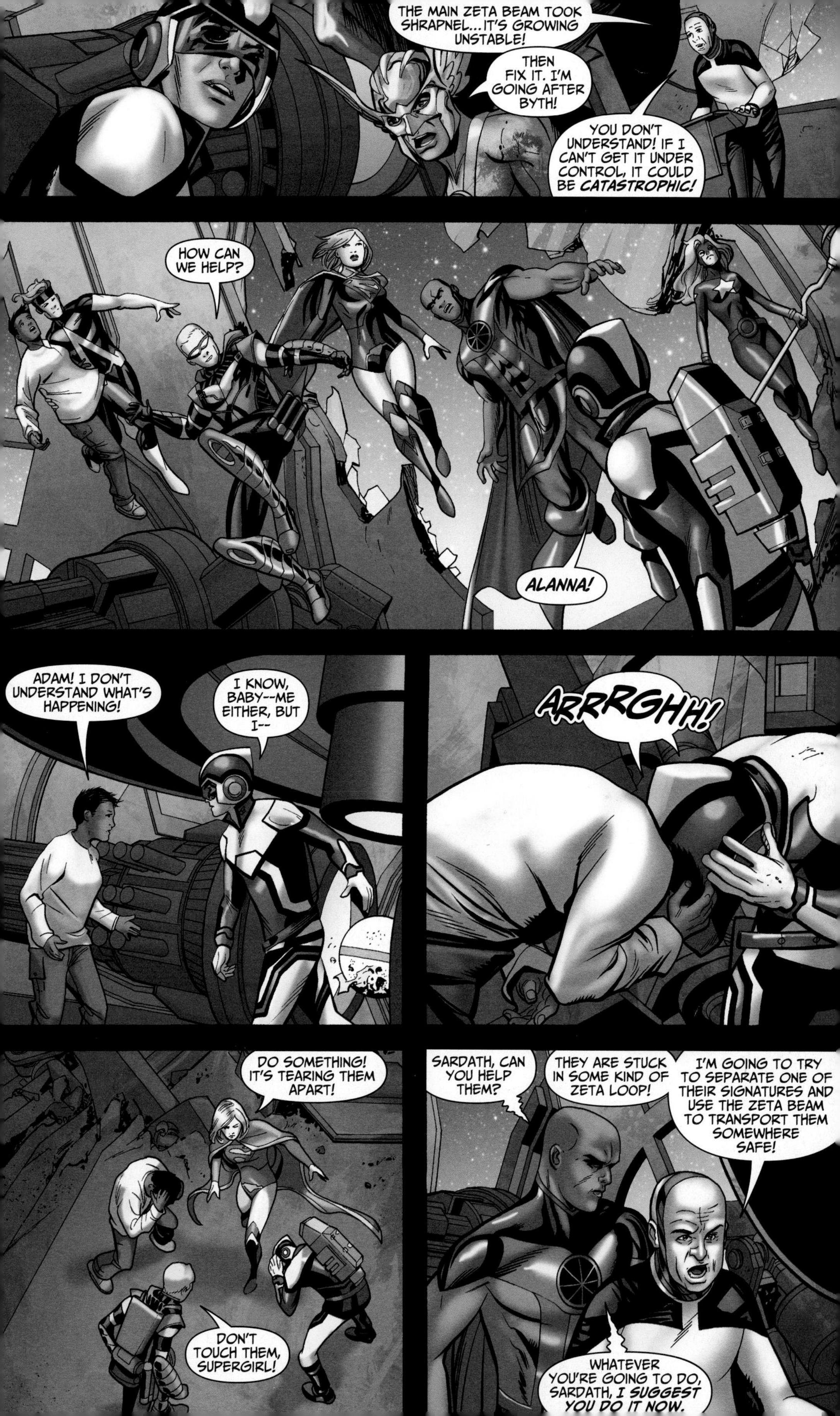
THE MAIN ZETA BEAM TOOK SHRAPNEL...IT'S GROWING UNSTABLE!
THEN FIX IT. I'M GOING AFTER BYTH!
YOU DON'T UNDERSTAND! IF I CAN'T GET IT UNDER CONTROL, IT COULD BE CATASTROPHIC!
HOW CAN WE HELP?
ALANNA!
ADAM! I DON'T UNDERSTAND WHAT'S HAPPENING!
I KNOW, BABY--ME EITHER, BUT I--
ARRRGHH!
DO SOMETHING! IT'S TEARING THEM APART!
DON'T TOUCH THEM, SUPERGIRL!
SARDATH, CAN YOU HELP THEM?
THEY ARE STUCK IN SOME KIND OF ZETA LOOP!
I'M GOING TO TRY TO SEPARATE ONE OF THEIR SIGNATURES AND USE THE ZETA BEAM TO TRANSPORT THEM SOMEWHERE SAFE!
WHATEVER YOU'RE GOING TO DO, SARDATH, I SUGGEST YOU DO IT NOW.

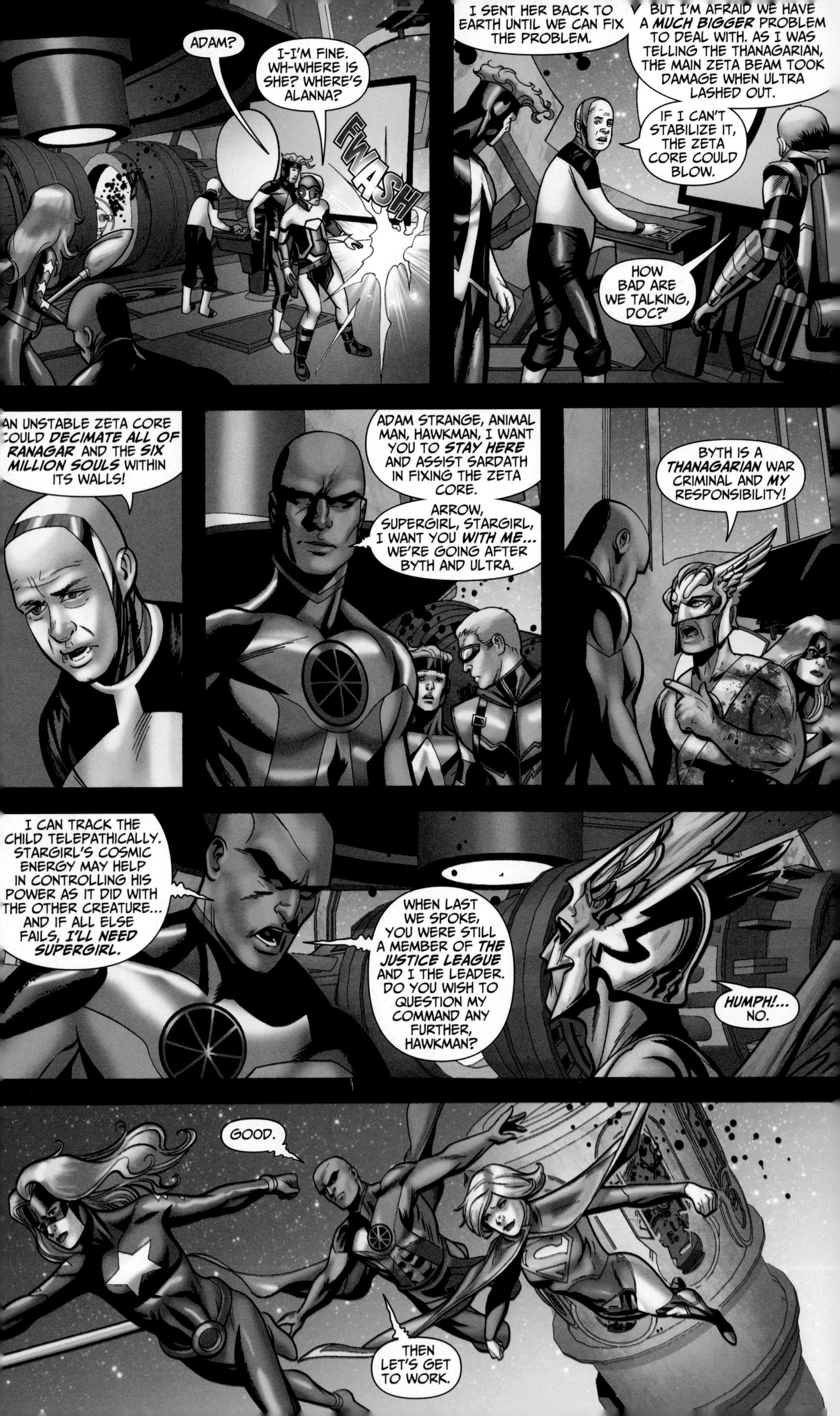
ADAM?
I-I'M FINE. WH-WHERE IS SHE? WHERE'S ALANNA?
FWASH
I SENT HER BACK TO EARTH UNTIL WE CAN FIX THE PROBLEM.
BUT I'M AFRAID WE HAVE A MUCH BIGGER PROBLEM TO DEAL WITH. AS I WAS TELLING THE THANAGARIAN, THE MAIN ZETA BEAM TOOK DAMAGE WHEN ULTRA LASHED OUT.
IF I CAN'T STABILIZE IT, THE ZETA CORE COULD BLOW.
HOW BAD ARE WE TALKING, DOC?'
AN UNSTABLE ZETA CORE COULD DECIMATE ALL OF RANAGAR AND THE SIX MILLION SOULS WITHIN ITS WALLS!
ADAM STRANGE, ANIMAL MAN, HAWKMAN, I WANT YOU TO STAY HERE AND ASSIST SARDATH IN FIXING THE ZETA CORE.
ARROW, SUPERGIRL, STARGIRL, I WANT YOU WITH ME... WE'RE GOING AFTER BYTH AND ULTRA.
BYTH IS A THANAGARIAN WAR CRIMINAL AND MY RESPONSIBILITY!
I CAN TRACK THE CHILD TELEPATHICALLY. STARGIRL'S COSMIC ENERGY MAY HELP IN CONTROLLING HIS POWER AS IT DID WITH THE OTHER CREATURE... AND IF ALL ELSE FAILS, I'LL NEED SUPERGIRL.
WHEN LAST WE SPOKE, YOU WERE STILL A MEMBER OF THE JUSTICE LEAGUE AND I THE LEADER. DO YOU WISH TO QUESTION MY COMMAND ANY FURTHER, HAWKMAN?
HUMPH!... NO.
GOOD.
THEN LET'S GET TO WORK.

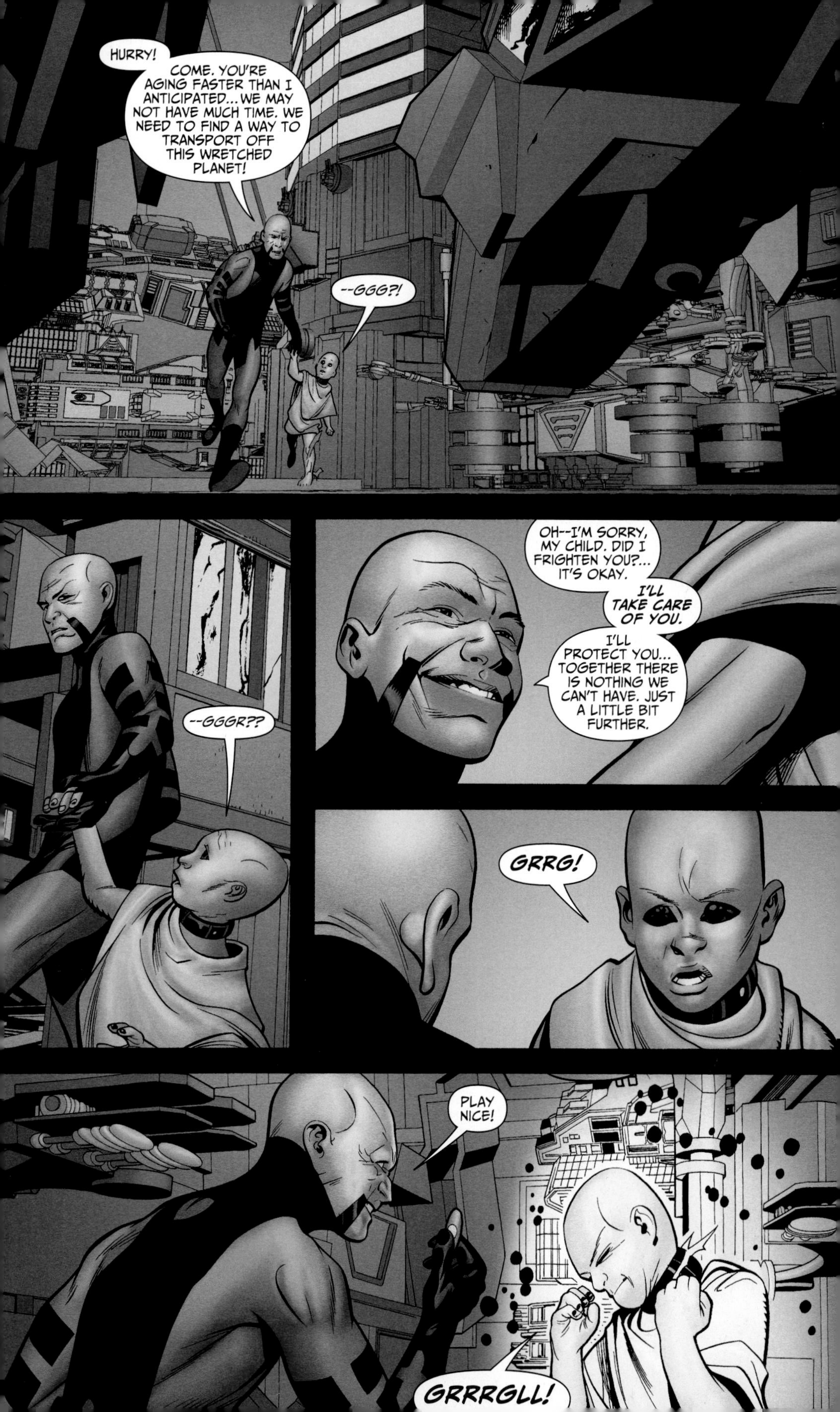
HURRY!
COME. YOU'RE AGING FASTER THAN I ANTICIPATED...WE MAY NOT HAVE MUCH TIME. WE NEED TO FIND A WAY TO TRANSPORT OFF THIS WRETCHED PLANET!
--GGG?!
--GGGR??
OH--I'M SORRY, MY CHILD. DID I FRIGHTEN YOU?... IT'S OKAY.
I'LL TAKE CARE OF YOU.
I'LL PROTECT YOU... TOGETHER THERE IS NOTHING WE CAN'T HAVE. JUST A LITTLE BIT FURTHER.
GRRG!
PLAY NICE!
GRRRGLL!

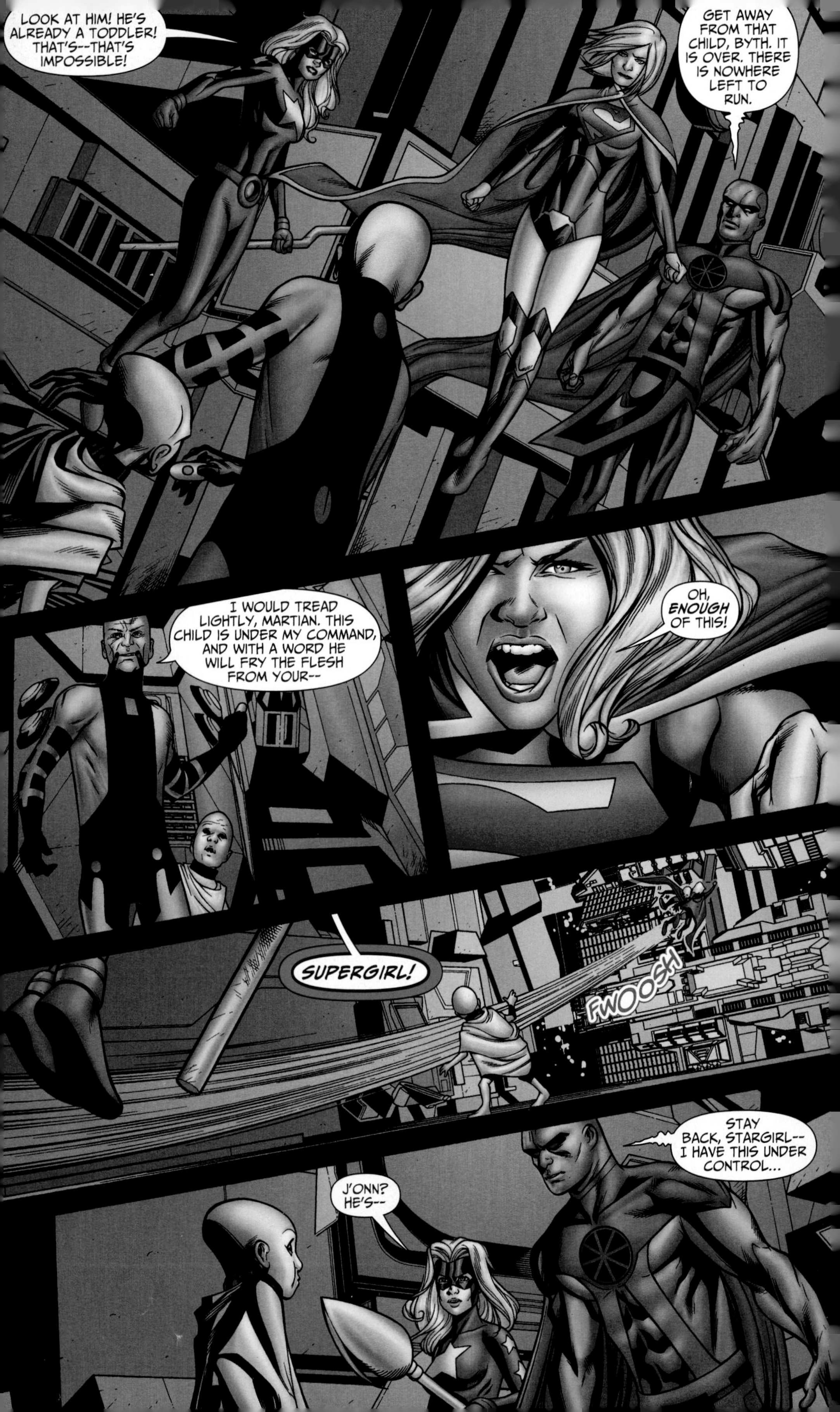
LOOK AT HIM! HE'S ALREADY A TODDLER! THAT'S--THAT'S IMPOSSIBLE!
GET AWAY FROM THAT CHILD, BYTH. IT IS OVER. THERE IS NOWHERE LEFT TO RUN.
I WOULD TREAD LIGHTLY, MARTIAN. THIS CHILD IS UNDER MY COMMAND, AND WITH A WORD HE WILL FRY THE FLESH FROM YOUR--
OH, ENOUGH OF THIS!
SUPERGIRL!
FWOOSH
STAY BACK, STARGIRL-- I HAVE THIS UNDER CONTROL...
J'ONN? HE'S--

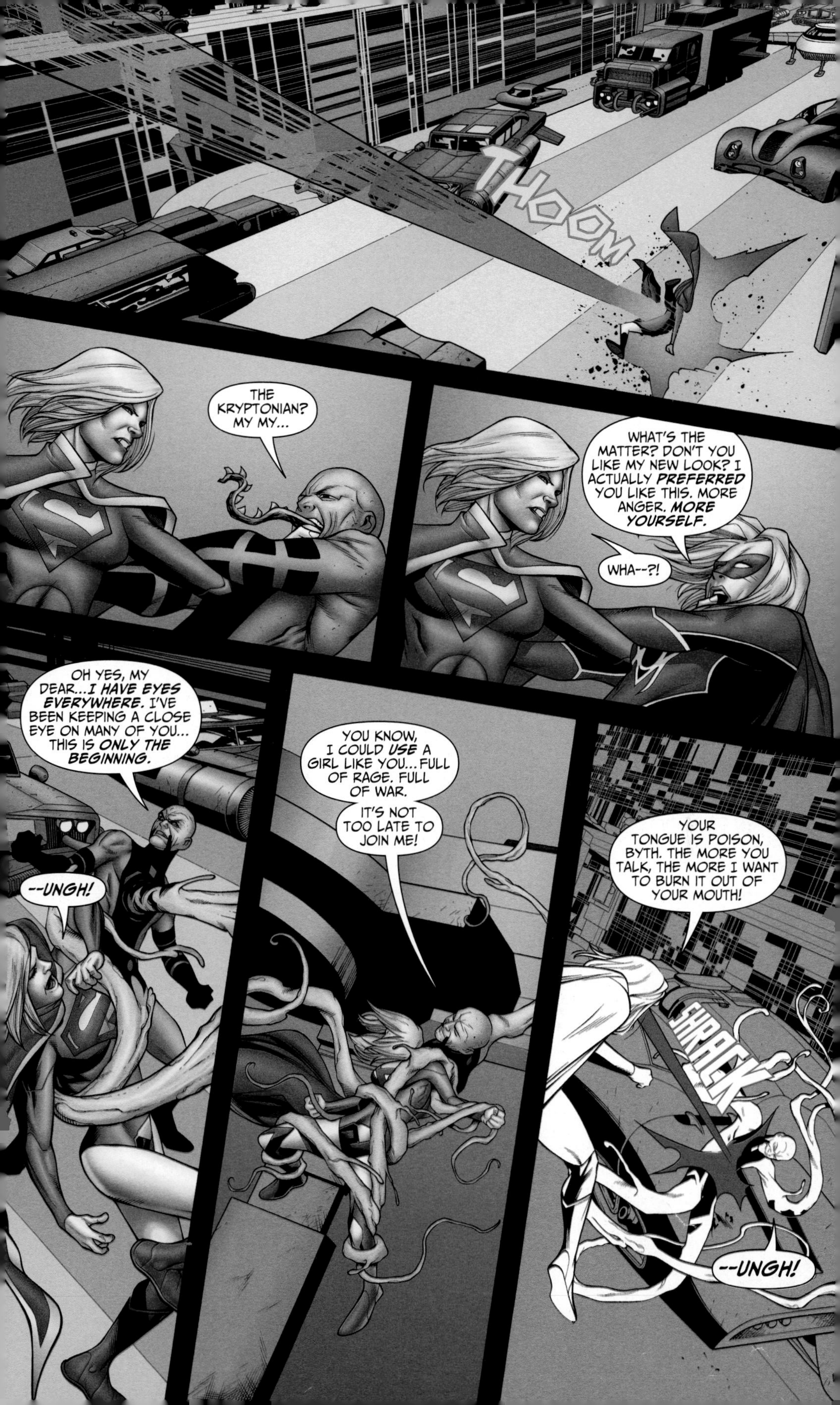
THOOM
THE KRYPTONIAN? MY MY...
WHAT'S THE MATTER? DON'T YOU LIKE MY NEW LOOK? I ACTUALLY PREFERRED YOU LIKE THIS. MORE ANGER. MORE YOURSELF.
WHA--?!
OH YES, MY DEAR...I HAVE EYES EVERYWHERE. I'VE BEEN KEEPING A CLOSE EYE ON MANY OF YOU... THIS IS ONLY THE BEGINNING.
--UNGH!
YOU KNOW, I COULD USE A GIRL LIKE YOU...FULL OF RAGE. FULL OF WAR.
IT'S NOT TOO LATE TO JOIN ME!
YOUR TONGUE IS POISON, BYTH. THE MORE YOU TALK, THE MORE I WANT TO BURN IT OUT OF YOUR MOUTH!
SHRACK
--UNGH!

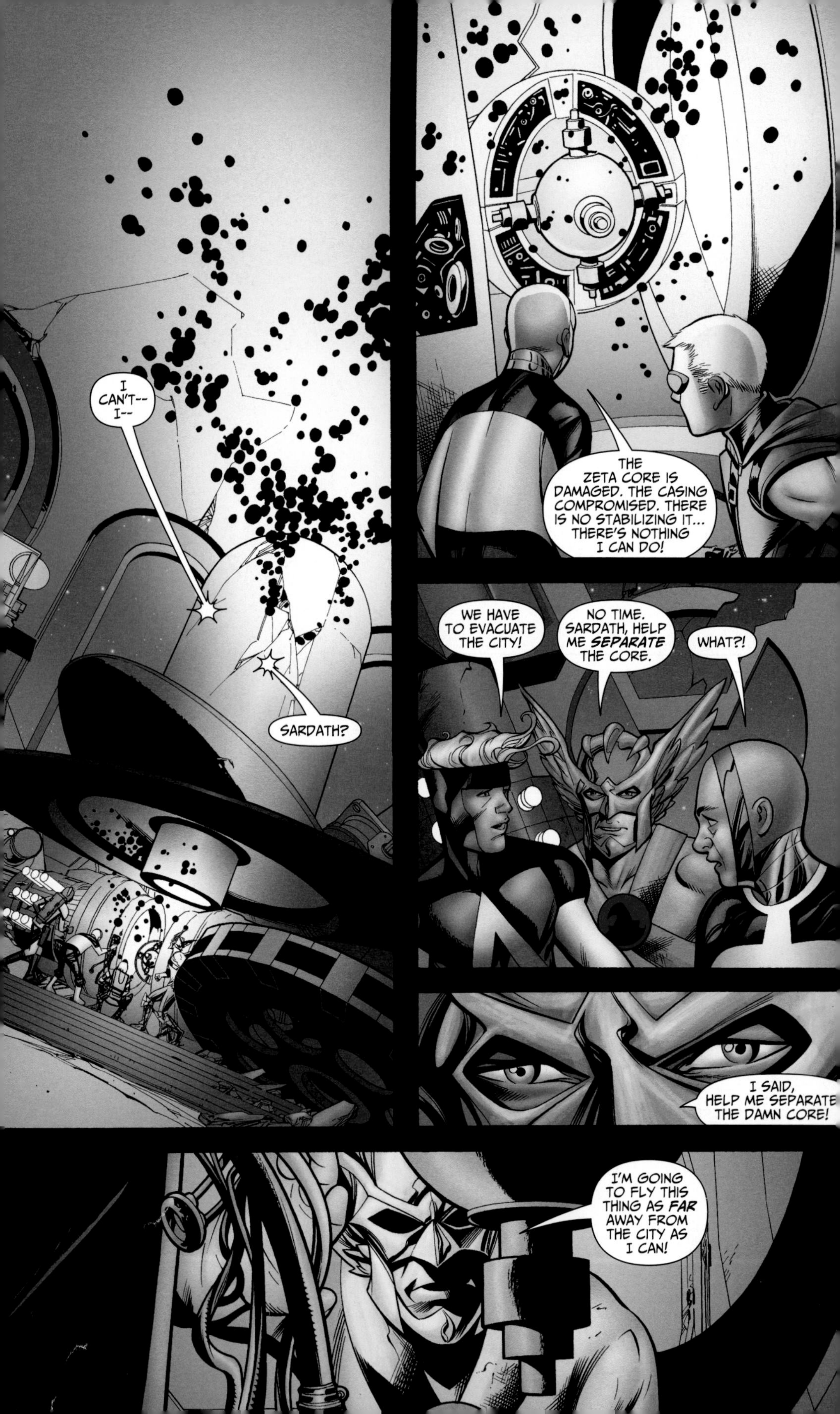
THE ZETA CORE IS DAMAGED. THE CASING COMPROMISED. THERE IS NO STABILIZING IT... THERE'S NOTHING I CAN DO!
I CAN'T-- I--
SARDATH?
WE HAVE TO EVACUATE THE CITY!
NO TIME. SARDATH, HELP ME SEPARATE THE CORE.
WHAT?!
I SAID, HELP ME SEPARATE THE DAMN CORE!
I'M GOING TO FLY THIS THING AS FAR AWAY FROM THE CITY AS I CAN!

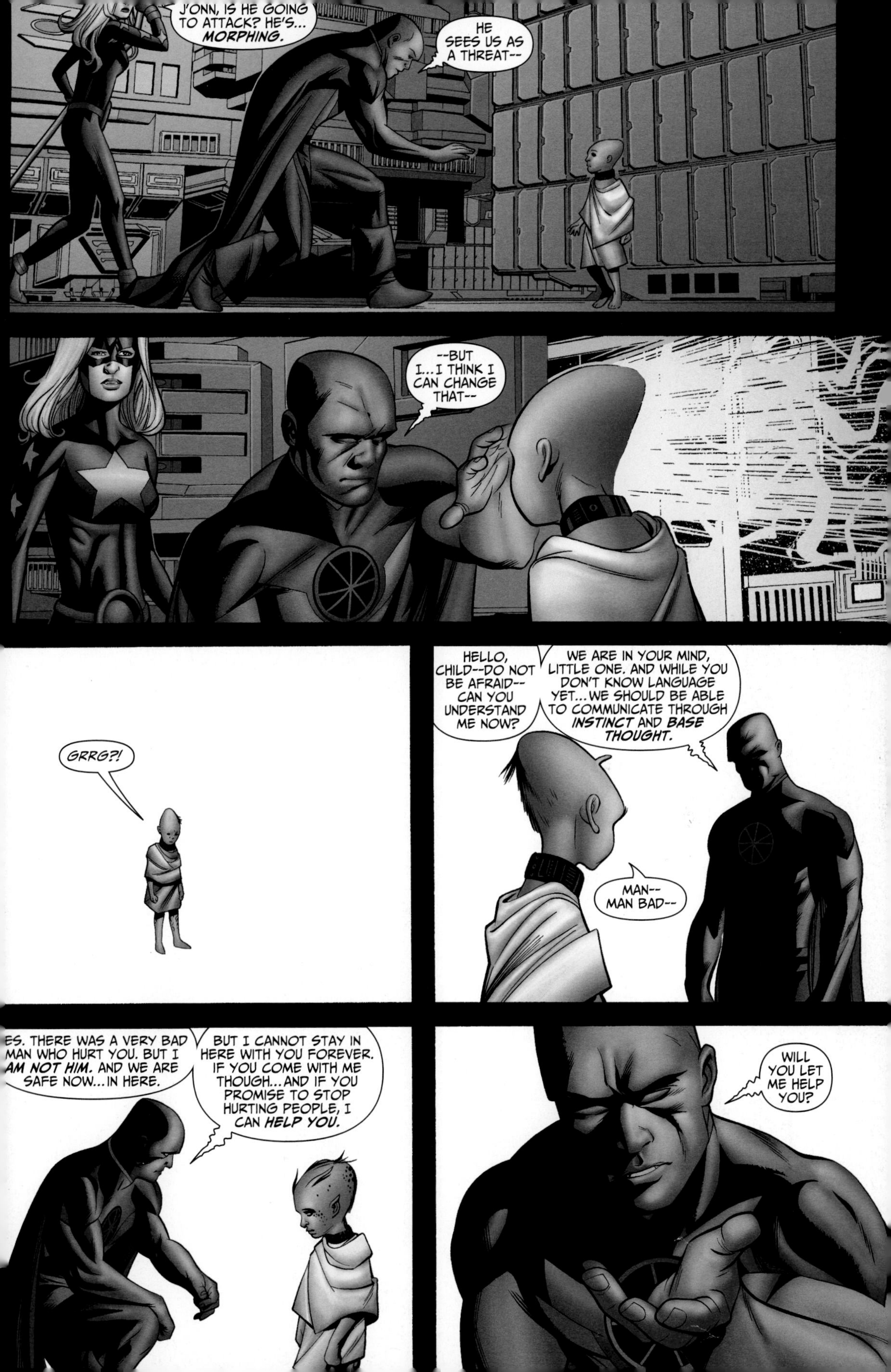

J'ONN, IS HE GOING TO ATTACK? HE'S... MORPHING.
HE SEES US AS A THREAT--
--BUT I...I THINK I CAN CHANGE THAT--
GRRG?!
HELLO, CHILD--DO NOT BE AFRAID--CAN YOU UNDERSTAND ME NOW?
WE ARE IN YOUR MIND, LITTLE ONE. AND WHILE YOU DON'T KNOW LANGUAGE YET...WE SHOULD BE ABLE TO COMMUNICATE THROUGH INSTINCT AND BASE THOUGHT.
MAN-- MAN BAD--
ES. THERE WAS A VERY BAD MAN WHO HURT YOU. BUT I AM NOT HIM. AND WE ARE SAFE NOW...IN HERE.
BUT I CANNOT STAY IN HERE WITH YOU FOREVER. IF YOU COME WITH ME THOUGH...AND IF YOU PROMISE TO STOP HURTING PEOPLE, I CAN HELP YOU.
WILL YOU LET ME HELP YOU?

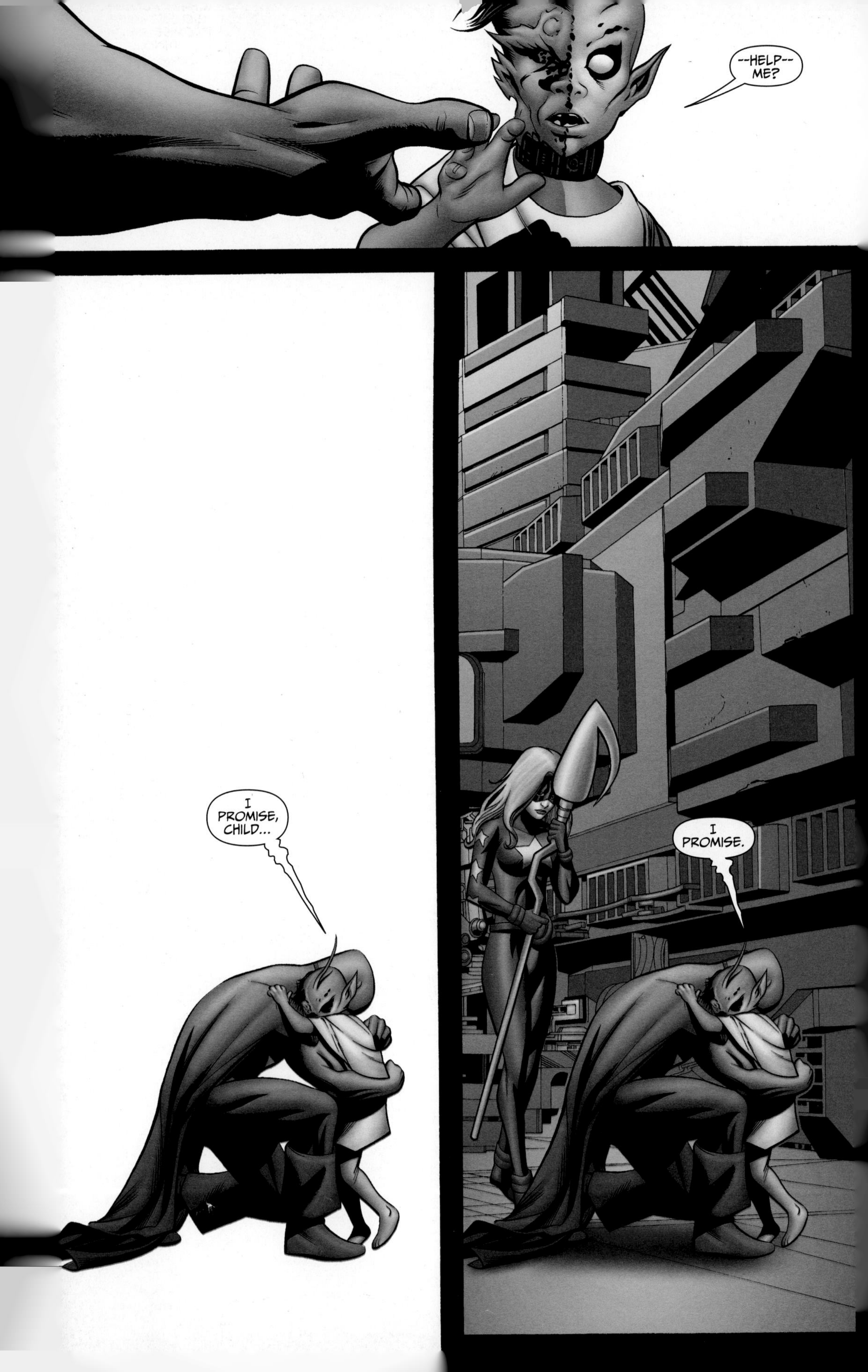
--HELP-- ME?
I PROMISE, CHILD...
I PROMISE.

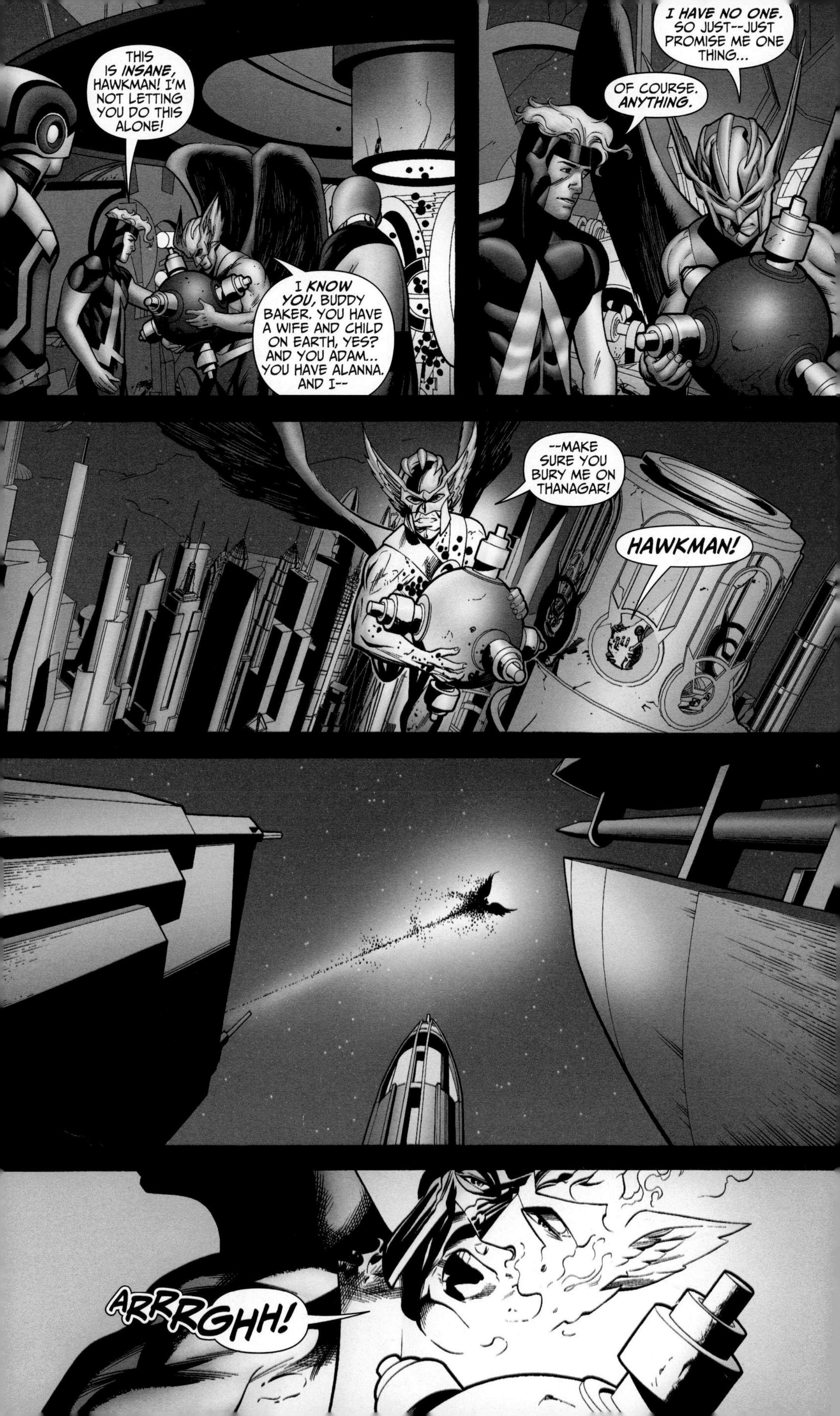
THIS IS INSANE, HAWKMAN! I'M NOT LETTING YOU DO THIS ALONE!
I KNOW YOU, BUDDY BAKER. YOU HAVE A WIFE AND CHILD ON EARTH, YES? AND YOU ADAM... YOU HAVE ALANNA. AND I--
I HAVE NO ONE. SO JUST--JUST PROMISE ME ONE THING...
OF COURSE. ANYTHING.
--MAKE SURE YOU BURY ME ON THANAGAR!
HAWKMAN!
ARRRGHH!

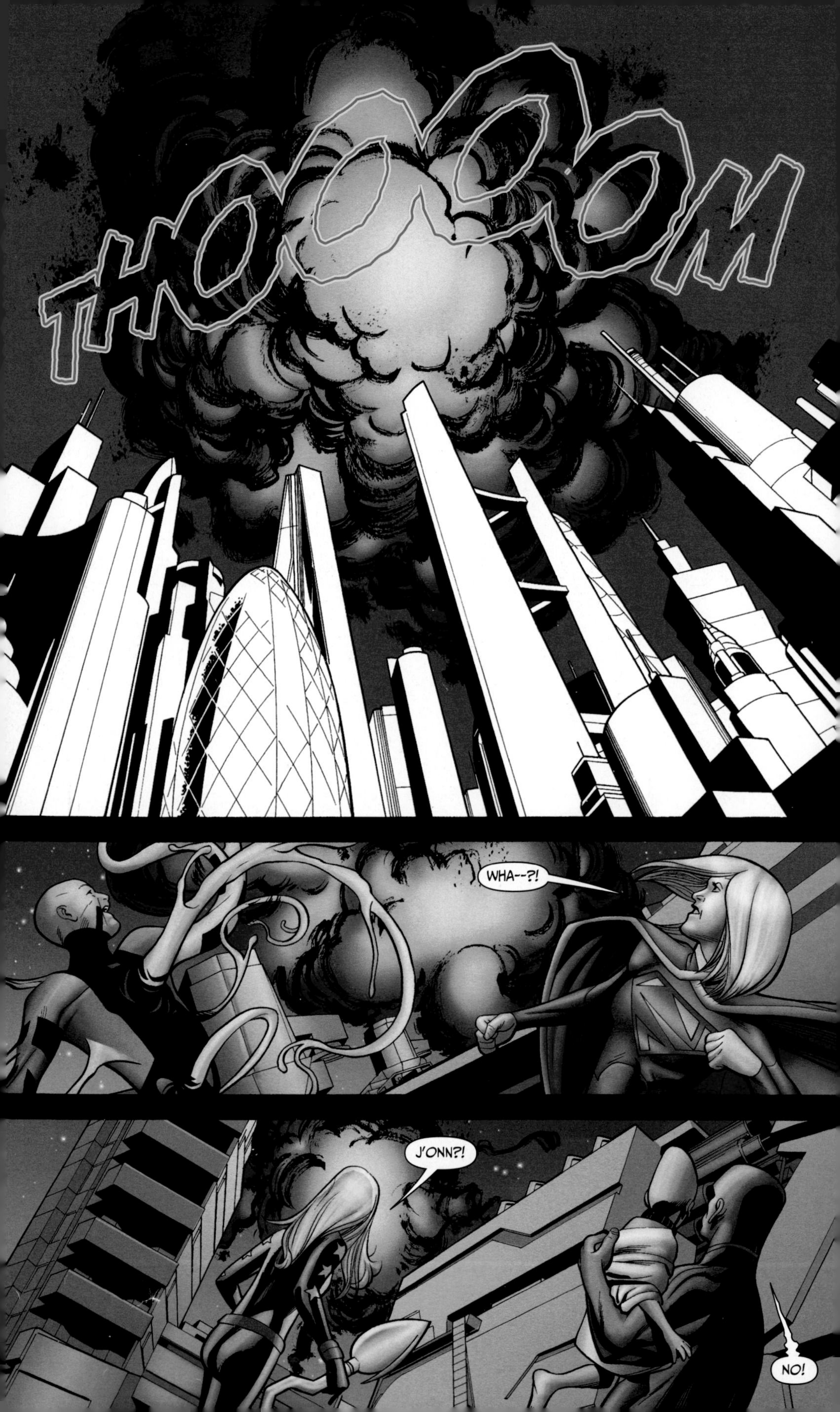
THOOOOOM
WHA--?!
J'ONN?!
NO!

--UNGGH!!

TOOK ME FOREVER TO FIND YOU, BYTH. I DON'T KNOW WHAT'S GOING DOWN HERE, BUT I THINK WE NEED TO MAKE OUR EXIT. *NOW.*

GO!

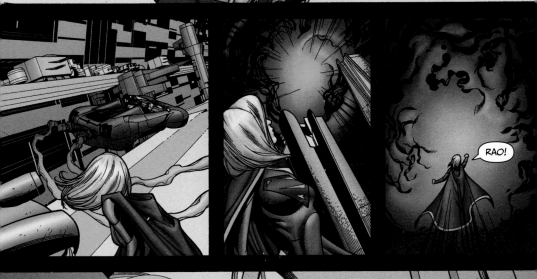

RAO!

ANIMAL MAN?!

MANHUNTER-- IT'S HAWKMAN! HE--

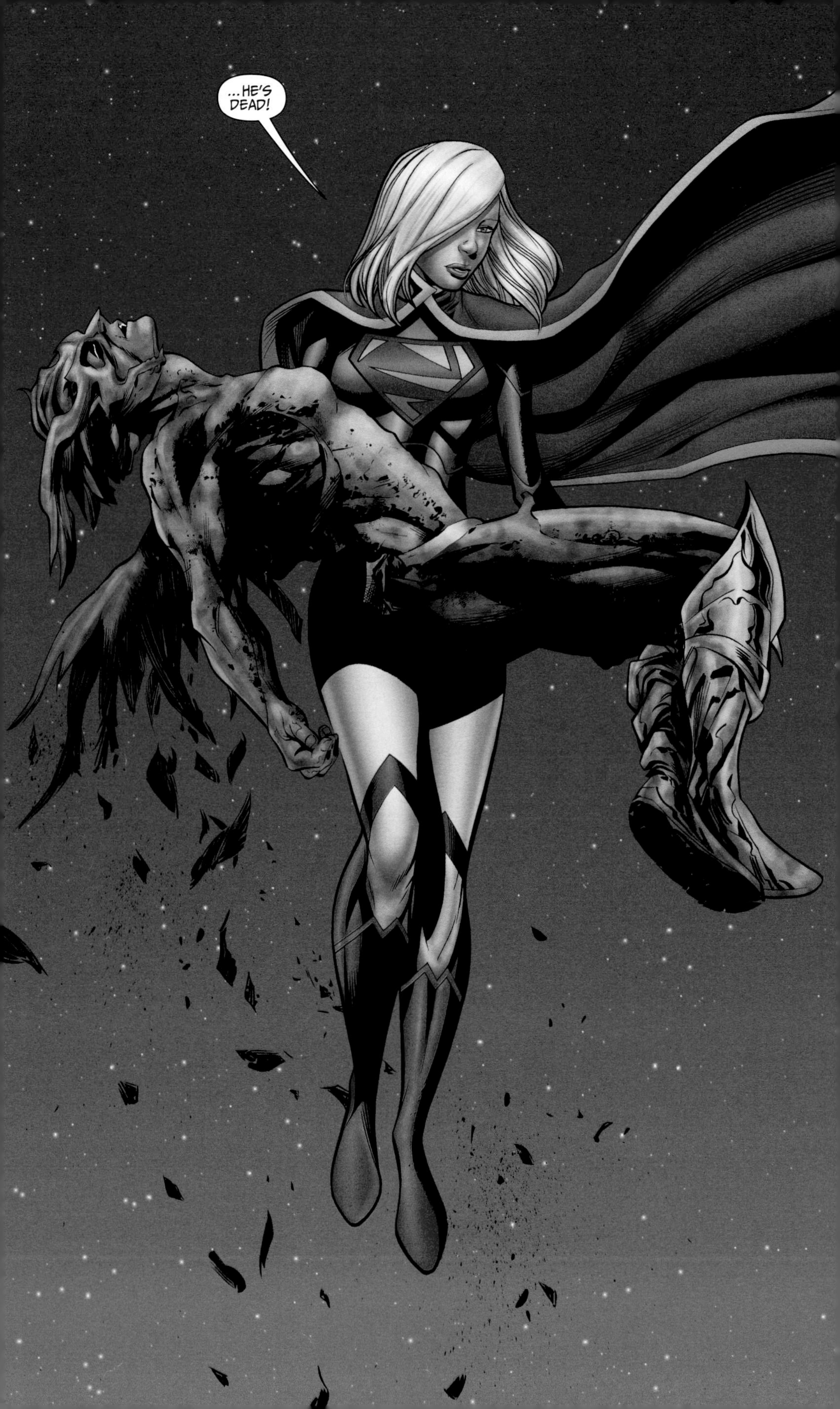
...HE'S DEAD!

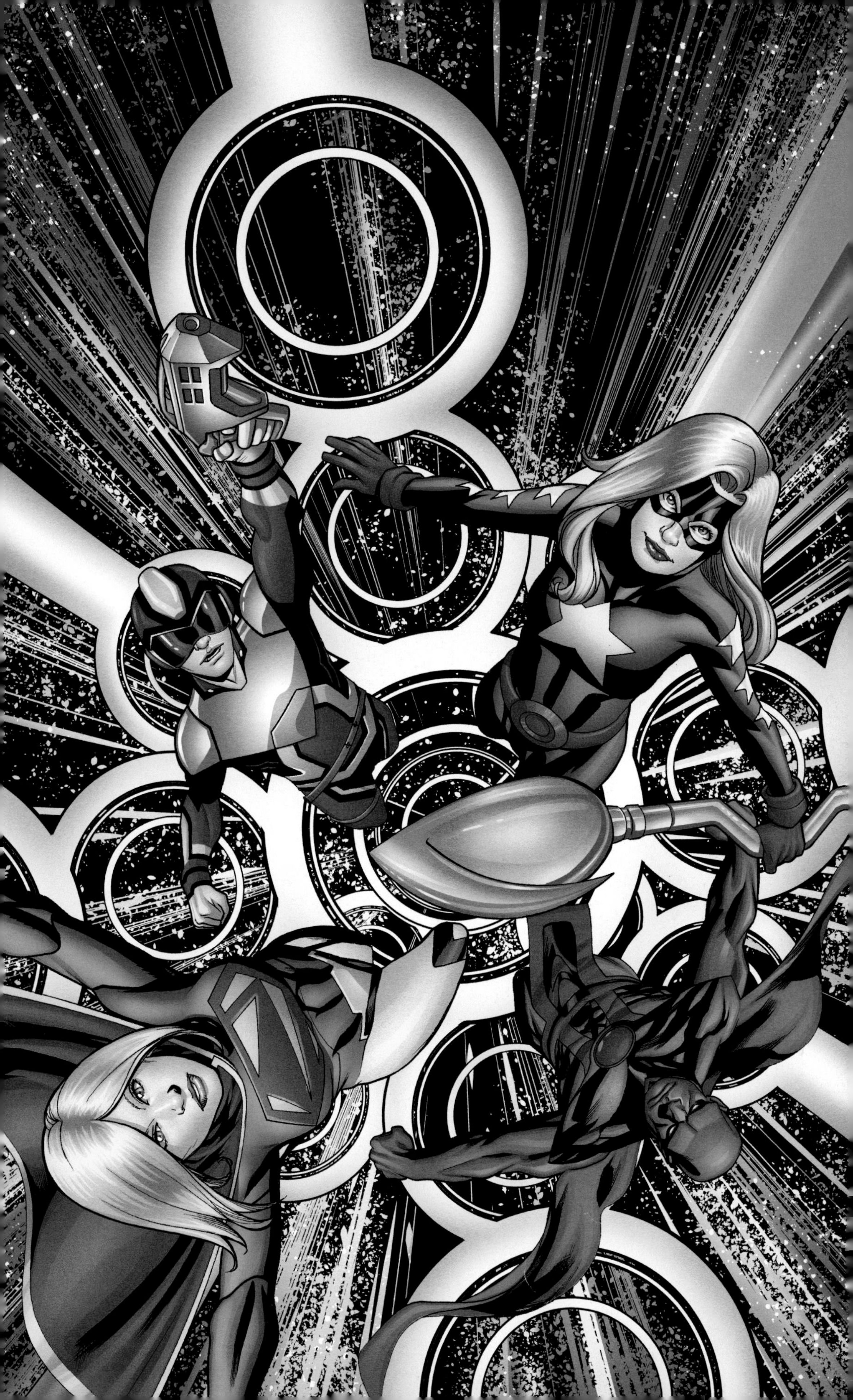

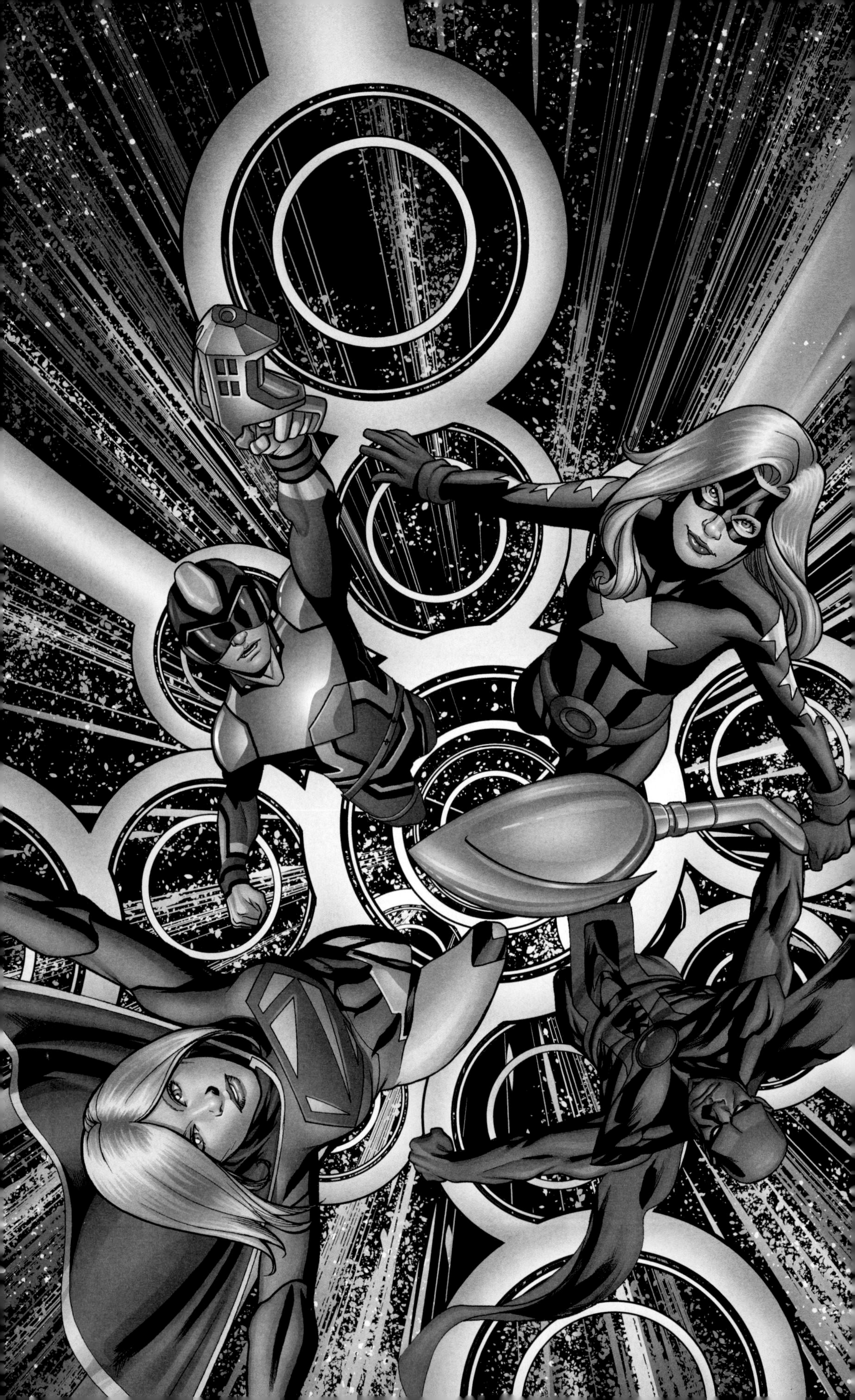

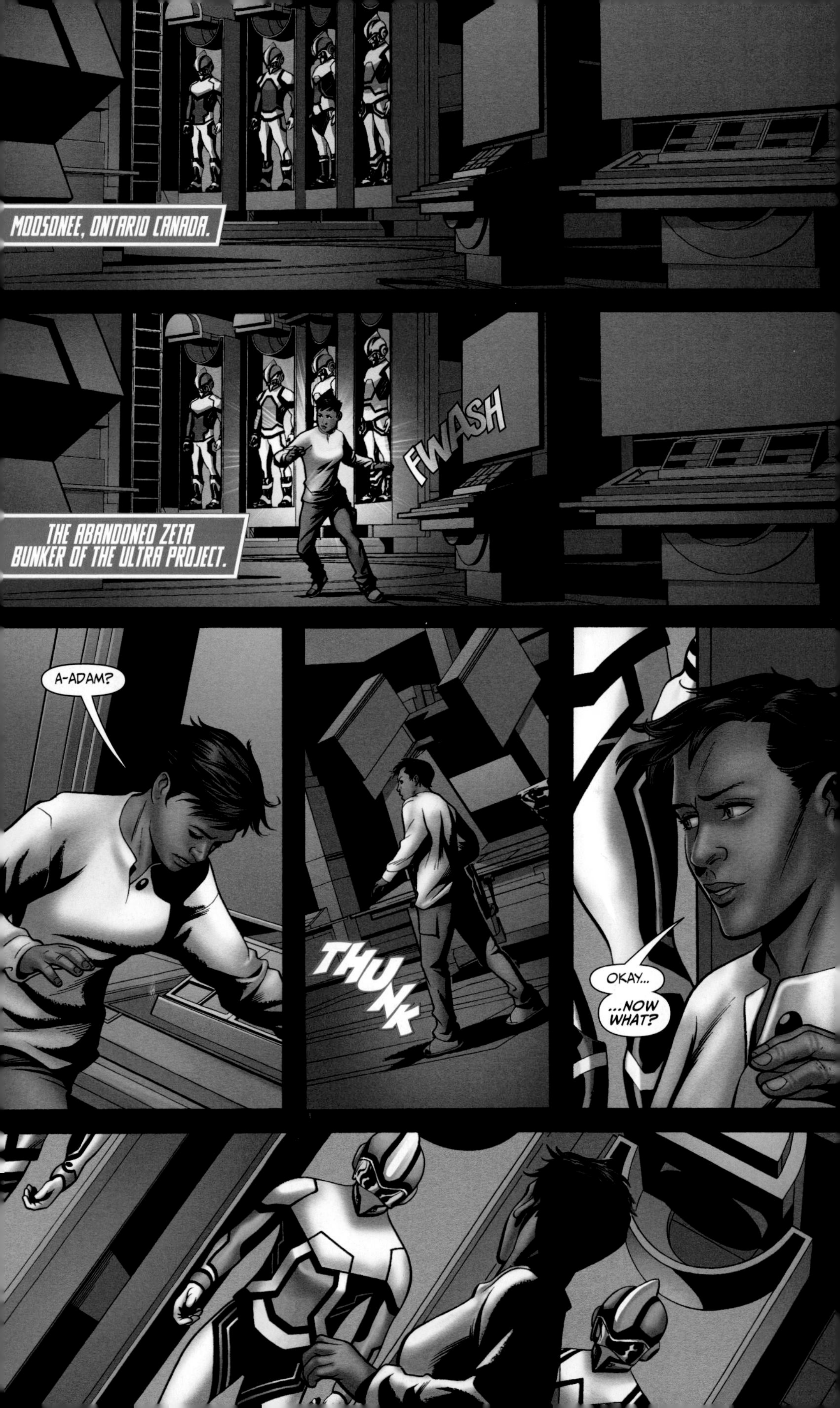

MOOSONEE, ONTARIO CANADA.
THE ABANDONED ZETA BUNKER OF THE ULTRA PROJECT.
FWASH
A-ADAM?
THUNK
OKAY...
...NOW WHAT?

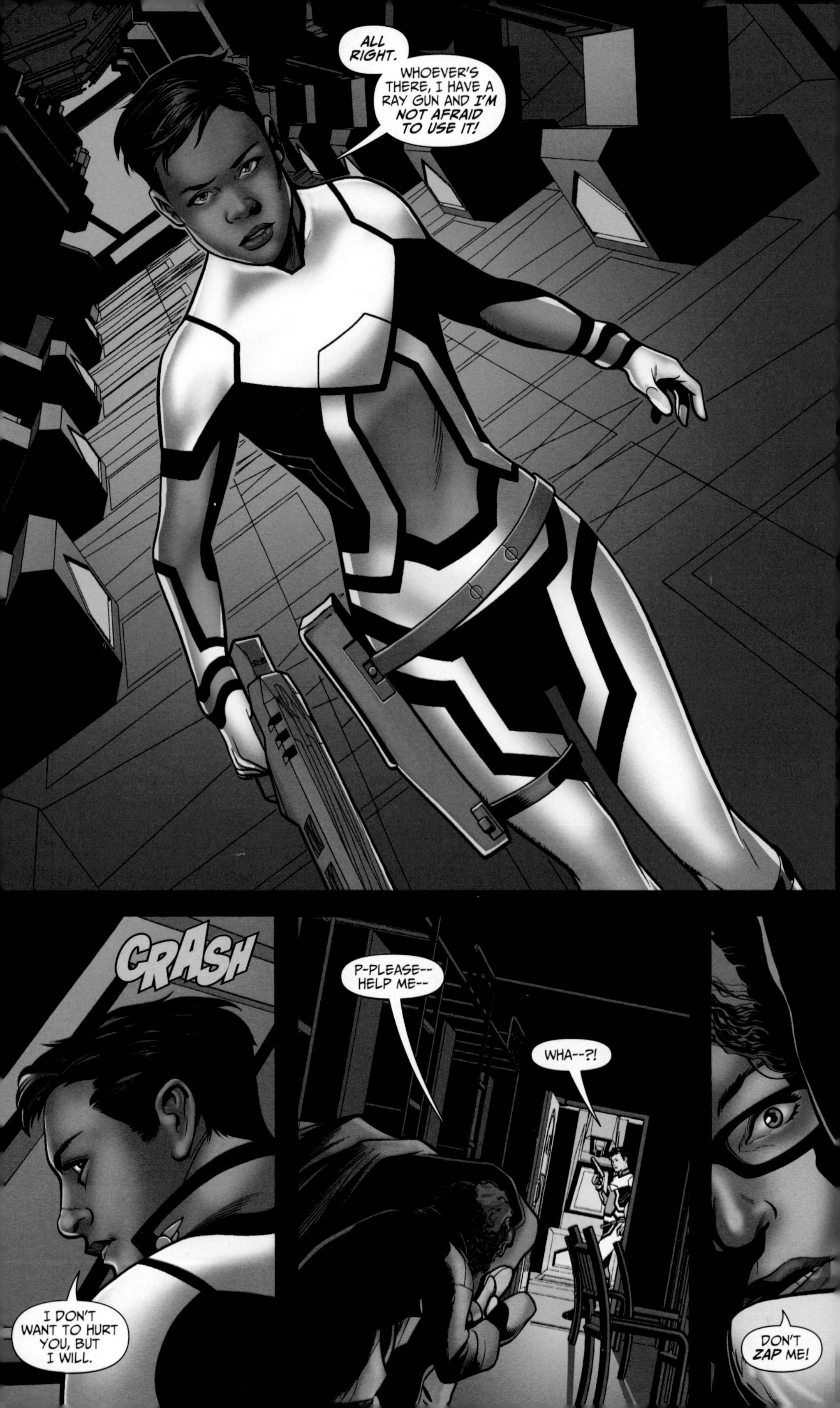
ALL RIGHT.
WHOEVER'S THERE, I HAVE A RAY GUN AND I'M NOT AFRAID TO USE IT!
CRASH
I DON'T WANT TO HURT YOU, BUT I WILL.
P-PLEASE-- HELP ME--
WHA--?!
DON'T ZAP ME!

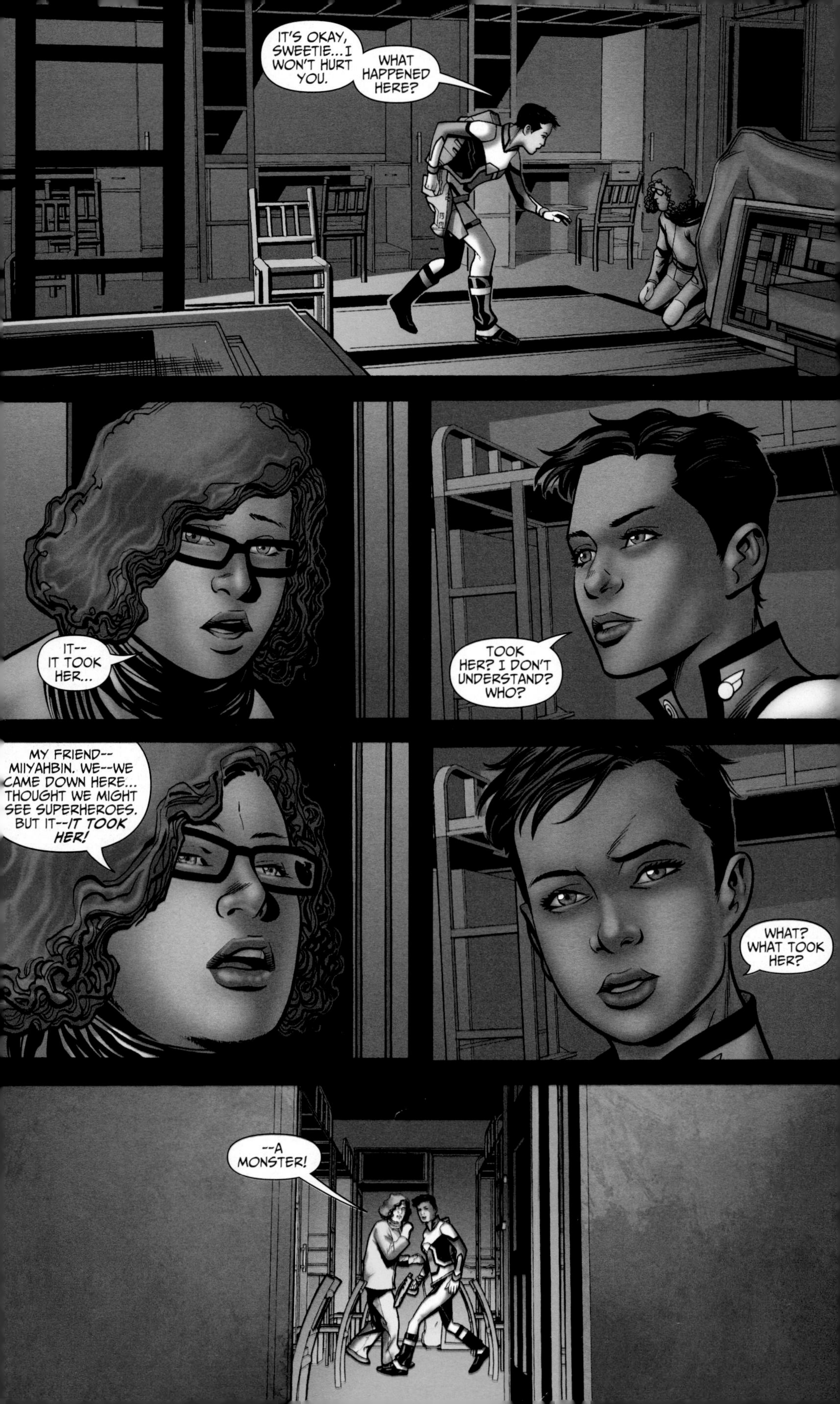
IT'S OKAY, SWEETIE...I WON'T HURT YOU.
WHAT HAPPENED HERE?
IT-- IT TOOK HER...
TOOK HER? I DON'T UNDERSTAND? WHO?
MY FRIEND-- MIIYAHBIN. WE--WE CAME DOWN HERE... THOUGHT WE MIGHT SEE SUPERHEROES. BUT IT--*IT TOOK HER!*
WHAT? WHAT TOOK HER?
--A MONSTER!

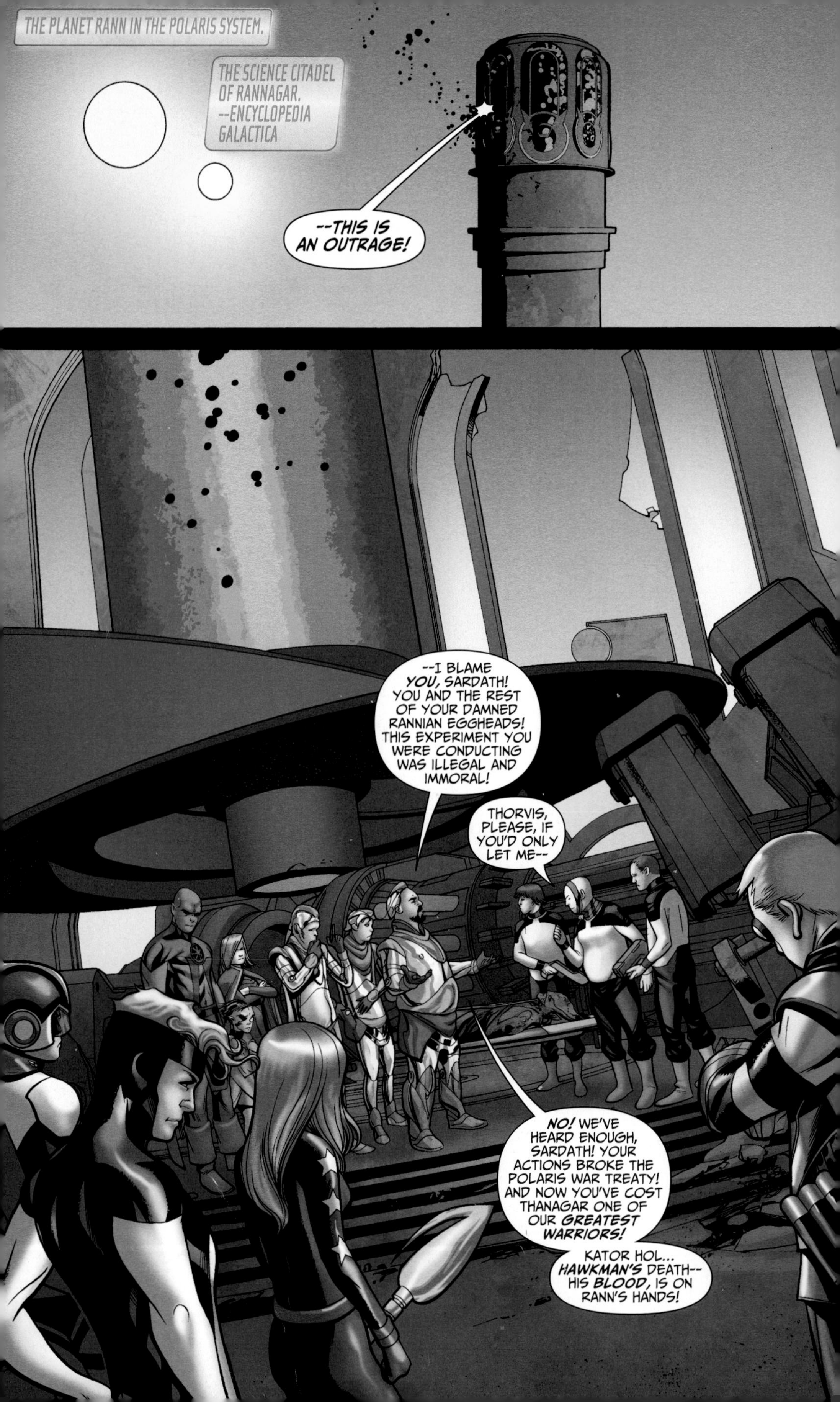
THE PLANET RANN IN THE POLARIS SYSTEM.
THE SCIENCE CITADEL OF RANNAGAR. --ENCYCLOPEDIA GALACTICA
--THIS IS AN OUTRAGE!
--I BLAME YOU, SARDATH! YOU AND THE REST OF YOUR DAMNED RANNIAN EGGHEADS! THIS EXPERIMENT YOU WERE CONDUCTING WAS ILLEGAL AND IMMORAL!
THORVIS, PLEASE, IF YOU'D ONLY LET ME--
NO! WE'VE HEARD ENOUGH, SARDATH! YOUR ACTIONS BROKE THE POLARIS WAR TREATY! AND NOW YOU'VE COST THANAGAR ONE OF OUR GREATEST WARRIORS!
KATOR HOL... HAWKMAN'S DEATH-- HIS BLOOD, IS ON RANN'S HANDS!

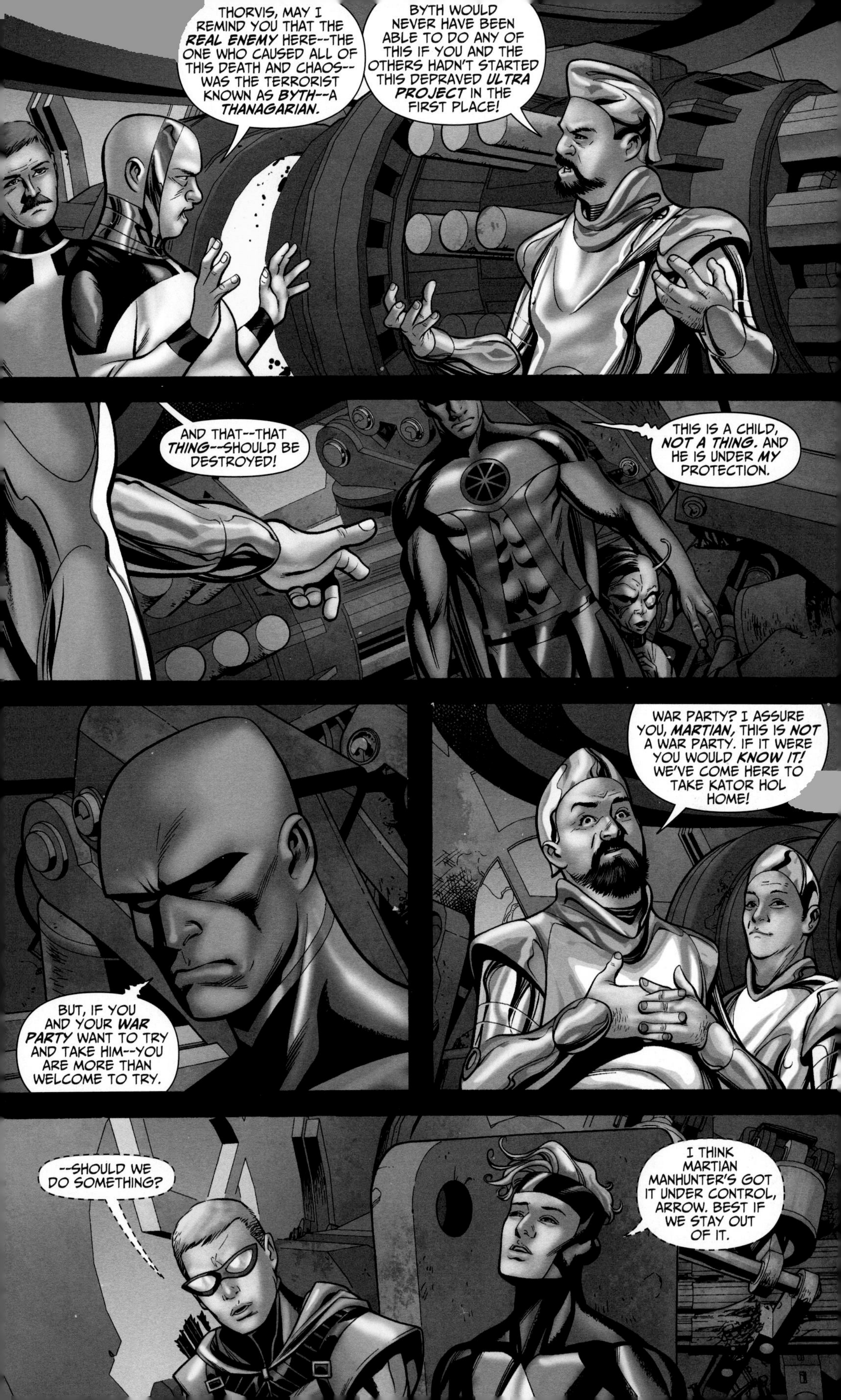

THORVIS, MAY I REMIND YOU THAT THE REAL ENEMY HERE--THE ONE WHO CAUSED ALL OF THIS DEATH AND CHAOS--WAS THE TERRORIST KNOWN AS BYTH--A THANAGARIAN.
BYTH WOULD NEVER HAVE BEEN ABLE TO DO ANY OF THIS IF YOU AND THE OTHERS HADN'T STARTED THIS DEPRAVED ULTRA PROJECT IN THE FIRST PLACE!
AND THAT--THAT THING--SHOULD BE DESTROYED!
THIS IS A CHILD, NOT A THING. AND HE IS UNDER MY PROTECTION.
BUT, IF YOU AND YOUR WAR PARTY WANT TO TRY AND TAKE HIM--YOU ARE MORE THAN WELCOME TO TRY.
WAR PARTY? I ASSURE YOU, MARTIAN, THIS IS NOT A WAR PARTY. IF IT WERE YOU WOULD KNOW IT! WE'VE COME HERE TO TAKE KATOR HOL HOME!
--SHOULD WE DO SOMETHING?
I THINK MARTIAN MANHUNTER'S GOT IT UNDER CONTROL, ARROW. BEST IF WE STAY OUT OF IT.

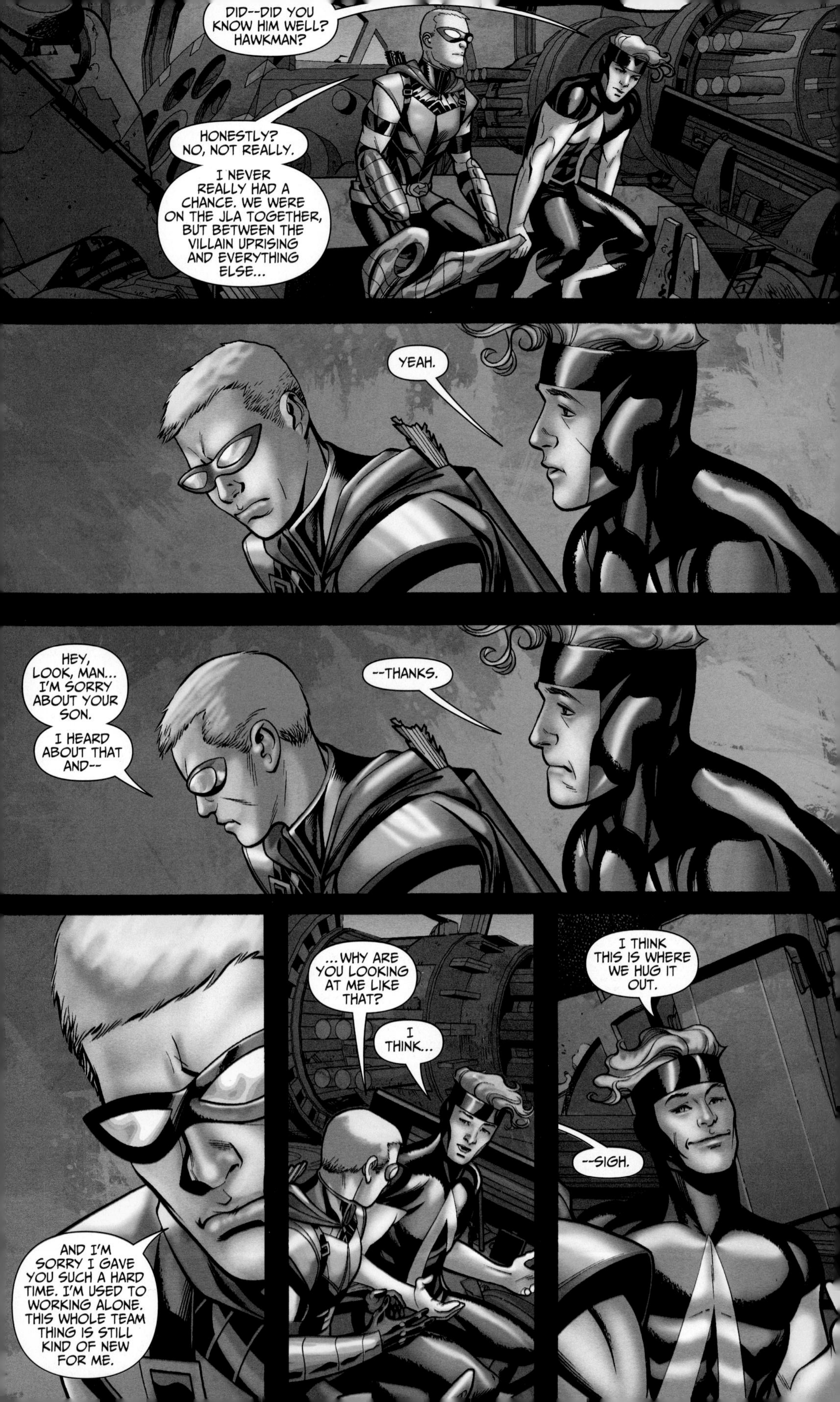
DID--DID YOU KNOW HIM WELL? HAWKMAN?
HONESTLY? NO, NOT REALLY.
I NEVER REALLY HAD A CHANCE. WE WERE ON THE JLA TOGETHER, BUT BETWEEN THE VILLAIN UPRISING AND EVERYTHING ELSE...
YEAH.
HEY, LOOK, MAN... I'M SORRY ABOUT YOUR SON.
I HEARD ABOUT THAT AND--
--THANKS.
AND I'M SORRY I GAVE YOU SUCH A HARD TIME. I'M USED TO WORKING ALONE. THIS WHOLE TEAM THING IS STILL KIND OF NEW FOR ME.
...WHY ARE YOU LOOKING AT ME LIKE THAT?
I THINK...
I THINK THIS IS WHERE WE HUG IT OUT.
--SIGH.

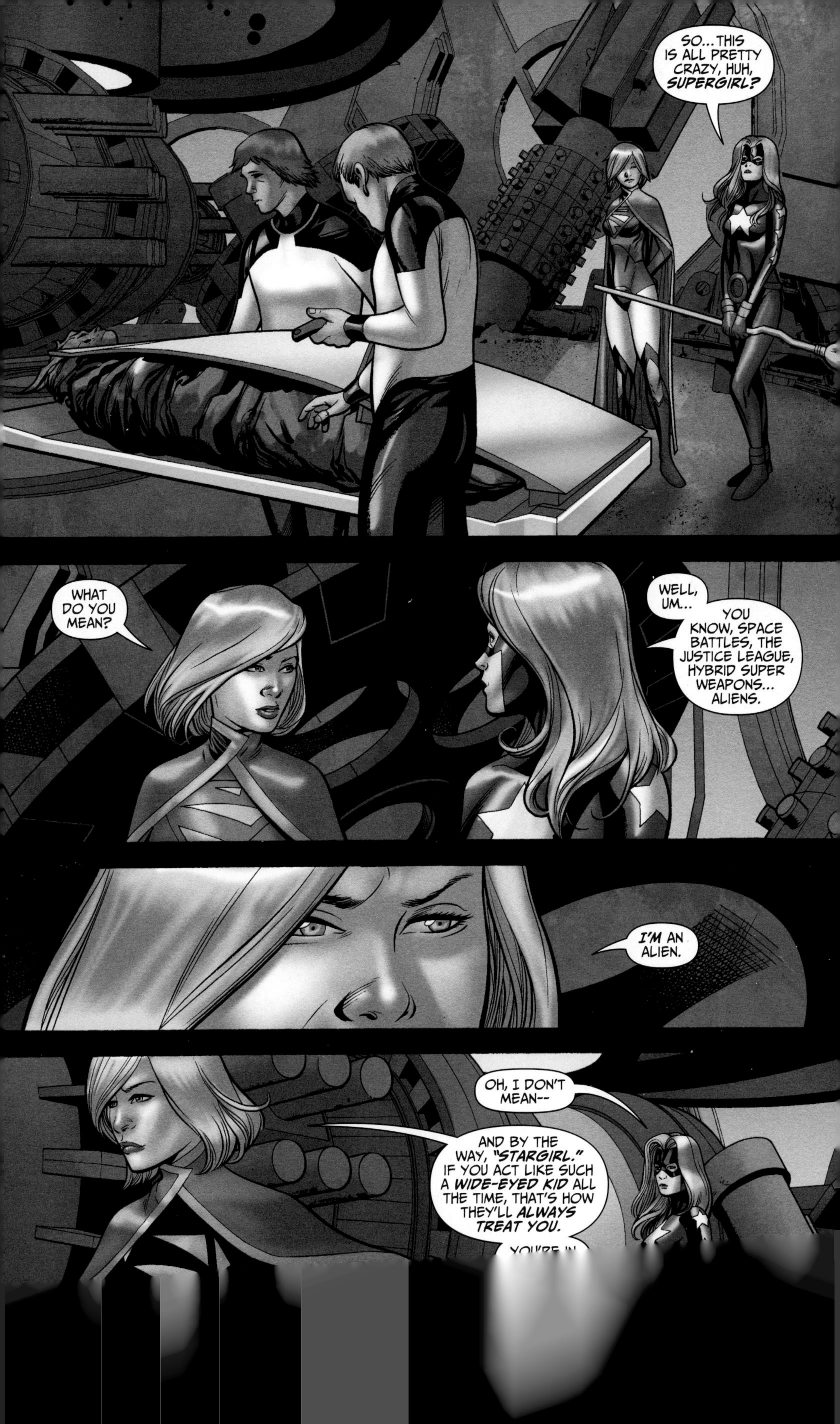
SO... THIS IS ALL PRETTY CRAZY, HUH, *SUPERGIRL?*
WHAT DO YOU MEAN?
WELL, UM...
YOU KNOW, SPACE BATTLES, THE JUSTICE LEAGUE, HYBRID SUPER WEAPONS... ALIENS.
I'M AN ALIEN.
OH, I DON'T MEAN--
AND BY THE WAY, *"STARGIRL."* IF YOU ACT LIKE SUCH A *WIDE-EYED KID* ALL THE TIME, THAT'S HOW THEY'LL *ALWAYS TREAT YOU.*

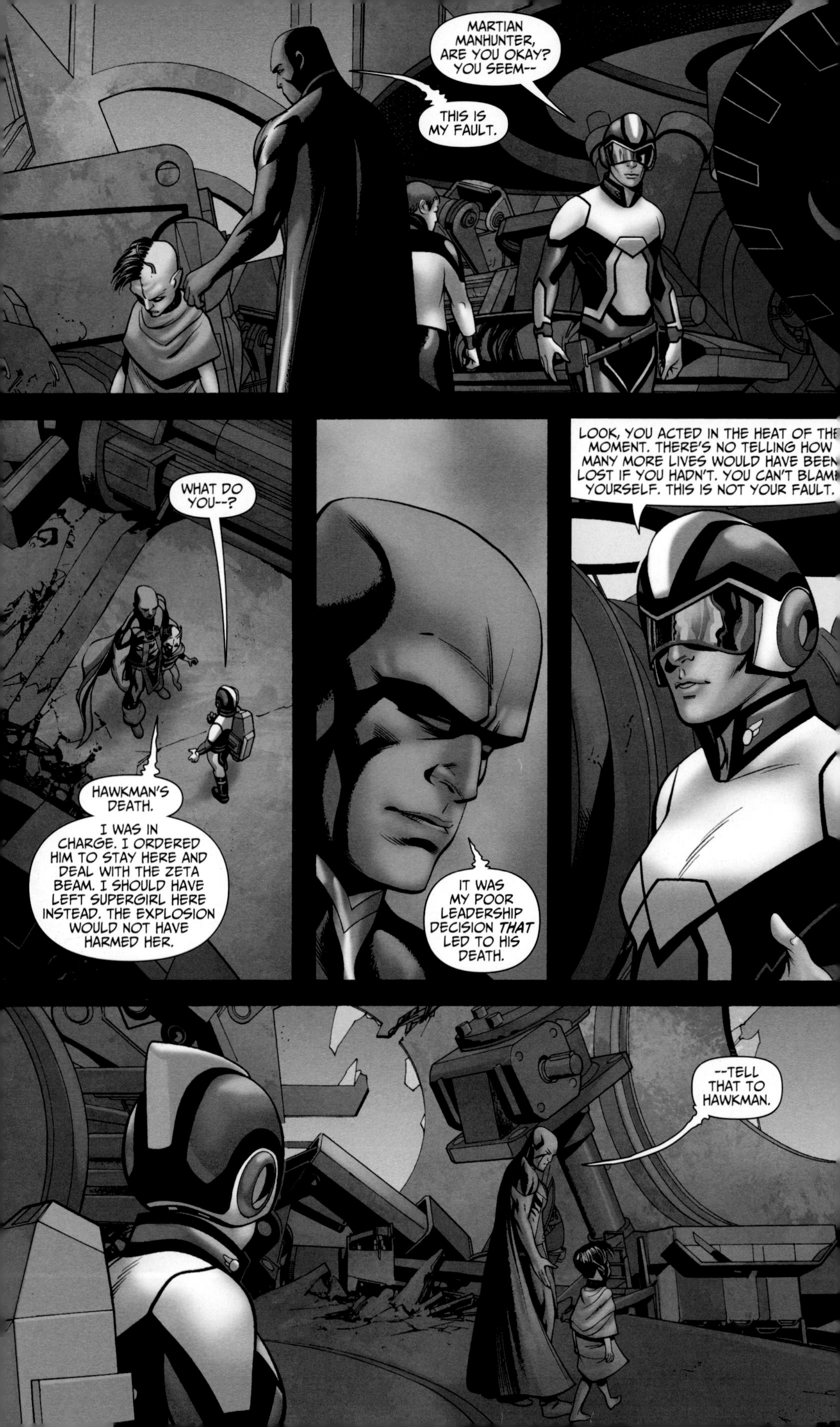
MARTIAN MANHUNTER, ARE YOU OKAY? YOU SEEM--
THIS IS MY FAULT.
WHAT DO YOU--?
HAWKMAN'S DEATH.
I WAS IN CHARGE. I ORDERED HIM TO STAY HERE AND DEAL WITH THE ZETA BEAM. I SHOULD HAVE LEFT SUPERGIRL HERE INSTEAD. THE EXPLOSION WOULD NOT HAVE HARMED HER.
IT WAS MY POOR LEADERSHIP DECISION *THAT* LED TO HIS DEATH.
LOOK, YOU ACTED IN THE HEAT OF THE MOMENT. THERE'S NO TELLING HOW MANY MORE LIVES WOULD HAVE BEEN LOST IF YOU HADN'T. YOU CAN'T BLAM YOURSELF. THIS IS NOT YOUR FAULT.
--TELL THAT TO HAWKMAN.

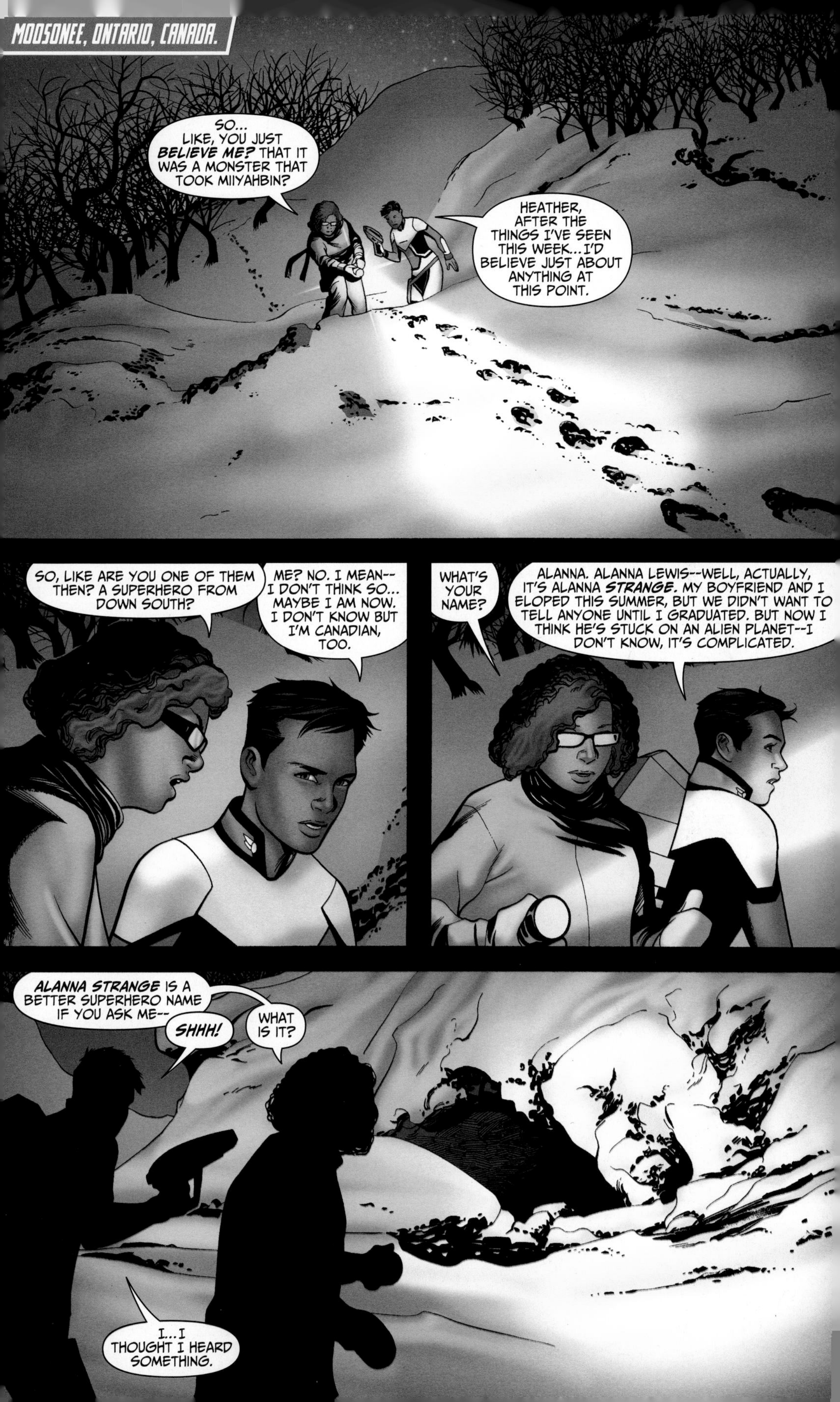

MOOSONEE, ONTARIO, CANADA.
SO... LIKE, YOU JUST BELIEVE ME? THAT IT WAS A MONSTER THAT TOOK MIIYAHBIN?
HEATHER, AFTER THE THINGS I'VE SEEN THIS WEEK...I'D BELIEVE JUST ABOUT ANYTHING AT THIS POINT.
SO, LIKE ARE YOU ONE OF THEM THEN? A SUPERHERO FROM DOWN SOUTH?
ME? NO. I MEAN-- I DON'T THINK SO... MAYBE I AM NOW. I DON'T KNOW BUT I'M CANADIAN, TOO.
WHAT'S YOUR NAME?
ALANNA. ALANNA LEWIS--WELL, ACTUALLY, IT'S ALANNA STRANGE. MY BOYFRIEND AND I ELOPED THIS SUMMER, BUT WE DIDN'T WANT TO TELL ANYONE UNTIL I GRADUATED. BUT NOW I THINK HE'S STUCK ON AN ALIEN PLANET--I DON'T KNOW, IT'S COMPLICATED.
ALANNA STRANGE IS A BETTER SUPERHERO NAME IF YOU ASK ME--
SHHH!
WHAT IS IT?
I...I THOUGHT I HEARD SOMETHING.

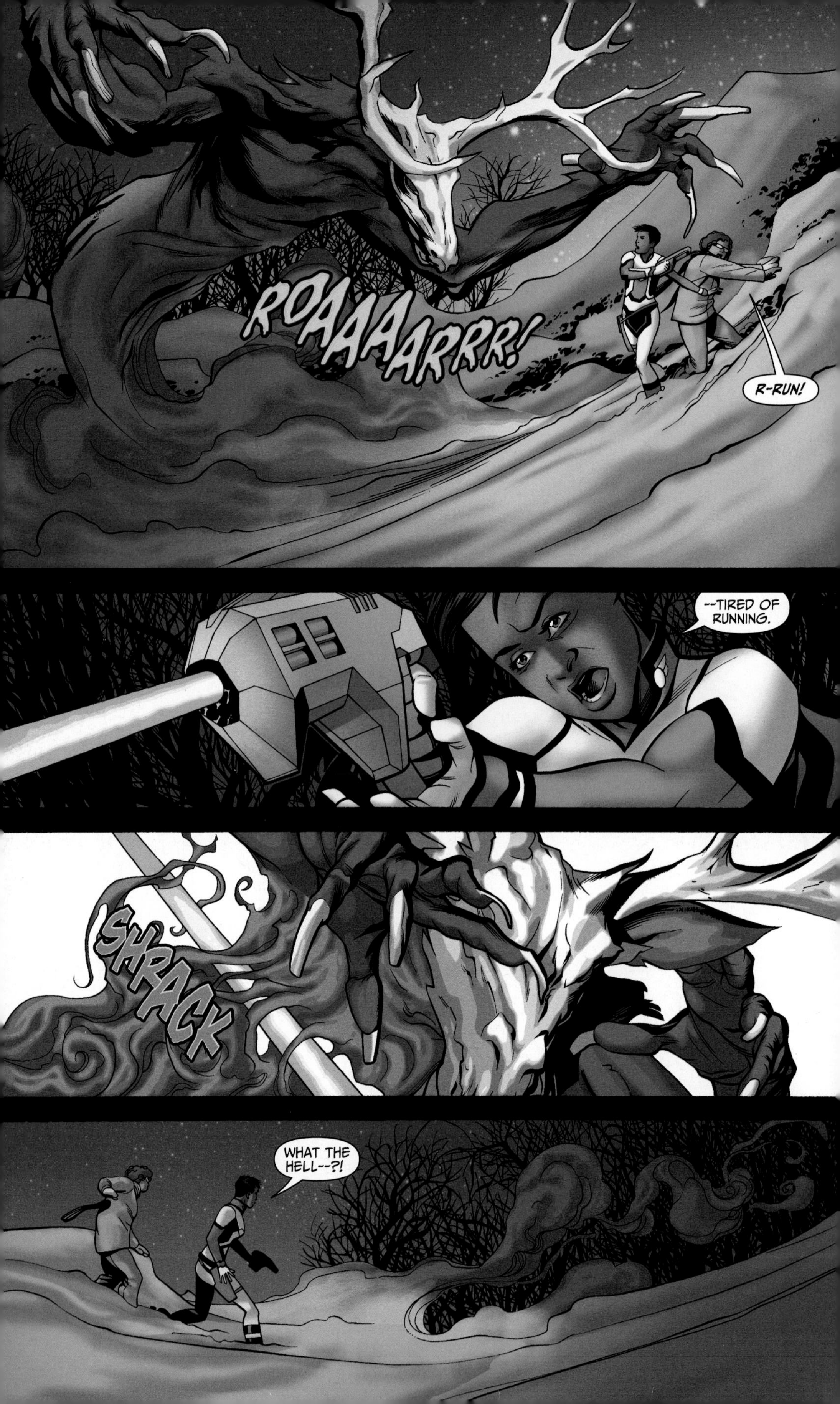
ROAAAARRRR!
R-RUN!
--TIRED OF RUNNING.
SHRACK
WHAT THE HELL--?!

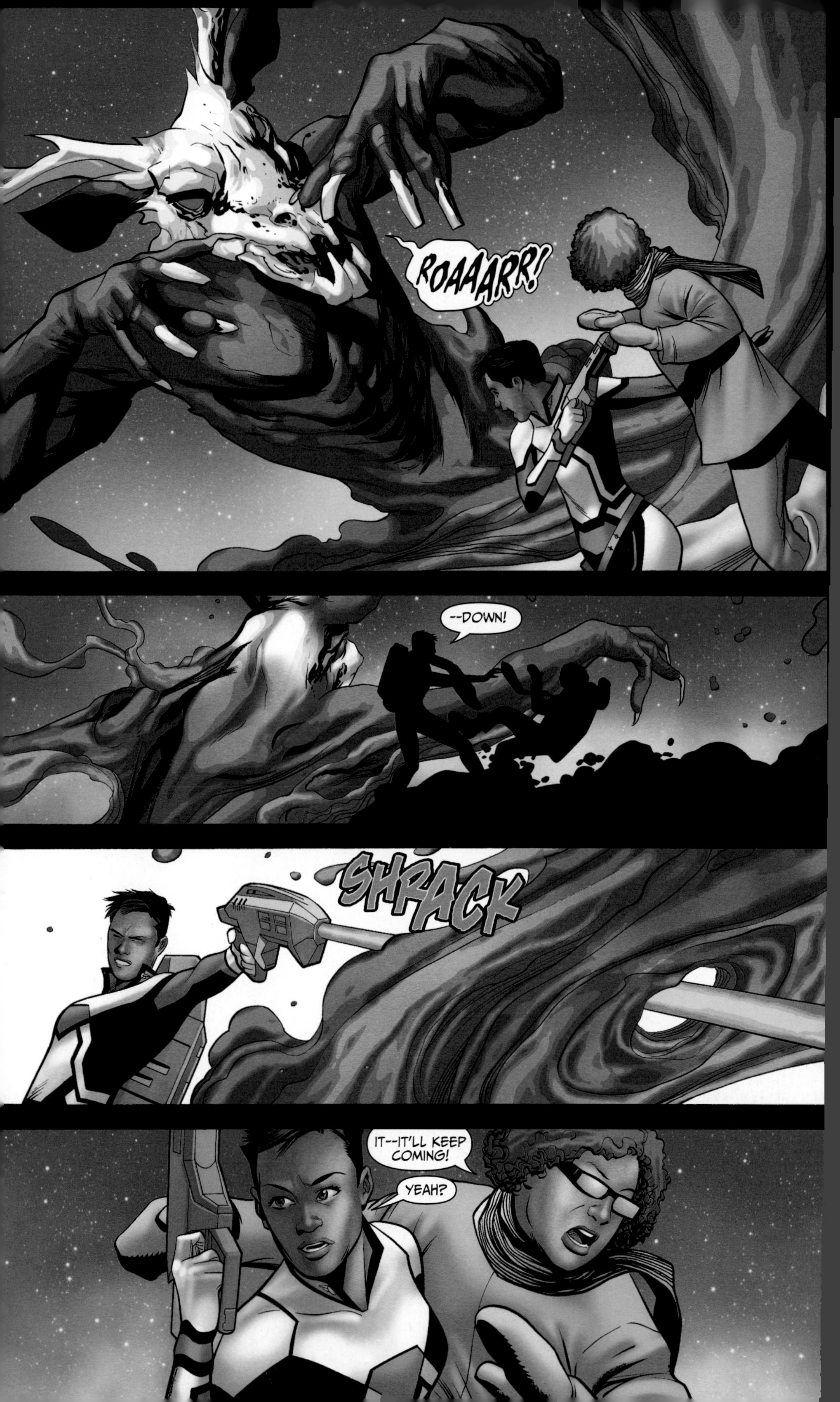
ROAAARR!
--DOWN!
SHRACK
IT--IT'LL KEEP COMING!
YEAH?

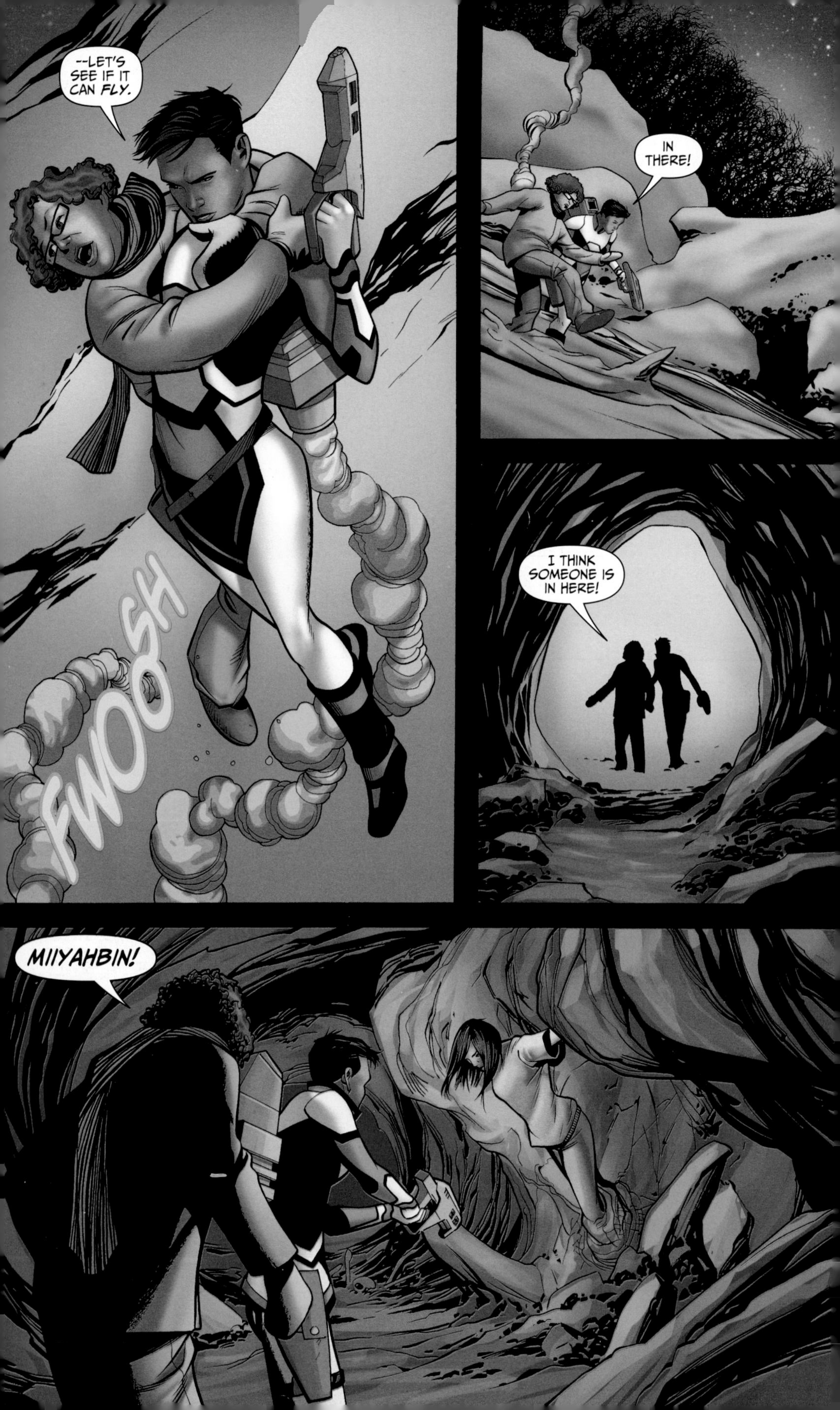
--LET'S SEE IF IT CAN FLY.
FWOOSH
IN THERE!
I THINK SOMEONE IS IN HERE!
MIIYAHBIN!

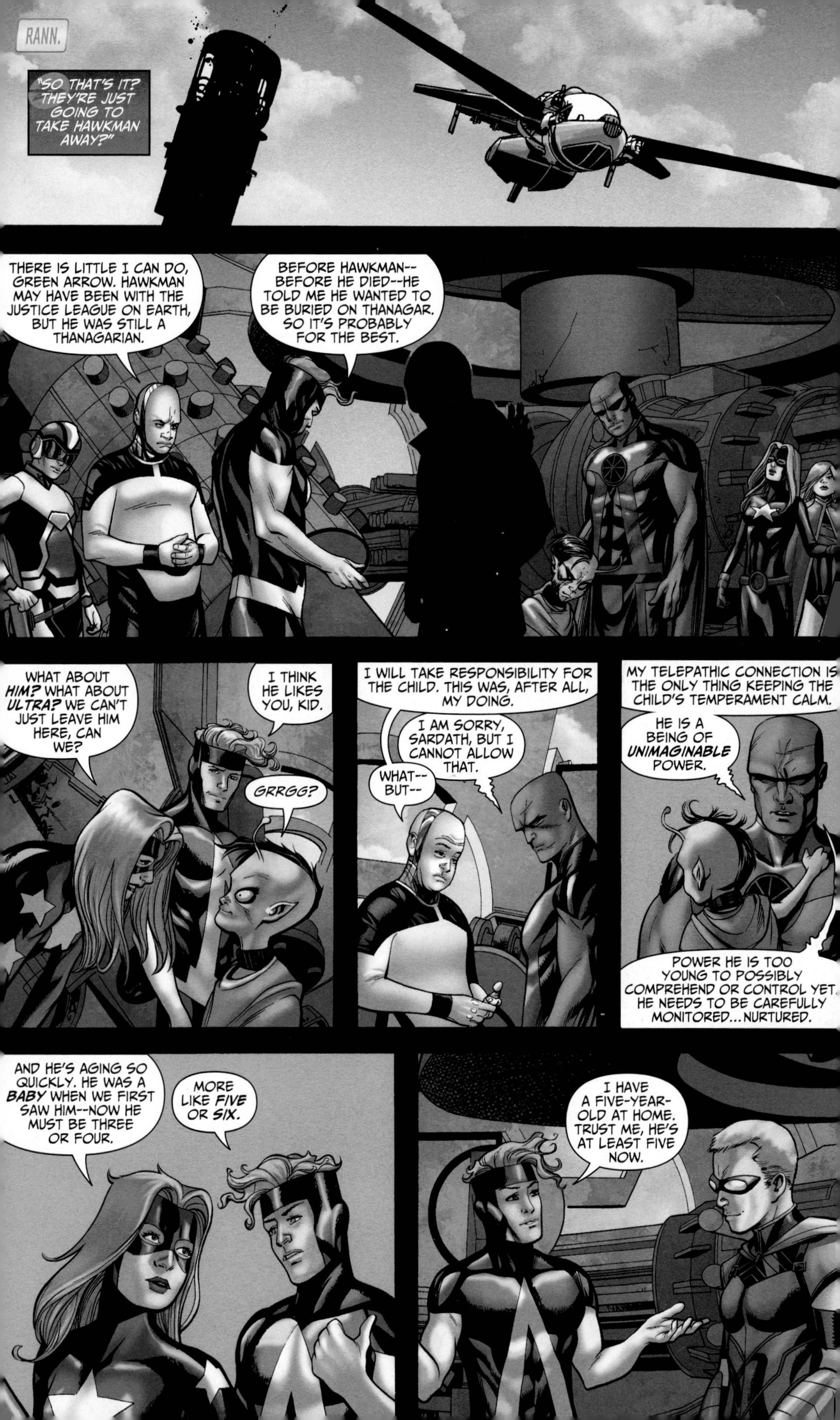
RANN.
"SO THAT'S IT? THEY'RE JUST GOING TO TAKE HAWKMAN AWAY?"
THERE IS LITTLE I CAN DO, GREEN ARROW. HAWKMAN MAY HAVE BEEN WITH THE JUSTICE LEAGUE ON EARTH, BUT HE WAS STILL A THANAGARIAN.
BEFORE HAWKMAN-- BEFORE HE DIED--HE TOLD ME HE WANTED TO BE BURIED ON THANAGAR. SO IT'S PROBABLY FOR THE BEST.
WHAT ABOUT *HIM?* WHAT ABOUT *ULTRA?* WE CAN'T JUST LEAVE HIM HERE, CAN WE?
I THINK HE LIKES YOU, KID.
GRRGG?
I WILL TAKE RESPONSIBILITY FOR THE CHILD. THIS WAS, AFTER ALL, MY DOING.
I AM SORRY, SARDATH, BUT I CANNOT ALLOW THAT.
WHAT-- BUT--
MY TELEPATHIC CONNECTION IS THE ONLY THING KEEPING THE CHILD'S TEMPERAMENT CALM.
HE IS A BEING OF *UNIMAGINABLE* POWER.
POWER HE IS TOO YOUNG TO POSSIBLY COMPREHEND OR CONTROL YET. HE NEEDS TO BE CAREFULLY MONITORED... NURTURED.
AND HE'S AGING SO QUICKLY. HE WAS A *BABY* WHEN WE FIRST SAW HIM--NOW HE MUST BE THREE OR FOUR.
MORE LIKE *FIVE* OR *SIX.*
I HAVE A FIVE-YEAR-OLD AT HOME. TRUST ME, HE'S AT LEAST FIVE NOW.

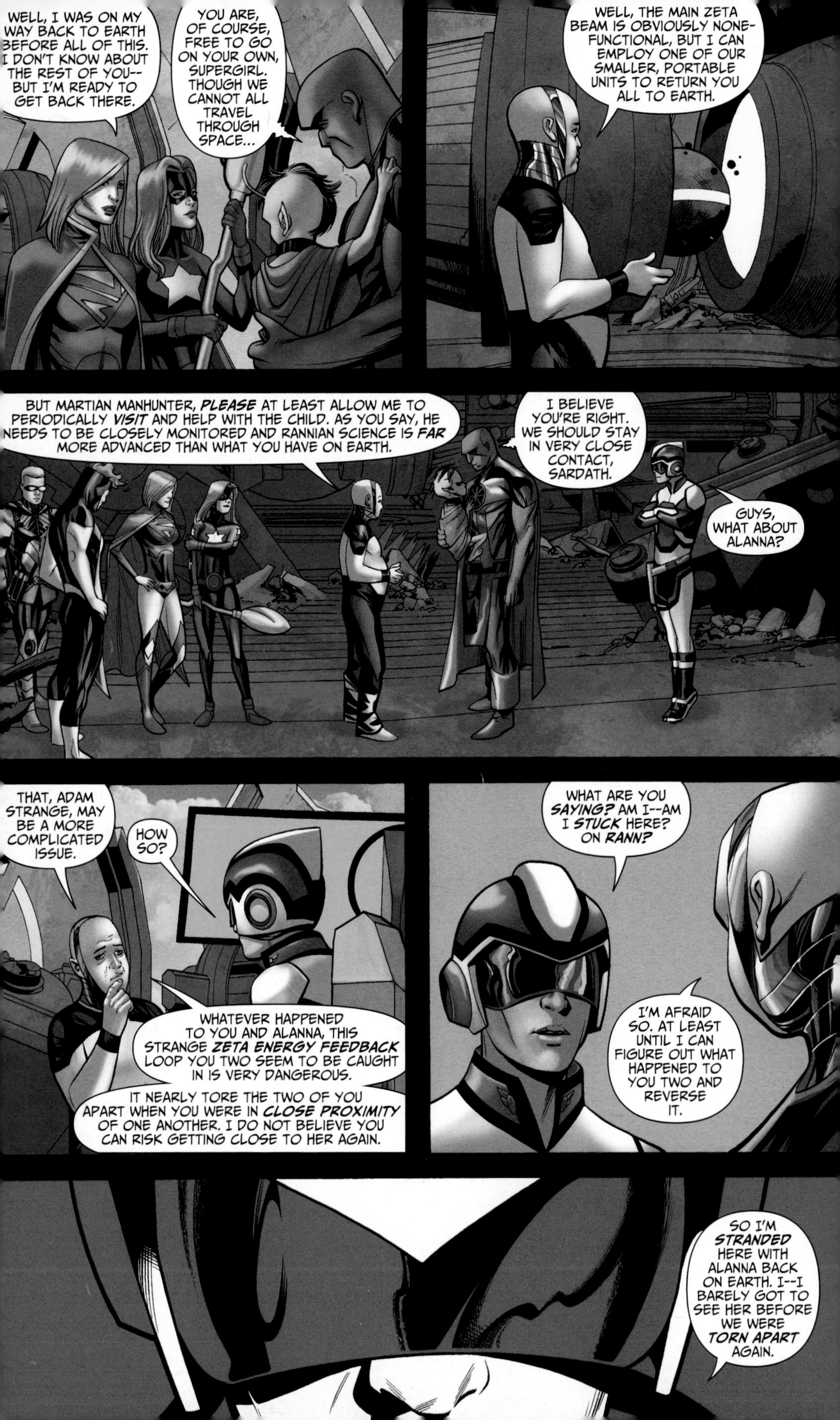
WELL, I WAS ON MY WAY BACK TO EARTH BEFORE ALL OF THIS. I DON'T KNOW ABOUT THE REST OF YOU-- BUT I'M READY TO GET BACK THERE.
YOU ARE, OF COURSE, FREE TO GO ON YOUR OWN, SUPERGIRL. THOUGH WE CANNOT ALL TRAVEL THROUGH SPACE...
WELL, THE MAIN ZETA BEAM IS OBVIOUSLY NONE-FUNCTIONAL, BUT I CAN EMPLOY ONE OF OUR SMALLER, PORTABLE UNITS TO RETURN YOU ALL TO EARTH.
BUT MARTIAN MANHUNTER, PLEASE AT LEAST ALLOW ME TO PERIODICALLY VISIT AND HELP WITH THE CHILD. AS YOU SAY, HE NEEDS TO BE CLOSELY MONITORED AND RANNIAN SCIENCE IS FAR MORE ADVANCED THAN WHAT YOU HAVE ON EARTH.
I BELIEVE YOU'RE RIGHT. WE SHOULD STAY IN VERY CLOSE CONTACT, SARDATH.
GUYS, WHAT ABOUT ALANNA?
THAT, ADAM STRANGE, MAY BE A MORE COMPLICATED ISSUE.
HOW SO?
WHATEVER HAPPENED TO YOU AND ALANNA, THIS STRANGE ZETA ENERGY FEEDBACK LOOP YOU TWO SEEM TO BE CAUGHT IN IS VERY DANGEROUS.
IT NEARLY TORE THE TWO OF YOU APART WHEN YOU WERE IN CLOSE PROXIMITY OF ONE ANOTHER. I DO NOT BELIEVE YOU CAN RISK GETTING CLOSE TO HER AGAIN.
WHAT ARE YOU SAYING? AM I--AM I STUCK HERE? ON RANN?
I'M AFRAID SO. AT LEAST UNTIL I CAN FIGURE OUT WHAT HAPPENED TO YOU TWO AND REVERSE IT.
SO I'M STRANDED HERE WITH ALANNA BACK ON EARTH. I--I BARELY GOT TO SEE HER BEFORE WE WERE TORN APART AGAIN.

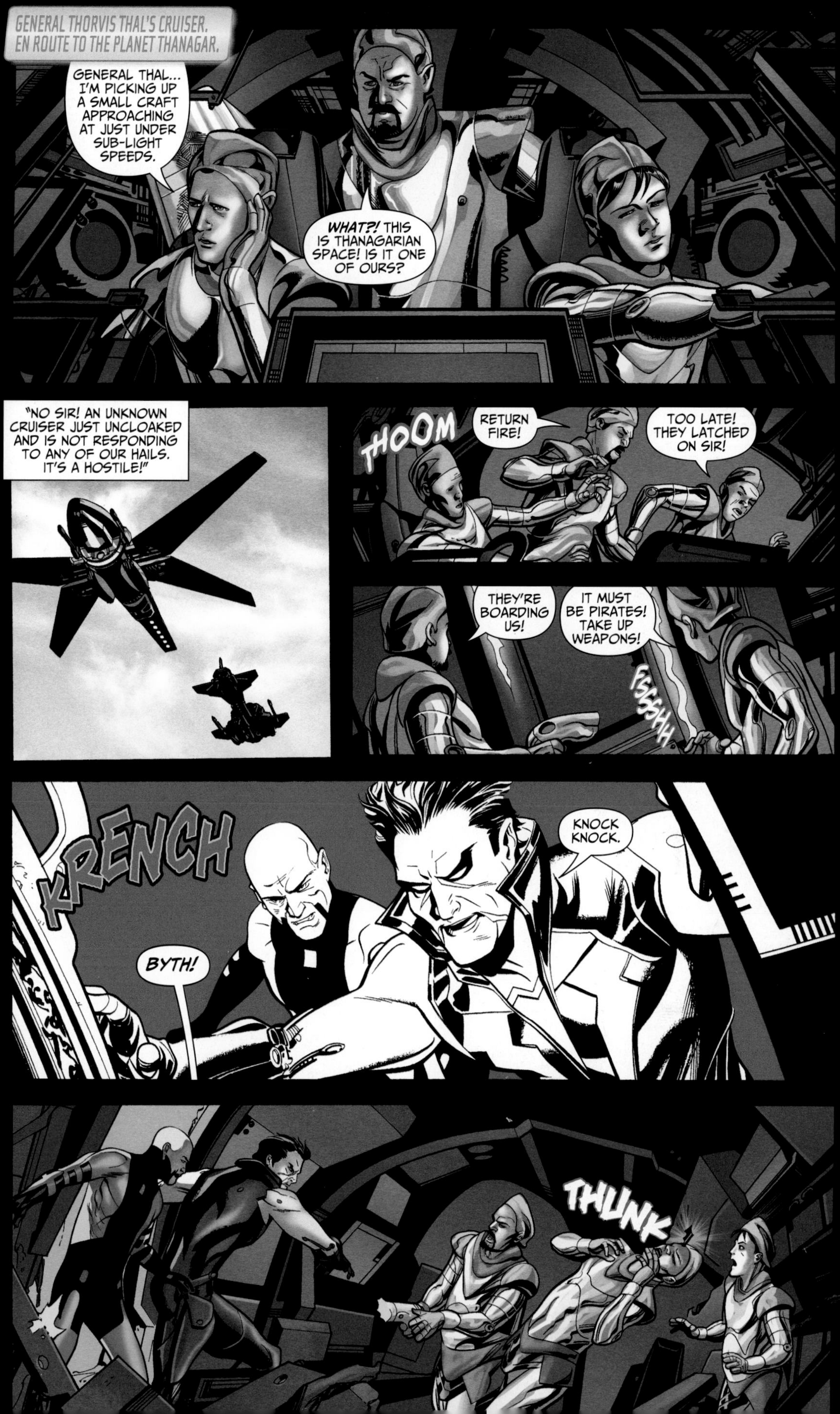
GENERAL THORVIS THAL'S CRUISER. EN ROUTE TO THE PLANET THANAGAR.
GENERAL THAL... I'M PICKING UP A SMALL CRAFT APPROACHING AT JUST UNDER SUB-LIGHT SPEEDS.
WHAT?! THIS IS THANAGARIAN SPACE! IS IT ONE OF OURS?
"NO SIR! AN UNKNOWN CRUISER JUST UNCLOAKED AND IS NOT RESPONDING TO ANY OF OUR HAILS. IT'S A HOSTILE!"
THOOM
RETURN FIRE!
TOO LATE! THEY LATCHED ON SIR!
THEY'RE BOARDING US!
IT MUST BE PIRATES! TAKE UP WEAPONS!
FSSSHH
KRENCH
KNOCK KNOCK.
BYTH!
THUNK

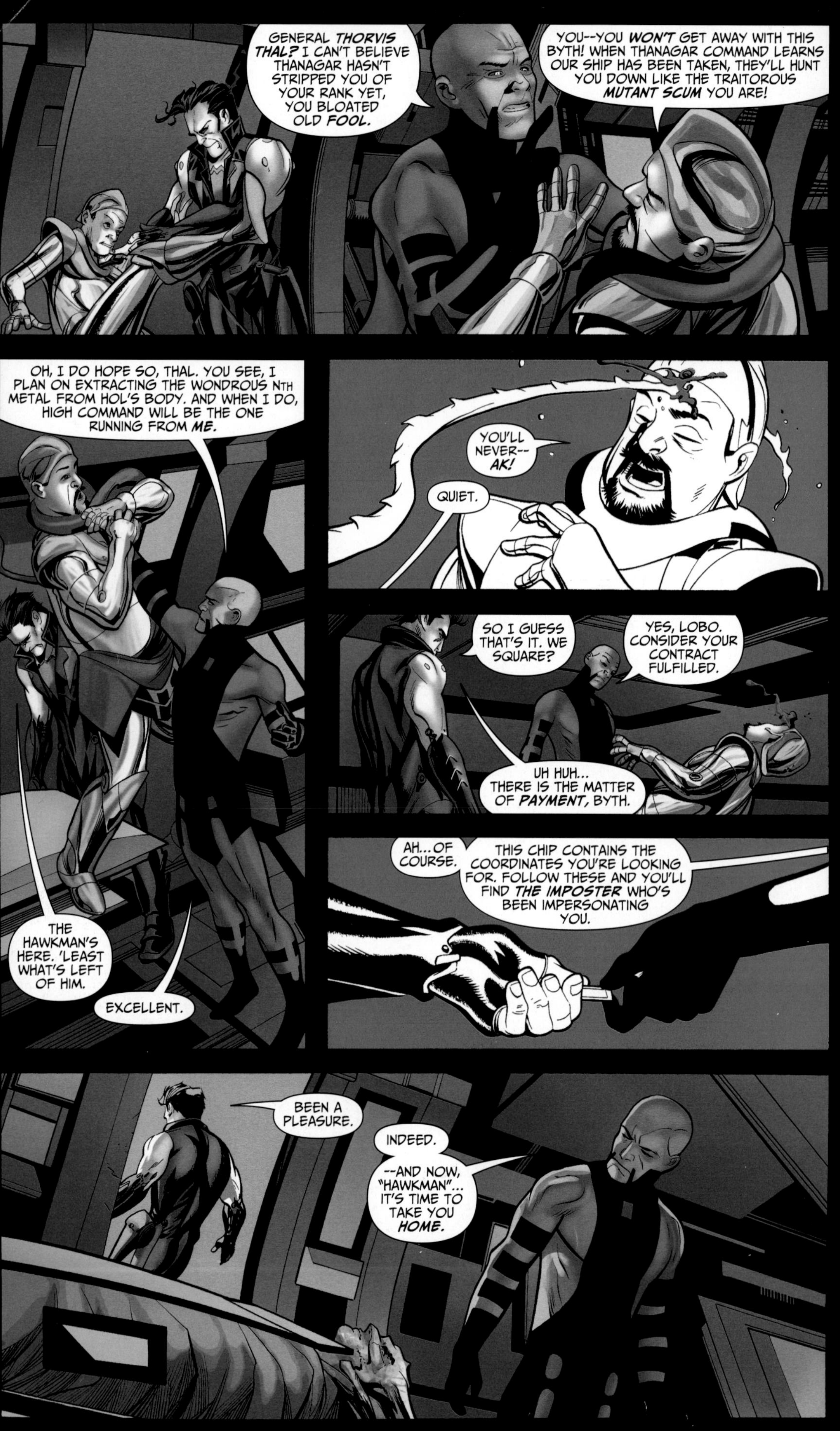
GENERAL THORVIS THAL? I CAN'T BELIEVE THANAGAR HASN'T STRIPPED YOU OF YOUR RANK YET, YOU BLOATED OLD FOOL.
YOU--YOU WON'T GET AWAY WITH THIS BYTH! WHEN THANAGAR COMMAND LEARNS OUR SHIP HAS BEEN TAKEN, THEY'LL HUNT YOU DOWN LIKE THE TRAITOROUS MUTANT SCUM YOU ARE!
OH, I DO HOPE SO, THAL. YOU SEE, I PLAN ON EXTRACTING THE WONDROUS NTH METAL FROM HOL'S BODY. AND WHEN I DO, HIGH COMMAND WILL BE THE ONE RUNNING FROM ME.
THE HAWKMAN'S HERE. 'LEAST WHAT'S LEFT OF HIM.
EXCELLENT.
YOU'LL NEVER-- AK!
QUIET.
SO I GUESS THAT'S IT. WE SQUARE?
YES, LOBO. CONSIDER YOUR CONTRACT FULFILLED.
UH HUH... THERE IS THE MATTER OF PAYMENT, BYTH.
AH...OF COURSE.
THIS CHIP CONTAINS THE COORDINATES YOU'RE LOOKING FOR. FOLLOW THESE AND YOU'LL FIND THE IMPOSTER WHO'S BEEN IMPERSONATING YOU.
BEEN A PLEASURE.
INDEED.
--AND NOW, "HAWKMAN"... IT'S TIME TO TAKE YOU HOME.

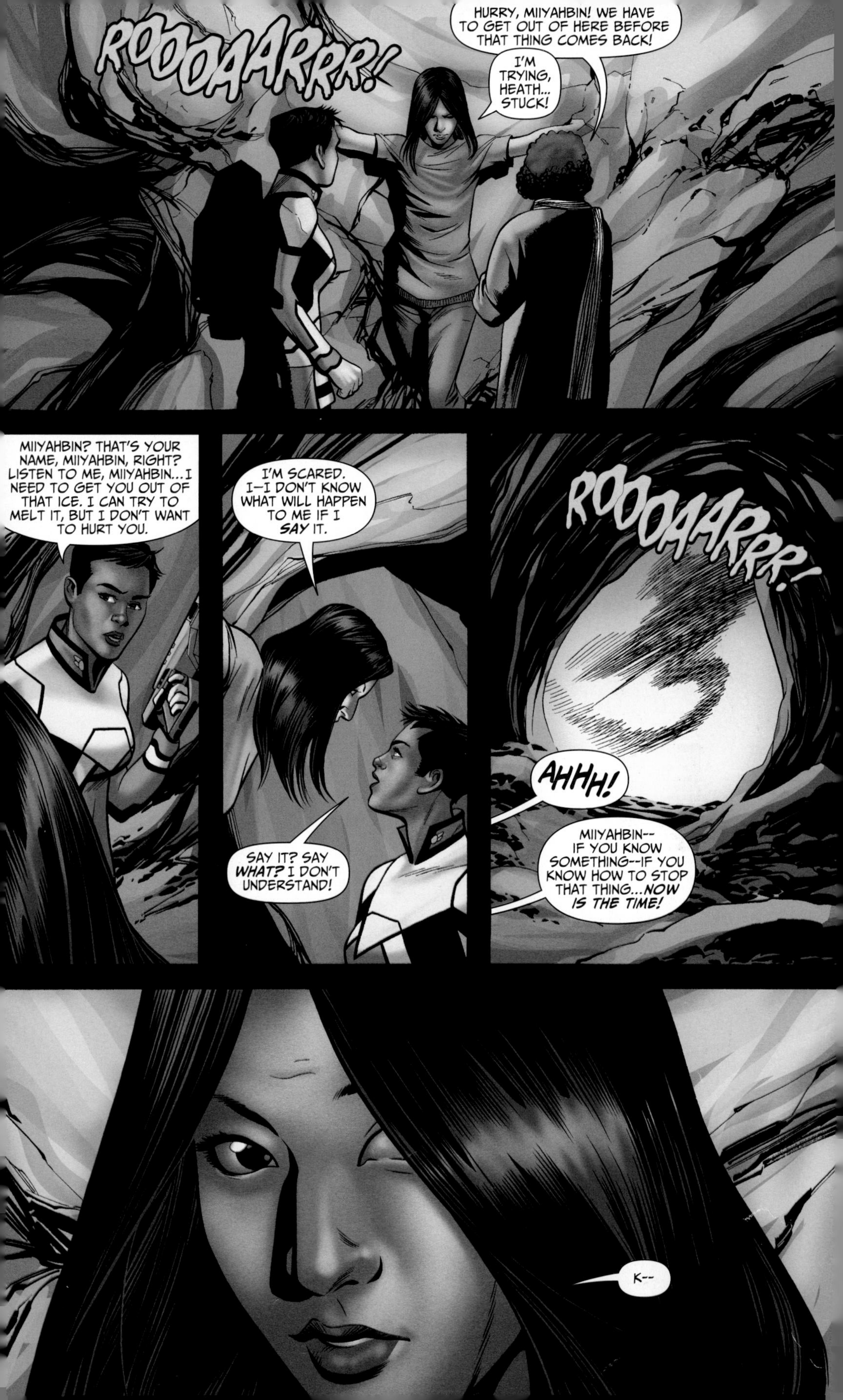
ROOOAARRR!
HURRY, MIIYAHBIN! WE HAVE TO GET OUT OF HERE BEFORE THAT THING COMES BACK!
I'M TRYING, HEATH... STUCK!
MIIYAHBIN? THAT'S YOUR NAME, MIIYAHBIN, RIGHT? LISTEN TO ME, MIIYAHBIN...I NEED TO GET YOU OUT OF THAT ICE. I CAN TRY TO MELT IT, BUT I DON'T WANT TO HURT YOU.
I'M SCARED. I--I DON'T KNOW WHAT WILL HAPPEN TO ME IF I SAY IT.
SAY IT? SAY WHAT? I DON'T UNDERSTAND!
ROOOAARRR!
AHHH!
MIIYAHBIN-- IF YOU KNOW SOMETHING--IF YOU KNOW HOW TO STOP THAT THING...NOW IS THE TIME!
K--

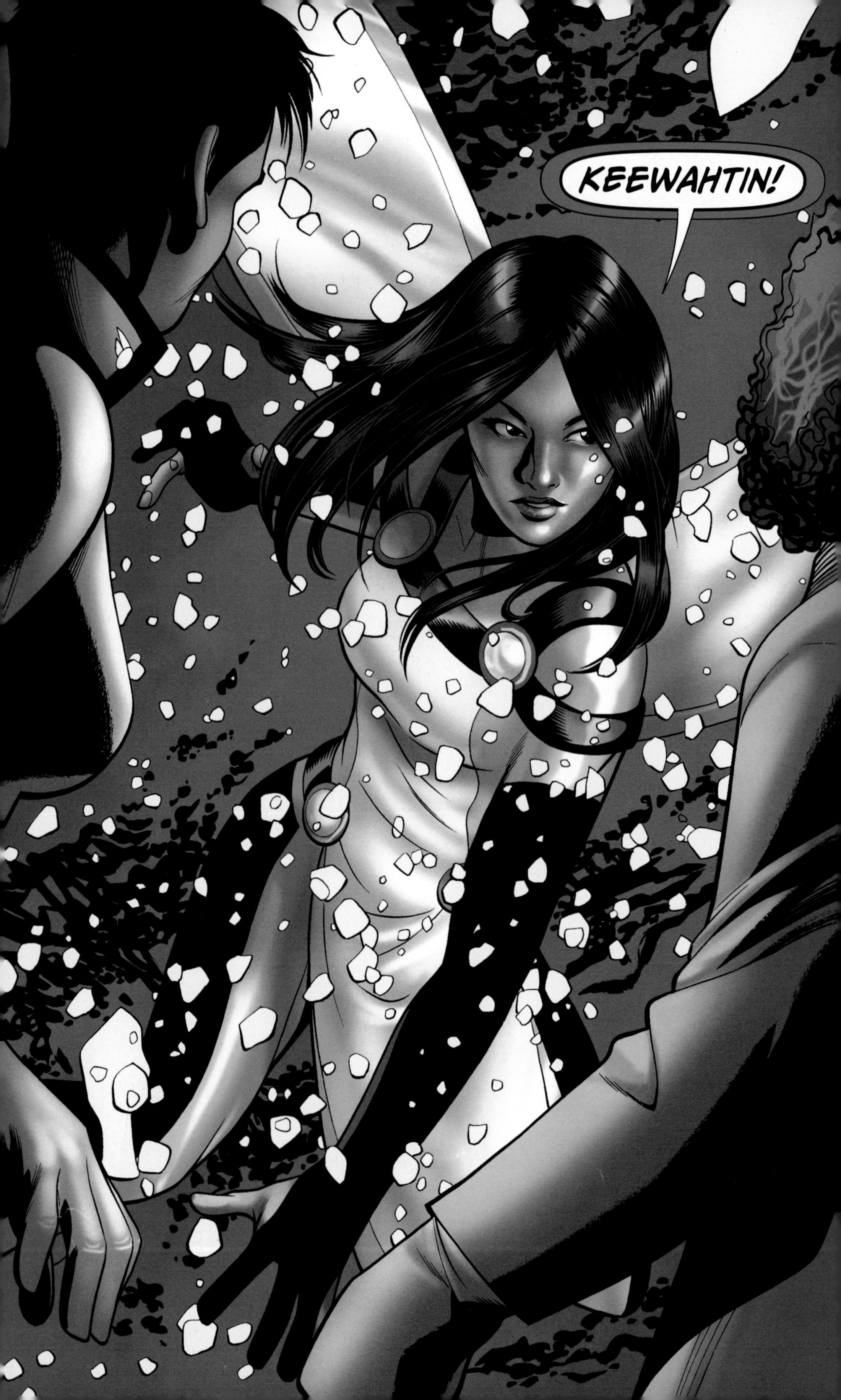
KEEWAHTIN!

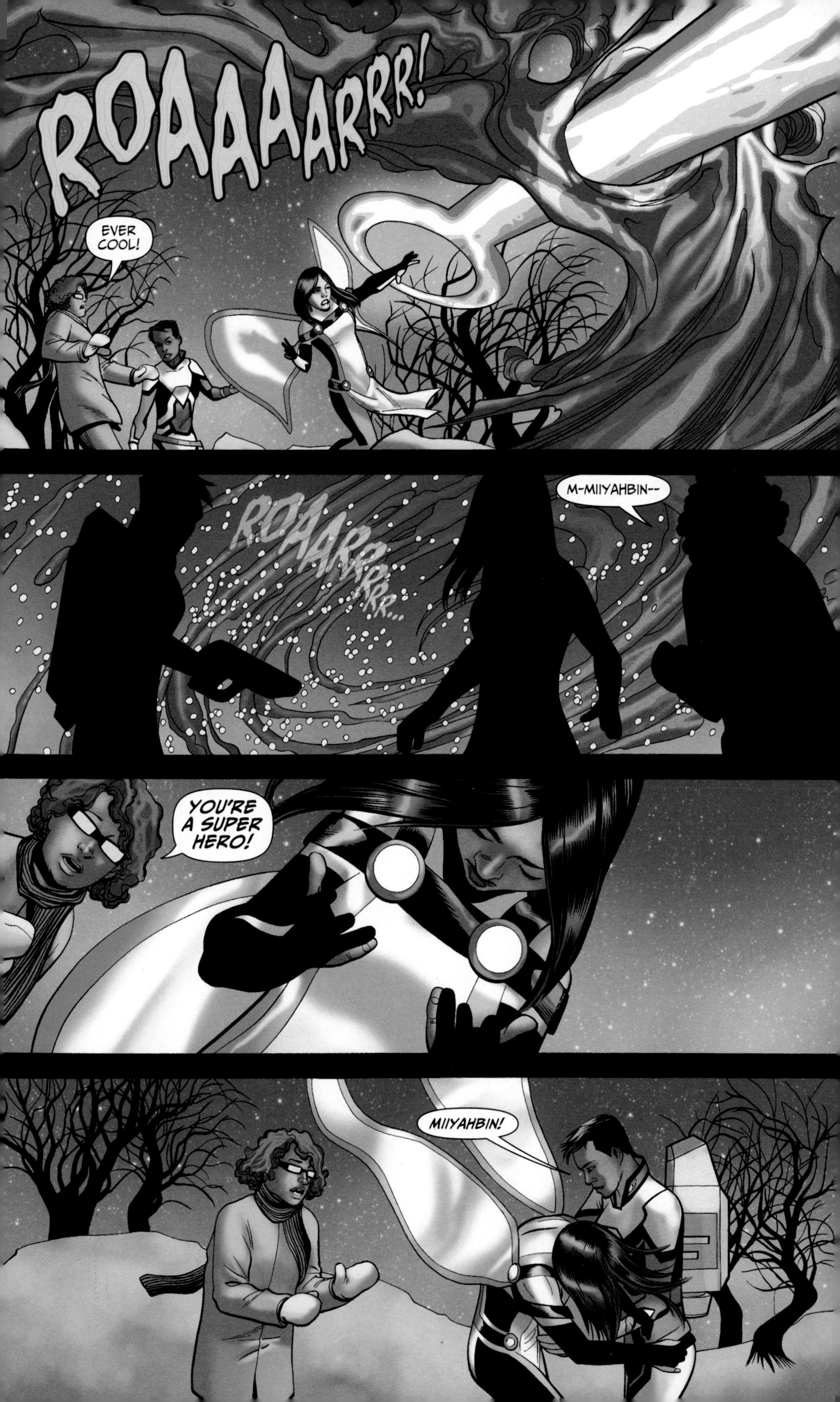
ROAAAARRR!
EVER COOL!
ROAARRRR...
M-MIIYAHBIN--
YOU'RE A SUPER HERO!
MIIYAHBIN!

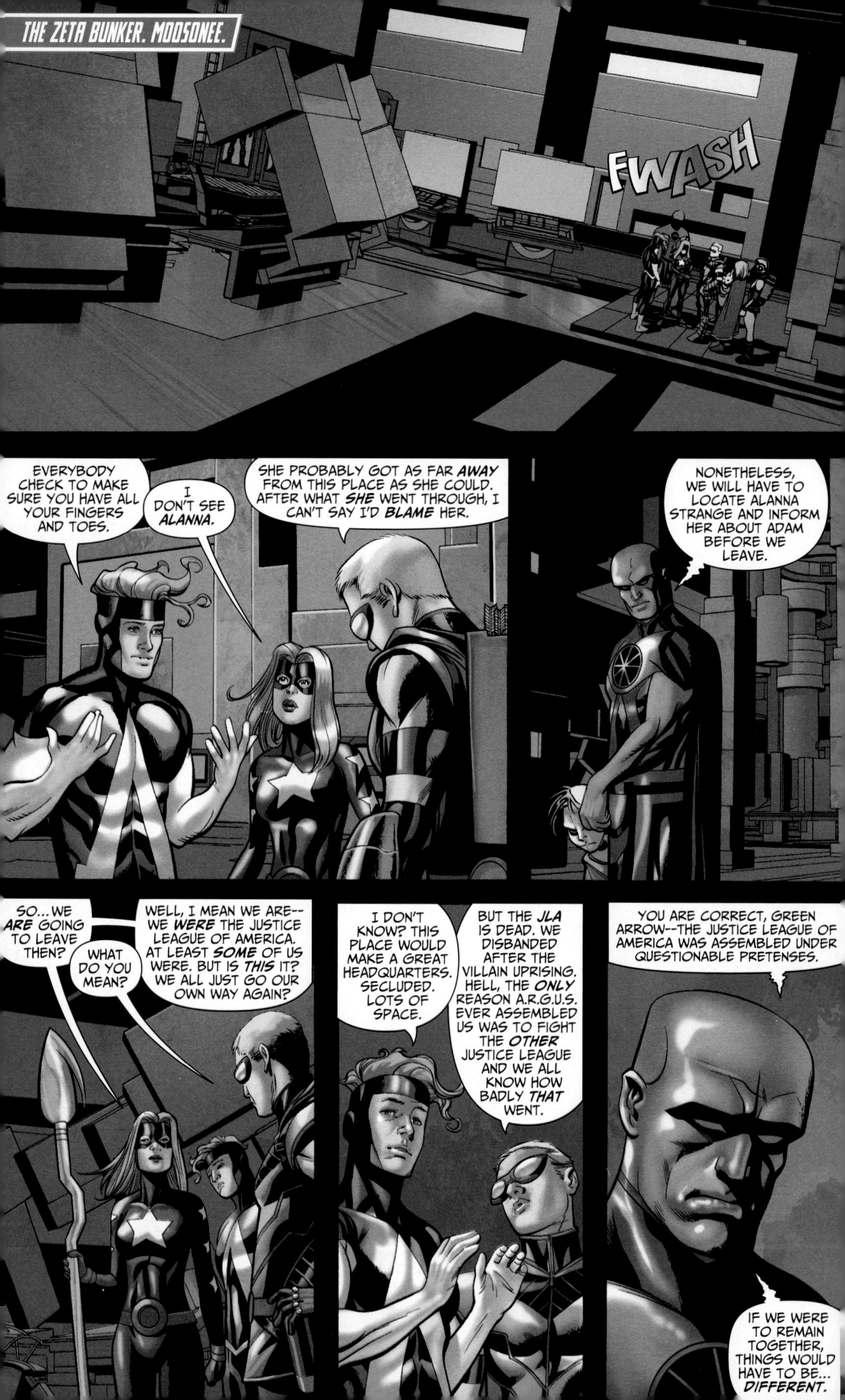
THE ZETA BUNKER. MOOSONEE.
FWASH
EVERYBODY CHECK TO MAKE SURE YOU HAVE ALL YOUR FINGERS AND TOES.
I DON'T SEE ALANNA.
SHE PROBABLY GOT AS FAR AWAY FROM THIS PLACE AS SHE COULD. AFTER WHAT SHE WENT THROUGH, I CAN'T SAY I'D BLAME HER.
NONETHELESS, WE WILL HAVE TO LOCATE ALANNA STRANGE AND INFORM HER ABOUT ADAM BEFORE WE LEAVE.
SO... WE ARE GOING TO LEAVE THEN?
WHAT DO YOU MEAN?
WELL, I MEAN WE ARE-- WE WERE THE JUSTICE LEAGUE OF AMERICA. AT LEAST SOME OF US WERE. BUT IS THIS IT? WE ALL JUST GO OUR OWN WAY AGAIN?
I DON'T KNOW? THIS PLACE WOULD MAKE A GREAT HEADQUARTERS. SECLUDED. LOTS OF SPACE.
BUT THE JLA IS DEAD. WE DISBANDED AFTER THE VILLAIN UPRISING. HELL, THE ONLY REASON A.R.G.U.S. EVER ASSEMBLED US WAS TO FIGHT THE OTHER JUSTICE LEAGUE AND WE ALL KNOW HOW BADLY THAT WENT.
YOU ARE CORRECT, GREEN ARROW--THE JUSTICE LEAGUE OF AMERICA WAS ASSEMBLED UNDER QUESTIONABLE PRETENSES.
IF WE WERE TO REMAIN TOGETHER, THINGS WOULD HAVE TO BE... DIFFERENT.

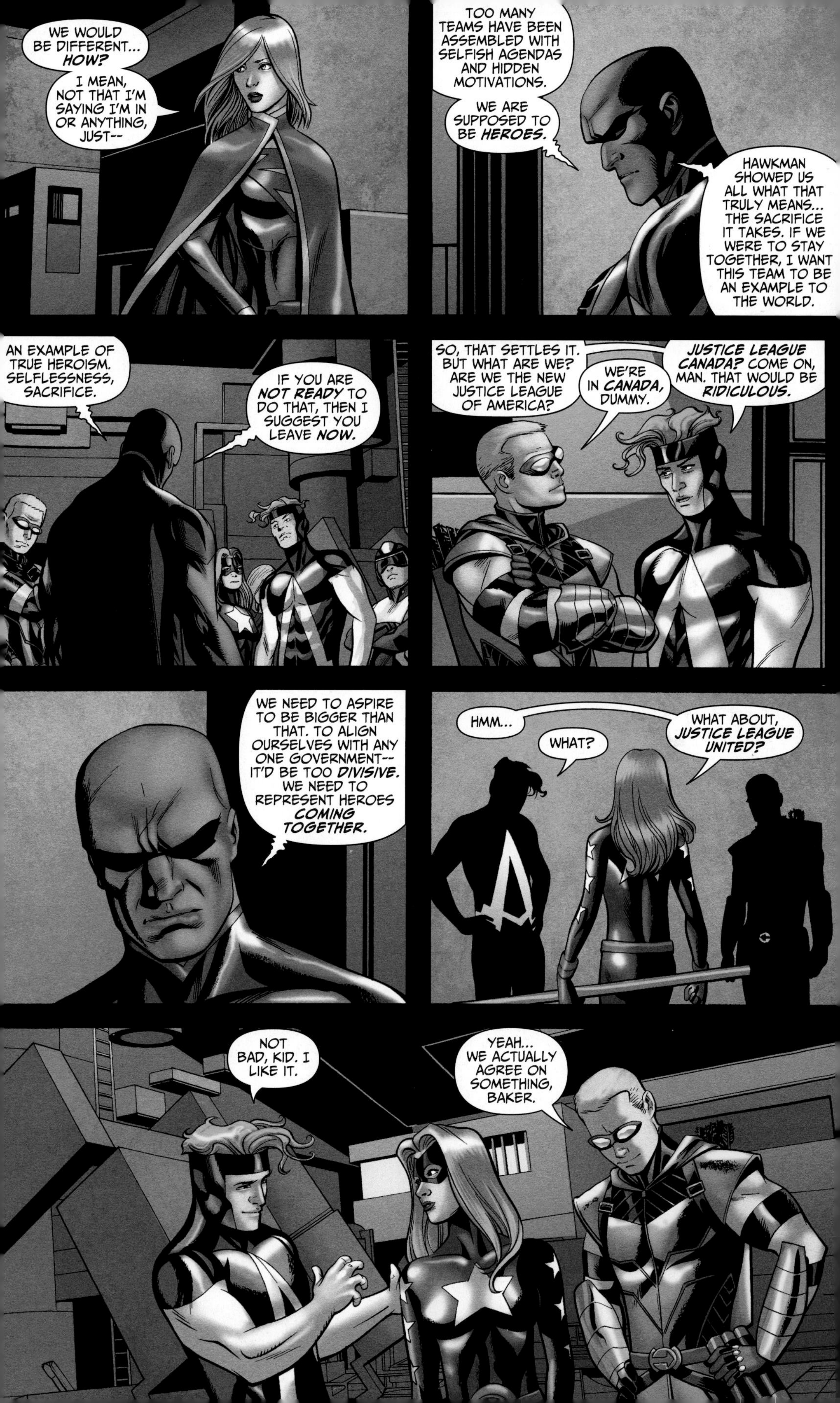
WE WOULD BE DIFFERENT... HOW?
I MEAN, NOT THAT I'M SAYING I'M IN OR ANYTHING, JUST--
TOO MANY TEAMS HAVE BEEN ASSEMBLED WITH SELFISH AGENDAS AND HIDDEN MOTIVATIONS.
WE ARE SUPPOSED TO BE HEROES.
HAWKMAN SHOWED US ALL WHAT THAT TRULY MEANS... THE SACRIFICE IT TAKES. IF WE WERE TO STAY TOGETHER, I WANT THIS TEAM TO BE AN EXAMPLE TO THE WORLD.
AN EXAMPLE OF TRUE HEROISM. SELFLESSNESS, SACRIFICE.
IF YOU ARE NOT READY TO DO THAT, THEN I SUGGEST YOU LEAVE NOW.
SO, THAT SETTLES IT. BUT WHAT ARE WE? ARE WE THE NEW JUSTICE LEAGUE OF AMERICA?
WE'RE IN CANADA, DUMMY.
JUSTICE LEAGUE CANADA? COME ON, MAN. THAT WOULD BE RIDICULOUS.
WE NEED TO ASPIRE TO BE BIGGER THAN THAT. TO ALIGN OURSELVES WITH ANY ONE GOVERNMENT-- IT'D BE TOO DIVISIVE. WE NEED TO REPRESENT HEROES COMING TOGETHER.
HMM...
WHAT?
WHAT ABOUT, JUSTICE LEAGUE UNITED?
NOT BAD, KID. I LIKE IT.
YEAH... WE ACTUALLY AGREE ON SOMETHING, BAKER.

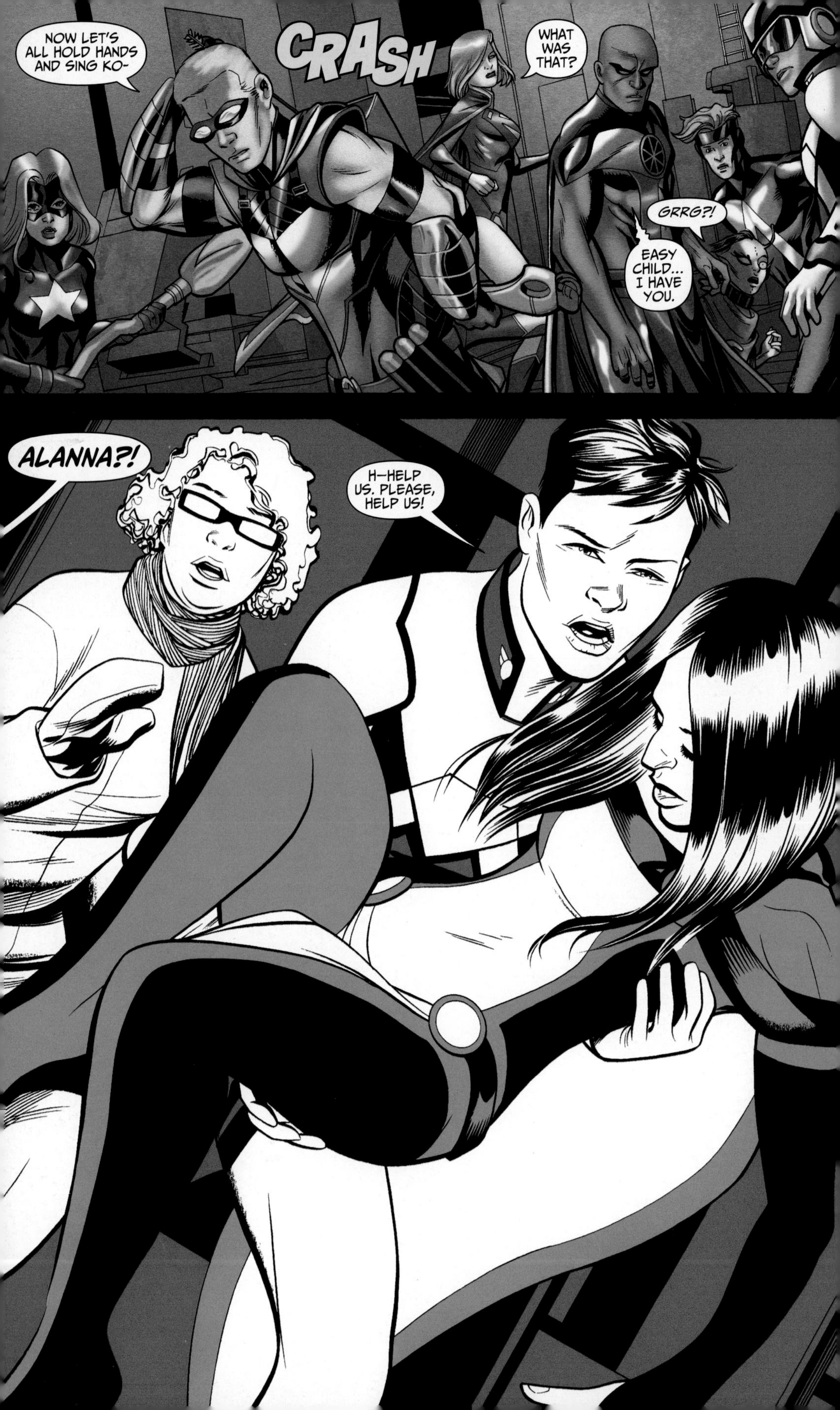
NOW LET'S ALL HOLD HANDS AND SING KO-
CRASH
WHAT WAS THAT?
GRRG?!
EASY CHILD... I HAVE YOU.
ALANNA?!
H--HELP US. PLEASE, HELP US!

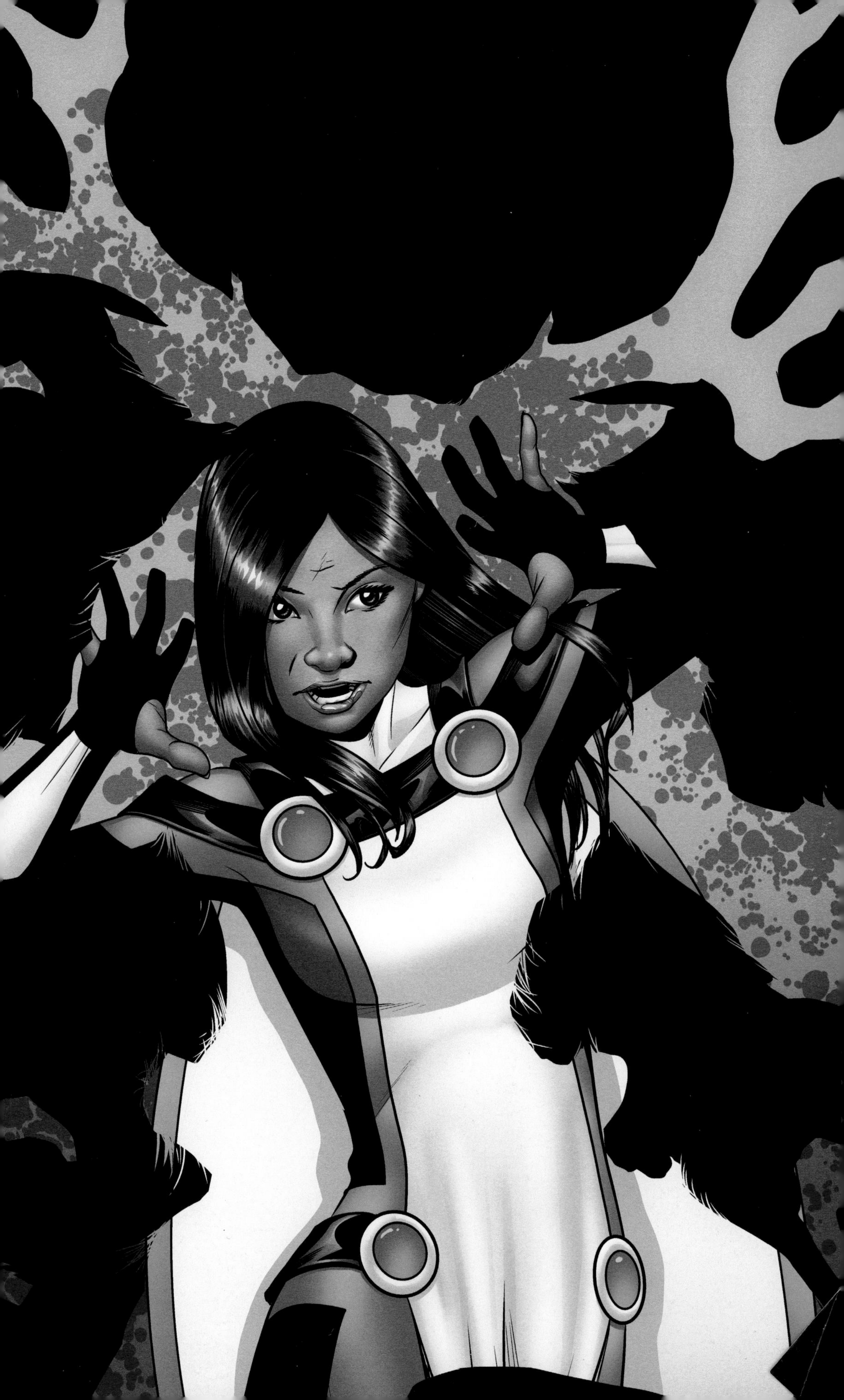

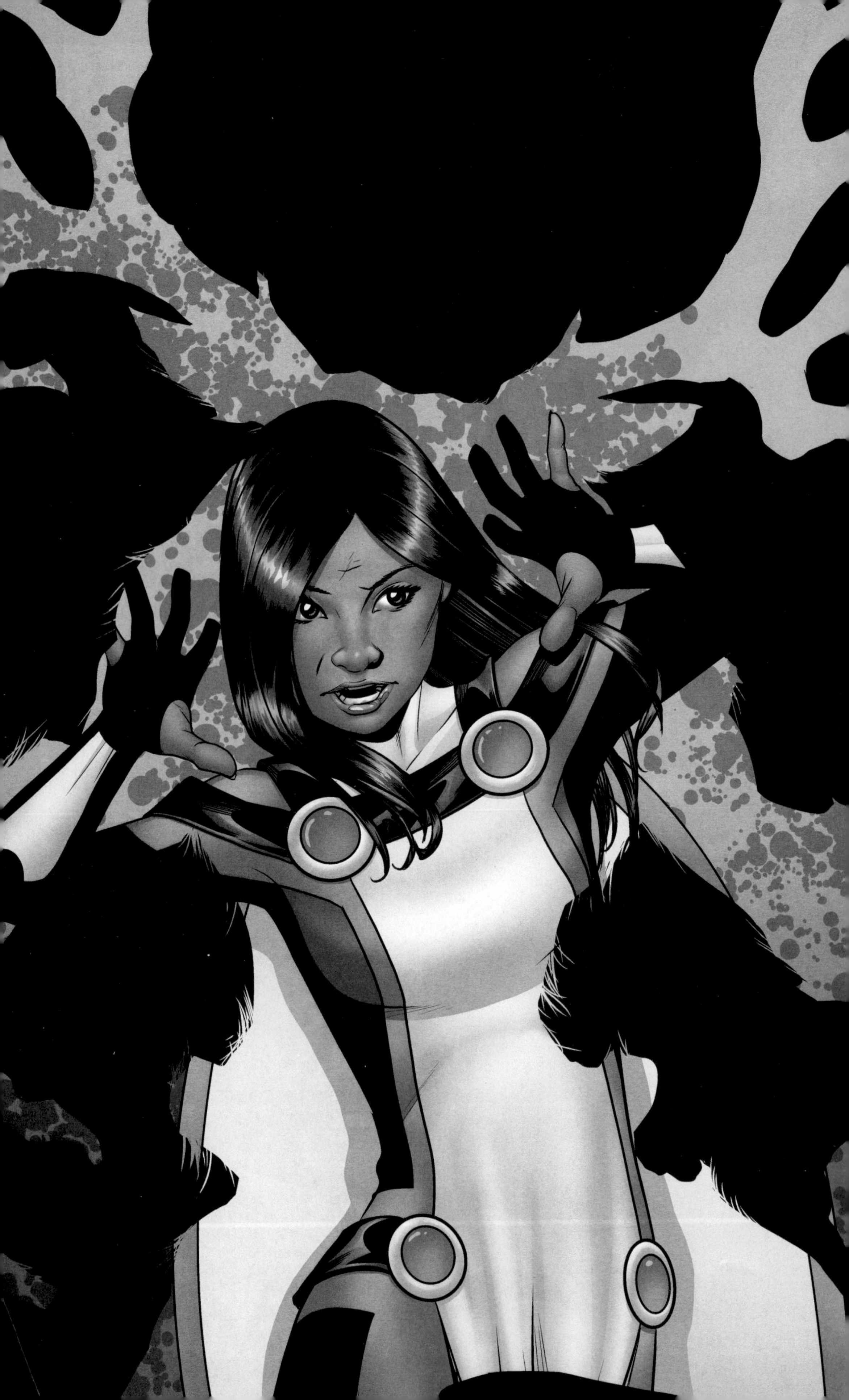

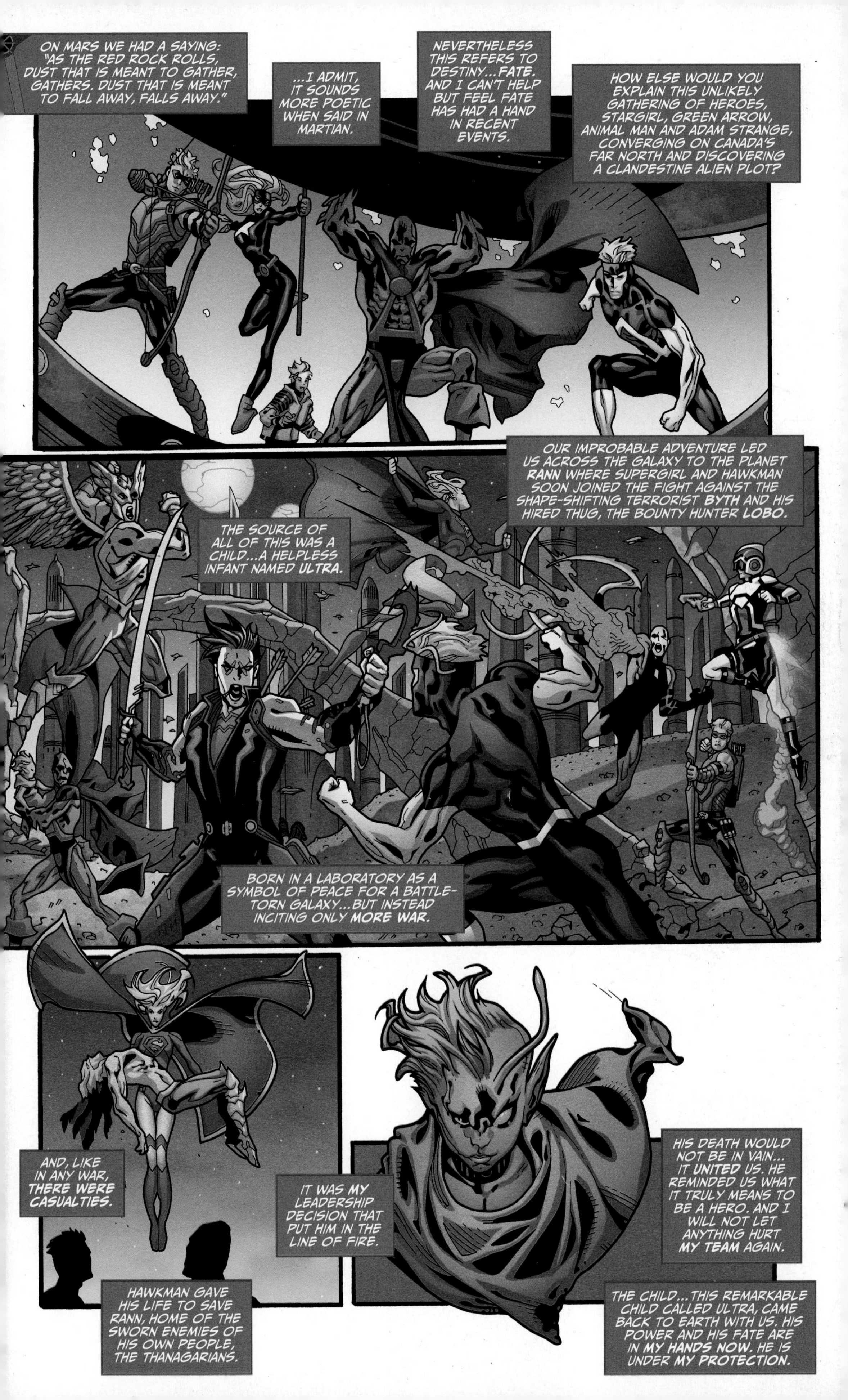

ON MARS WE HAD A SAYING: "AS THE RED ROCK ROLLS, DUST THAT IS MEANT TO GATHER, GATHERS. DUST THAT IS MEANT TO FALL AWAY, FALLS AWAY."
...I ADMIT, IT SOUNDS MORE POETIC WHEN SAID IN MARTIAN.
NEVERTHELESS THIS REFERS TO DESTINY...FATE. AND I CAN'T HELP BUT FEEL FATE HAS HAD A HAND IN RECENT EVENTS.
HOW ELSE WOULD YOU EXPLAIN THIS UNLIKELY GATHERING OF HEROES, STARGIRL, GREEN ARROW, ANIMAL MAN AND ADAM STRANGE, CONVERGING ON CANADA'S FAR NORTH AND DISCOVERING A CLANDESTINE ALIEN PLOT?
OUR IMPROBABLE ADVENTURE LED US ACROSS THE GALAXY TO THE PLANET RANN WHERE SUPERGIRL AND HAWKMAN SOON JOINED THE FIGHT AGAINST THE SHAPE-SHIFTING TERRORIST BYTH AND HIS HIRED THUG, THE BOUNTY HUNTER LOBO.
THE SOURCE OF ALL OF THIS WAS A CHILD...A HELPLESS INFANT NAMED ULTRA.
BORN IN A LABORATORY AS A SYMBOL OF PEACE FOR A BATTLE-TORN GALAXY...BUT INSTEAD INCITING ONLY MORE WAR.
AND, LIKE IN ANY WAR, THERE WERE CASUALTIES.
HAWKMAN GAVE HIS LIFE TO SAVE RANN, HOME OF THE SWORN ENEMIES OF HIS OWN PEOPLE, THE THANAGARIANS.
IT WAS MY LEADERSHIP DECISION THAT PUT HIM IN THE LINE OF FIRE.
HIS DEATH WOULD NOT BE IN VAIN... IT UNITED US. HE REMINDED US WHAT IT TRULY MEANS TO BE A HERO. AND I WILL NOT LET ANYTHING HURT MY TEAM AGAIN.
THE CHILD...THIS REMARKABLE CHILD CALLED ULTRA, CAME BACK TO EARTH WITH US. HIS POWER AND HIS FATE ARE IN MY HANDS NOW. HE IS UNDER MY PROTECTION.

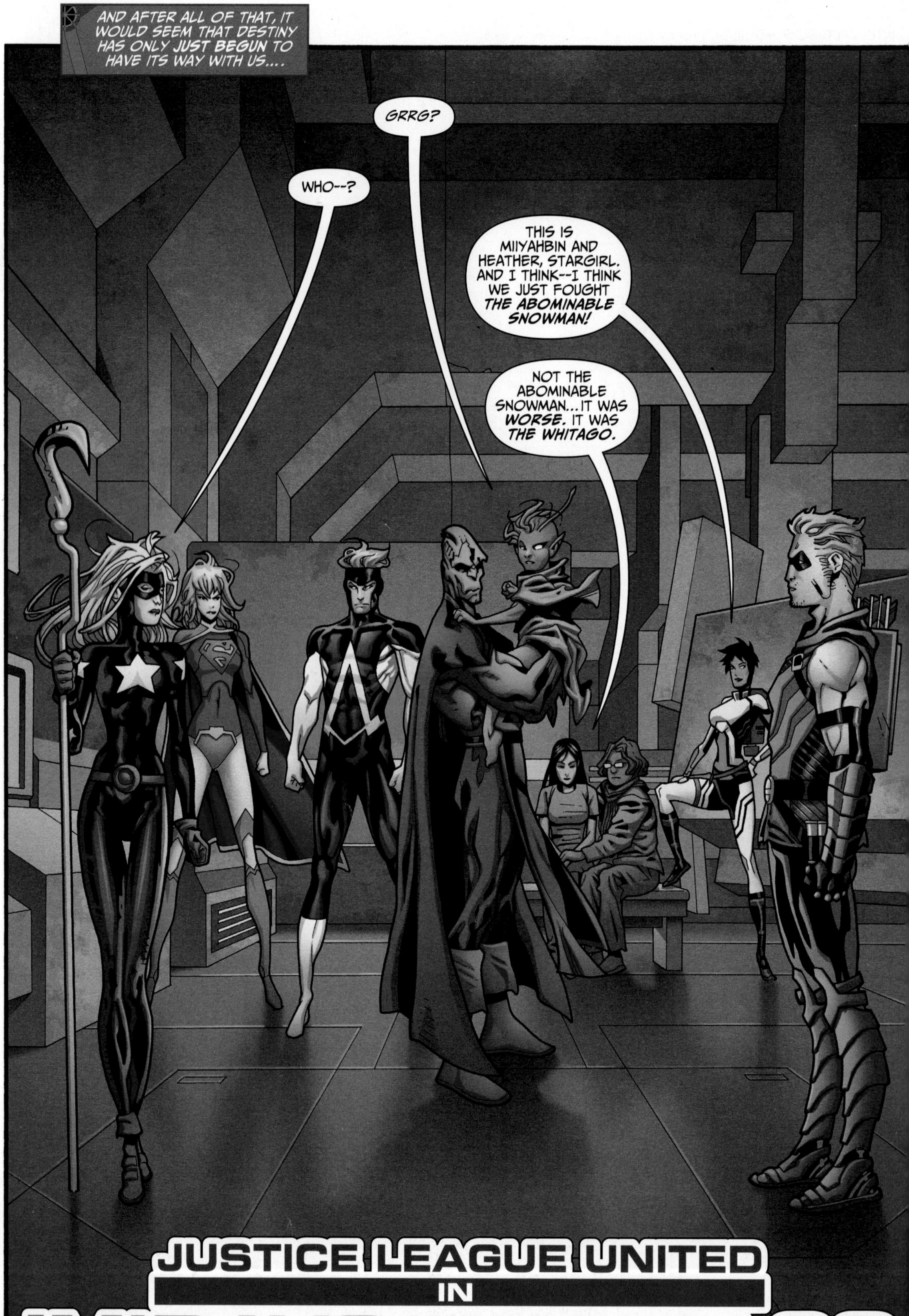
AND AFTER ALL OF THAT, IT WOULD SEEM THAT DESTINY HAS ONLY JUST BEGUN TO HAVE ITS WAY WITH US....
WHO--?
GRRG?
THIS IS MIIYAHBIN AND HEATHER, STARGIRL. AND I THINK--I THINK WE JUST FOUGHT THE ABOMINABLE SNOWMAN!
NOT THE ABOMINABLE SNOWMAN...IT WAS WORSE. IT WAS THE WHITAGO.
JUSTICE LEAGUE UNITED
IN
THE MIDAYO AND THE WHITAGO

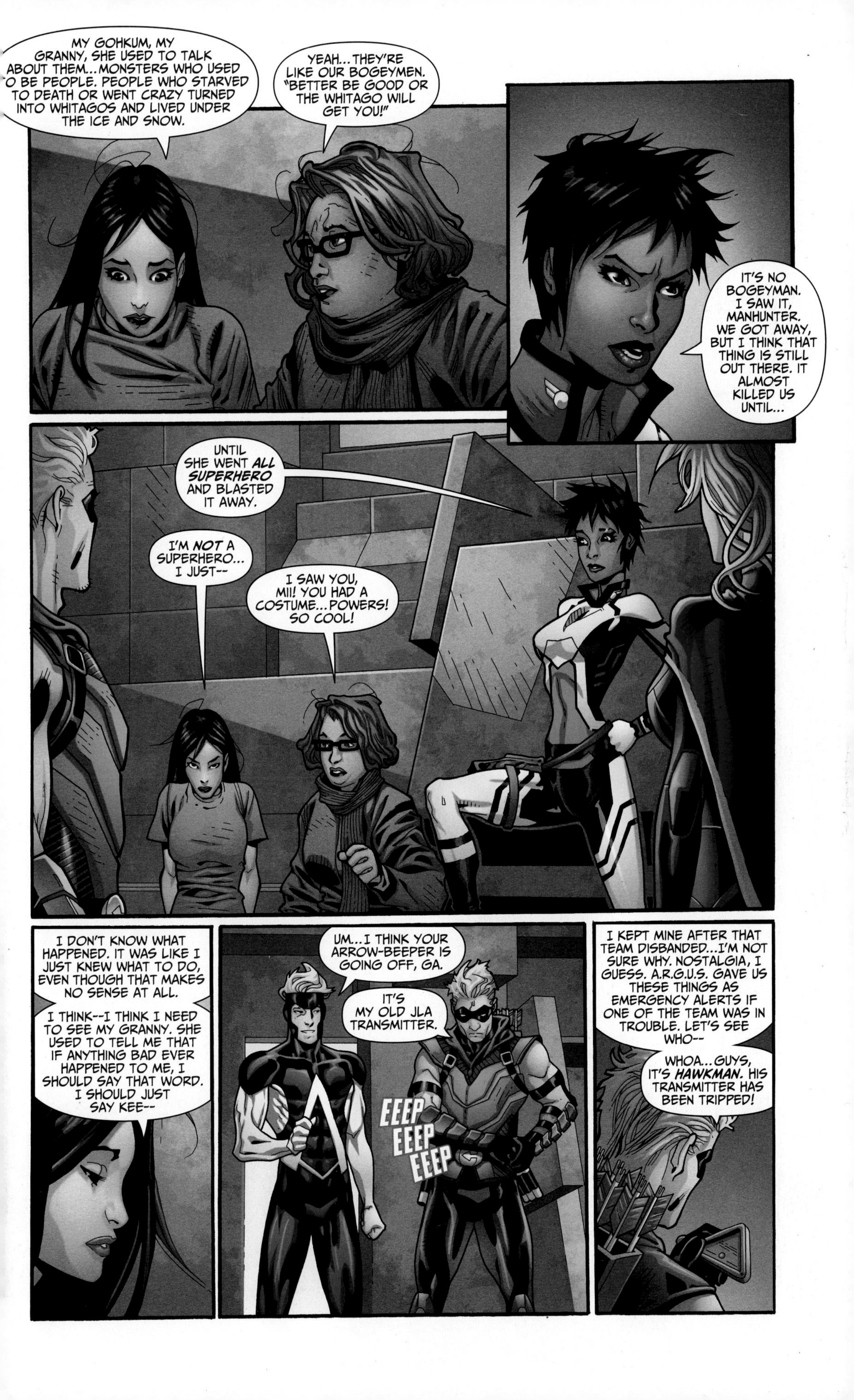
MY GOHKUM, MY GRANNY, SHE USED TO TALK ABOUT THEM... MONSTERS WHO USED TO BE PEOPLE. PEOPLE WHO STARVED TO DEATH OR WENT CRAZY TURNED INTO WHITAGOS AND LIVED UNDER THE ICE AND SNOW.
YEAH... THEY'RE LIKE OUR BOGEYMEN. "BETTER BE GOOD OR THE WHITAGO WILL GET YOU!"
IT'S NO BOGEYMAN. I SAW IT, MANHUNTER. WE GOT AWAY, BUT I THINK THAT THING IS STILL OUT THERE. IT ALMOST KILLED US UNTIL...
UNTIL SHE WENT ALL SUPERHERO AND BLASTED IT AWAY.
I'M NOT A SUPERHERO... I JUST--
I SAW YOU, MII! YOU HAD A COSTUME... POWERS! SO COOL!
I DON'T KNOW WHAT HAPPENED. IT WAS LIKE I JUST KNEW WHAT TO DO, EVEN THOUGH THAT MAKES NO SENSE AT ALL.
I THINK--I THINK I NEED TO SEE MY GRANNY. SHE USED TO TELL ME THAT IF ANYTHING BAD EVER HAPPENED TO ME, I SHOULD SAY THAT WORD. I SHOULD JUST SAY KEE--
UM... I THINK YOUR ARROW-BEEPER IS GOING OFF, GA.
IT'S MY OLD JLA TRANSMITTER.
EEEP EEEP EEEP
I KEPT MINE AFTER THAT TEAM DISBANDED... I'M NOT SURE WHY. NOSTALGIA, I GUESS. A.R.G.U.S. GAVE US THESE THINGS AS EMERGENCY ALERTS IF ONE OF THE TEAM WAS IN TROUBLE. LET'S SEE WHO--
WHOA... GUYS, IT'S HAWKMAN. HIS TRANSMITTER HAS BEEN TRIPPED!

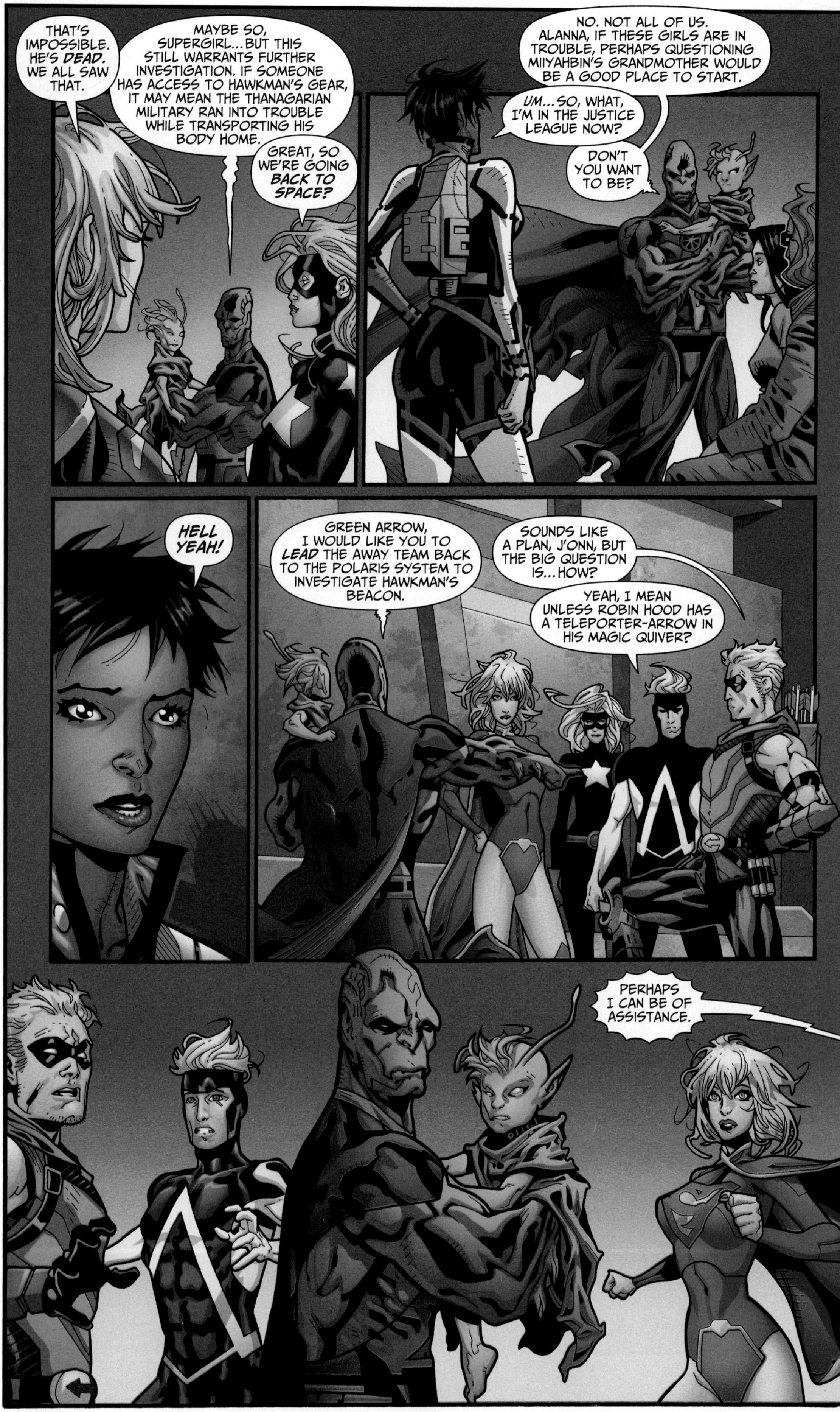
THAT'S IMPOSSIBLE. HE'S *DEAD.* WE ALL SAW THAT.
MAYBE SO, SUPERGIRL...BUT THIS STILL WARRANTS FURTHER INVESTIGATION. IF SOMEONE HAS ACCESS TO HAWKMAN'S GEAR, IT MAY MEAN THE THANAGARIAN MILITARY RAN INTO TROUBLE WHILE TRANSPORTING HIS BODY HOME.
GREAT, SO WE'RE GOING *BACK TO SPACE?*
NO. NOT ALL OF US. ALANNA, IF THESE GIRLS ARE IN TROUBLE, PERHAPS QUESTIONING MIIYAHBIN'S GRANDMOTHER WOULD BE A GOOD PLACE TO START.
UM... SO, WHAT, I'M IN THE JUSTICE LEAGUE NOW?
DON'T YOU WANT TO BE?
HELL YEAH!
GREEN ARROW, I WOULD LIKE YOU TO *LEAD* THE AWAY TEAM BACK TO THE POLARIS SYSTEM TO INVESTIGATE HAWKMAN'S BEACON.
SOUNDS LIKE A PLAN, J'ONN, BUT THE BIG QUESTION IS...HOW?
YEAH, I MEAN UNLESS ROBIN HOOD HAS A TELEPORTER-ARROW IN HIS MAGIC QUIVER?
PERHAPS I CAN BE OF ASSISTANCE.

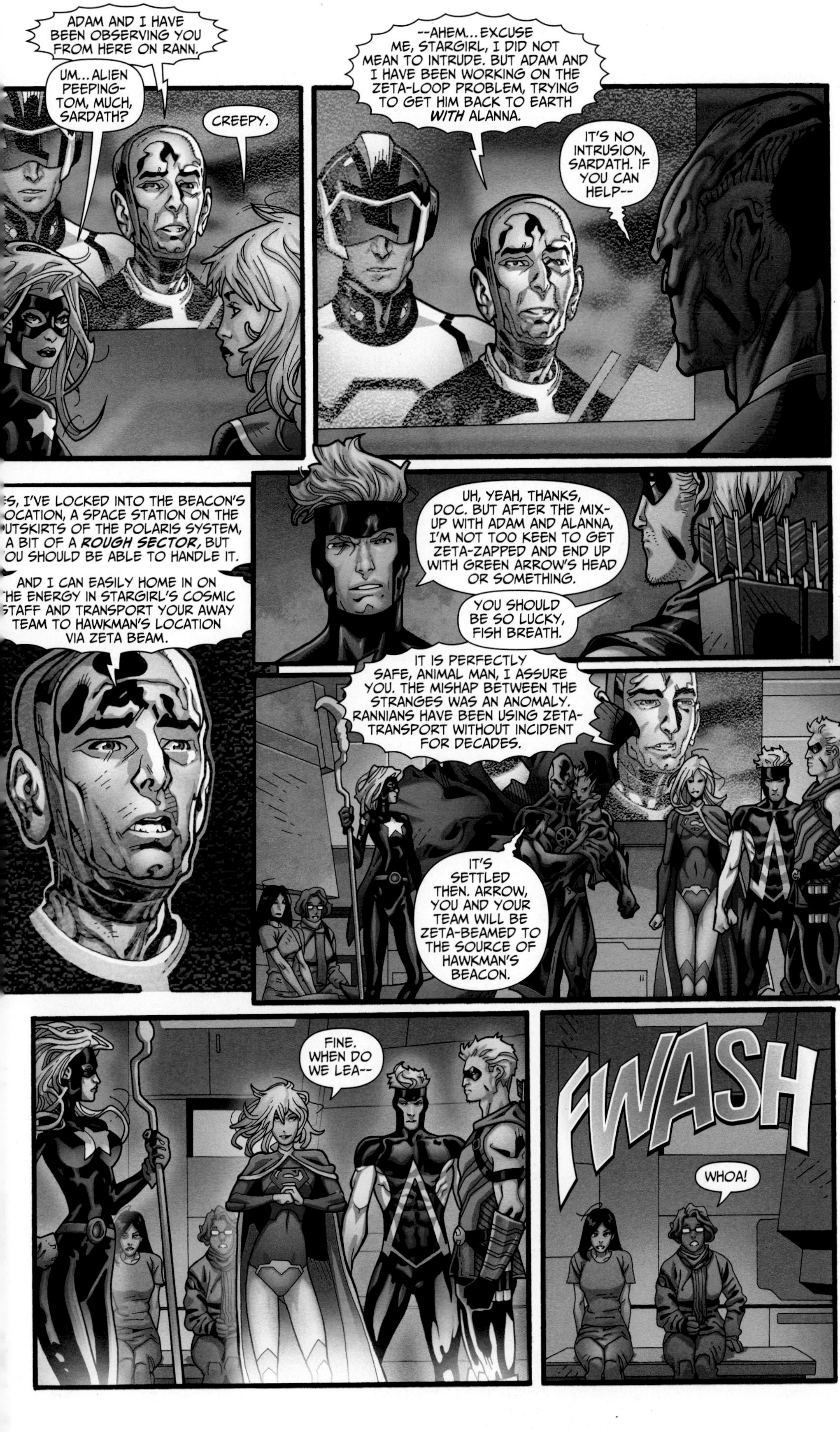
ADAM AND I HAVE BEEN OBSERVING YOU FROM HERE ON RANN.
UM...ALIEN PEEPING-TOM, MUCH, SARDATH?
CREEPY.
--AHEM...EXCUSE ME, STARGIRL, I DID NOT MEAN TO INTRUDE. BUT ADAM AND I HAVE BEEN WORKING ON THE ZETA-LOOP PROBLEM, TRYING TO GET HIM BACK TO EARTH WITH ALANNA.
IT'S NO INTRUSION, SARDATH. IF YOU CAN HELP--
S, I'VE LOCKED INTO THE BEACON'S OCATION, A SPACE STATION ON THE UTSKIRTS OF THE POLARIS SYSTEM, A BIT OF A ROUGH SECTOR, BUT OU SHOULD BE ABLE TO HANDLE IT.
AND I CAN EASILY HOME IN ON HE ENERGY IN STARGIRL'S COSMIC STAFF AND TRANSPORT YOUR AWAY TEAM TO HAWKMAN'S LOCATION VIA ZETA BEAM.
UH, YEAH, THANKS, DOC. BUT AFTER THE MIX-UP WITH ADAM AND ALANNA, I'M NOT TOO KEEN TO GET ZETA-ZAPPED AND END UP WITH GREEN ARROW'S HEAD OR SOMETHING.
YOU SHOULD BE SO LUCKY, FISH BREATH.
IT IS PERFECTLY SAFE, ANIMAL MAN, I ASSURE YOU. THE MISHAP BETWEEN THE STRANGES WAS AN ANOMALY. RANNIANS HAVE BEEN USING ZETA-TRANSPORT WITHOUT INCIDENT FOR DECADES.
IT'S SETTLED THEN. ARROW, YOU AND YOUR TEAM WILL BE ZETA-BEAMED TO THE SOURCE OF HAWKMAN'S BEACON.
FINE. WHEN DO WE LEA--
FWASH
WHOA!

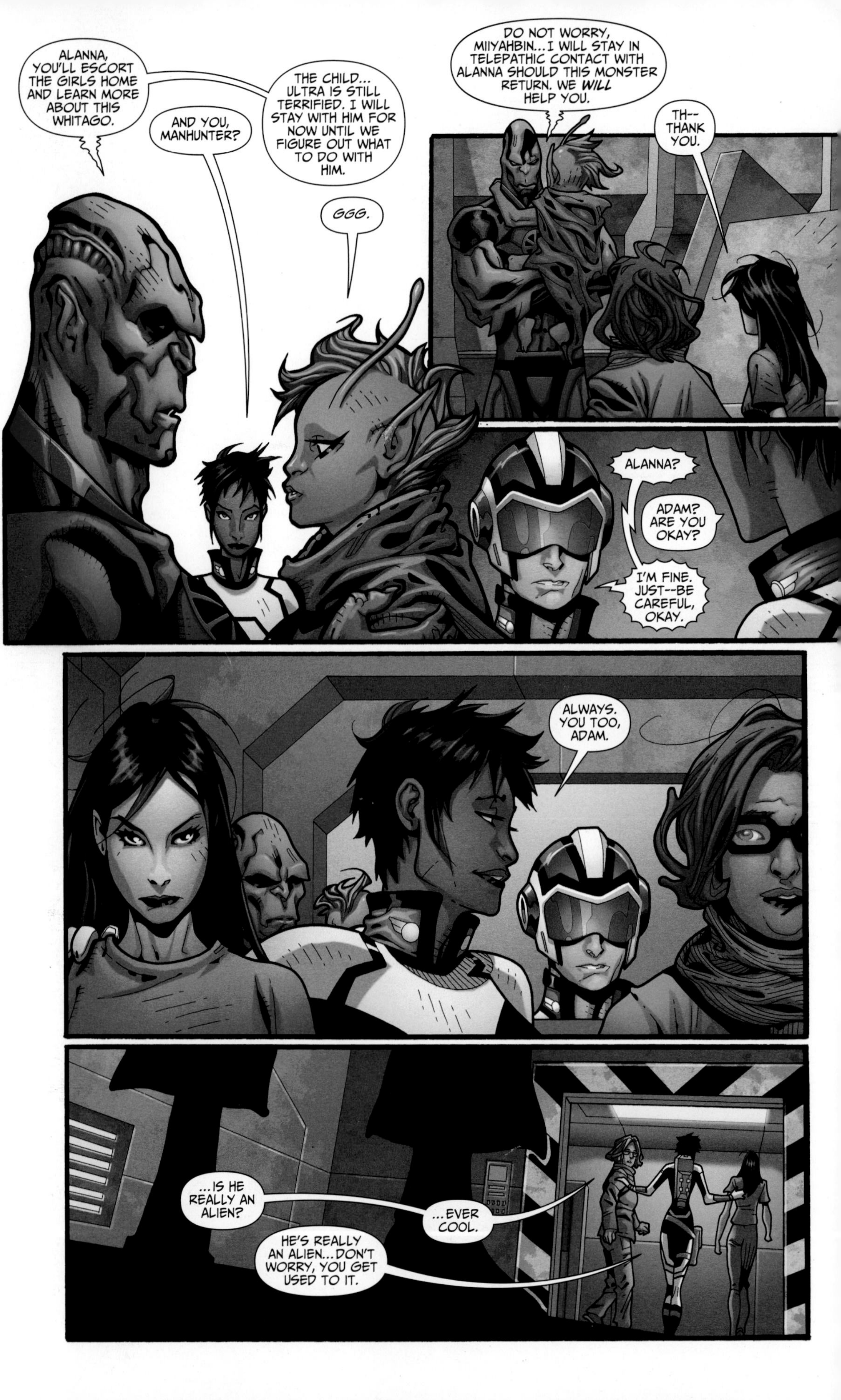
ALANNA, YOU'LL ESCORT THE GIRLS HOME AND LEARN MORE ABOUT THIS WHITAGO.
AND YOU, MANHUNTER?
THE CHILD... ULTRA IS STILL TERRIFIED. I WILL STAY WITH HIM FOR NOW UNTIL WE FIGURE OUT WHAT TO DO WITH HIM.
GGG.
DO NOT WORRY, MIIYAHBIN... I WILL STAY IN TELEPATHIC CONTACT WITH ALANNA SHOULD THIS MONSTER RETURN. WE *WILL* HELP YOU.
TH--THANK YOU.
ALANNA?
ADAM? ARE YOU OKAY?
I'M FINE. JUST--BE CAREFUL, OKAY.
ALWAYS. YOU TOO, ADAM.
...IS HE REALLY AN ALIEN?
...EVER COOL.
HE'S REALLY AN ALIEN...DON'T WORRY, YOU GET USED TO IT.

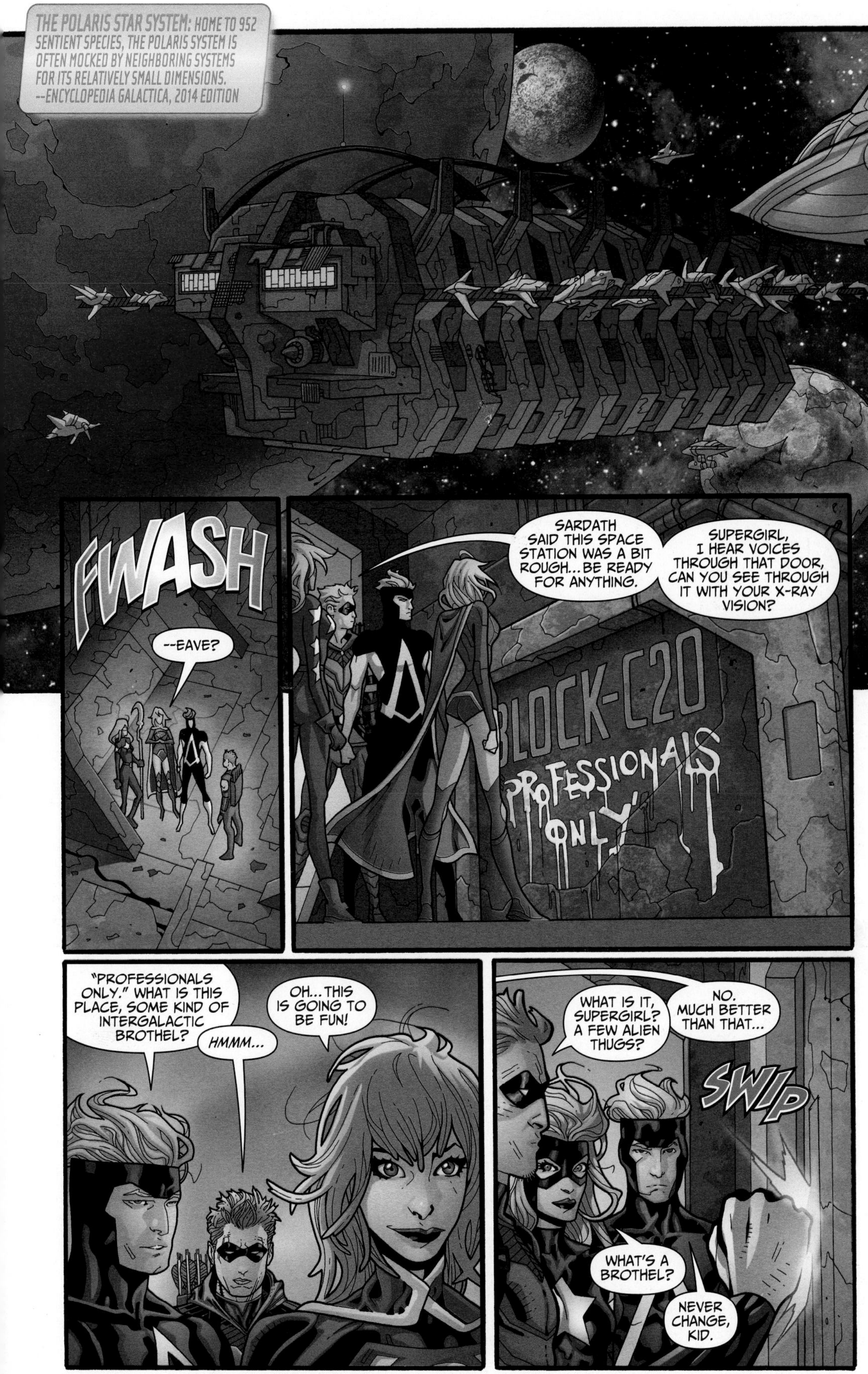
THE POLARIS STAR SYSTEM: HOME TO 952 SENTIENT SPECIES, THE POLARIS SYSTEM IS OFTEN MOCKED BY NEIGHBORING SYSTEMS FOR ITS RELATIVELY SMALL DIMENSIONS. --ENCYCLOPEDIA GALACTICA, 2014 EDITION
FWASH
--EAVE?
SARDATH SAID THIS SPACE STATION WAS A BIT ROUGH...BE READY FOR ANYTHING.
SUPERGIRL, I HEAR VOICES THROUGH THAT DOOR, CAN YOU SEE THROUGH IT WITH YOUR X-RAY VISION?
BLOCK-C20
PROFESSIONALS ONLY
"PROFESSIONALS ONLY." WHAT IS THIS PLACE, SOME KIND OF INTERGALACTIC BROTHEL?
HMMM...
OH...THIS IS GOING TO BE FUN!
WHAT IS IT, SUPERGIRL? A FEW ALIEN THUGS?
NO. MUCH BETTER THAN THAT...
SWIP
WHAT'S A BROTHEL?
NEVER CHANGE, KID.

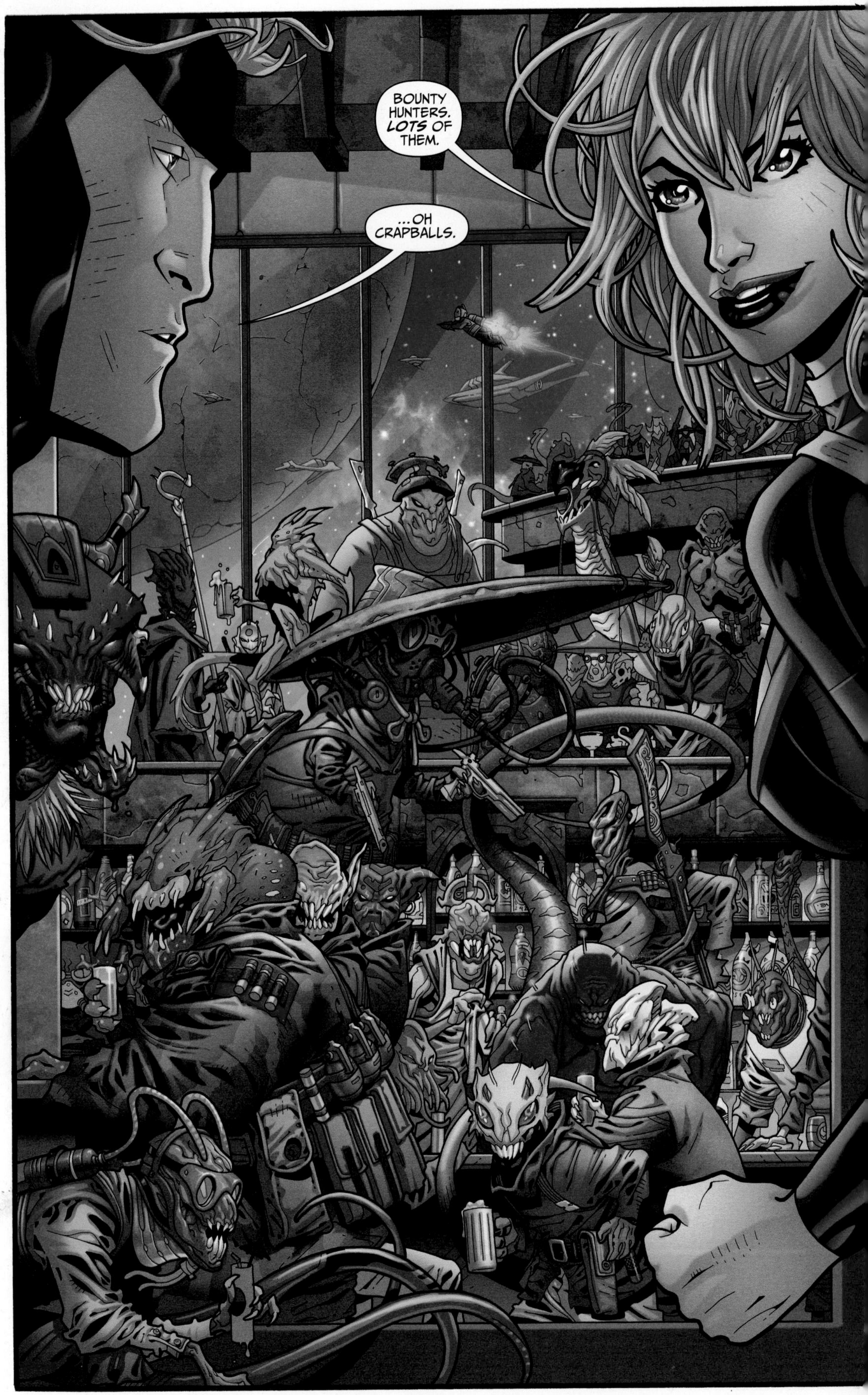
BOUNTY HUNTERS. LOTS OF THEM.
...OH CRAPBALLS.

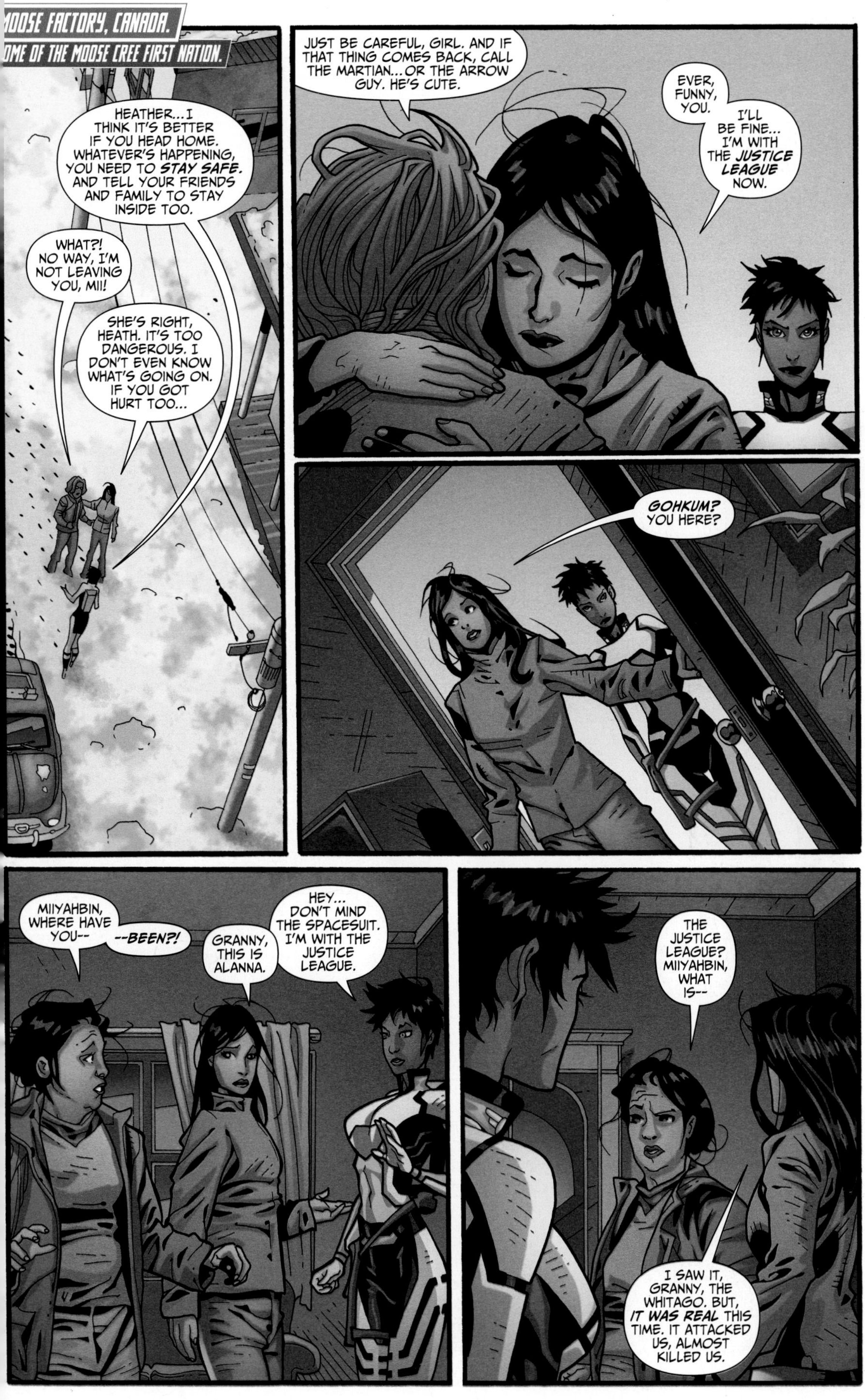
MOOSE FACTORY, CANADA.
OME OF THE MOOSE CREE FIRST NATION.
HEATHER... I THINK IT'S BETTER IF YOU HEAD HOME. WHATEVER'S HAPPENING, YOU NEED TO STAY SAFE. AND TELL YOUR FRIENDS AND FAMILY TO STAY INSIDE TOO.
WHAT?! NO WAY, I'M NOT LEAVING YOU, MII!
SHE'S RIGHT, HEATH. IT'S TOO DANGEROUS. I DON'T EVEN KNOW WHAT'S GOING ON. IF YOU GOT HURT TOO...
JUST BE CAREFUL, GIRL. AND IF THAT THING COMES BACK, CALL THE MARTIAN... OR THE ARROW GUY. HE'S CUTE.
EVER, FUNNY, YOU.
I'LL BE FINE... I'M WITH THE JUSTICE LEAGUE NOW.
GOHKUM? YOU HERE?
MIIYAHBIN, WHERE HAVE YOU--
--BEEN?!
GRANNY, THIS IS ALANNA.
HEY... DON'T MIND THE SPACESUIT. I'M WITH THE JUSTICE LEAGUE.
THE JUSTICE LEAGUE? MIIYAHBIN, WHAT IS--
I SAW IT, GRANNY, THE WHITAGO. BUT, IT WAS REAL THIS TIME. IT ATTACKED US, ALMOST KILLED US.

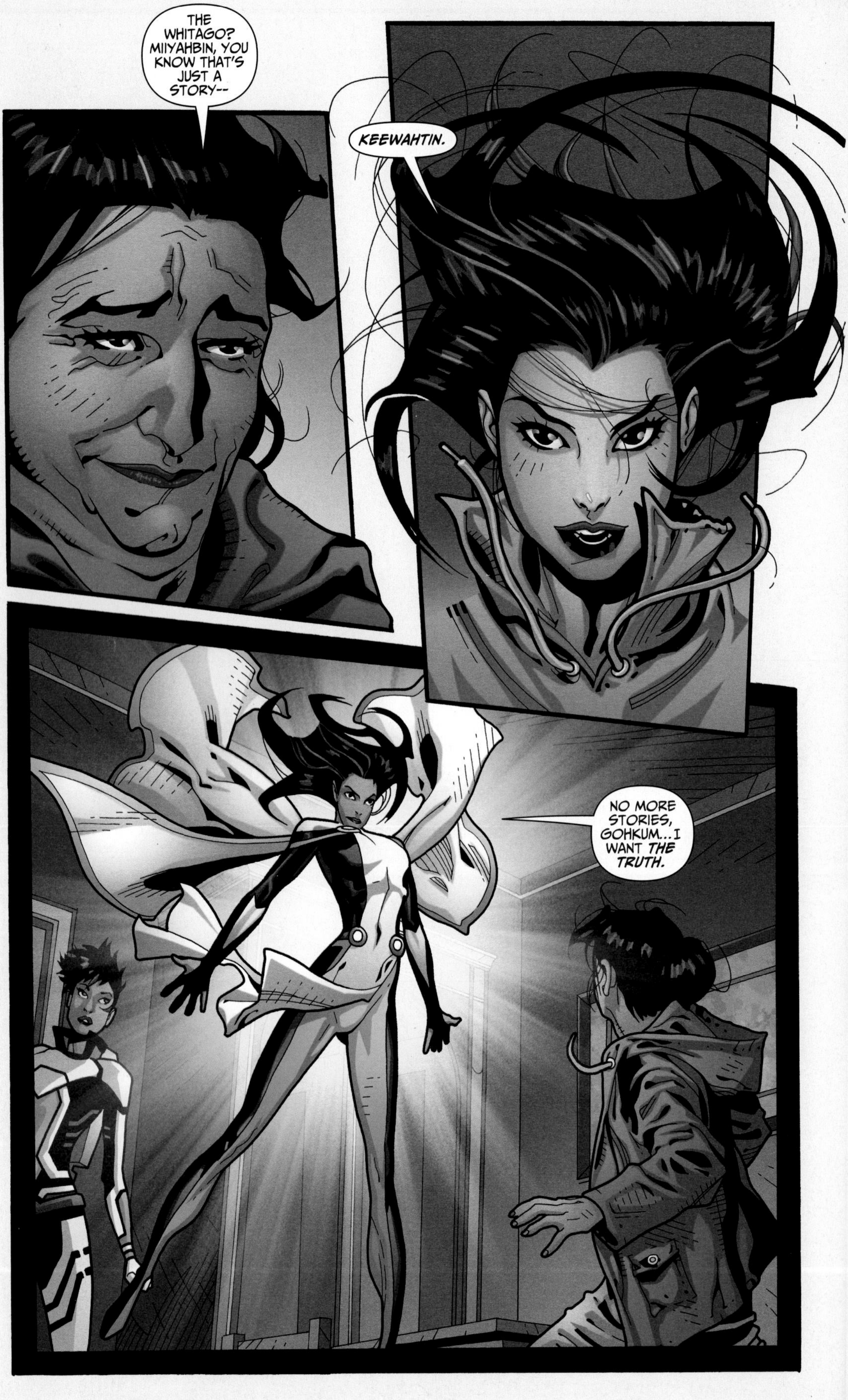
THE WHITAGO? MIIYAHBIN, YOU KNOW THAT'S JUST A STORY--
KEEWAHTIN.
NO MORE STORIES, GOHKUM...I WANT THE TRUTH.

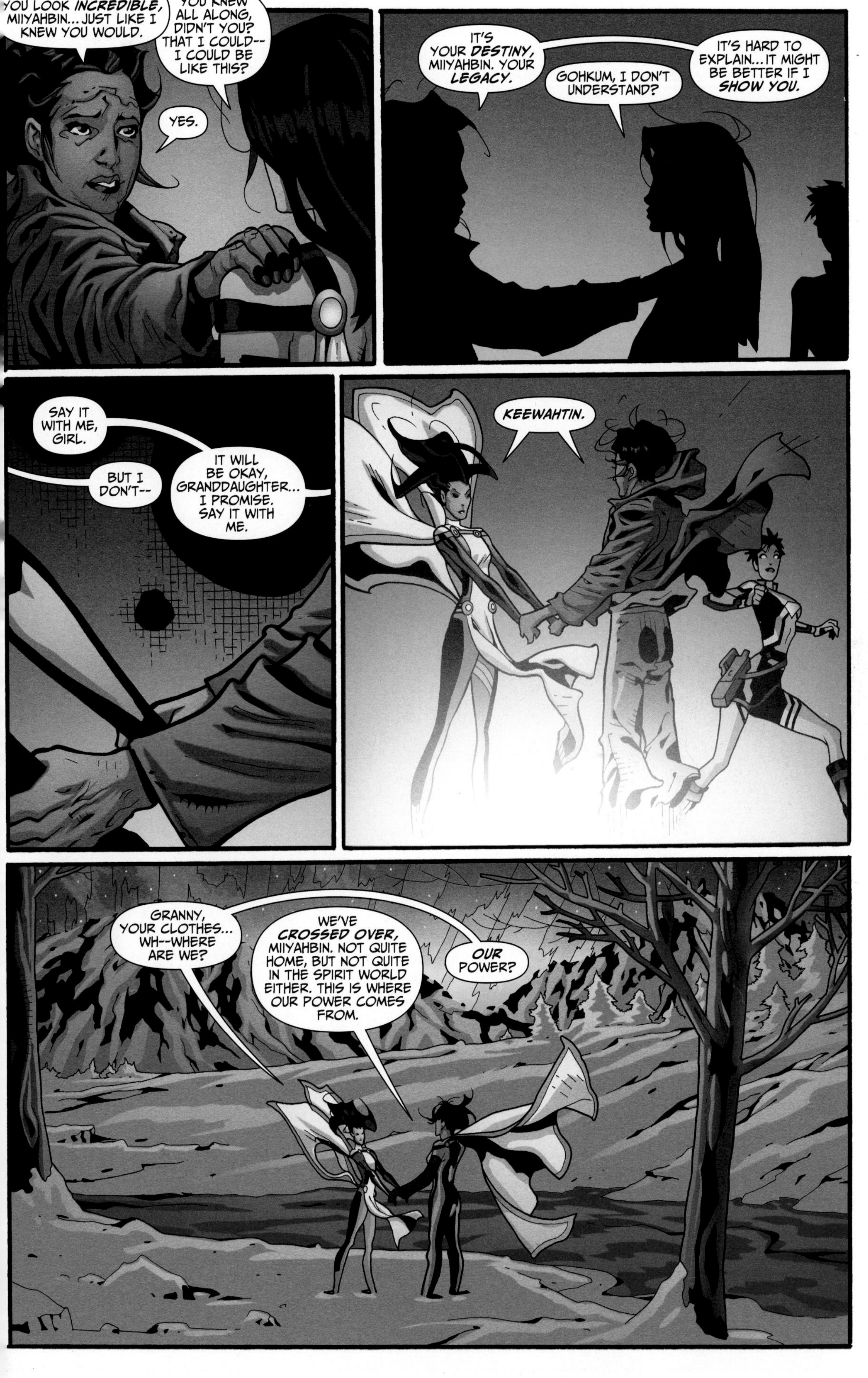
SO, IT'S HAPPENED. YOU LOOK INCREDIBLE, MIIYAHBIN... JUST LIKE I KNEW YOU WOULD.
YOU KNEW ALL ALONG, DIDN'T YOU? THAT I COULD-- I COULD BE LIKE THIS?
YES.
IT'S YOUR DESTINY, MIIYAHBIN. YOUR LEGACY.
GOHKUM, I DON'T UNDERSTAND?
IT'S HARD TO EXPLAIN... IT MIGHT BE BETTER IF I SHOW YOU.
SAY IT WITH ME, GIRL.
BUT I DON'T--
IT WILL BE OKAY, GRANDDAUGHTER... I PROMISE. SAY IT WITH ME.
KEEWAHTIN.
GRANNY, YOUR CLOTHES... WH--WHERE ARE WE?
WE'VE CROSSED OVER, MIIYAHBIN. NOT QUITE HOME, BUT NOT QUITE IN THE SPIRIT WORLD EITHER. THIS IS WHERE OUR POWER COMES FROM.
OUR POWER?

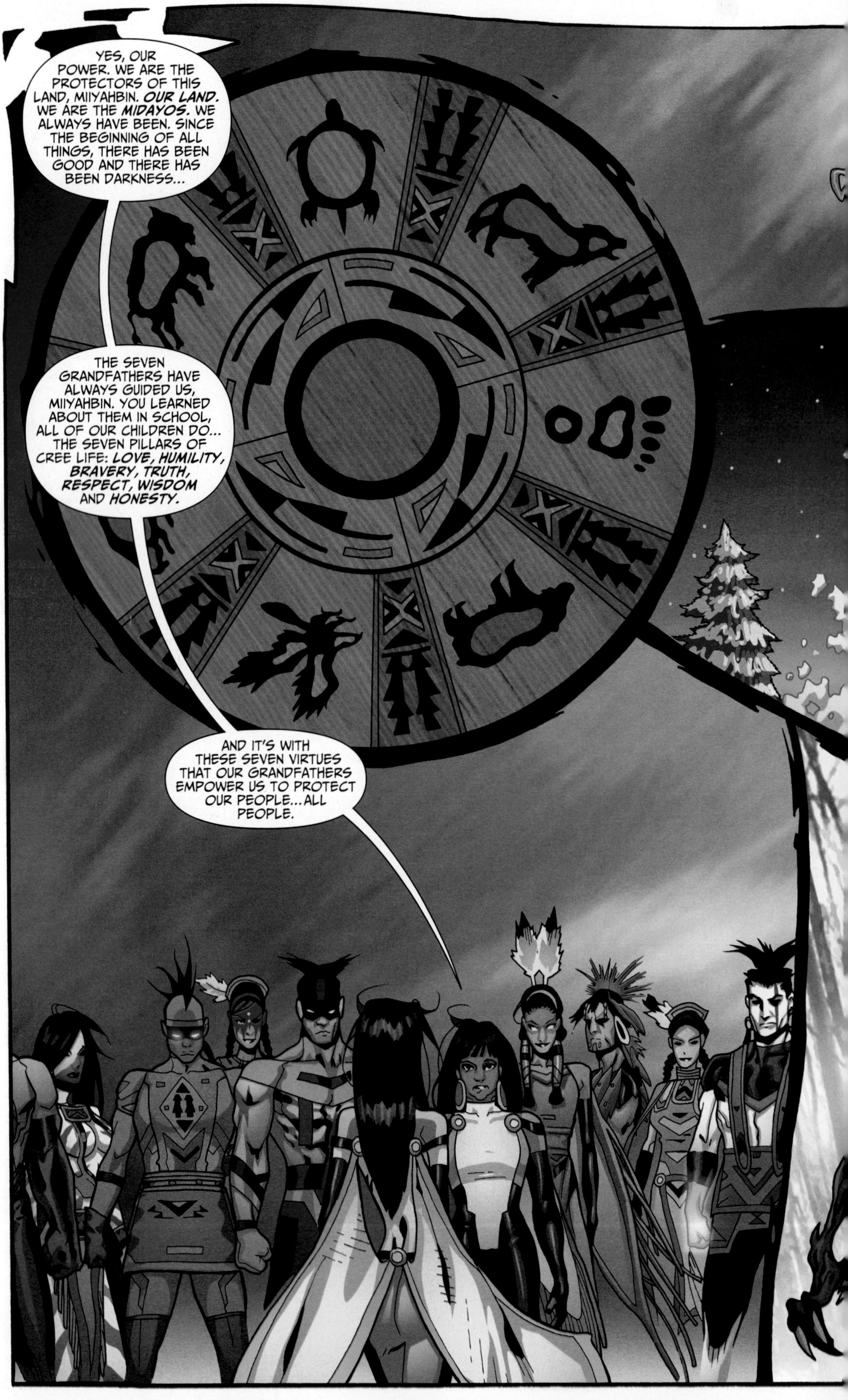
YES, OUR POWER. WE ARE THE PROTECTORS OF THIS LAND, MIIYAHBIN. *OUR LAND.* WE ARE THE *MIDAYOS.* WE ALWAYS HAVE BEEN. SINCE THE BEGINNING OF ALL THINGS, THERE HAS BEEN GOOD AND THERE HAS BEEN DARKNESS...
THE SEVEN GRANDFATHERS HAVE ALWAYS GUIDED US, MIIYAHBIN. YOU LEARNED ABOUT THEM IN SCHOOL, ALL OF OUR CHILDREN DO... THE SEVEN PILLARS OF CREE LIFE: *LOVE, HUMILITY, BRAVERY, TRUTH, RESPECT, WISDOM* AND *HONESTY.*
AND IT'S WITH THESE SEVEN VIRTUES THAT OUR GRANDFATHERS EMPOWER US TO PROTECT OUR PEOPLE...ALL PEOPLE.

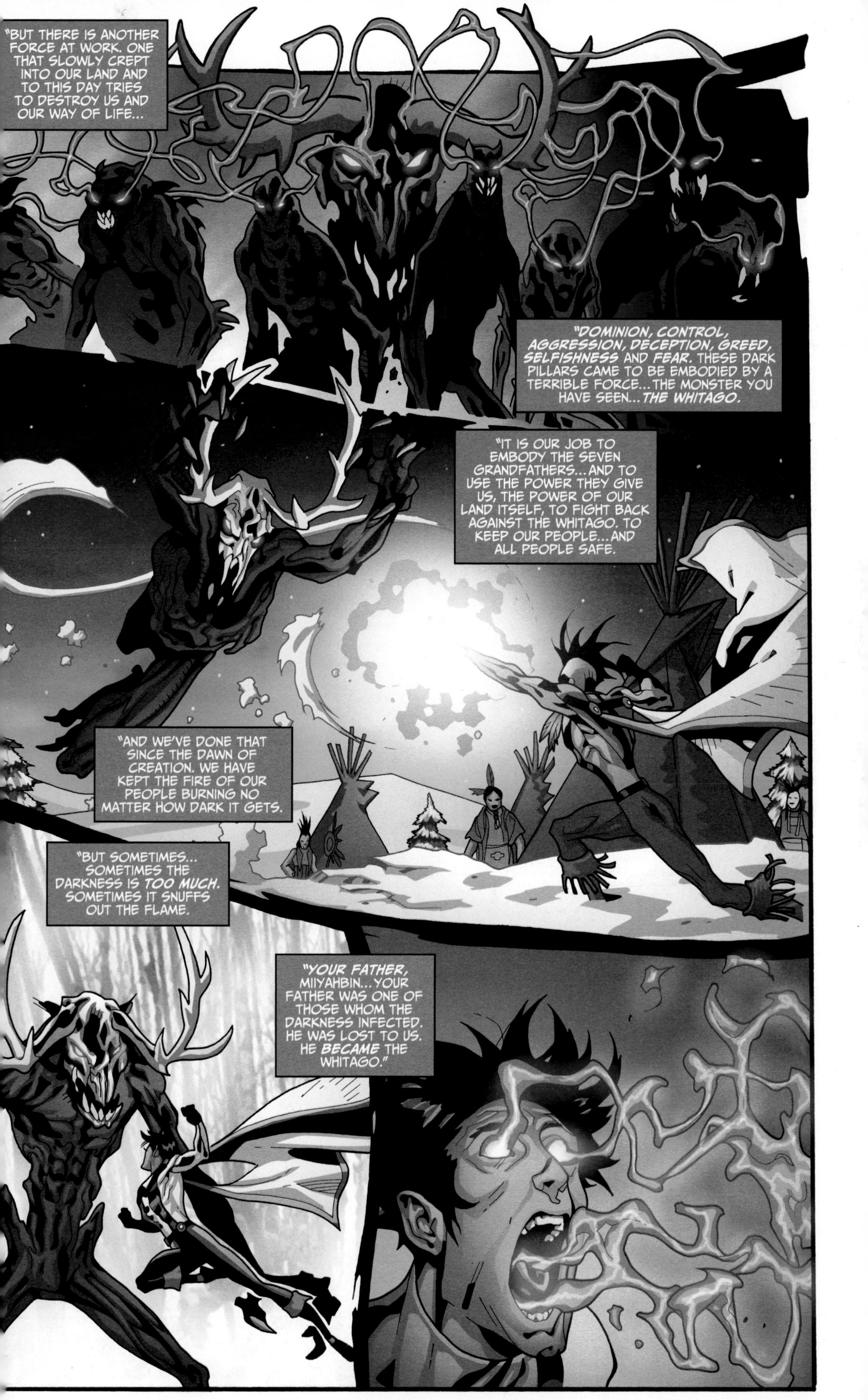
"BUT THERE IS ANOTHER FORCE AT WORK. ONE THAT SLOWLY CREPT INTO OUR LAND AND TO THIS DAY TRIES TO DESTROY US AND OUR WAY OF LIFE...
"DOMINION, CONTROL, AGGRESSION, DECEPTION, GREED, SELFISHNESS AND FEAR. THESE DARK PILLARS CAME TO BE EMBODIED BY A TERRIBLE FORCE...THE MONSTER YOU HAVE SEEN...THE WHITAGO.
"IT IS OUR JOB TO EMBODY THE SEVEN GRANDFATHERS...AND TO USE THE POWER THEY GIVE US, THE POWER OF OUR LAND ITSELF, TO FIGHT BACK AGAINST THE WHITAGO. TO KEEP OUR PEOPLE...AND ALL PEOPLE SAFE.
"AND WE'VE DONE THAT SINCE THE DAWN OF CREATION. WE HAVE KEPT THE FIRE OF OUR PEOPLE BURNING NO MATTER HOW DARK IT GETS.
"BUT SOMETIMES... SOMETIMES THE DARKNESS IS TOO MUCH. SOMETIMES IT SNUFFS OUT THE FLAME.
"YOUR FATHER, MIIYAHBIN...YOUR FATHER WAS ONE OF THOSE WHOM THE DARKNESS INFECTED. HE WAS LOST TO US. HE BECAME THE WHITAGO."

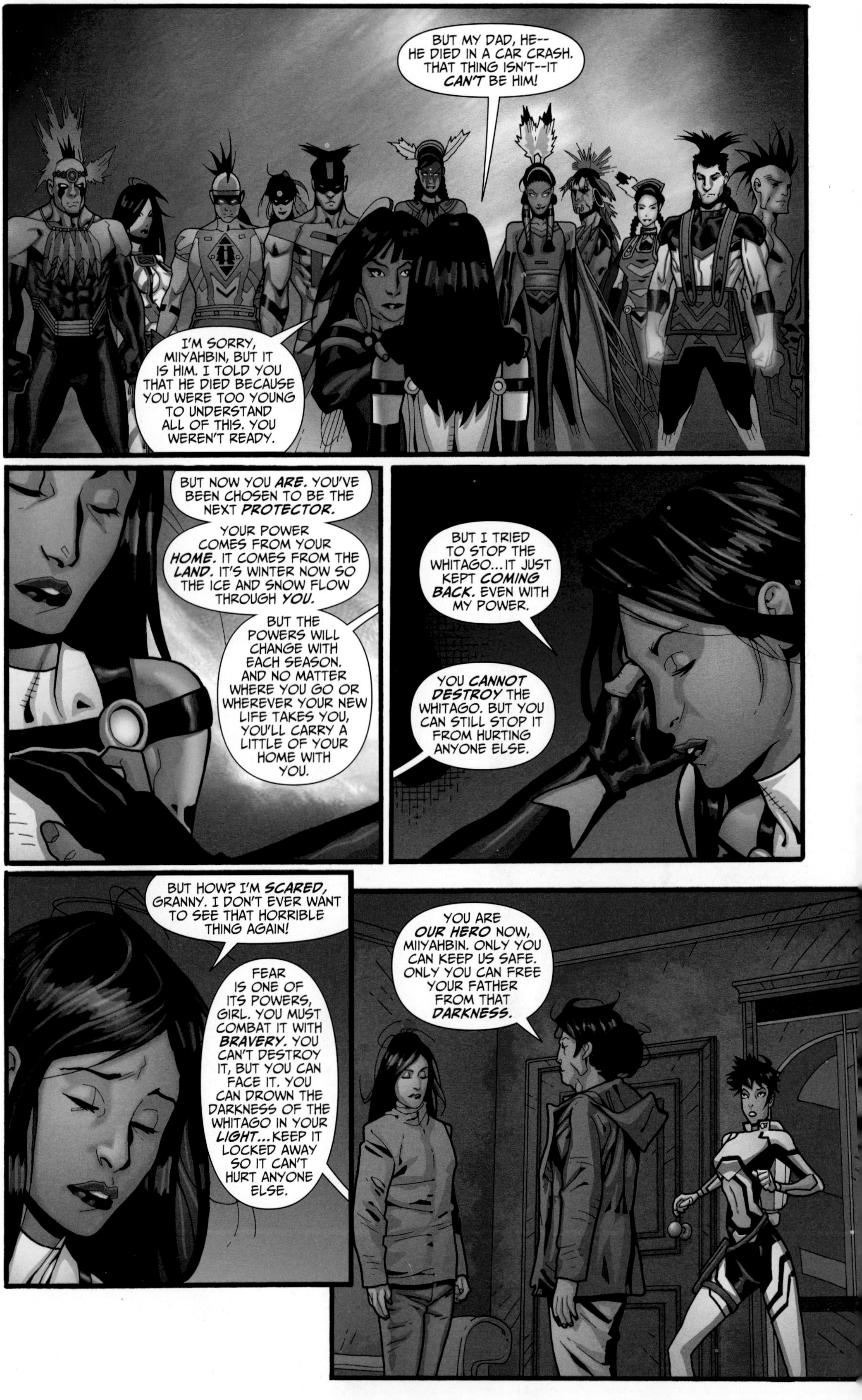
BUT MY DAD, HE-- HE DIED IN A CAR CRASH. THAT THING ISN'T--IT CAN'T BE HIM!
I'M SORRY, MIIYAHBIN, BUT IT IS HIM. I TOLD YOU THAT HE DIED BECAUSE YOU WERE TOO YOUNG TO UNDERSTAND ALL OF THIS. YOU WEREN'T READY.
BUT NOW YOU ARE. YOU'VE BEEN CHOSEN TO BE THE NEXT PROTECTOR.
YOUR POWER COMES FROM YOUR HOME. IT COMES FROM THE LAND. IT'S WINTER NOW SO THE ICE AND SNOW FLOW THROUGH YOU.
BUT THE POWERS WILL CHANGE WITH EACH SEASON. AND NO MATTER WHERE YOU GO OR WHEREVER YOUR NEW LIFE TAKES YOU, YOU'LL CARRY A LITTLE OF YOUR HOME WITH YOU.
BUT I TRIED TO STOP THE WHITAGO... IT JUST KEPT COMING BACK. EVEN WITH MY POWER.
YOU CANNOT DESTROY THE WHITAGO. BUT YOU CAN STILL STOP IT FROM HURTING ANYONE ELSE.
BUT HOW? I'M SCARED, GRANNY. I DON'T EVER WANT TO SEE THAT HORRIBLE THING AGAIN!
FEAR IS ONE OF ITS POWERS, GIRL. YOU MUST COMBAT IT WITH BRAVERY. YOU CAN'T DESTROY IT, BUT YOU CAN FACE IT. YOU CAN DROWN THE DARKNESS OF THE WHITAGO IN YOUR LIGHT... KEEP IT LOCKED AWAY SO IT CAN'T HURT ANYONE ELSE.
YOU ARE OUR HERO NOW, MIIYAHBIN. ONLY YOU CAN KEEP US SAFE. ONLY YOU CAN FREE YOUR FATHER FROM THAT DARKNESS.

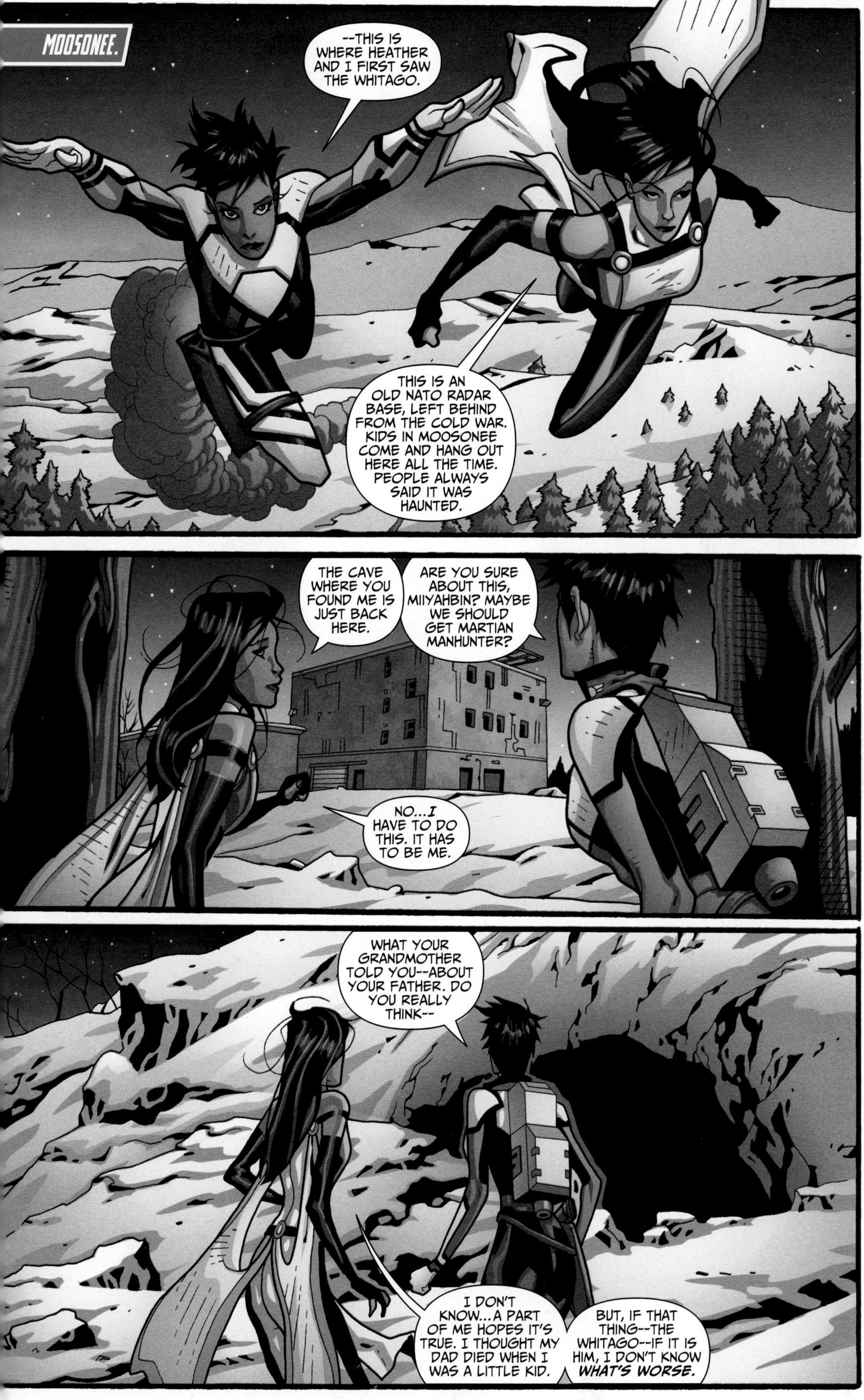
MOOSONEE.
--THIS IS WHERE HEATHER AND I FIRST SAW THE WHITAGO.
THIS IS AN OLD NATO RADAR BASE, LEFT BEHIND FROM THE COLD WAR. KIDS IN MOOSONEE COME AND HANG OUT HERE ALL THE TIME. PEOPLE ALWAYS SAID IT WAS HAUNTED.
THE CAVE WHERE YOU FOUND ME IS JUST BACK HERE.
ARE YOU SURE ABOUT THIS, MIIYAHBIN? MAYBE WE SHOULD GET MARTIAN MANHUNTER?
NO...*I* HAVE TO DO THIS. IT HAS TO BE ME.
WHAT YOUR GRANDMOTHER TOLD YOU--ABOUT YOUR FATHER. DO YOU REALLY THINK--
I DON'T KNOW...A PART OF ME HOPES IT'S TRUE. I THOUGHT MY DAD DIED WHEN I WAS A LITTLE KID.
BUT, IF THAT THING--THE WHITAGO--IF IT IS HIM, I DON'T KNOW ***WHAT'S WORSE.***

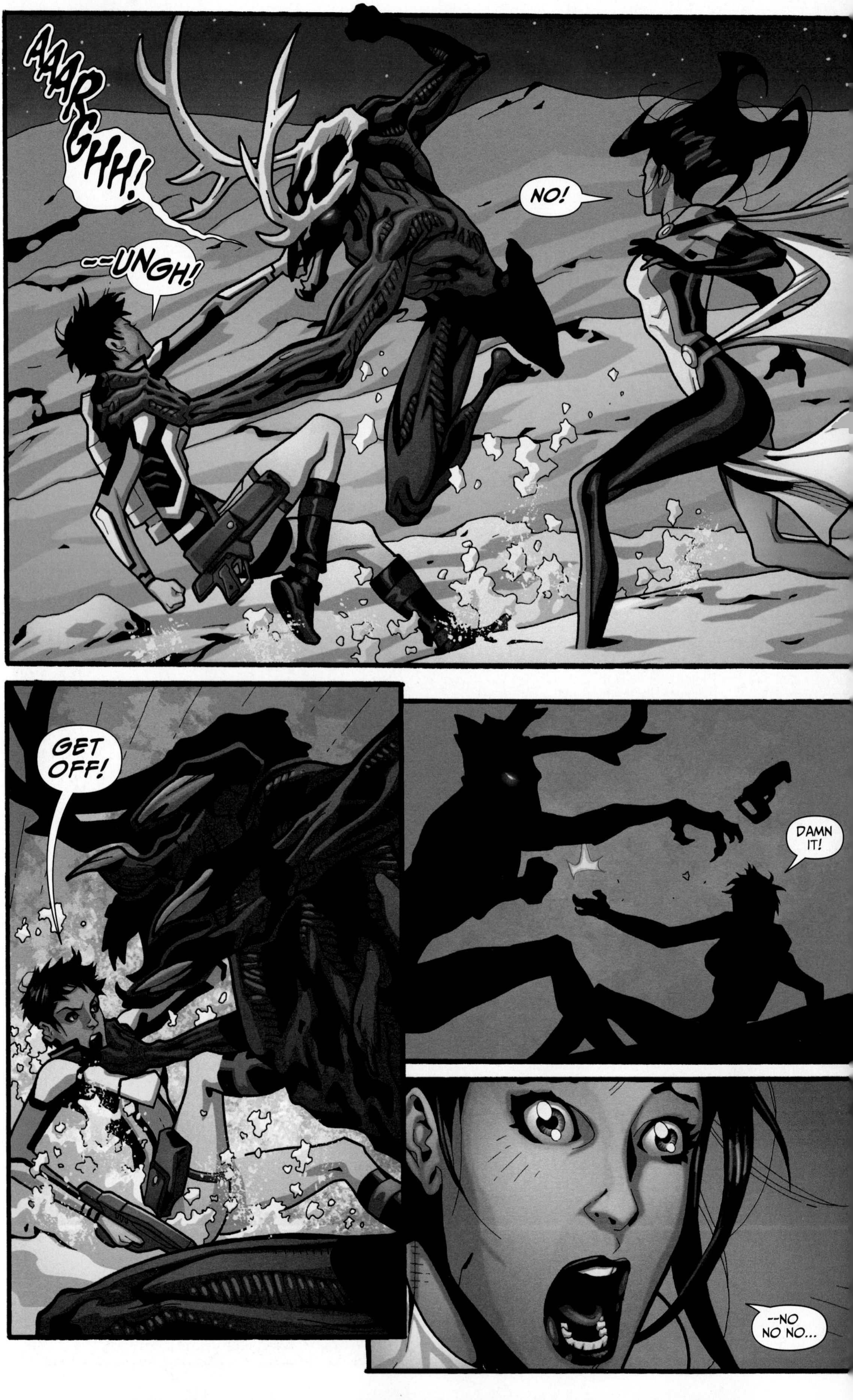
AAARGHH!
--UNGH!
NO!
GET OFF!
DAMN IT!
--NO NO NO...

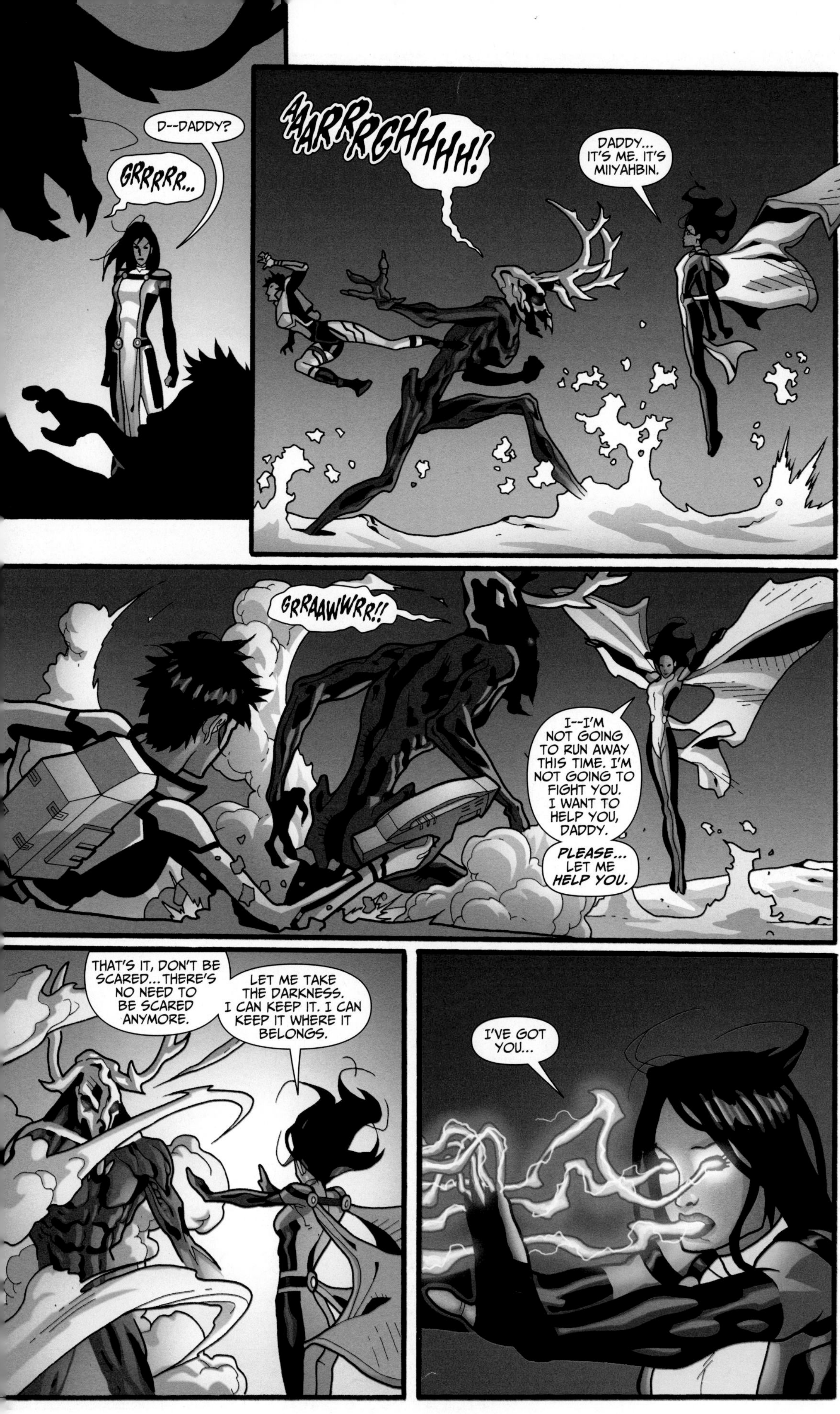
D--DADDY?
GRRRRR...
AAARRRRGHHHHH!
DADDY... IT'S ME. IT'S MIIYAHBIN.
GRRAAWRR!!
I--I'M NOT GOING TO RUN AWAY THIS TIME. I'M NOT GOING TO FIGHT YOU. I WANT TO HELP YOU, DADDY.
PLEASE... LET ME HELP YOU.
THAT'S IT, DON'T BE SCARED...THERE'S NO NEED TO BE SCARED ANYMORE.
LET ME TAKE THE DARKNESS. I CAN KEEP IT. I CAN KEEP IT WHERE IT BELONGS.
I'VE GOT YOU...

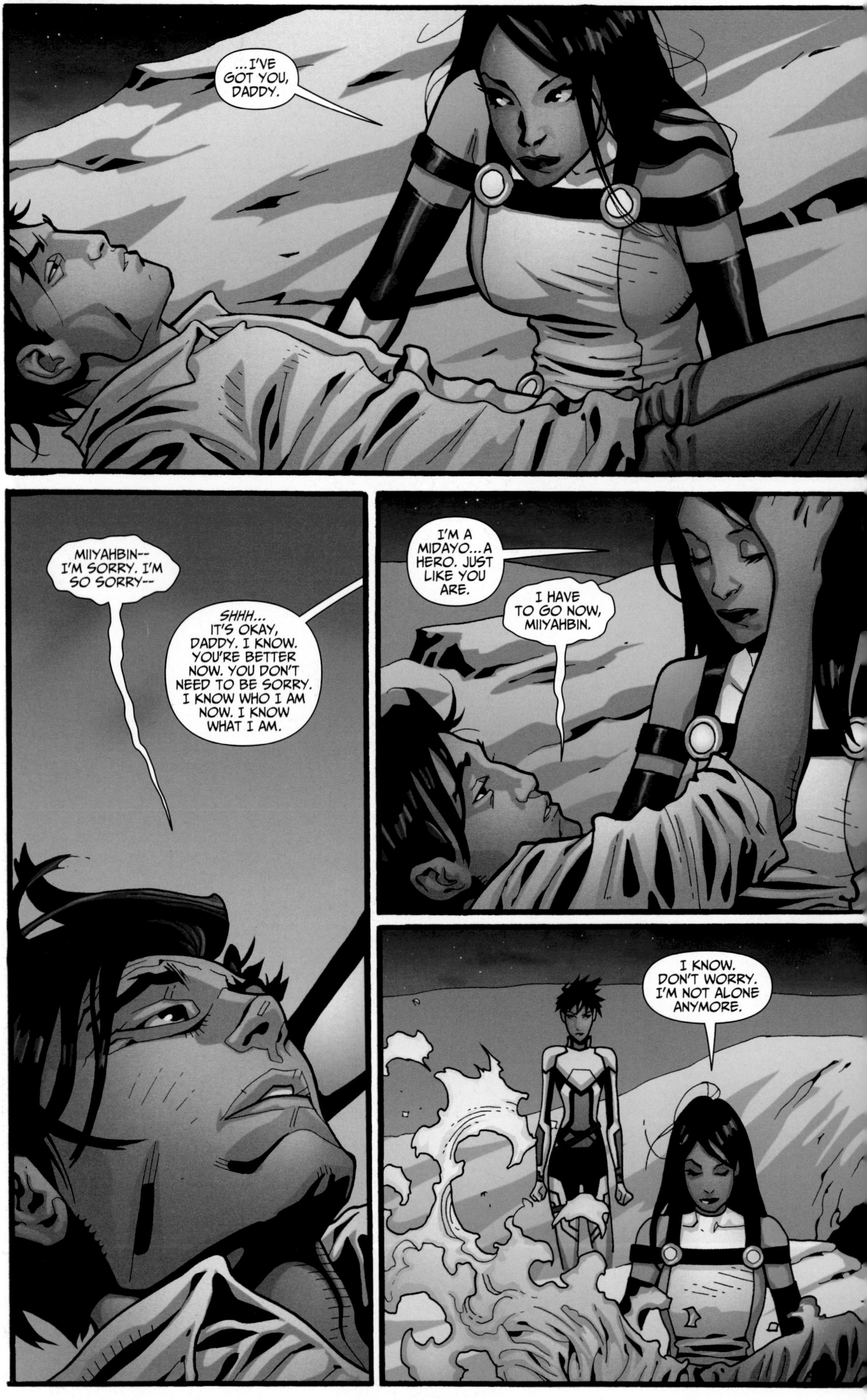
...I'VE GOT YOU, DADDY.
MIIYAHBIN-- I'M SORRY. I'M SO SORRY--
SHHH... IT'S OKAY, DADDY. I KNOW. YOU'RE BETTER NOW. YOU DON'T NEED TO BE SORRY. I KNOW WHO I AM NOW. I KNOW WHAT I AM.
I'M A MIDAYO...A HERO. JUST LIKE YOU ARE.
I HAVE TO GO NOW, MIIYAHBIN.
I KNOW. DON'T WORRY. I'M NOT ALONE ANYMORE.

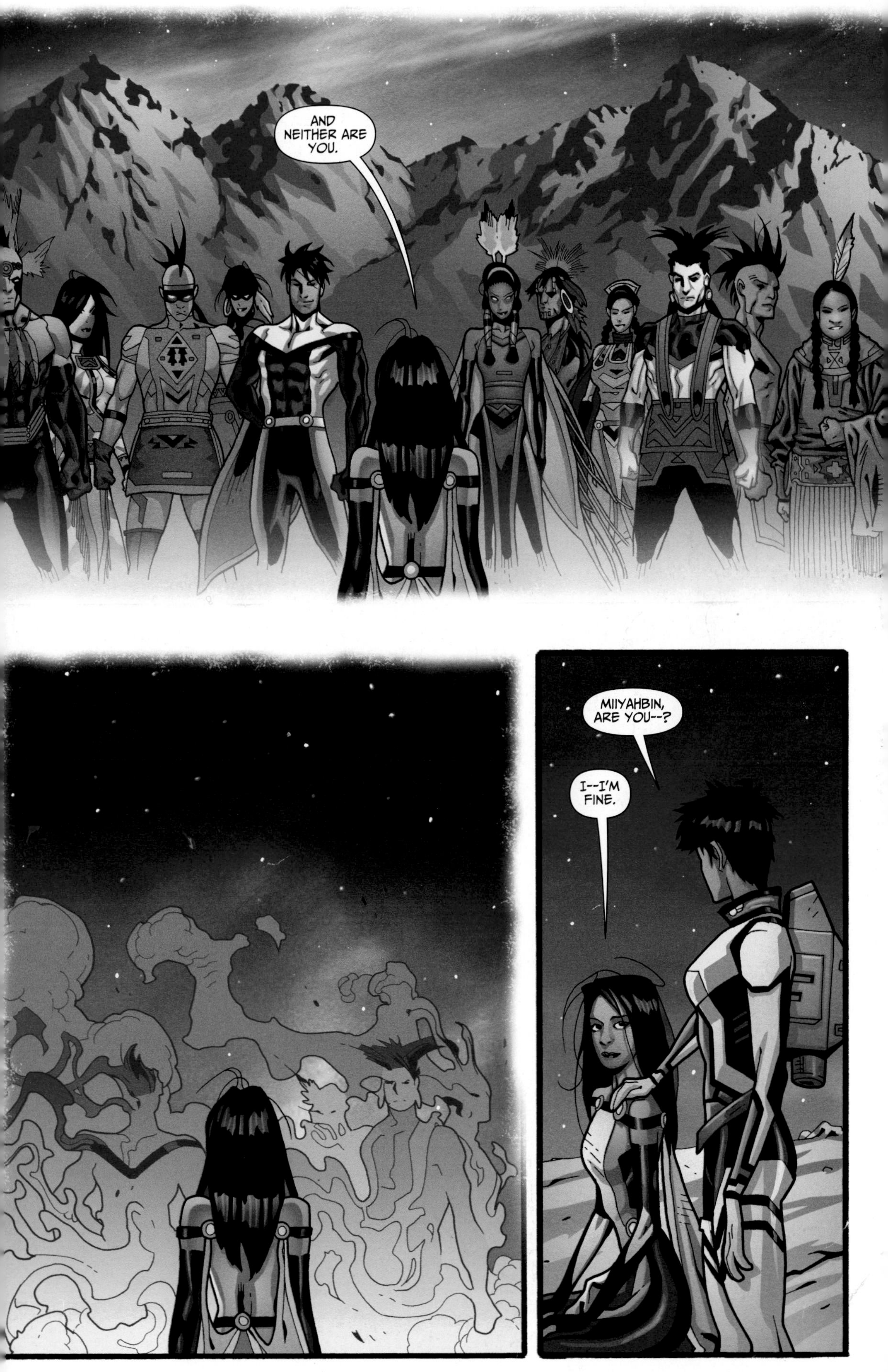
AND NEITHER ARE YOU.
MIIYAHBIN, ARE YOU--?
I--I'M FINE.

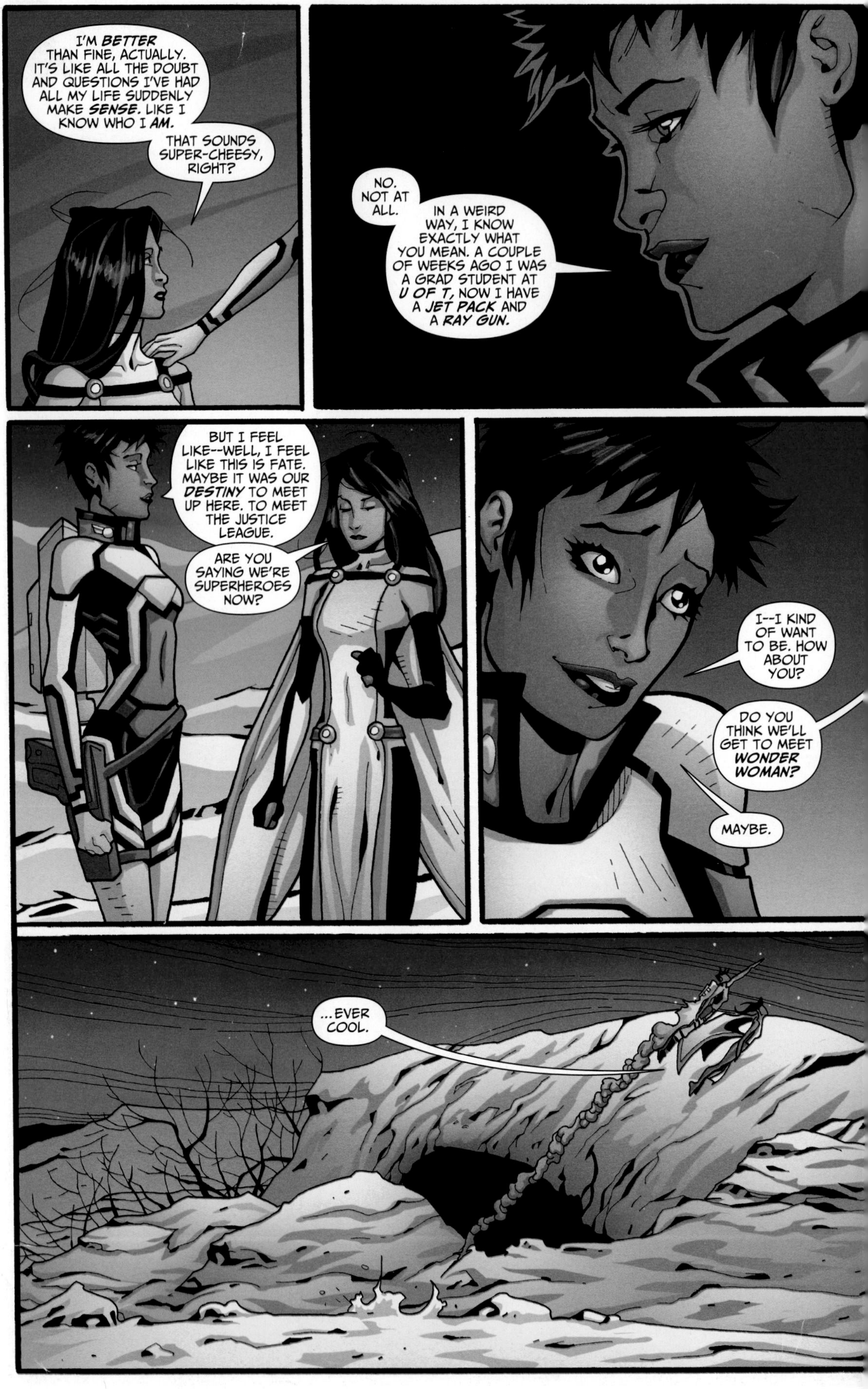
I'M **BETTER** THAN FINE, ACTUALLY. IT'S LIKE ALL THE DOUBT AND QUESTIONS I'VE HAD ALL MY LIFE SUDDENLY MAKE **SENSE.** LIKE I KNOW WHO I **AM.**
THAT SOUNDS SUPER-CHEESY, RIGHT?
NO. NOT AT ALL.
IN A WEIRD WAY, I KNOW EXACTLY WHAT YOU MEAN. A COUPLE OF WEEKS AGO I WAS A GRAD STUDENT AT ***U OF T,*** NOW I HAVE A ***JET PACK*** AND A ***RAY GUN.***
BUT I FEEL LIKE--WELL, I FEEL LIKE THIS IS FATE. MAYBE IT WAS OUR ***DESTINY*** TO MEET UP HERE. TO MEET THE JUSTICE LEAGUE.
ARE YOU SAYING WE'RE SUPERHEROES NOW?
I--I KIND OF WANT TO BE. HOW ABOUT YOU?
DO YOU THINK WE'LL GET TO MEET ***WONDER WOMAN?***
MAYBE.
...EVER COOL.

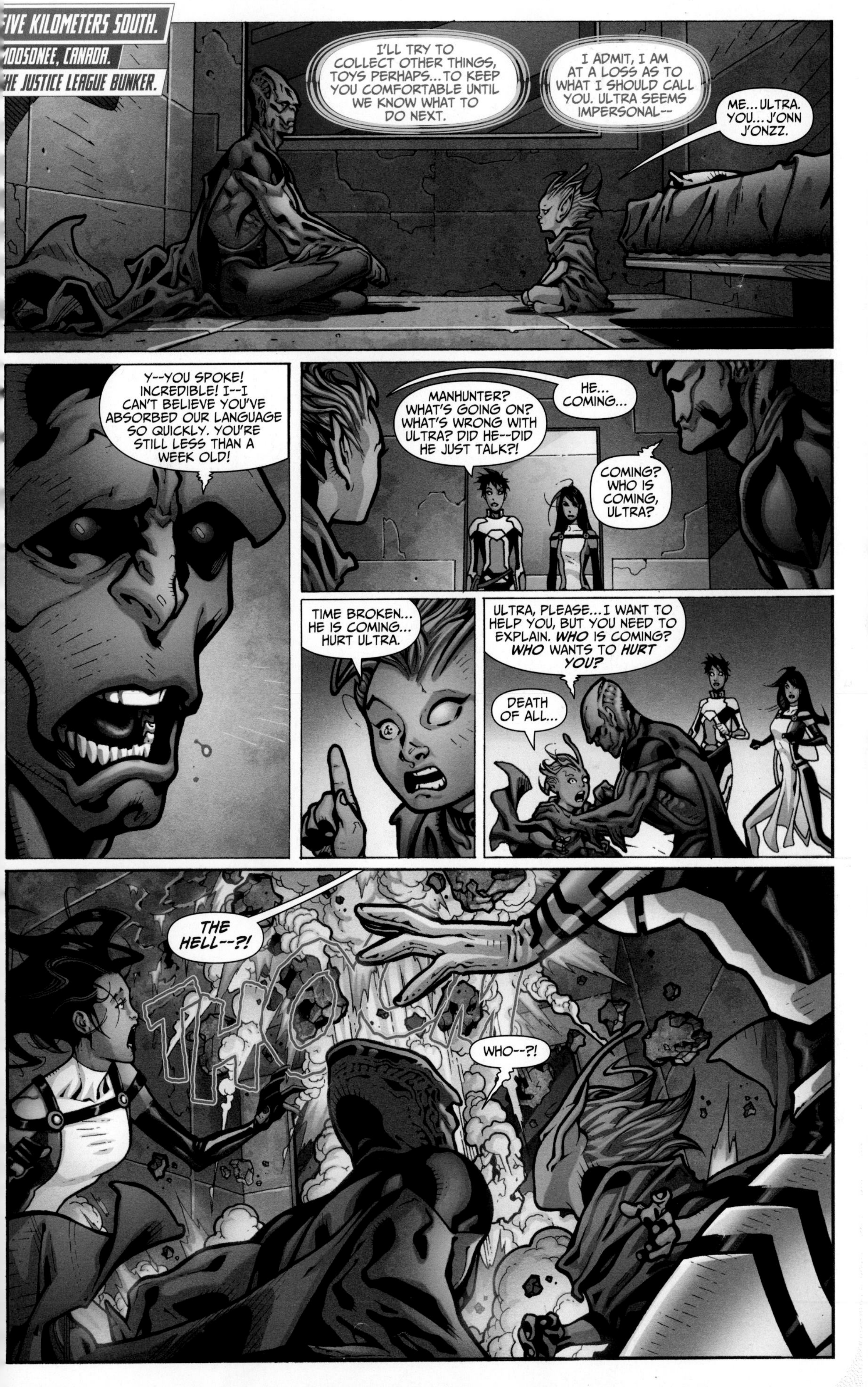
FIVE KILOMETERS SOUTH.
MOOSONEE, CANADA.
THE JUSTICE LEAGUE BUNKER.
I'LL TRY TO COLLECT OTHER THINGS, TOYS PERHAPS...TO KEEP YOU COMFORTABLE UNTIL WE KNOW WHAT TO DO NEXT.
I ADMIT, I AM AT A LOSS AS TO WHAT I SHOULD CALL YOU. ULTRA SEEMS IMPERSONAL--
ME...ULTRA. YOU...J'ONN J'ONZZ.
Y--YOU SPOKE! INCREDIBLE! I--I CAN'T BELIEVE YOU'VE ABSORBED OUR LANGUAGE SO QUICKLY. YOU'RE STILL LESS THAN A WEEK OLD!
MANHUNTER? WHAT'S GOING ON? WHAT'S WRONG WITH ULTRA? DID HE--DID HE JUST TALK?!
HE... COMING...
COMING? WHO IS COMING, ULTRA?
TIME BROKEN... HE IS COMING... HURT ULTRA.
ULTRA, PLEASE...I WANT TO HELP YOU, BUT YOU NEED TO EXPLAIN. *WHO* IS COMING? *WHO* WANTS TO *HURT* *YOU?*
DEATH OF ALL...
THE HELL--?!
THOOM
WHO--?!

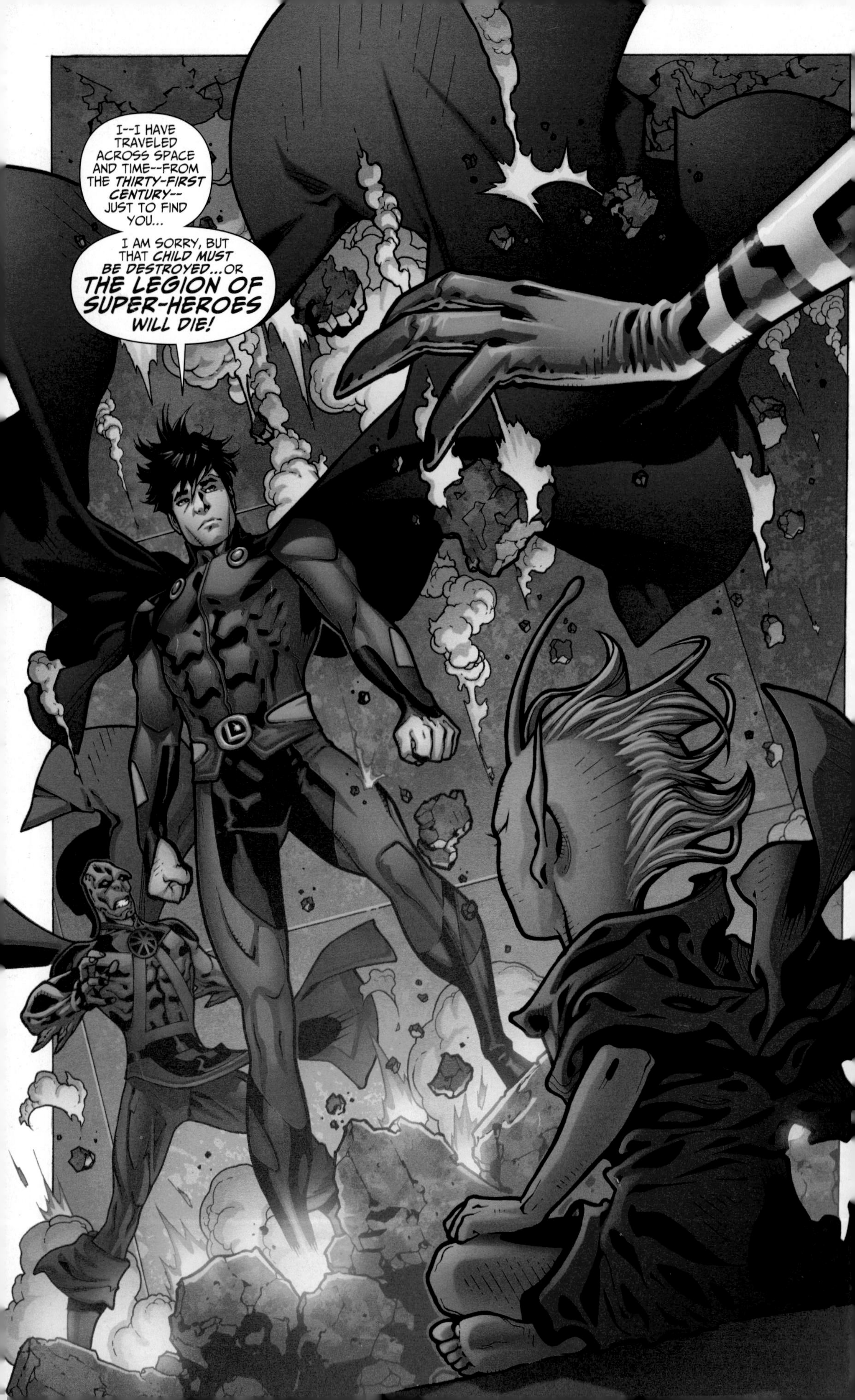
I--I HAVE TRAVELED ACROSS SPACE AND TIME--FROM THE THIRTY-FIRST CENTURY--JUST TO FIND YOU...
I AM SORRY, BUT THAT CHILD MUST BE DESTROYED...OR THE LEGION OF SUPER-HEROES WILL DIE!

VARIANT COVER GALLERY

JUSTICE LEAGUE UNITED 0
Variant cover by Mike McKone with Gabe Eltaeb

JUSTICE LEAGUE UNITED 1
Variant cover by Gene Ha

JUSTICE LEAGUE UNITED 2
Variant cover by Ben Oliver

JUSTICE LEAGUE UNITED 2
Bombshell variant cover by Ant Lucia

JUSTICE LEAGUE UNITED 3
Variant cover by Jeff Lemire

JUSTICE LEAGUE UNITED 3
Batman 75th anniversary variant cover by Mario Alberti

JUSTICE LEAGUE UNITED 4
Variant cover by Karl Kerschl

JUSTICE LEAGUE UNITED 4
Selfie variant cover by Emanuela Lupacchino & Alex Sinclair

JUSTICE LEAGUE UNITED 5
Variant cover by Cameron Stewart & Nathan Fairbairn

JUSTICE LEAGUE UNITED 5
Monster variant cover by Kelley Jones

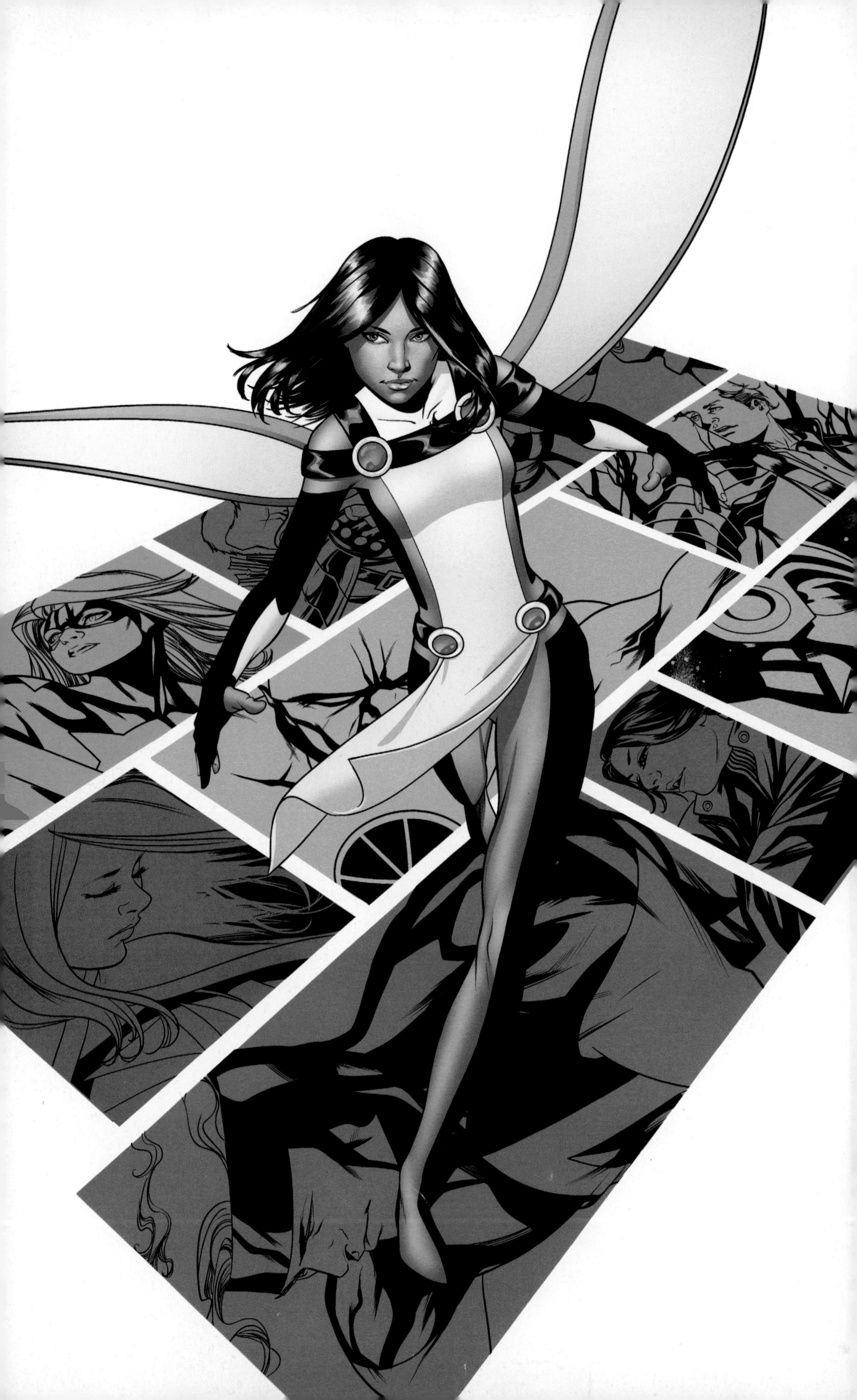

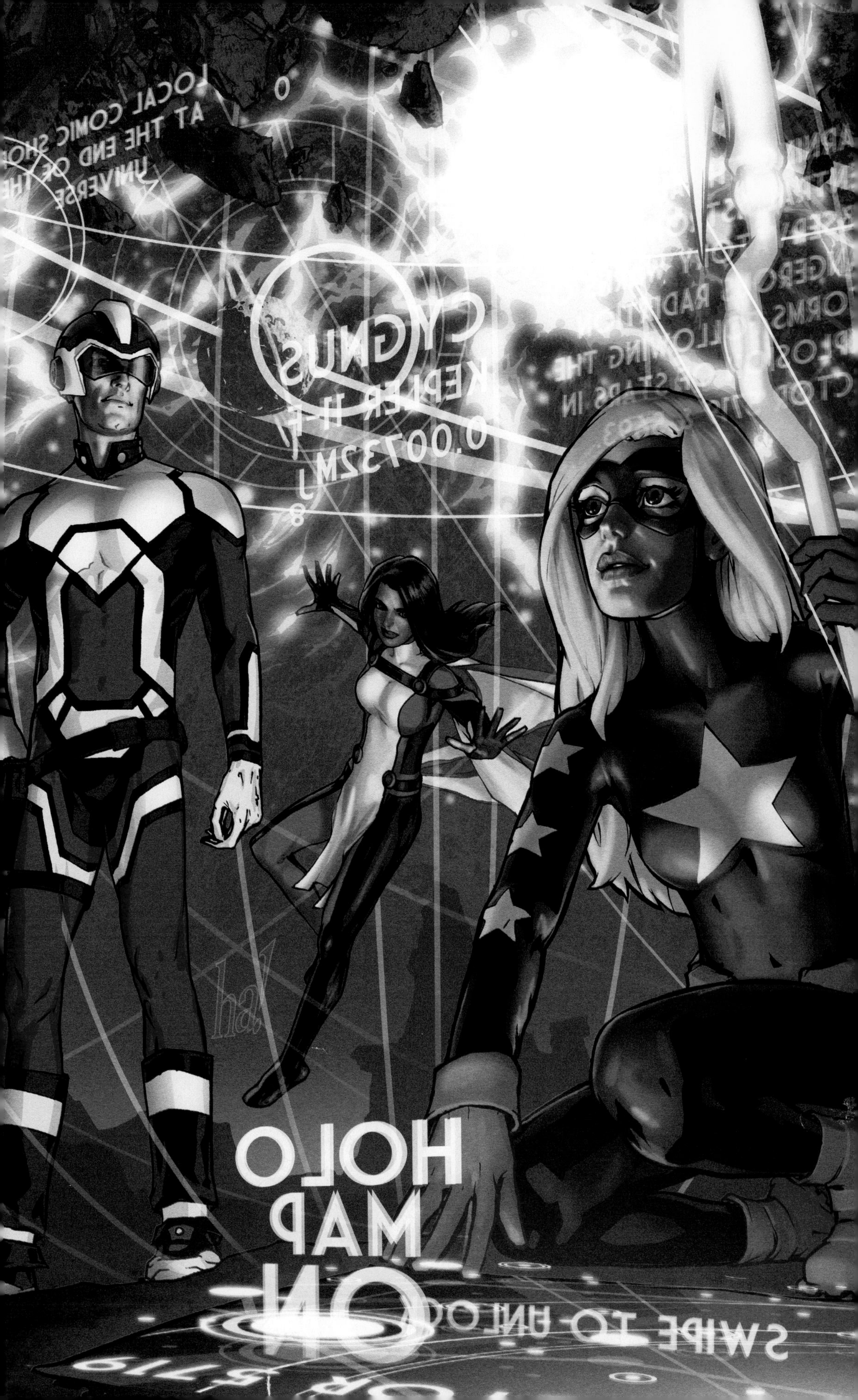
HOLO
MAP
ON
CYGNUS
KEPLER 11-F

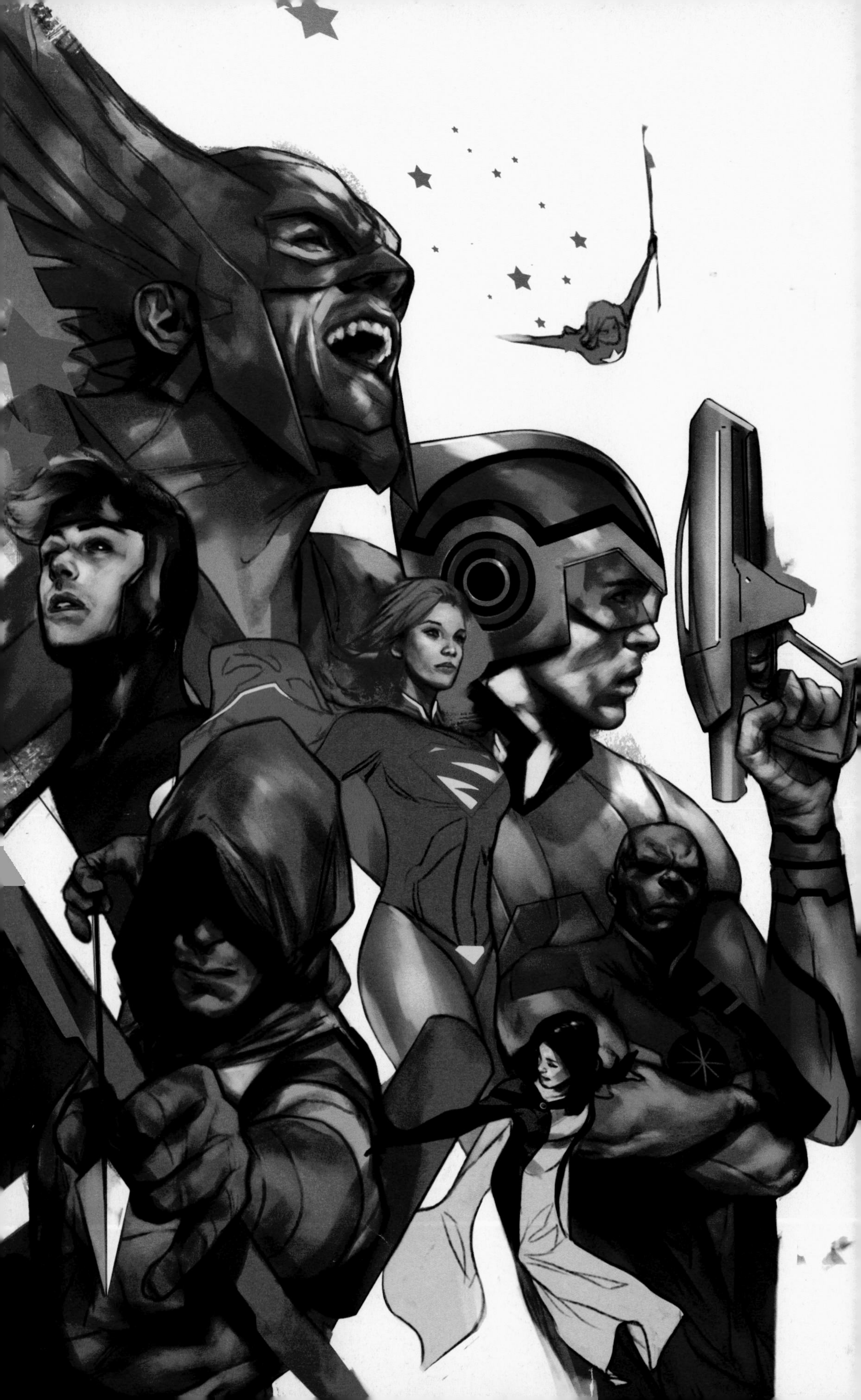

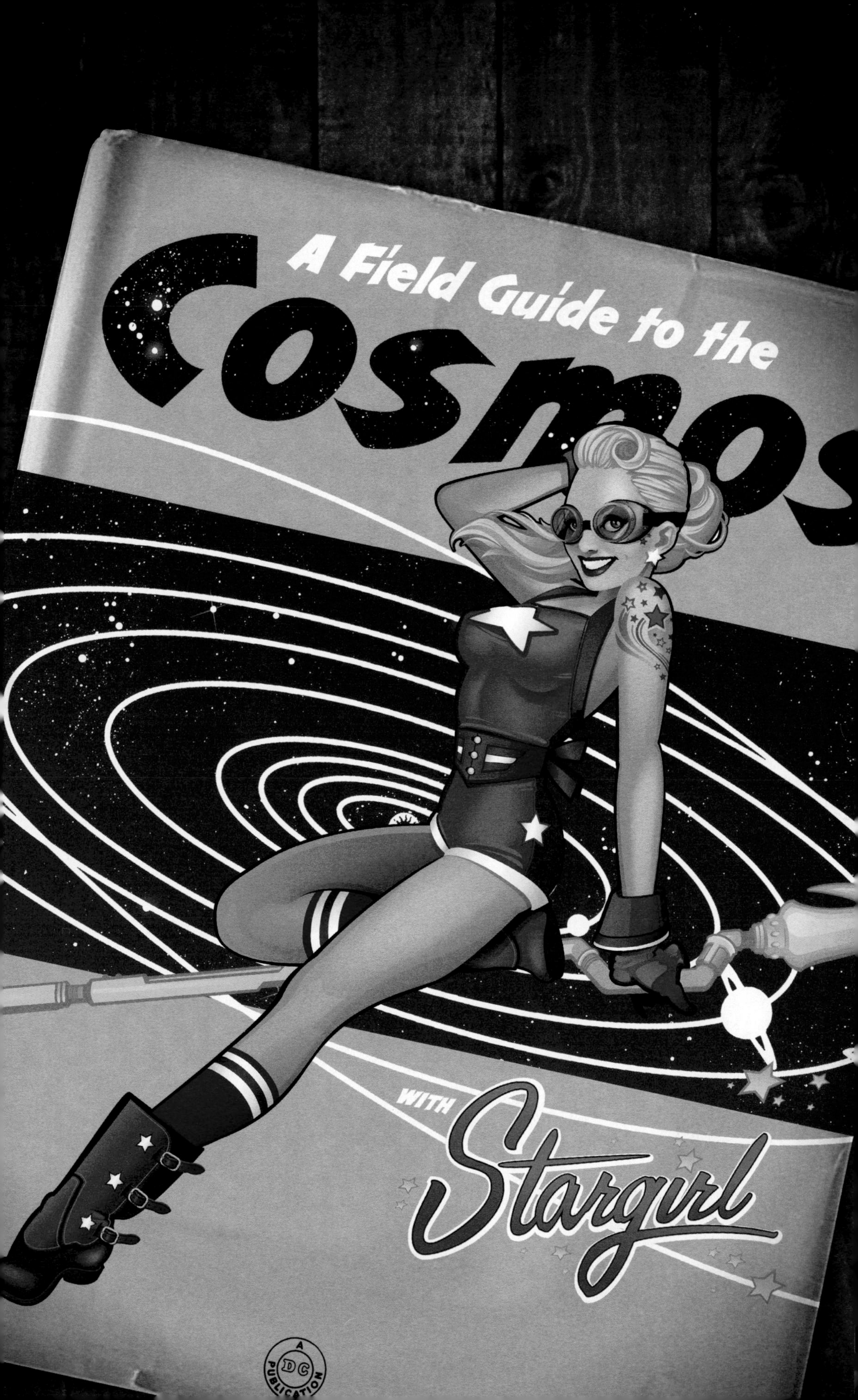
A Field Guide to the
Cosmos
WITH
Stargirl
A DC PUBLICATION

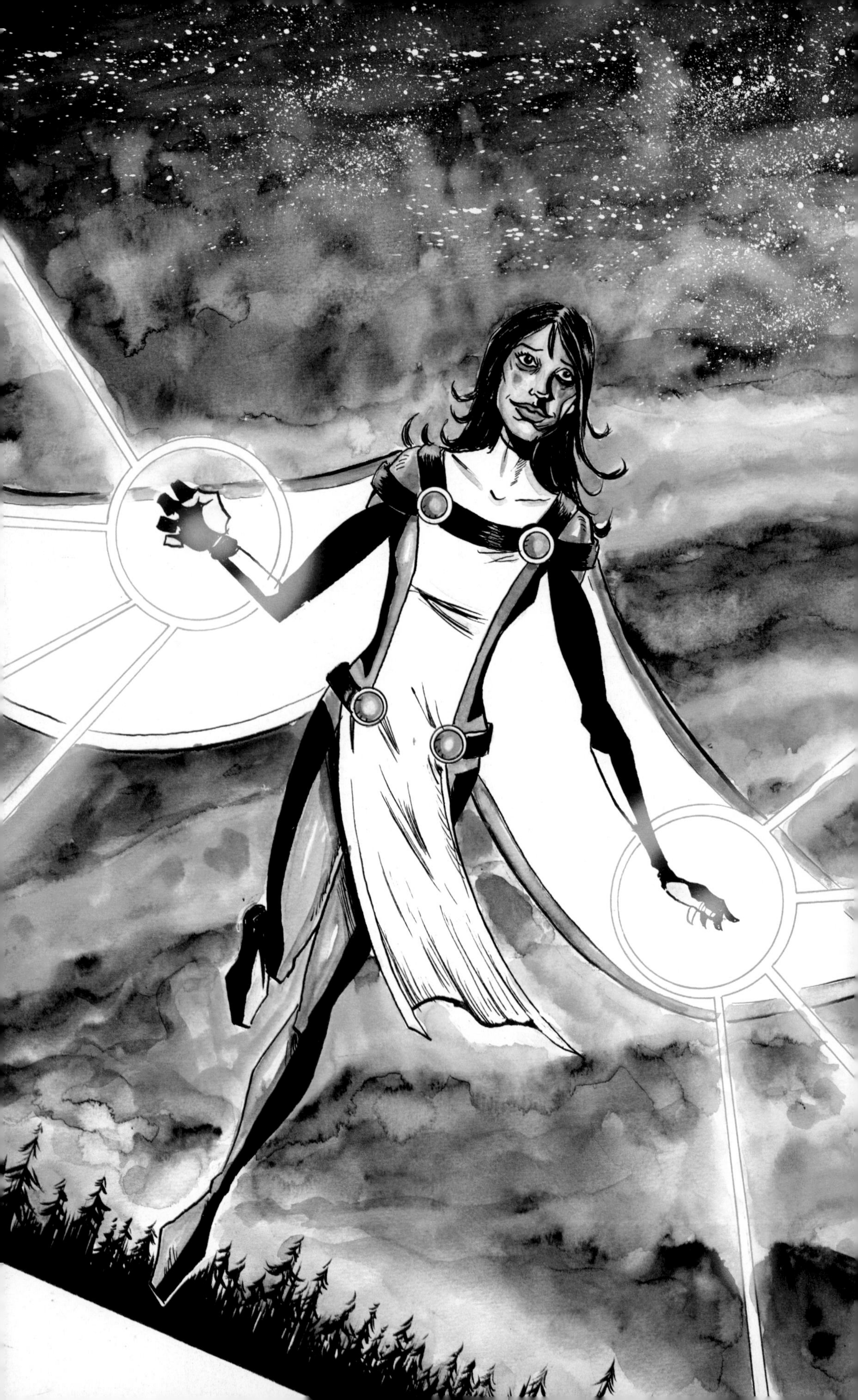

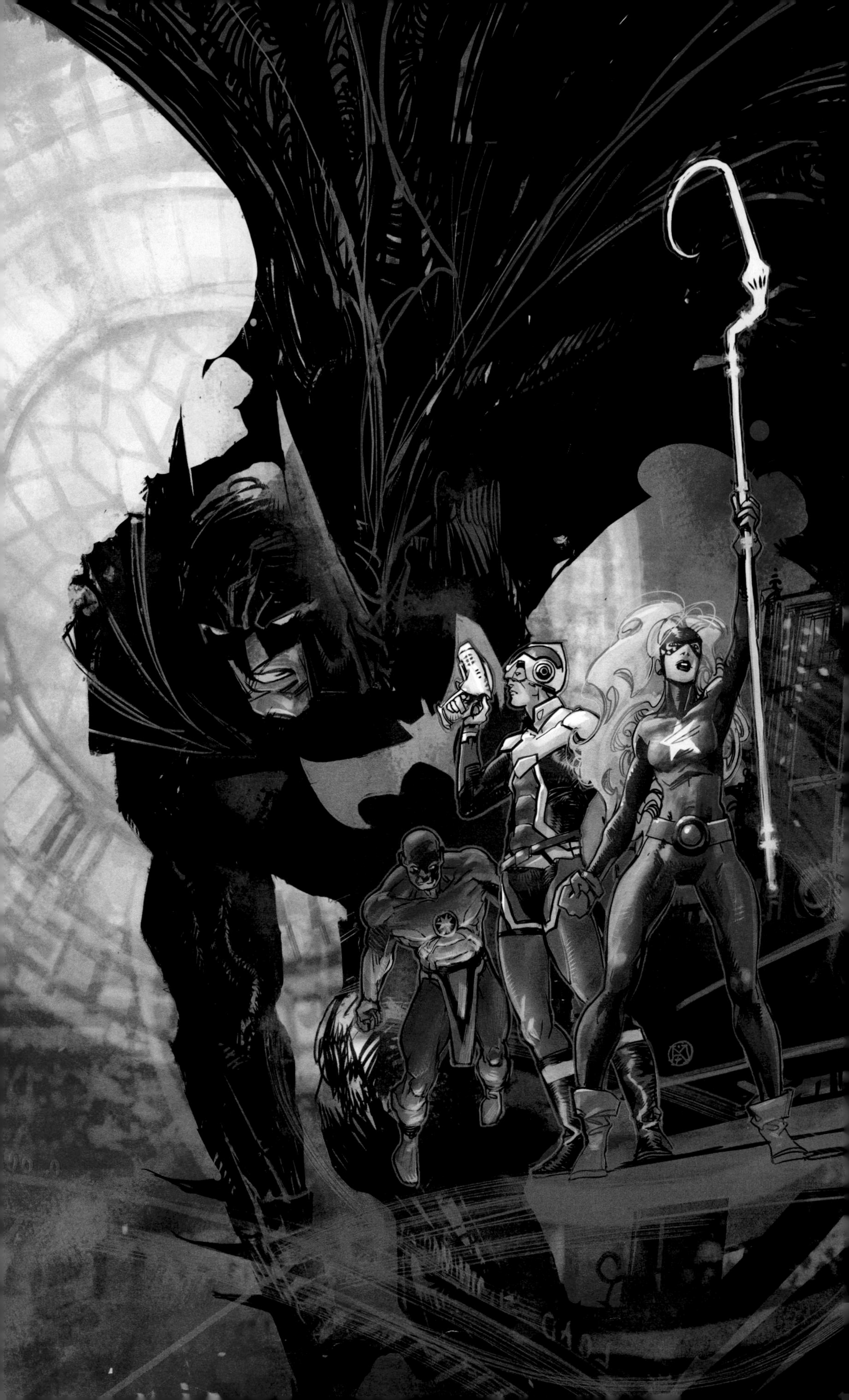

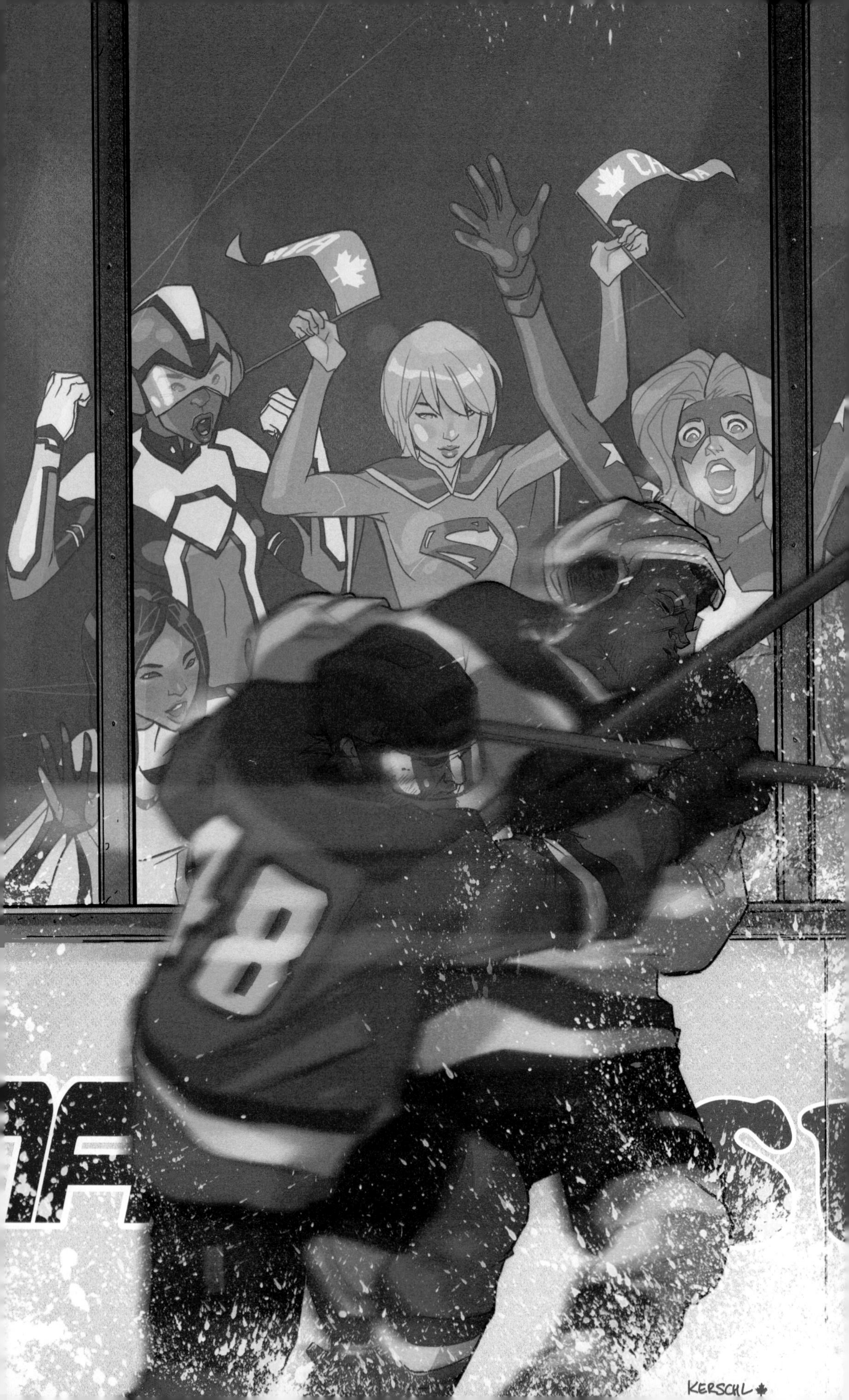
KERSCHL

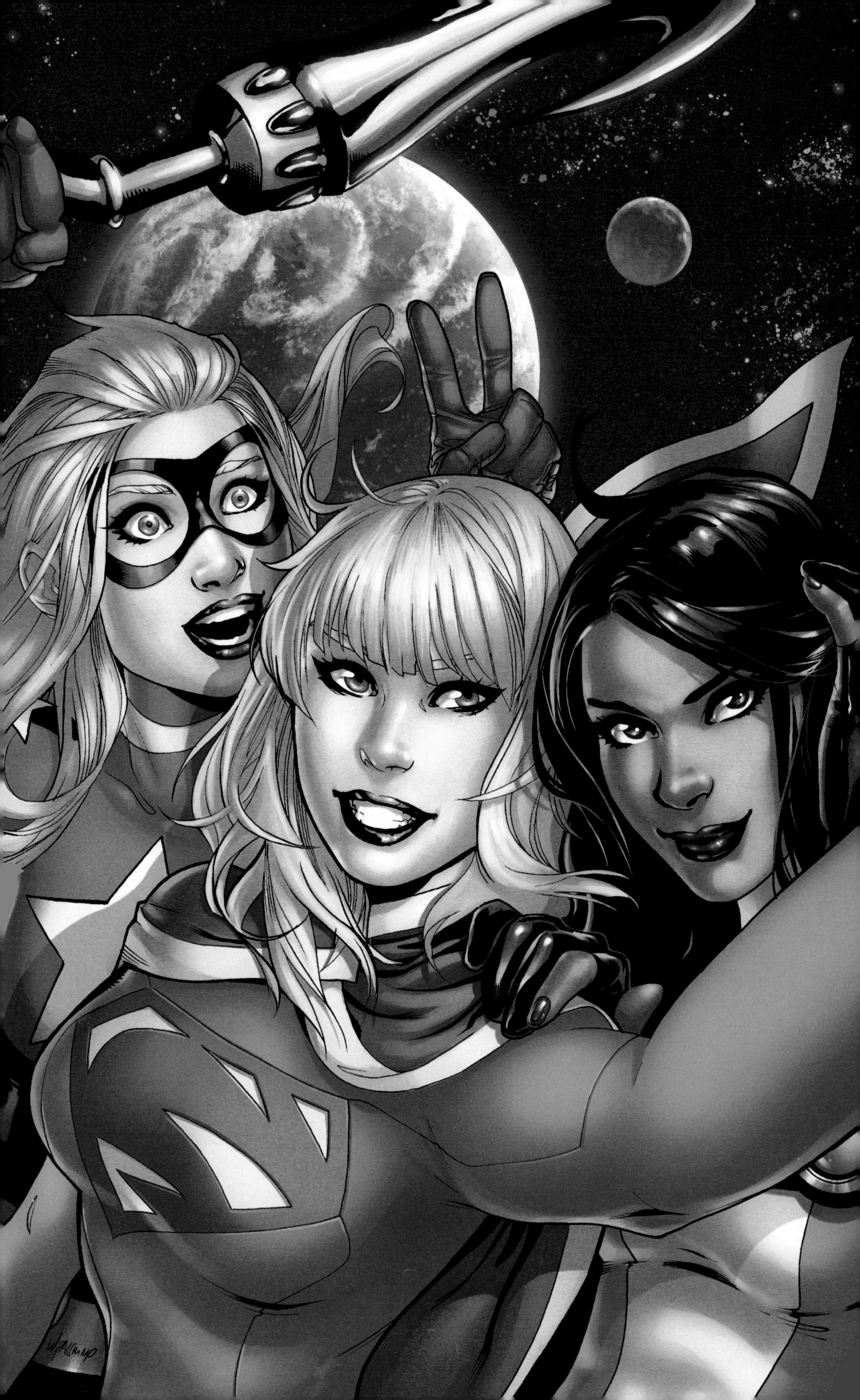

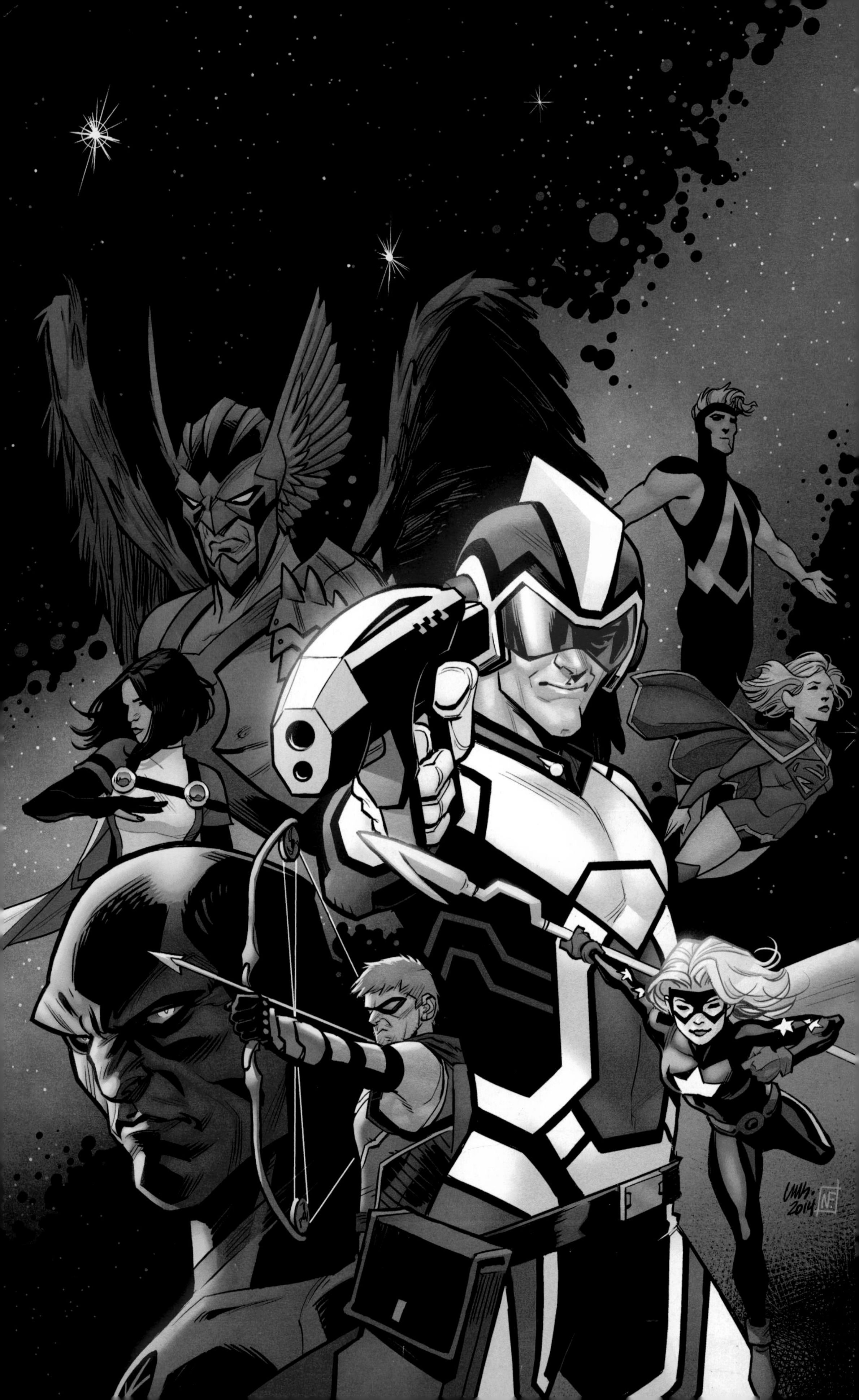

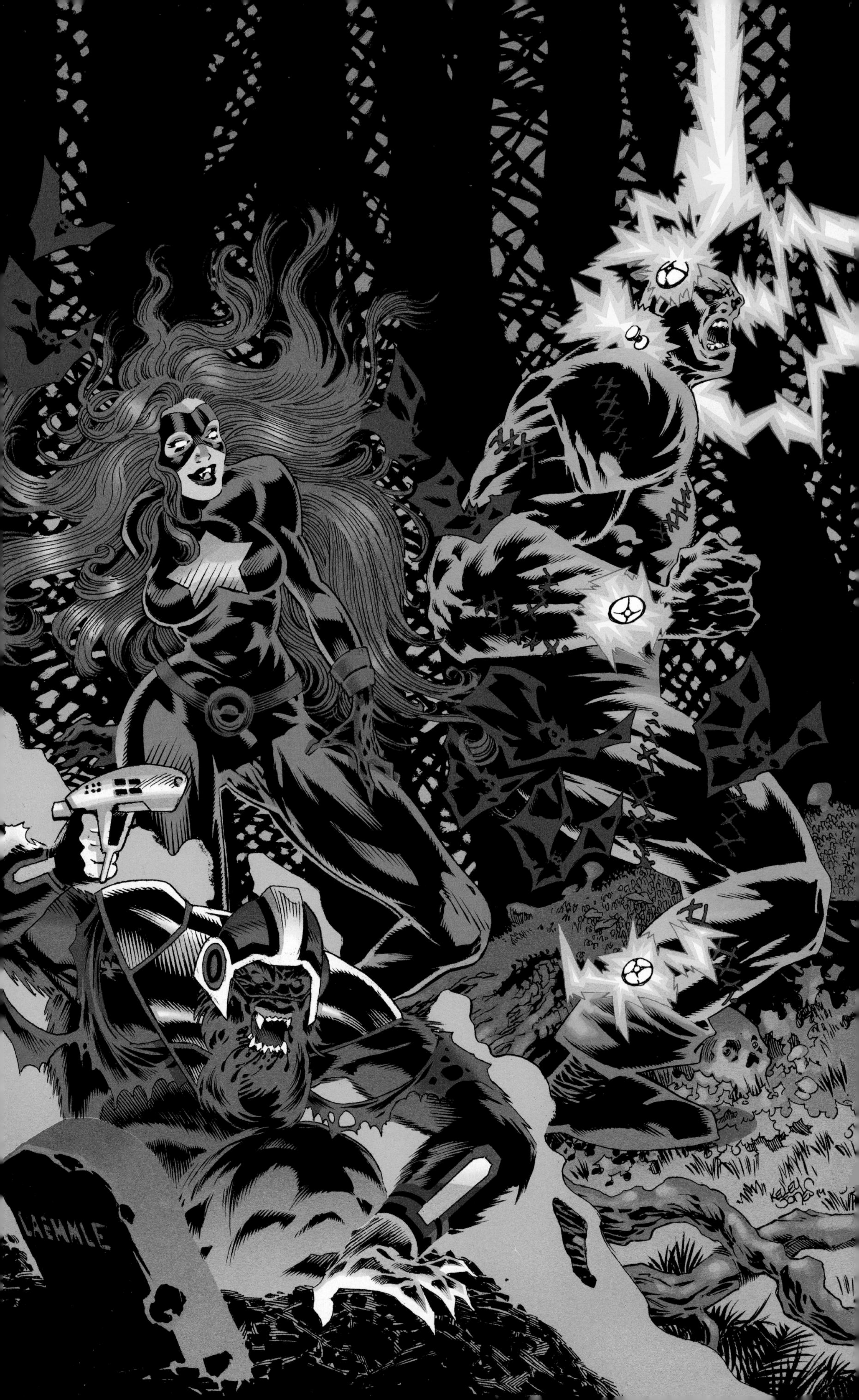
LAEMMLE

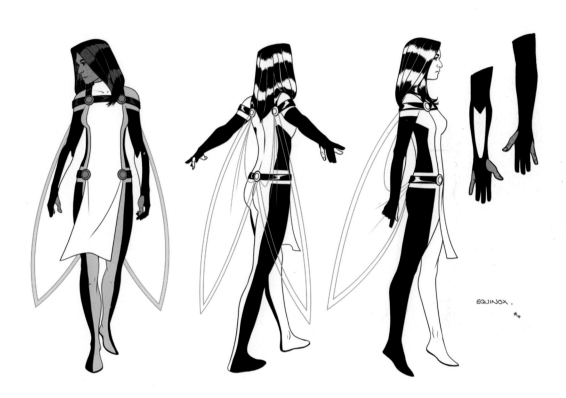

EQUINOX.
MᵂH

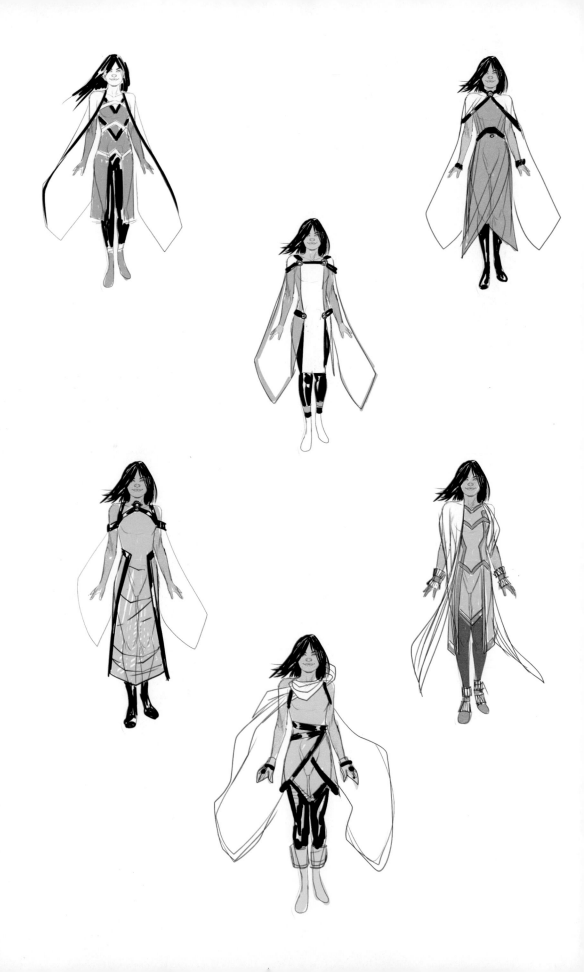

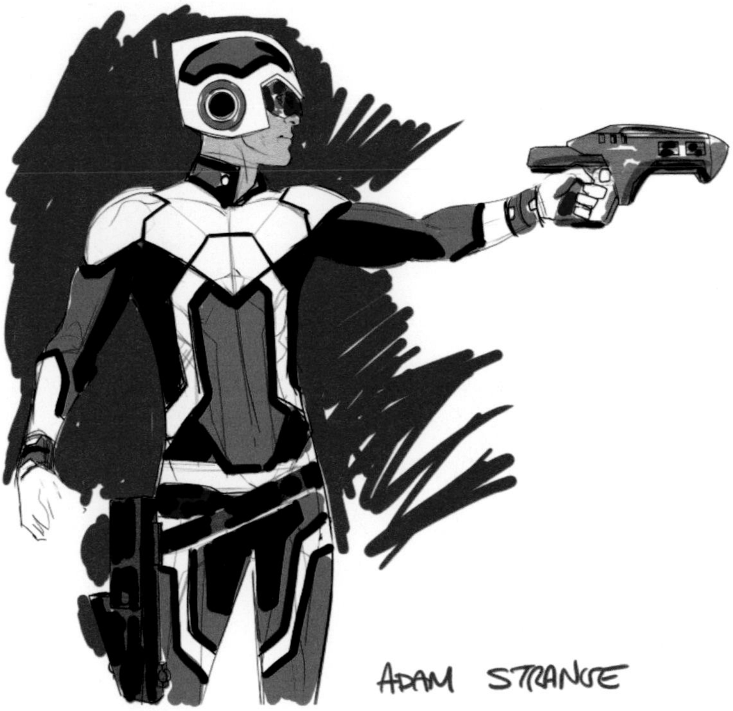
ADAM STRANGE

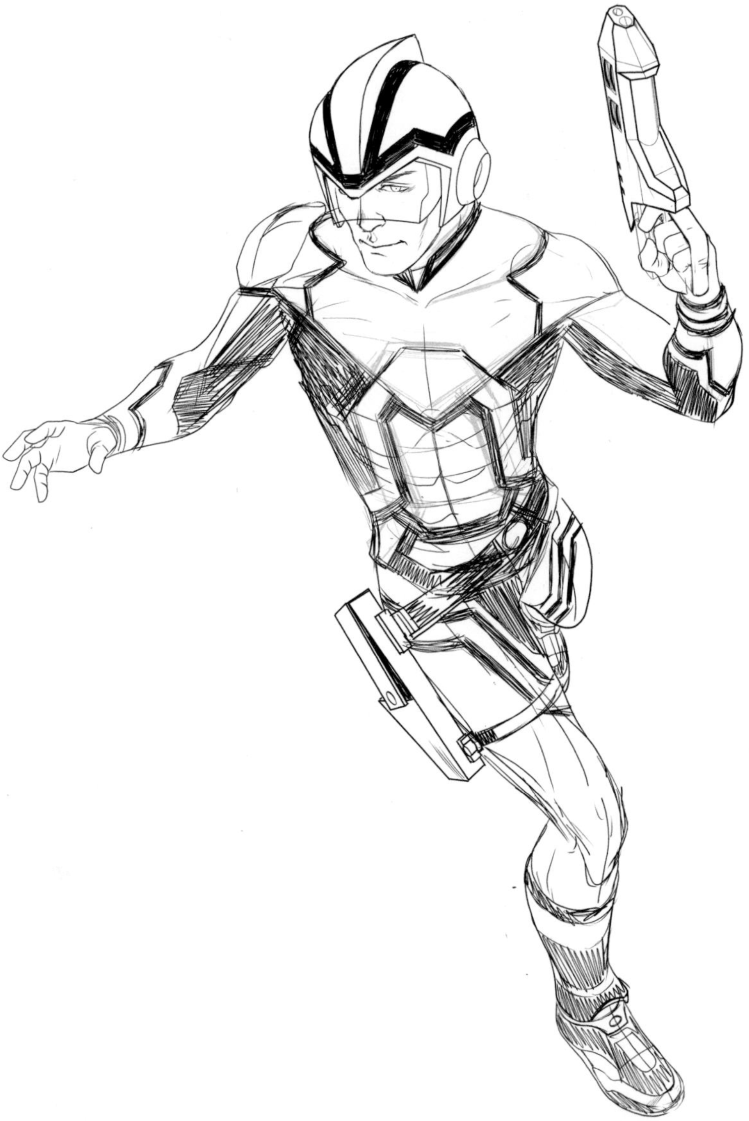

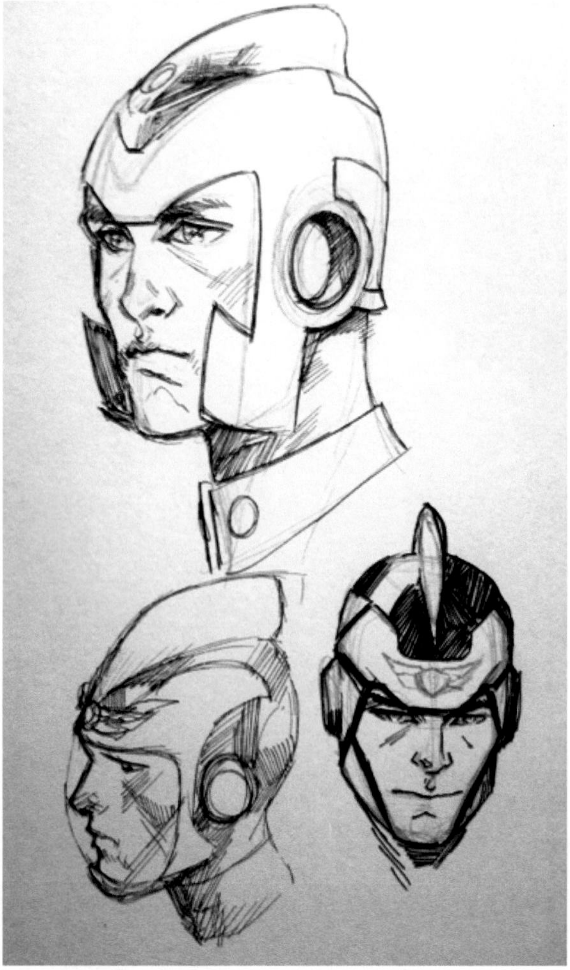
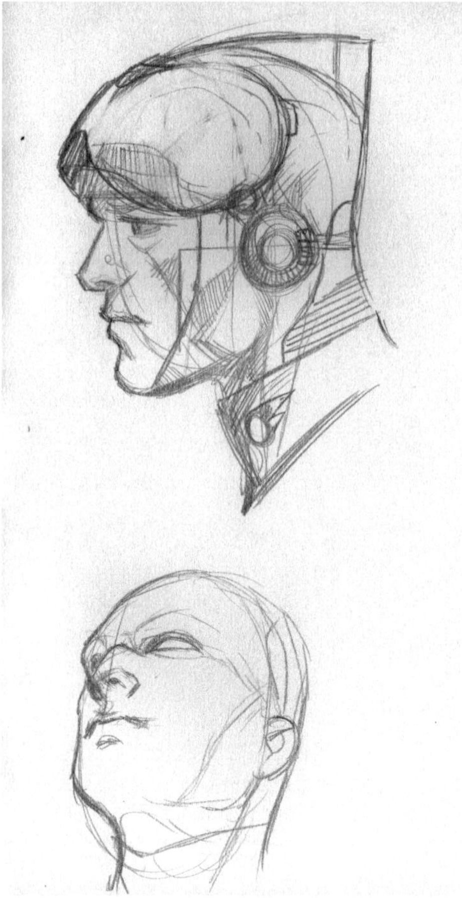
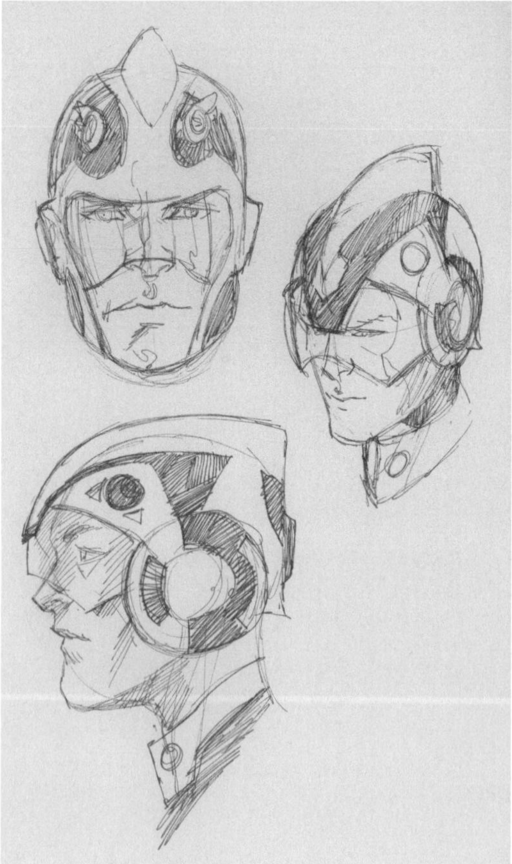

Unused Red Lantern design

Some aliens to inhabit the story

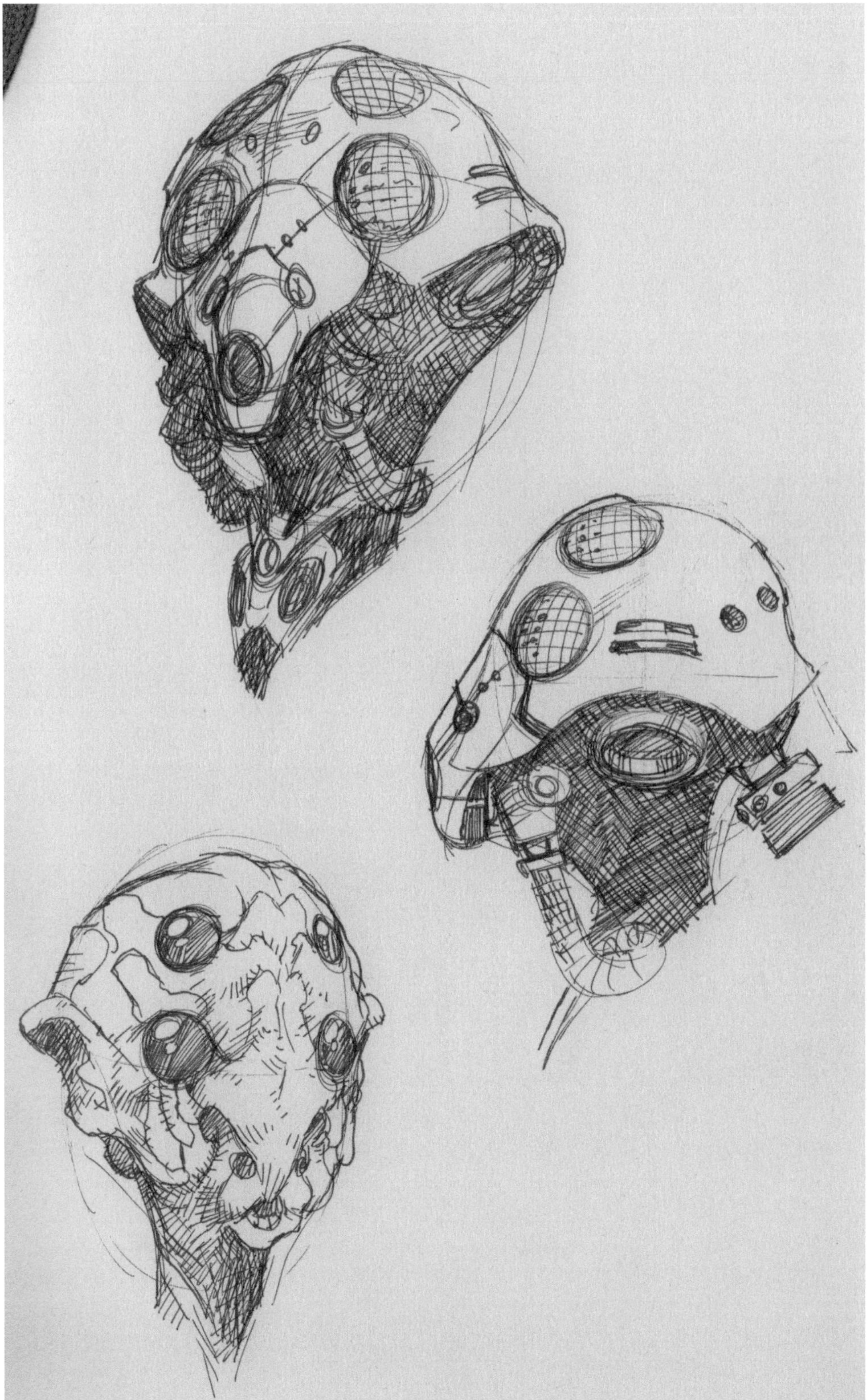

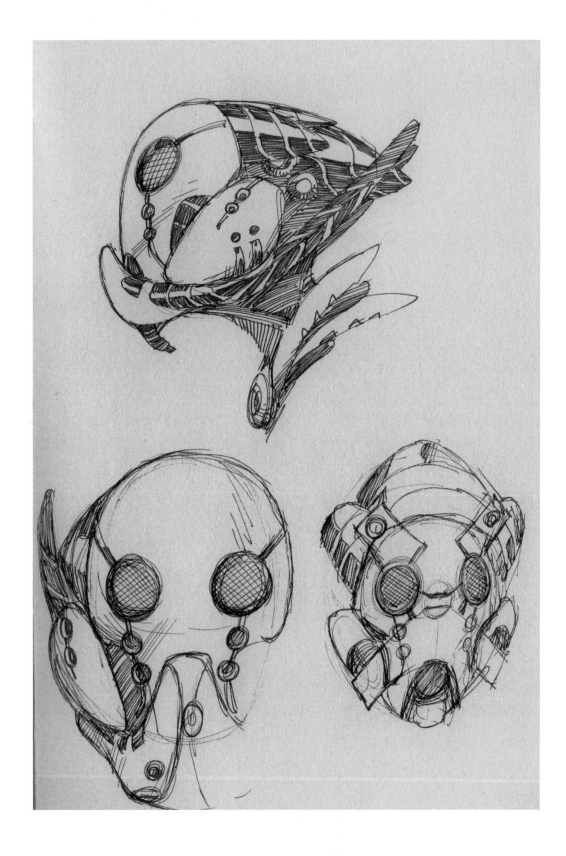

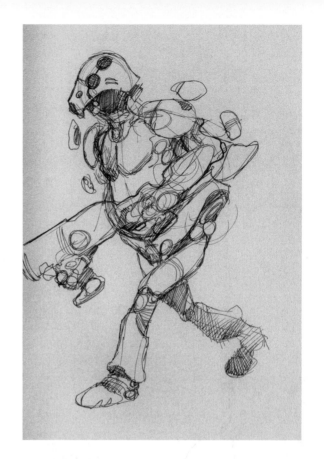

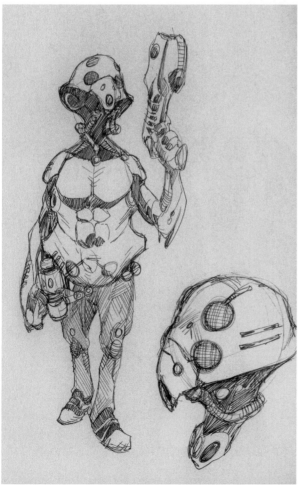

The DC Heroes

As imagined by the bright young minds of Canada!

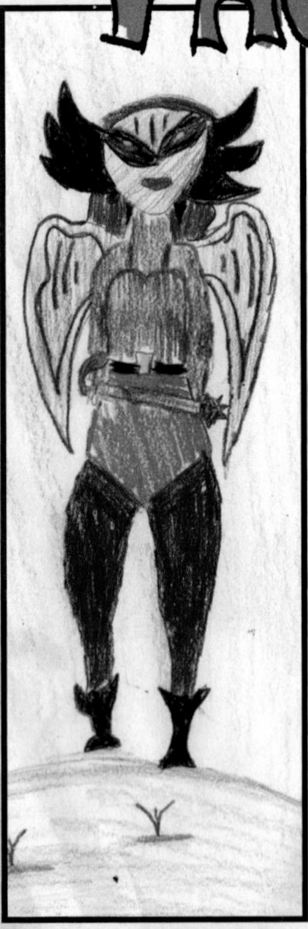

Hawkgirl by GWEN NAKOGEE
Grade 5/6 Moosonee Public School

Getting to write a Justice League comic is a childhood dream come true, but getting to set that comic in my home country of Canada and introduce a ***new Canadian super hero*** is beyond my wildest dreams.

Early on in the process of writing JLU, I decided to set the book, and its eclectic cast, in an isolated part of Northern Ontario called Moosonee/Moose Factory. This area is home to the Moose Cree First Nation, and I wanted to create a new character that would represent all the grace, humor, resilience and courage of the Cree people I've had the pleasure of coming to know.

I've made two trips to the area so far and in addition to marathon snowmobile trips, helicopter rides and my first taste of Moose stew (don't tell Animal Man!), I've spent time in a number of schools, talking to kids about comics and art and sharing my story with them. And in turn the kids shared some of their stories, their art and their amazing culture with me. Traveling north has been one of the most rewarding experiences of my life, and I'm pleased to share with you these wonderful renditions of some of DC's brightest stars by some of the brightest kids in the north! Enjoy and come back next month to learn more about the character these kids inspired...the mysterious teenager from Moose Factory, Miiyahbin Marten aka ***EQUINOX***, and how she'll change the Justice League forever!

-Jeff Lemire

Batman by KHORBIN MCCOMB
Grade 4/5 Moosonee Public School

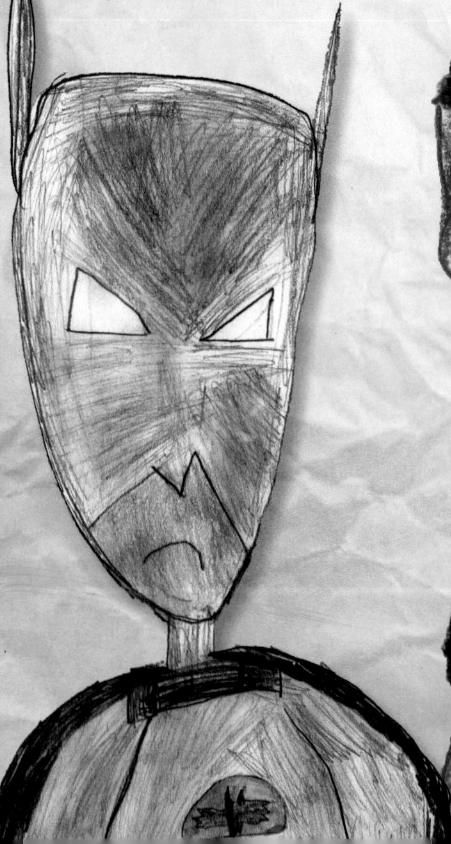

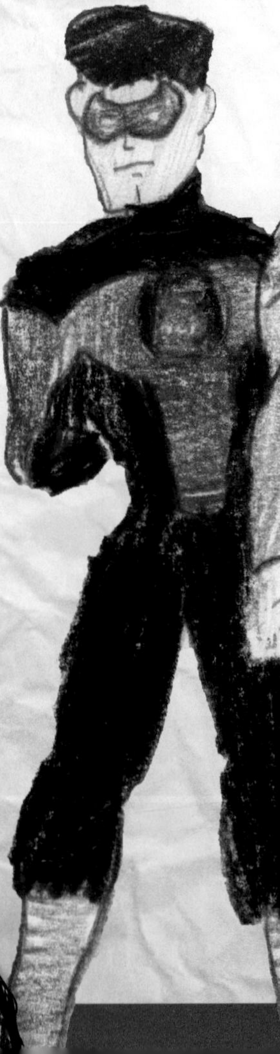

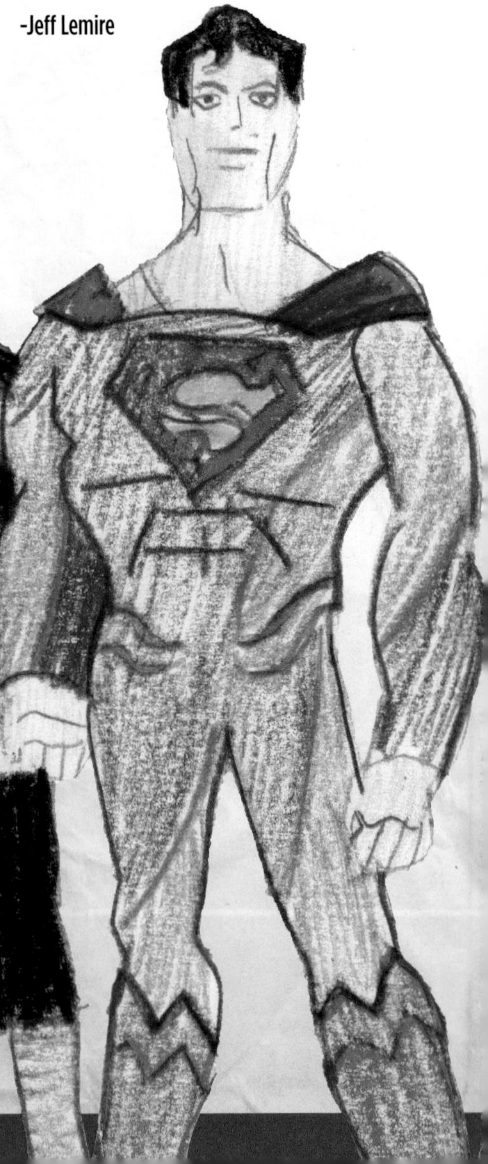

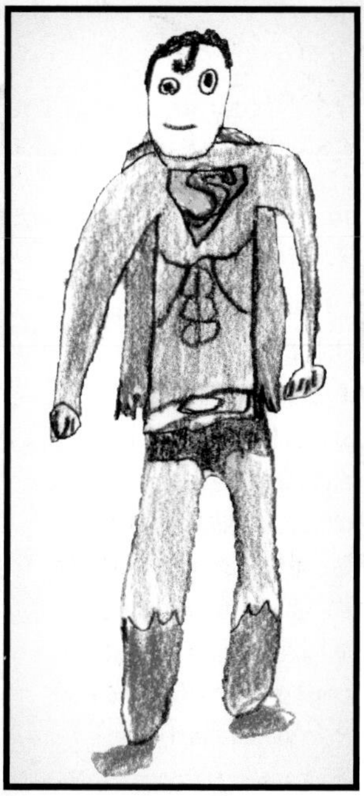

Supes by
MARTIN NAKOGEE
Grade 5 St. Andrew's
Kashechewan, Ontario

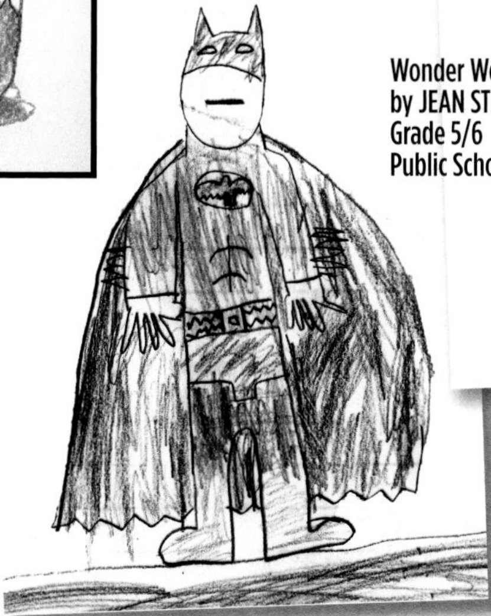

Batman
by WADLE KOOSTACHIN
Grade 4 St. Andrew's
Kashechewan, Ontario

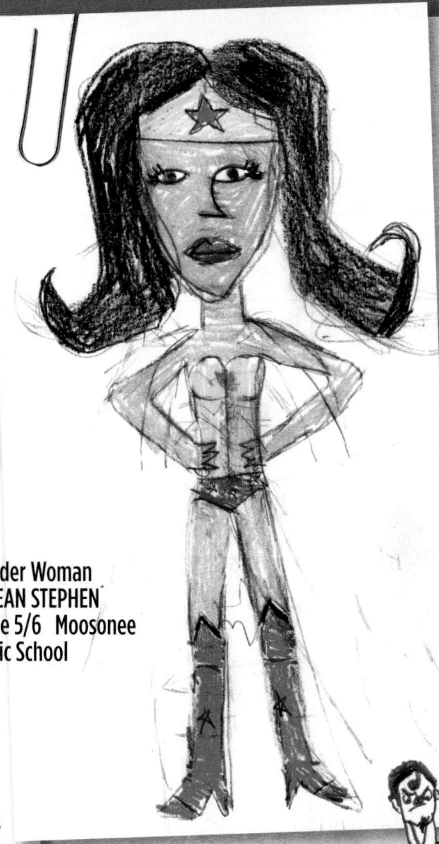

Wonder Woman
by JEAN STEPHEN
Grade 5/6 Moosonee
Public School

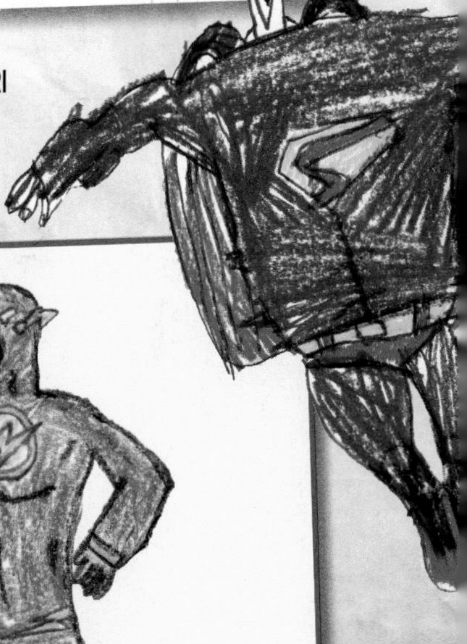

Superman
by ADAM TIBERI
Grade 5/6
Moosonee
Public School

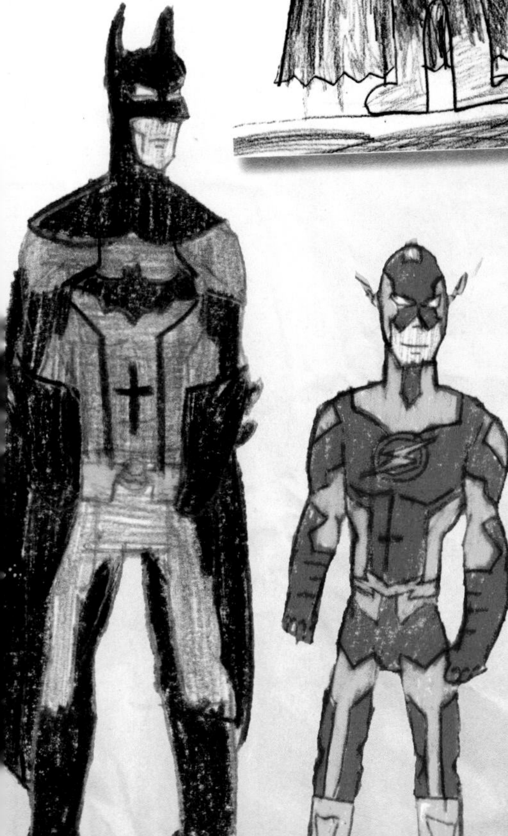

JLA by CODEN SOLOMON
Grade 5/6 Moosonee Public School

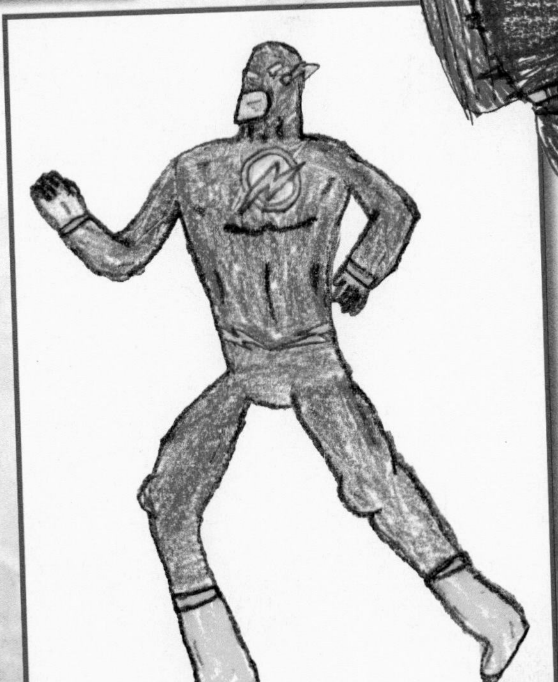

Flash by RUSSELL MITCHELL
Grade 5/6 Moosonee Public School

DC COMICS™

"Writer Geoff Johns and artist Jim Lee toss you–and their heroes–into the action from the very start and don't put on the brakes. DC's über-creative team craft an inviting world for those who are trying out a comic for the first time. Lee's art is stunning."—USA TODAY

"A fun ride."—IGN

START AT THE BEGINNING!

JUSTICE LEAGUE VOLUME 1: ORIGIN

GEOFF JOHNS and JIM LEE

THE NEW 52!
DC COMICS™
JUSTICE LEAGUE
VOLUME 1 ORIGIN
"WRITTEN BY GEOFF JOHNS, WITH ART BY THE GODLY JIM LEE, JUSTICE LEAGUE IS A MUST READ."
— COMPLEX MAGAZINE
GEOFF JOHNS JIM LEE SCOTT WILLIAMS

JUSTICE LEAGUE VOL. 2: THE VILLAIN'S JOURNEY

THE NEW 52!
JUSTICE LEAGUE
GEOFF JOHNS JIM LEE SCOTT WILLIAMS

JUSTICE LEAGUE VOL. 3: THRONE OF ATLANTIS

THE NEW 52!
JUSTICE LEAGUE
GEOFF JOHNS IVAN REIS PAUL PELLETIER TONY S. DANIEL

JUSTICE LEAGUE OF AMERICA VOL. 1: WORLD'S MOST DANGEROUS

THE NEW 52!
JUSTICE LEAGUE OF AMERICA
VOLUME 1 WORLD'S MOST DANGEROUS
GEOFF JOHNS DAVID FINCH BRETT BOOTH DOUG MAHNKE

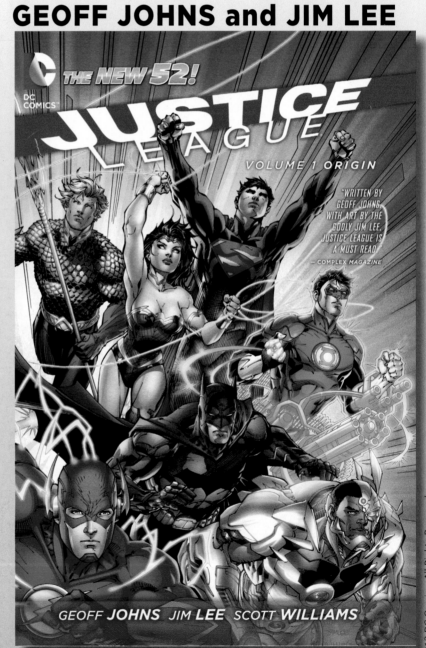